THE SINGER RESUMES
THE TALE

A volume in the series Myth and Poetics, edited by Gregory Nagy.
A list of titles appears at the end of the book.

Avdo Međedović, the singer, and Albert Lord at Avdo's house at Obrov, 1951. Photo by Mary Louise Lord.

THE SINGER RESUMES THE TALE

ALBERT BATES LORD

Edited by MARY LOUISE LORD

CORNELL UNIVERSITY PRESS

ITHACA AND LONDON

Copyright © 1995 by Cornell University

All rights reserved. Except for brief quotations in a review, this book, or parts thereof, must not be reproduced in any form without permission in writing from the publisher. For information, address Cornell University Press, Sage House, 512 East State Street, Ithaca, New York 14850.

First published 1995 by Cornell University Press.

Library of Congress Cataloging-in-Publication Data
Lord, Albert Bates.
    The singer resumes the tale / Albert Bates Lord ; edited by Mary Louise Lord.
       p. cm. — (Myth and poetics)
    Includes bibliographical references and index.
    ISBN 0-8014-3103-4 (cloth)
    1. Folk poetry—History and criticism. 2. Poetry, Medieval—History and criticism. 3. Oral tradition—History and criticism. 4. Oral-formulaic analysis. I. Lord, Mary Louise, 1916– II. Title. III. Series.
PN1341.L67 1995
809.1—dc20   94-45608

Printed in the United States of America

⊗ The paper in this book meets the minimum requirements of the American National Standard for Information Sciences—Permanence of Paper for Printed Library Materials, ANSI Z39.48-1984.

Frontispiece photograph by Mary Louise Lord from *Serbo-Croatian Heroic Songs*, collected by Milman Parry, vol. 3, *The Wedding of Smailagić Meho*, by Avdo Međedović, trans. Albert B. Lord (Cambridge: Harvard University Press, 1974). Reprinted by permission of the publisher.

Excerpts from *Italian Folktales: Selected and Retold by Italo Calvino*, copyright © 1956 by Giulio Einaudi editore, s.p.a., English translation by George Martin copyright © 1980 by Harcourt Brace & Company, reprinted by permission of Harcourt Brace & Company.

Passages from Albert Bates Lord, *Epic Singers and Oral Tradition*, copyright © 1991 by Cornell University, are reprinted by permission of the publisher, Cornell University Press.

For Nathan and Mark

Contents

	Foreword by Gregory Nagy	ix
	Preface by Mary Louise Lord	xi
1	The Nature and Kinds of Oral Literature	1
2	Oral Traditional Lyric Poetry	22
3	Homer and the Muses: Oral Traditional Poetics, a Mythic Episode, and Arming Scenes in the *Iliad*	69
4	*Beowulf* and Oral Epic Tradition	96
5	The Formula in Anglo-Saxon Poetry	117
6	The Theme in Anglo-Saxon Poetry	137
7	The Ballad: Textual Stability, Variation, and Memorization	167
8	Rebuttal	187
9	Two Versions of the Theme of the Overnight Visit in *The Wedding of Smailagić Meho*	203
10	The Transitional Text	212
	Bibliography	239
	Index	253

Foreword

Gregory Nagy

The Singer Resumes the Tale, by Albert B. Lord, is a book in progress. The author died on July 29, 1991, before he could put the finishing touches on what he had intended as a sequel to his 1960 masterpiece, *The Singer of Tales.* The loss was incalculably painful, but a remedy appeared. His cherished wife and partner, Mary Louise Lord, undertook the difficult task of collecting and meticulously editing the various drafts the author had composed to achieve the book that he had intended. Thanks to her heroic accomplishment, the current work of Albert Lord emerges in all its clarity of vision. I say "current" because he had meant this book to be a statement of work in progress. Throughout *The Singer Resumes the Tale* Lord again and again reveals his openness to finding new ways of looking at oral traditions. Most striking is his sustained vision of literature as a concept that encompasses oral as well as written traditions. Whether he agrees or disagrees with various scholars, senior and junior alike, in their various approaches to the complex problem of establishing the relationships of oral and written traditions, he does so with a strong sense that continuing debate about this problem will lead to an ever deeper understanding of literature itself. The debate proceeds each time the reader reopens this book, each time the singer resumes the tale.

Preface

This is Albert B. Lord's book. It is not quite the same book that would have resulted had he lived to crown it with his finishing touches, but it comes as close to that book as I could help to make it. He had completed almost all the chapters, to which I have added two, "*Beowulf* and Oral Epic Tradition" and "Rebuttal," which consist of unpublished lectures that he had recently delivered. It is appropriate, I believe, to incorporate into his book these lectures, and parts of lectures, as in "The Formula in Anglo-Saxon Poetry," "The Ballad: Textual Stability, Variation, and Memorization" and "The Transitional Text"; for he considered them as preparation for the work that he long intended as a sequel to *The Singer of Tales*. What little is mine in *The Singer Resumes the Tale* is easily distinguished by being set off by square brackets. The sections with the label "Editor's Addendum" are an attempt to fill in what my husband would have treated much more gracefully and perceptively had he been able to do so. Notes pertaining to publications dating after his death in 1991 have also been placed in brackets.

The Singer Resumes the Tale, as will be readily apparent, includes many citations from the various kinds of poetry discussed throughout the volume. It had to be thus; for Albert Lord believed firmly in literary criticism based closely upon the text. He was wary of theories and analyses that hover high in the stratosphere without ever descending to the terra firma of the poet's own words. He also was skeptical of abstruse, verbose, and unnecessarily complex critical terminology. The more direct the definition, the better.

Portions of this book will sound familiar, as they continue arguments begun in *The Singer of Tales*, in subsequent articles, and in *Epic Singers and Oral Tradition*. If they seem in any way repetitious, they illustrate my husband's belief that repetition in oral tradition is always significant! Such repetition reveals an underlying and vital message that is further developed here. The present volume advances and redefines two important topics broached in *The Singer of Tales*, namely, "the theme" and "the transitional text." The phenomenon of "blocks of lines," intermediate between the formula and the theme, also receives attention and ample illustration. The theme is examined in Homer, in *Beowulf*, and in Russian *byliny* and Latvian *dainas* as well as in the South Slavic heroic epic of Avdo Međedović and in the "Women's Songs." New to this book are the chapters on traditional lyrical poetry and on the ballad. The "transitional text" is the subject of the last chapter, but, as the concluding paragraphs indicate, the term *transitional* does not describe the poetry, epic and lyric, that forms the basis of the book.

Many years ago a reader of one of the first articles submitted by my husband for publication recommended that it contain "more Parry and less thrust!" Throughout his career Albert Lord adhered to that advice all too steadfastly, even when friends strongly urged that he respond to his critics. For the most part, instead of answering attacks on the Parry-Lord approach to oral poetics, he resolutely proceeded to "cultivate his garden." Recently, however, he ventured a few "thrusts." By allowing them a place in this book, I hope that I am being faithful to the memory both of Milman Parry and of Albert Lord.

My husband deliberately emphasized the present tense "resumes" for the title of this book. No matter how many texts he collected, transcribed, translated, and studied, the "song" is far from having run its course. Its words and rhythms must ever be made to reverberate by friends of oral traditional poetry, both by those known and revered by Albert Lord and by those many scholars unknown to him but nonetheless to be esteemed for their contributions to this discipline.

The Singer Resumes the Tale would never have seen the light of day without the enthusiastic help of Gregory Nagy, who has given this book a place in his series, "Myth and Poetics," and who has constantly provided encouragement and advice. My profound thanks for his guidance and friendship. I gratefully acknowledge the assistance of the Harvard Department of the Classics, through the kindness of Richard J. Tarrant and Zeph Stewart, in providing a subsidy from the Loeb Publication Fund for the preparation of the manuscript. The keyboarding of the book has been in the capable hands of Pamela Marshall.

I owe a very special debt to many of Albert's colleagues for supplying information on substantive matters occasioned by the several languages involved in the book. David E. Bynum has been a constant and ever-ready resource for the South Slavic texts and has checked them with a discerning eye. From his abundant knowledge of this poetry, he has contributed greatly to the present volume. Thomas J. Butler also has been an invaluable help in this regard and has generously assisted in the solution of a number of problems. Horace Lunt's advice on several linguistic matters is much appreciated.

I am most grateful to Daniel Donoghue, who faithfully read through and improved the portions dealing with Anglo-Saxon poetry. John M. Foley has also provided helpful advice on the chapters dealing with Old English. Vladimir Alexandrov has kindly aided with the passages in Russian, and Kristine Konrad and Morris Halle have assisted with the Latvian *dainas*. I am greatly indebted to Stephen A. Mitchell for his interest in this book and for his many fine suggestions with regard to Germanic poetry. Richard Janko and Jan Ziolkowski deserve especially warm mention for reading and commenting on several parts of the book.

Marshall Poe, teaching fellow in the Department of History at Harvard, and Claire Waters, an advanced undergraduate student, have been intrepid scouts, combing the stacks and scanning the catalogs of Widener Library. Matthew Kay and Russell Martin have also been loyally at hand. My heartfelt thanks to one and all for their devotion to the memory of Albert Lord and to the principles that guided his research.

Cornell University Press and especially Bernhard Kendler have been wonderfully responsive and friendly in their reception of this book. Elizabeth Holmes and Janet Mais have resourcefully coped with the abundant problems occasioned by citations in several languages, some of them not normally encountered in everyday American usage. No detail has been too slight for their careful attention. I thank them for their patience and their steady guidance.

In the Editor's Preface to Volume 1 of *Serbo-Croatian Heroic Songs*, Albert Lord dedicated the books in the series to the living voices of Milman Parry, the scholar and collector, to his assistant, Nikola Vujnović, and to the South Slavic singers themselves. In carrying forward their work, Albert Lord's voice is also still living and keeps the song resounding.

MARY LOUISE LORD

Cambridge, Massachusetts

THE SINGER RESUMES THE TALE

CHAPTER I

The Nature and Kinds of Oral Literature

Epics, ballads, prose tales, ritual and lyric songs, as genres, existed orally before writing was invented. We do not have a special word to designate them before they were manifested in writing, so we are left with the paradox of "oral literature." But if literature can be defined as "carefully constructed verbal expression," carefully structured oral verbal expression can surely qualify as literature. This is common sense. People did not wait until there was writing before they told stories and sang songs. Moreover, when these genres first appeared in writing, their metric base, their poetic and compositional devices, were already fully developed and none of them could have been invented by any one person at any one time. They are too complicated for that. Oral literature, then, consists of the songs and stories, and other sayings, that people have heard and listened to, sung and told, without any intervention of writing. The creator or transmitter did not write the song or the story but sang or told it; the receiver did not read the song or story but heard it. These stories and songs are, therefore, not only oral but also aural; they are not only told, they are also heard.

Beginning with oral traditional epic, I should like to focus on the "performance," at the moment of performing in a traditional setting and with a traditional audience. The word *traditional* is important in the phrase oral traditional epic (or literature), implying, as it does, a depth of meaning set into that literature, from its origin, by previous generations. Text and context are inseparable. Without a sympathetic knowledge of context, the text may be misunderstood. Yet it is not sufficient to study performance and contextuality without an understanding of the tradition underlying them.

I prefer the term *listeners* instead of "audience," because "audience" seems to imply a more formal type of event. I want to think of the place and times when a truly traditional singer ordinarily sings epic songs to traditional listeners in his community who ordinarily listen to his and others' singing of epic.[1] They have listened to him before, and he has sung for them since he first began to sing; some of them are also singers and he has listened to them; they know him and his songs and vice versa; they like to listen to him and he likes to sing to them. They form a small and intimate group; they are the ideal "traditional" group.

The circumstances will be different to some extent in each traditional culture, but speaking for the one that I know best, that of the Slavic Balkans, I would find one of the most normal places for singing to be the house in a small village where neighbors gather for an evening and sit and talk and listen to a singer. Epics are sung also at weddings and to help celebrate the Slava, the family feast for its patron saint. Another informal setting is the coffeehouse in Moslem communities, where men gather, especially during Ramadan, and listen, after a day of fasting, to epic songs that may continue for a whole night. The singers and the listeners are all "insiders"; that is, they are part of the same tradition.

Perhaps these settings do not seem at first to fit the ancient Greek case. We learn in Homer of the singing of epic in the court of a king. One thinks of Demodocus in Alcinous's palace in Phaeacia or Phemius, who sang for the suitors in Ithaca.[2] There is also Achilles, keeping apart in his tent before Troy, singing of the κλέα ἀνδρῶν, "the famous deeds of heroes."[3] Yet I see no reason why what I have said about traditional performer and traditional audience cannot apply just as well to the singer in a small king's court as to the singer in a neighborhood gathering. The kingdoms in ancient Greece were small, the number of listeners surely not very great.

Exceptions were occasions like the Ionian festival mentioned in the Homeric *Hymn to Apollo*, at which the maidens "sing a strain telling of men

---

1. I refer to the epic singer by the masculine pronoun because the epics discussed in this book were sung by men. For Homeric bards one can cite Phemius and Demodocus in the *Odyssey*. In *Beowulf* we hear the Anglo-Saxon scop reciting tales of Sigemund and Heremod. The minstrel who performs the lay of Finn likewise provides entertainment in Heorot. The byliny, Russian folk epics, were regularly sung by men, although some women were performers, especially in the period of the tradition's decline. The South Slavic heroic songs are performed by men. The poems are stichic and, among the Moslems, are long and are sung in the coffeehouses by men for men. The so-called women's songs, as distinguished from epics, can be performed by men as well as women. They are stanzaic and usually short and either lyric, or, when narrative, classed as ballads.

2. For more on epic singing as depicted in the *Odyssey*, see A. Lord, 1962, 182–84. This reference includes mention of a former South Slavic tradition of Moslem singers at the courtly circles of beys and pashas.

3. *Iliad* 9.189.

and women of past days, and charm the tribes of men." The singer says then, of himself, words that have become famous:

> Remember me in after time whenever any one of men on earth, a stranger who has seen and suffered much, comes here and asks of you: "Whom think ye, girls, is the sweetest singer that comes here, and in whom do you most delight?" Then answer, each and all, with one voice: "He is a blind man, and dwells in rocky Chios: his lays are evermore supreme." As for me, I will carry your renown as far as I roam over the earth to the well-placed cities of man, and they will believe also; for indeed this thing is true.[4]

It is important that the traditional group was generally homogeneous.[5] The kings and princes and those who gathered in the court formed the community; the singers and their listeners shared knowledge and had the same sense of values. They shared stories and myths. In short, they shared the tradition.

Let me explain what I mean by "tradition" in respect to epic song. For any individual singer the tradition consists of all the performances of all the songs of all the singers he has ever heard. *All* the singers encompasses the worst, the best, and all in between. Homer was the best of the traditional singers of whom we know in ancient Greece. He was not outside the tradition or "making use of the tradition"; he was part of it, in it. A tradition is dynamic and ongoing. It lasts as long as there are singers and listeners.

The singing of epic songs is very ancient. It is clear that it began before writing was invented. The ancient Greek tradition was very highly developed by Homer's time. Though traditions start in the distant past and retain the strength of their roots, they are not *of* the past, until there are no longer any truly traditional singers and listeners. Traditions are subject to change: the reforming of old stories, the telling of new ones that may seem much like the old. A really living tradition has no need of "preservation" because it is always being preserved with every truly traditional performance by a truly traditional singer.

There are several categories of traditionality, that is, of elements that may persist over generations. I suggest five aspects of oral tradition, which I shall first enumerate, later returning to enlarge upon the second, third, and fifth categories, which call for special emphasis.

First, the *practice* of storytelling itself, be it in prose or verse, be it spoken,

---

4. Homeric *Hymn to Apollo*, ll. 166–76, Evelyn-White, 1943, 337. For the great Panathenaean festivals at which rhapsodes recited the Homeric poems, see Nagy, 1990b; consult the General Index under "Festivals" and "Panathenaia." [See also Janko, 1992, 30–31.]

5. See Chapter 2 for the circumstances of the performance of Latvian lyric poems, the *dainas*.

sung, or chanted, and of singing songs of various kinds, can be traditional. This means that for generations in a given community or culture people have found a time, a place, and an audience for such a practice. Telling or singing has long had a place in their social behavior patterns. Laments, for example, are sung or chanted as part of the rituals practiced at times of death, and this custom has been kept since time immemorial.

Second, the *art of composing* songs and stories is itself handed down from one generation of creator-transmitters to the next. This is a crucial category for distinguishing some oral traditional songs or stories from their later literary—that is, "written literary"—counterparts. The traditional process of composition and transmission of oral traditional poetry or prose varies from genre to genre and is treated in detail when we look more closely, for example, at lyric, nonnarrative songs in Chapter 2. In general, lines are constructed with the help of "formulas," and poems, or stories, or songs, are made up of "themes."

Third, there is a category of *traditional content* of traditional literature. Here we find traditional story patterns, traditional generic secular and mythic narratives, and traditional generic types of nonnarrative songs, such as lyric or ritual songs.

Fourth, there are the *specific works*, the specific oral traditional stories, songs, and short literary forms in all their variants. By that I mean the ballad of "Barbara Allen," the epic of "Marko Kraljević and Musa the Highwayman," the tale of "The Three Princesses," and so forth. I do not believe that this category needs elaboration, but it is necessary to insist that it contain *all* variants, recorded or not, of each work, because we cannot point to any one of them as the "correct" or "original" text.

The fifth category of traditionality is *oral traditional poetics*. It may be that from the beginning, some stories and songs were simple, brief, and ephemeral. They consisted of loosely structured, short-lived anecdotes and songs with a limited frame of reference. Yet it is certain that there came into being, as time went on, well-structured narratives and songs of wider reference and deeper meaning told or sung by skillful creator-storytellers or singers. In short, there emerged eventually an "oral literature" in the qualitative sense of the term. We can suppose that repetitions of sounds and patterns of words put together to be imitative and to have the power of magic came to set models of duplication and of balance and proportion which had an appeal to an innate human aesthetic sense.

To retrace my steps and return to the second aspect of traditionality, the art of composing songs and stories, I shall illustrate the "formulas" and "themes," by which songs are created. Formulas, in Milman Parry's definition, consist of "a group of words which is regularly employed under the same metrical conditions to express a given essential idea."⁶ A theme is a repeated passage with a varying, but fairly high, degree of verbal correspondence each time it is used.⁷ In reality the formulas and clusters of formulas that have evolved in any particular culture over a long period of time make it possible for the singer to fit essential ideas into the metrical lines. The addition of an epithet to a noun, or of an adverb to a verb, can make it possible to use that noun or verb under a variety of metrical situations. Because singers, like other people, think in terms of sentences, that is, of ideas linked together, rather than single ideas, clusters of formulas have arisen to express one or more groups of ideas.

A few examples clarify these generalities. I take the first from the collection of Russian byliny made by A. F. Hilferding in 1871.⁸ Trofim Grigor'evich Rjabinin began four of his eighteen songs in Volume 2 with the description of a feast held by Prince Vladimir. The first line in three of them is a bona fide whole-line formula, the essential idea of which is Prince Vladimir himself:

> No. 76   Slavnyja Vladymir stol'ne-kievskoj
> Glorious Vladimir of the capital Kiev
>
> No. 80   A Vladymir knjaz' da stol'njo-kievskoj
> Prince Vladimir of the capital Kiev
>
> No. 81   A Vladymir knjaz' stol'ne-kievskoj
> Prince Vladimir of the capital Kiev.

He uses a different construction at the opening of

> No. 84   A j vo slavnojom vo gorodi vo Kievi
> Slavnogo u knjazja Vladymira
>
> In the glorious city Kiev
> At the glorious prince Vladimir's.

but Vladimir keeps his epithet *slavnyj* 'glorious' and his title *knjaz'* 'prince'. In Nos. 76, 80, and 81, Vladimir also has the compound epithet *stol'ne-kievskoj* 'of the capital Kiev'.

The second line of the "theme" of the feast (which I shall analyze as a theme shortly) is another well-established formula:

---

6. Milman Parry, "Studies in the Epic Technique of Oral Verse-Making, 1, Homer and Homeric Style," 1930, in Parry, 1971, 272. See also A. Lord, 1960, chap. 3, "The Formula," 30–67.
7. For an earlier treatment of the theme, see A. Lord, 1960, chap. 4, "The Theme," 68–98. See also A. Lord, 1991, 84–93.
8. Hilferding, 1938.

> No. 76 Sobiral-to on slavnyj pochesten pir,
> He assembled a glorious, honorable feast,
>
> No. 80 Zavodil pochesten pir da j pirovan'ice,
> He held an honorable feast, and a feasting,
>
> No. 81 Zavodil on pochesten pir pirovan'ico,
> He held an honorable feast, a feasting,
>
> No. 84 Zavodilsja u knjazja pochesten pir.
> There was held at the prince's an honorable feast.

The "feast" at Vladimir's is always "honorable." *Pochesten pir* 'honorable feast' is clearly a common formula for Rjabinin (and for others), and one of the commonest verbs used with it is *zavodil* 'held' or, in the passive, *zavodilsja* 'was held'. In No. 76 another verb is used, *sobiral* 'he gathered', and to *pochesten* 'honorable' is added for the sake of the meter another epithet, the ubiquitous *slavnyj* 'glorious'. And in Nos. 80 and 81 an appositive is added, also for the sake of the meter, *pirovan'ice* 'feasting'. These are clearly formulas, and taking two (or three) lines together, as one must, one has a cluster of formulas as well.

Some of the above lines are not limited to the theme of a feast at Vladimir's court. Rjabinin's version of "Il'ja Muromec and Car' Kalin" begins with the line

> No. 75 Kak Vladimir knjaz' da stol'njo-kievskoj
> As Prince Vladimir of the capital Kiev

and continues:

Porozgnevalsja na starago kazaka Il'ju Muromca,	Was angered at the old Cossack Il'ja Muromec,
Zasadil ego vo pogreb vo glubokii,	He put him in a deep cellar
Vo glubokij pogreb vo holodnyi	In a deep cellar, a cold one,
Da na tri-to godu pory vremeni.	For three years' time.
A u slavnago u knjazja u Vladymira	The glorious prince Vladimir
Byla doch' da odinakaja,	Had an only daughter.

Other examples of those two lines can be easily found.

At this point No. 84 parts company with the other three songs by telling that at the feast there were two widows, and the activity centers on their conversations and the results of them. But No. 76 continues with Nos. 80 and 81 for two more lines before diverging in its turn:

No. 76   Na mnogih knjazej on i bojarov
         Slavnyh sil'nyih moguchiih bogatyrej;

         Many princes and boyars,
         Glorious, mighty, powerful bogatyrs;

No. 80   Na mnogih knjazej da na vsih bojarov,
         Na vsih sil'nih rus'skiih moguchih na bogatyrej.

         Many princes and all boyars,
         All mighty, Russian, powerful bogatyrs.

No. 81   A j na vseh-to na knjazej na bojarov,
         Da j na rus'skih moguchih bogatyrej,

         All princes and boyars,
         And Russian, powerful bogatyrs.

The princes and boyars are "many" or "all," and the bogatyrs are *slavnyj* 'glorious', of course—though only once—*sil'nyj* 'mighty', *rus'skii* 'Russian', and *moguchii* 'powerful'.

The formulaic style is well illustrated in the foregoing lines, both in respect to individual formulas, such as *pochesten pir* 'honorable feast', and clusters of formulas, namely, this group of lines itself, which consists of formulas frequently associated with one another. No. 76 now leaves the other texts to recount that Vladimir did not invite to the feast the old Cossack Il'ja Muromec, and the story develops from that fact.[9]

I now move from formula to theme, using the remainder of the theme of a feast in Nos. 80 and 81 from Trofim Rjabinin to illustrate an example of that form of the theme in which a messenger, or ambassador, is chosen to undertake a dangerous mission. One is reminded of the council theme in *The Song of Roland* in which Ganelon is chosen to carry Charlemagne's answer to Marsile.

But first the description of those invited to the feast continues for one more line:

---

9. The following example from medieval poetry may also be instructive. In Anglo-Saxon, *Beowulf maðelode* expresses the idea "Beowulf spoke" in the *a* verse, the first half of the line. If one does not wish to introduce a new idea in the *b* verse, the second half of the line, one can simply use the common alliterating patronymic for Beowulf, and the line then reads *Beowulf maðelode/ bearn Ecgðeowes* 'Beowulf spoke/ the son of Ecgðeow'. Each verse is a formula, and the whole line is also a formula, because they are regular ways of saying "Beowulf spoke." See A. Lord, 1991, chap. 9, "The Formulaic Structure of Introductions to Direct Discourse in *Beowulf* and *Elene*," 147–69.

8   The Singer Resumes the Tale

80	81
Aj na slavnyh poljanic da na udalyih.	Na vseh slavnyh poljanic na udalyih.
Glorious, bold warriors from afar.	All glorious bold warriors from afar.

At this point the two stories begin to diverge, but they both present a speech from Vladimir. There is further setting for it in No. 81:

> A sidjat-to molodci na chestnom piru,
> Vse-to sidjat p'jany vesely;
>
> The fine, brave fellows sit at the honorable feast,
> They sit drunk and merry.

80	81
Na chestnom piru Vladymir stal pohazhivat'	Vladymir knjaz' po gorenki pohazhival,
	Poslovechno gosudar' vygovarival:
At the honorable feast Vladimir began to walk up and down the room.	Prince Vladimir walked up and down the room.
	The lord began to speak carefully.

The speeches are, of course, different in each song. In No. 80, Vladimir needs someone to collect tribute; in No. 81 he wants someone to find him a wife. The reaction, however, is the same.

80	81
Vse bogatyri za stolikom umolknuli,	Vse bogatyri za stolikom umolknuli,
Vse umolknuli i priutihnuli,	Vse molodci da priutihnuli,
Kak bogatyri za stolikom-to pritul'jalisja,	Za stolom-to sidjat zatul'jalisja;
A bol'shaja-to tulitsja za serednjuju,	Bol'shaja tulitsja k serednjuju,
A serednja tulitsja za men'shuju,	Serednjuju tulitsja za men'shuju,
A ot men'shojoj ot tulicy otvetu net.	A ot men'shoj tulicy otvetu net.
Iz-za tyh li-to za stolichkov dubovyih,	Z-za togo [z] za stolichka dubovago,
Iz-za tyh li-to skameechek okol'nyih	Iz-za tyh skameechek okol'niih
Vyshel staryja Permin da syn Ivanovich,	Vyshel staryja Permin syn Ivanovich,
Stal po gorenke jon Permin da pohazhivat',	Ponizeshen'ku knjazju poklonjaetsja:
A Vladymiru knjazju da stal jon pogovarivat':	
"Ty, Vladymir knjaz' da stol'njo-kievskoj!	"Vladymir knjaz' i stol'ne-kievskoj!

Blaslovi-tko gosudar' mne slovce vymolvit'.	Blagoslovi-ko gosudar' mni slovce vymolvit'.
A 'shche znaju ja kogo poslat' poehati	A 'shche znaju ja tobi suprotivnichku:"
A j vo dal'nie-ty zemli v sorochinskii."	
All the bogatyrs at the table were silent,	All the bogatyrs at the table were silent,
They were silent and hushed,	All the fine, brave fellows were hushed.
As the bogatyrs sit at the table hiding,	They sit at the table hiding;
The bigger hide behind the medium-sized,	The bigger hide behind the medium-sized,
And the medium-sized hide behind the smaller.	The medium-sized hide behind the smaller,
And from the smaller there was no answer.	And from the smaller there was no answer.
From behind the oak tables,	From behind the oak table,
From behind the surrounding benches,	From behind the surrounding benches
Came old Permin Ivanovich.	Came old Permin Ivanovich.
Permin began to walk up and down the room,	He bowed low before the prince:
And he began to speak to Prince Vladimir:	
"You, Prince Vladimir of capital Kiev,	"Vladimir, prince of capital Kiev!
Give me your blessing, lord, to speak.	Give me your blessing, lord, to speak.
I know whom to send to go	I know a wife for you."
To the distant lands of Sorochinsk."	

At this point, each song develops its own story in the respective speeches of Permin. In No. 80, Permin suggests that Vasiliij Kazimirov is the person to send on the mission to Botijan Botijanov, and in No. 81 he says that he knows a good wife for Vladimir, namely, Opraks'ja, daughter of the king of Lithuania. Thereupon, Vladimir asks the company whom to send to the king of Lithuania, a question like that in No. 80, whom to send to Botijan Botijanov. At this juncture there is in No. 81 a repetition of the two lines:

> Vse za stolom sidjat umolknuli,
> Vse molodci priutihnuli.
>
> All sitting at the table are silent,
> All the fine, brave, fellows are hushed.

depicting the reaction of the company to the request for a messenger on a possibly dangerous mission, which we have seen before. And once again appears:

> Staryja Permin syn Ivanovich,
> A po gorenke Permin jon pohazhivaet,
> Poslovechno knjazju jon vygovarivaet:
> "Ty Vladymir knjaz' stol'ne-kievskoj!
> Blagoslovi mne gosudar' slovcjo molviti.
> A j to znaju ja poslat' kogo posvatat'sja."
>
> Old Permin Ivanovich,
> And Permin walked up and down the room,
> He began to speak to the prince carefully:
> "You, Vladimir, prince of capital Kiev!
> Give me your blessing, lord, to speak.
> I know whom to send as wedding broker."[10]

It is to be noted that within the verbal repetitions there is a subtle kaleidoscopic mutation and recombination of elements.

Now the two songs are on the same level again and the choice of messenger or ambassador is made for the separate undertakings. There is no need to follow in detail the ceremony of choice and acceptance with which the full theme is concluded. It is clear that the singer has a store of verses repeated more or less exactly to describe a feast at which a question is asked by the prince, messengers are proposed, and they are chosen with due ceremony. He needs only to fill in the specifics peculiar to each story. The process of composition of oral literature by using formulas and themes constitutes a traditional art, which one generation passes on to the next.

The theme of the feast at which a messenger or ambassador is chosen for a dangerous mission, which is a large theme, particularly if it is described fully, may contain smaller themes within it. If a section of a larger scheme can be found as a discernible unit elsewhere, either independent or as part of another large theme, it constitutes a theme in its own right. This is a principle worked out by David Bynum.[11] Thus it could be argued that the beginning lines of the four songs from the Hilferding collection form an independent theme, because they are a discernible unit in three distinct forms of the theme of a feast at Prince Vladimir's court.

Tradition, that is to say, all singers before and around him, bequeathed to

---

10. I am indebted to Professor Vladimir Alexandrov of Yale University for checking, correcting, and improving my translations from Russian.
11. Bynum, 1964.

each singer/performer, including Homer, a technique of composing songs in performance which is *not* improvisation, if the latter is understood as impromptu, extempore creation. Let there be no more misunderstanding on this point.[12] What I have just described is not improvisation on the spur of the moment but a very special type of composition in performance made possible by the singer's command of formulas and themes. They are not mastered by a conscious process of rote memorization, but they are remembered from frequent use and practice. Formulas do not exist to make memorization easier, but rather they make memorization unnecessary.

The aspect of traditionality I develop next is category three, the content of traditional literature. If a singer has not memorized a fixed text—there is no fixed text to remember—what does he hold in his mind? One should reply, I believe, "First the story." That is what the performance is about; the tale or the narrative, is at the center of the performance. A specialist in Arabic epic, Dwight Reynolds, who has collected oral epic in the Nile Delta, in a lecture at Harvard helped explain the importance of the story. He told how in that tradition an older singer, while walking along with a young boy who was learning to sing the epic, would say to him, "Now tell me what happened at such and such a point in the story." The boy would then have to tell him that part of the story. This was the first thing he had to absorb to the point of being able to tell it himself.[13]

Traditional story patterns reside in the stories themselves but can be distilled for purposes of research. There is a pattern consisting of (1) absence of a powerful figure (or disabled elder), (2) devastation, (3) arrival (or return) of a powerful figure, and (4) justice or restoration of order. This pattern fits parts of *Beowulf*, the *Iliad*, and the *Odyssey*. In *Beowulf*, for example, (1) Hrothgar is powerless to handle (2) the depredations of Grendel, until (3) Beowulf arrives and (4) overcomes the evil Grendel and his mother and restores order to Hrothgar's kingdom. Or, to use an illustration from living epic tradition, in the South Slavic song of "The Captivity of Đulić Ibrahim," (1) while Đulić is in prison his wife despairs and (2) is about to marry again, when Đulić hears of this and contrives to be released to collect ransom, (3) returns home for that purpose, and (4) (a) either brings revenge on the suitor—if he be a bad one—and on his wife—if she be a bad one—or (b) is reunited with his wife while the suitor is married to Đulić's sister. The story pattern consists of these elements, and the generic story is the story without names of specific individuals. I believe that the pattern I have chosen for an example is a mythic

---

12. For more on the question of improvisation, see A. Lord, 1991, 76–77.
13. See Reynolds, 1990 and 1995.

pattern, representing the absence of a god, such as a god of vegetation, the calamities and death that result, and the restoration of life on the god's return from the land of the dead.[14]

Oral traditional epic is not merely entertainment but has a serious function in its society.[15] It contains the ideals and values of the society, as well as a concern for the basic problems of both the community and the individual, and how to solve them or to become reconciled to those that are insoluble. These are embodied in the myths with which, in my opinion, epics, including Homer's and others in ancient Greece, originated.

The *Iliad* and *Odyssey* depict the valiant actions of heroes, their prowess in combat, their courage in facing the unknown and the supernatural, their skill in overcoming obstacles. These are "the best of the Achaeans," to quote the title of a distinguished book by my colleague Gregory Nagy. In war and in council they were preeminent. Most of them were mortals like the rest of us, but some, like Achilles, had one divine parent; and some, like Odysseus, had a god or goddess "on their side," a divine protector. These connections with gods and goddesses may in part at least account for their being able to accomplish what they did. They should, however, be credited with being of the caliber to merit the assistance of the deities. Sometimes the heroes found themselves in narrative patterns created for gods and later assumed by humans—or half-humans. The god Marduk in the Babylonian creation epic fought with the primeval dragon Tiamat and with the help of supernatural weapons overcame her and created the universe from her carcass. Zeus subdued the monster Typhoeus. In the next generation or so in Mesopotamia, Gilgamesh, two-thirds god and one-third man, killed—with the help of his friend Enkidu, a fully human being—the monster Humbaba. The Greek hero Heracles, a son of Zeus and Alcmena, a mortal woman, was a famed monster slayer. Odysseus, with no immortal parents, had a loyal and powerful protector in Athena. It is not surprising that heroes, like the gods, came to have cults of their own.

Myth, a narrative in the "sacred" realm (using "sacred" in Mircea Eliade's sense of the opposite of "profane") is a strong force in oral traditional epic.[16] I

---

14. See A. Lord, 1960, chap. 9, "The *Iliad*," 186–97, for an elaboration of the story pattern of absence, devastation, and return; see also M. L. Lord, 1967. Chapter 3 below, at n.5, contains a discussion of mythic patterns inherent in the episode of Achilles' fight with the river Xanthus, *Iliad*, bk. 21.

15. In *The Singer of Tales*, I may have given undue emphasis to the element of entertainment when I spoke of epic poetry in Yugoslavia "at the present time, or until very recently, as the chief entertainment of the adult male population in the villages and small towns" (A. Lord, 1960, 14). Yet I tempered this statement with the observation that "this poetry would seem even from its origins to have belonged to serious ceremonial occasions, to ritual, to celebration" (ibid., 6).

16. See Eliade, 1961.

venture to say that its role is stronger than that of history, because, in my view, epic was born with myth, whereas history entered it at a later stage. It is clear, for example, that the Trojan War provides the *background* of the *Iliad* of Homer, but *not* its subject.

Yet it is important to be aware that not all story patterns are mythic; some are secular. Jesse Byock has pointed out a completely secular traditional pattern of narrative dealing with the way in which feuds were conducted in medieval Iceland.[17] He calls the elements "feudemes," and the pattern consists of the series (1) conflict, (2) advocacy, (3) resolution. What is common to both the mythic and the secular patterns is that they present a significant problem in the society, be it that of mortality or the basic legal contract that binds the group together and makes it work. The pattern dramatizes a fundamental anxiety or need of its culture.

To illustrate further the content of traditional literature, I wish to mention lyric or ritual songs such as those in which a lover asks his beloved a series of riddles, or those incantations that are counting-out rhymes. These are separate "classes," as it were, of lyric and ritual songs respectively. There is a group of lyric songs known as "dawn songs," in which lovers bewail the coming of day.[18] Laments are clearly a distinct and important class of traditional ritual songs.[19]

The fifth category of traditionality, the poetics of oral literature, requires particular attention. In attempting to trace the unfolding of oral traditional aesthetics, one realizes that some storytellers or singers were more talented than others and that they influenced the way in which stories were told and songs sung by introducing what have later been called figures of speech, thus establishing artistic norms and enriching the tale or song. Rhyme, both end and internal; alliteration; and assonance were repetitions of sound which were soon appreciated for their own sake and became regular features of many oral styles. This was true also for such tropes as anaphora and epiphora, for example, which involve repetitions of words at the beginning or end of lines and are much beloved in Slavic oral traditional poetry and elsewhere.

It is to these gifted tellers and singers that we owe also the elaboration of descriptions of heroes and maidens, of horses, and their trappings, of assemblies of men, of catalogs of chieftains, and of detailed accounts of battles. And they too over the centuries were responsible for working out what we know of as "ring composition" and "chiastic arrangement," or chiasmus, for which they themselves, of course, had no terms. By "ring composition" is meant a

17. Byock, 1982.
18. See Hatto, 1965.
19. See Alexiou, 1974.

structure that can be diagramed as *abcba*; the elements *a* and *b* lead to a central element *c*, after which elements *b* and *a* recur in one form or another, but in reverse order, thus closing a "ring." Ring composition differs from "chiastic arrangement" in that it "revolves" around a center, whereas in chiasmus there is no center, no *c*, but only *abba*. Such structures could be used within a single line, in a couplet, in a larger theme, in groups of themes, or in an entire song, forming ever expanding circles of relationships. In practice, chiasmus tends to be more common in short compass, especially in a single line, but ring composition belongs to longer passages.

An example of chiasmus on the level of the line is found in the following from one of Murat Žunić's songs from northern Bosnia collected by Milman Parry:

> Pa ćeš vidit' što vidijo nisi.
> Then you will see what seen you have not.[20]

The auxiliary is *a* and the verb "to see" is *b*.

Although Murat's song as a whole can be analyzed in terms of ring composition, it is sufficient merely to outline a single series of episodes that converge in a center. In "The Capture of Temišvar" the serfs complain to the viziers in Buda that King Rakocija is oppressing them. The viziers write to him, asking him to desist. He replies that he will not do so but will gather the seven Christian kingdoms and drive the sultan from Stambol. The viziers write to the sultan, but their letter is intercepted and never reaches him. Now a "ring" begins (within a larger ring):

a. King Rakocija gathers his forces.
b. The viziers write again to the sultan and this time make sure that the letter is delivered to him in person.
c. The sultan recalls the grand vizier, Ćuprilić, who has been removed to Konya.
b. The sultan executes the traitors.
a. The sultan gathers his forces.

The recalling of the "exiled" grand vizier is the center of the ring, because this action is the turning point against the traitors. Their doom is sealed. In the first *b*, the exposing of the traitors is set in motion, and in the second *b*, the judgment on them is executed. The outer circle that frames this ring consists of the gathering of opposing forces in both *a*s.

20. Parry, 1979, *Uzimanje Temišvara*, "The Capture of Temišvar," 246, l. 384.

Thus, in the course of time, developed the high quality of oral traditional literature which in the end was bequeathed to written literature; for all these elements came into being before writing was invented.

The stories and songs thus created were not only oral; they were also traditional. Young people learned from their elders how to tell stories and sing songs skillfully and with a sense of the special style that was theirs alone. One generation passed on to the next the technique, or art, of composing tales and songs, together with the appropriate story, ritual, or song material. Writing was not needed. The art was perfected without it and was never dependent on it. It is vastly important that this be understood. It is a technique that preserves essential patterns and associations and presents them in such a way as to make them most meaningful, most effective, and at the same time in a manner both pleasing and suitable, which happens also to be easy to remember.

Oral traditional poetics has some special characteristics because of the way in which it was created from the matrix of oral tradition. The opening lines of Hilferding No. 76 with their repetition of *slavnyj* 'glorious' would not be considered as good style in the poetics of written literature, but they are natural and right in the poetics of oral traditional literature:

Slavnyja Vladymir stol'ne-kievskoj	Glorious Vladimir of the capital Kiev
Sobiral-to on slavnyj pochesten pir	Held a glorious, honorable feast
Na mnogih knjazej on i bojarov,	For many princes and boyars,
Slavnyh sil'nyih moguchiih bogatyrej;	Glorious, mighty, powerful bogatyrs.

Written literature can, of course, easily imitate this usage of noun-epithet formulas, which arises from the necessity of being able to use the needed noun in a variety of metrical circumstances, but it would be imitation of the oral traditional style. No poet in a written literary style would create such lines. Were he to do so, he would be severely criticized. We cannot employ the criteria of written poetics to such a passage without doing an injustice to the oral traditional poetics that formed it and that finds it normal and "right."

Almost every time Vladimir appears, he has the epithet as above *stol'ne-kievskoj* 'of the capital Kiev'; and Il'ja Muromec is always the 'old Cossack' (*staroj kazak*). Poets in written literature do not favor even more or less fixed, "stereotyped," epithets. It is a different, oral, special poetics that does favor such epithets, understanding their necessity and feeling their appropriateness.

Moreover, to indicate another characteristic construction in Slavic oral traditional poetry, when in the same song Rjabinin sings:

> A j krichit-to ved' Il'ja on vo vsju golovu,
> Vo vsju golovu krichit on gromkim golosom:
>
> And Il'ja shouted with all his might,
> With all his might he shouted in a loud voice.

the repetition of the words at the end of one line at the beginning of the next would seem unnatural in written poetics. It is, however, an accepted, even preferred, device in oral traditional poetry, to which it is special, because it was created to allow three ideas to be expressed in two lines, namely, (1) 'he shouted' (*krichit*), (2) 'with all his might' (*vo vsju golovu*), and (3) 'in a loud voice' (*gromkim golosom*).

These are some of the devices of oral traditional poetics that are different from the poetics of written literature and stem from the method of oral composition by formula and theme. Associated with these peculiar differences is the impression that the oral style was inferior to the written. The examples given above indicate differences in devices but not in quality, although the critic of written literature might disagree.

Evidence for appreciation of the difference between oral traditional poetics and written literary poetics has come from an unexpected but very important source, an editor of oral traditional South Slavic epics. One of the finest collections from northern Bosnia was made by Luka Marjanović in the last quarter of the nineteenth century. His collection is among those in the Matica Hrvatska in Zagreb. The Milman Parry Collection was graciously allowed to microfilm the unpublished texts in the Marjanović collection.[21] In some cases we have the manuscript as it was edited by Marjanović for publication.

Marjanović made many changes in the manuscript. He left out lines and added lines; he left out blocks of five to ten lines. He changed all eleven-syllable lines to ten syllables, and sometimes he combined two lines. His edited texts do not represent the exact words of the singer who dictated them. Marjanović brought to the editing criteria different from those of the singer. Sometimes he omitted "awkward" lines, such as "Then you should see Beg Mustajbeg," lines the singer used frequently in performance and, interestingly enough, continued to use in dictating the text for a scribe. This fact, incidentally, speaks eloquently for the high quality of collecting involved. Marjanović's collection is one of the most scrupulously gathered ones that I have seen.

---

21. The Milman Parry Collection of Oral Literature, Widener Library, Harvard University, Cambridge, Mass.

The Nature and Kinds of Oral Literature   17

The changes Marjanović introduced as editor in order to make the text conform to "written poetics" are instructive. For example, in Salko Vojniković's song *Janković Stojan udaje posestrimu Turkinju djevojku za Kurtagić Hasana*, "Janković Stojan Weds His Blood-Sister, a Turkish Maiden, to Kurtagić Hasan,"[22] he made the following two lines into one:

> Jer vid' dere Uzeira sina,
> Uzeira Korlatova sina!
>
> Then see son Uzeir,
> Uzeir, Korlat's son!

They became:

> Vidi dere Korlatova sina!
> Then see Korlat's son!

The construction of the two lines, repeating *Uzeira* from the end of one line at the beginning of the next, is characteristic of Slavic oral traditional poetics, as we saw above in a Russian example, and arises from the fact that it is impossible to say "See Korlat's son Uzeir" in one line. The repetition is necessary, but from necessity has come an approved and favored poetic device. The editor has eliminated the element that is characteristic of oral traditional poetics, transforming it into something more ordinary, more compatible with his notion of written poetics.

In the next example, also from Salko Vojniković,[23] the editor has omitted a line as superfluous; yet its presence gave a typical rhythm to the expression of the ideas. Here is the setting:

	Editor's changes
Vid'im age starca Ćejvanage!	
Otišće aga u džepove ruke,	On otišće u džepove ruke,
Iz džepova knjigu izvadio.	Iz džepova knjigu izvadio.
A kad aga knjigu izvadio,	[line omitted]
On je imam' pruži efendiji.	
Kad je uze imam efendija,	
Jer razmota, a niz nju pogleda.	Razmota je, a niz nju pogleda.

---

22. Marjanović collected 104 songs from Salko Vojniković Perić, including 11 women's songs. The text quoted is No. 38, and the edited line is 896. The text was never published.

23. No. 36, *Sužanjstvo bega Mustabega u bana Zadranina; izbavi ga Ćelebijć Hasan*, "The Imprisonment of Bey Mustajbey; Ćelebijć Hasan Rescues Him," ll. 20–25.

> See the old man, aga Ćejvanaga!
> The aga put his hand in his pockets,
> He took the letter from his pockets.
> And when the aga had taken out the letter,
> He held it out to the imam.
> When the imam had taken it,
> He opened it and looked at it.

Marjanović's changes are not many, but they are symptomatic. Line two above has eleven syllables; Marjanović made it into ten by omitting *aga* and adding *on* 'he' at the beginning of the line. He then omitted line four as superfluous; yet the construction is typical, reflecting the rhythm of the thought. It does no harm to leave out the line, but it does change the tempo of narration and the shape of the thought as the singer himself had expressed it. Strangely enough, the editor kept the same construction in the last two lines quoted: "When the imam had taken it, he opened it and looked at it." Perhaps he objected to having two instances of the construction so close together and omitted one. If so, he reflected the taste of a "written poetics," which seeks to avoid repetitions within such brief compass, whereas the oral poetics of the singer found no difficulty with the repetition of the construction.

Finally, the last line was changed by omitting *jer* 'because' at the beginning and adding *je* 'it' after *razmota* 'opened', literally, 'unwound'. This change is different from the other two, and its acceptability could be argued. The singer introduces many lines with *jer* 'because' quite ungrammatically and illogically. From the point of view of oral traditional poetics, his doing so could legitimately be held to be poor style. In short, oral traditional poetics has its own standards as well; it is not true that anything done by singers is necessarily good. But the criteria for making such judgments should be those of oral traditional poetics, not those of written poetics. We are in fact dealing with two separate poetics. It is our task to set forth the particulars of their differences and especially to describe oral traditional poetics as specifically as possible, as it is the less well known.

Yet because some of the elements of oral traditional poetics were inherited by written literature, the illusion was created that the poetics of both literatures was the same.[24] They do indeed share many figures of speech, which we can see in the following passage, sung by Sulejman Makić in his "Song of Bagdad" in November 1934.[25]

---

24. For the view that "oral" and "written" poetics are alike, see Finnegan, 1977, 126–33.
25. Parry, 1953, No. 26, *Pjesma od Bagdata*, ll. 243–56.

Janjičari, veliki junaci,	The Janisseries, great heroes,
Prifatiše malog Ibrahima.	They took little Ibrahim.
Kod šeha ga. jadan. dovedoše.	To the priest, poor boy, they led him.
Svečevu mu kapu nataknuše.	The ceremonial cap they put on him.
Svečevom ga hrkom ogrnuše.	The ceremonial cloak they placed on him.
Svečevu mu kapu nataknuše.	The ceremonial cap they put on him.
Odveli ga na mesto babovo.	They led him to his father's place.
Primiše ga boža amaneta.	They received him under God's protection.
Pukoše mu sto topova, kaže,	For him a hundred cannon were fired, 'tis said,
Pa je zemlja čula carevina.	And so the whole empire heard.
Stari care đe je preselijo.	That the old sultan had died.
A sina mu malog nastavili.	And that they had invested his little son.
Navaljiše carski komandari.	Then the imperial commanders thronged in.
E dodjoše. cara udvoriše.	They came and waited on the sultan.

The anaphora in lines 4–6 of the passage can be matched in written literature, of course. Such figures of speech, however, are not the property of written literature alone, nor did they originate in written literature. They were used in oral literature long before writing was invented. This passage of investiture, moreover, shows a typical traditional pattern of positioning of verbs and of alteration of a group in final position with one in initial position. The close of the passage is marked, again traditionally, by internal rhyme. I have underlined the verbs to make this patterning clear. Makić put those words in those positions following a traditional poetics, not an individual one of his own making. The configurations in the passage are part and parcel of the formulaic style and are learned together with the art of making lines and clusters of lines and the technique of moving forward from one line to another. The poetics Makić was using was that of the traditional process of composition. Therefore, though the two literatures, oral and written, share many figures of speech, each has its own particular characteristics.

Notable also in the above passage is the paratactic construction. The necessary enjambment between lines one and two is followed by a series of twelve independent lines, each containing a complete thought. It is the whole constellation of elements found in the lines quoted, their combination into a special structure, that constitutes the particular quality of oral traditional poetics.

It is now time to turn to the genres themselves: oral traditional epics, oral traditional ballads, oral traditional lyrics and ritual poetries, oral traditional praise poems, oral traditional wisdom poetry (for example, proverbs and riddles), oral traditional verse and prose used in games, and oral traditional prose stories, such as folk tales. In some of these genres the poem or tale is conceived of as a more or less fixed entity, with its own wording, and in these cases the poem—more rarely also a story—is itself transmitted as a verbal entity. This applies particularly to wisdom poetry and prose, but it is also applicable to ritual, lyric, and game songs. There may be variation, and generally there is, but there is also on the part of the singers or reciters themselves a sense that such poems have, or should have, a given set of words. These poems, of which there are many, are ordinarily comparatively short and consist primarily of oral traditional nonnarrative songs. It is worth repeating that these poems are transmitted from one generation to another in a traditional society as verbal entities with a certain distinctive verbal content; each has its own more or less stable set of words, its own identity, and, if this be true, it would be perfectly correct to say here that songs, meaning *texts* of songs, are transmitted.

With epic, ballad, and prose narrative the situation is different. The oral traditional narrative genres transmit stories and story materials together with the art of creating a text, that is, of making verses, themes, and songs. In these cases what is remembered is a story and/or themes. In this context a poem, or song, means a story, not a given set of words, not a given text. It must be admitted that these characteristics apply especially to epic and to prose narrative. Ballad seems to partake of something of both categories in respect to what is transmitted.[26]

It may seem superfluous to insist on reminding ourselves at this point that memory does not always involve conscious exact memorization of a text fixed in only one form. In the world of everyday communication we remember with many degrees of exactness; we even say, "I could not repeat it word for word, but I can tell you the gist of it." That means that we did not bother to memorize the exact words of what was heard or read, but we remembered its essential meaning. It also means that we had a way through everyday speech of expressing what we had heard. I pay considerable attention to this phenomenon in the realm of the *forms* of verbal art in which oral literature is couched, attempting to define as precisely as possible and as specifically as possible what the "more or less" means.

Questions about such concepts as textuality, fixity or fluidity of text, and

---

26. See Chapter 7 for a discussion of stability and variation in the text of ballads.

memory demand that we consider the composition of nonnarrative genres in some detail. By textuality I mean that awareness, on the part of the composer, of the words he is using, of a text as such—as against content. One of the important concerns that arises is the "span" of textuality. How many lines, for example, how much text, does the composer's sense of textuality cover? In stanzaic poetry does it go beyond the stanza, or can it embrace several stanzas? Is it, perhaps, limited to couplets? The only way to answer these questions is to look at specific examples of repeated texts in lyric poetry.

CHAPTER 2

Oral Traditional Lyric Poetry

In this chapter we seek to understand the composition and transmission of some oral traditional nonnarrative songs, which would be classed as lyrics. They are generally short and *could* be easily memorized. I should like to stress that what I am using is primary material from "pure" tradition, from living tradition, untouched, or comparatively untouched, by "outside" influences. Such material is not now easy to find. One of the important principles to note at the outset is the necessity to understand where, on the scale of pure oral tradition → transitional stages → written tradition, any body of material or any given song is to be placed. Its value for comparative study, I believe, resides in part on that determination.

I have had ready access to two large collections of lyric texts. One is Milman Parry's collection of South Slavic oral traditional songs,[1] to which may be added the published collections of Vuk Stefanović Karadžić[2] and of the Matica Hrvatska.[3] The other is the Krišjānis Barons collection of Latvian *dainas*, published between 1894 and 1915. The majority of the *dainas* are quatrains, which frequently consist of parallel couplets. There are numerous

---

1. The Milman Parry Collection has more than ten thousand lyric songs, mostly in manuscript, taken down from dictation; but there are some on the phonograph records from 1934–35 and a few on tape from later years. I was present at the singing and collecting of these songs. The great majority of them are from Moslem women in Gacko, Herzegovina. Some were published with musical transcriptions and a lengthy and important analysis of the music by Béla Bartók in Bartók and A. Lord, 1951.
2. Karadžić, 1932–36, vol. 1 (1932) and vol. 5 (1935). These are the editions from which I quote throughout this chapter. The edition of vol. 1, published by Prosveta, Belgrade, 1958, is based on the 1841 Vienna edition and is to be recommended.
3. *Hrvatske narodne pjesme*, 1896–1942 (vols. 1–4, 8–9, contain heroic songs); Andrić, 1909–42.

variants. In 1915, Barons differentiated 35,789 "type-songs" and about 182,000 variants. Barons's work was continued by Pēteris Šmits, who added more type-songs and a few more variants. The Imanta edition, known as the Copenhagen edition because of its place of publication, combines Barons's and Šmits's type-songs but has fewer selected variants. It contains 60,080 type-songs and about 10,000 variants.[4] As a matter of fact, Barons's type-songs are often what we would term variants rather than separate songs. We shall see some examples shortly.

I have been especially interested in the fact that there are so many variants of the *dainas*. With these poems two questions arose: If these are ritual songs—and many of them are—they should, as we are sometimes told, be word-for-word exact in order to satisfy the ritual requirements. They should be like incantations, which are supposed not to work unless repeated exactly. Then how come the variants? The second question: If it is true that short forms are easily memorized, one would expect that eight lines would be stable, so how come the variants? Something else seems to be at work here, and one has to ask the questions again: Is it necessary to postulate word-for-word exactness, or is that making an untrue assumption with reference not to reality but only to a guesswork theory based on a misunderstanding of what the practitioners of the form have said under inept questioning? Is shortness a real criterion for memorization, or is another process of transmission at work here?

Perhaps we are wrong in thinking of exact memorization as the only means of transmission, just as we may be wrong in supposing that a fixed text is the only possible state in which a song or poem can exist. The two concepts, of course, go together; if one believes in a fixed text, then the idea of variants—even the word—indicates a deviation from a fixed entity. In one's thinking of the composition of oral traditional poetry, the word *multiform* is more accurate than "variant," because it does not give preference or precedence to any one word or set of words to express an idea; instead it acknowledges that the idea may exist in several forms.[5] The very existence of these thousands of variants or multiforms is dramatic proof of the fluidity of the Latvian oral *daina* tradition.

---

4. Barons and Visendorfs, 1894–1915. Material accumulated since 1915 was published by Šmits, 1936–39; he adds only 7,758 variants. Barons's collection was printed in Gothic type; Šmits introduced Latin type. In this chapter, "*Ld*" (*Latvju dainas*) refers to the Barons edition, whereas "*Ltd*" (*Latviešu tautas dziesmas*) refers to the Copenhagen edition; see Švabe, Straubergs, and Hauzenberga-Šturma, 1952–56. For more details about *dainas* and their collecting, see Vīķis-Freibergs, 1981.

5. See A. Lord, 1991, 76, 102, 130, 209.

Because of their brevity, then, and because of their sheer numbers, I turn first to the Latvian *dainas*. In 1783, Gotthard Friedrich Stender wrote, "No feast, no wedding, St. John- and harvest festival, no Talkus (that is, when a number of people from the neighborhood are brought together and entertained for some day's work in common), no working of the flax, no spinning at the farm, and the like, can be carried on without the singing of these little songs."[6] He added, rather enigmatically: "It is only a shame that sometimes, especially at weddings, abuse is made of the guests in song, but the guests do not take this age-old custom with bad grace, but rather observe it rigidly, so that the ceremonial usage of their great-grandfathers is not denied its right."[7] Is he referring to a custom like the "flyting" in Old Norse, which consists of an exchange of insults between a newcomer and his host?[8]

Uriah Katzenelenbogen gives more detailed accounts of the people who sang the *dainas* and of the occasions on which they were sung:[9]

> To celebrations (as weddings and baptisms), there came two groups of girl-singers of which each sought to surpass the other in singing—not only the songs they chose, but also in the cleverness of their choice of *dainas*—especially when there were guests from afar. They sang in turn; when one group finished a *daina*, the other would continue. The married women and the young girls stood apart. One girl was chosen as the reciter, who was proud to be thus selected. She stood in the centre; the others accompanied her.

The following *daina*, Katzenelenbogen's No. 174, appears to have been sung by two girls, one singing among her in-laws at some distance from the other, who is at her brother's farm.

Ld 244.1

Dziedi, dziedi, tautas meita,	Sing, sing, young maiden!
Es pretim gavilēju;	I answer you with joy;
Tu dziedāji tautiņās,	You are singing afar among your husband's kin,

---

6. Stender, 1783: "Kein Schmauss, keine Hochzeit, keine Johannis- und Erndtefeyer, kein Talkus (das ist, wo eine Menge Personen aus der Nachbarschaft, zu einer allgemeinen Tagesarbeit, zusammen gebeten und traktirt werden), keine Flachsarbeit und Spinnerey im Hofe, und desgleichen, kan ohne Gesang dieser Liederchen abgehen" (272).

7. Ibid.: "Nur Schade, dass sie bisweilen, insonderheit auf den Hochzeiten, die Gäste schimpflich zu besingen missbraucht werden, welches aber diese, als einen uralten Gebrauch gar nicht übel nehmen, sondern vielmehr steif darüber halten, dass dem urgrossväterlichen Ceremoniell sein Recht wiederfahre."

8. For more on the flyting, see Harris, 1979 and 1981a.

9. Katzenelenbogen, 1935, 111.

	Oral Traditional Lyric Poetry 25
Es brālīšu laukmalā.	While I am here at the edge of my brother's field.

Katzenelenbogen continues:

> Into the darkly-lit room in the peasant hut, each girl would come with her work; one with her spinning, a second with her sewing, a third with her knitting. . . . They would also gather in the bath. Each person would bring meat, groats, milk. The girls would cook the supper, while the others would do their work. Then there would be much singing. Or they would gather in the inn for dancing and singing to make one another's acquaintance.
>
> The Lithuanian and Latvian girls used to keep among their most prized possessions note-books in which were written the *dainos* which pleased them. Though they themselves might not write, they asked to have their favourite *dainas* written in.
>
> The men sang tavern and table songs. The following is a vivid example of such a singing occasion. From all the men, twelve noted for the excellence of their singing were chosen; they seated themselves around an oaken table. The master of the house would place on the table an oaken bucket filled with beer, from which small oaken cups were filled. Each of the twelve men had to sing twelve *dainas* about the oak tree; all the others would accompany them. On ending each set of twelve *dainas*, the young man who had sung would drink a jug of beer, and let each of the remaining ones at the table drink his health. Then the others would continue as before. This lasted until each had sung twelve songs. All the songs had to be about the oak, and no one could repeat a song previously sung. If any of the chosen ones could not complete his set of twelve, another would be chosen to take his place, who (with twelve songs about the oak) must show that he could take the place of the discarded one.[10]

Lalita Lace Muižniece tells more about the occasions for singing:

> Unlike the tales and riddles which were for the most part reserved for fall and winter evenings with the participating audience engaged in various domestic crafts in the communal chambers of the farmhouses, the folk songs could be created and performed anywhere, anytime—in groups or in solitude, during festivities or work. The verses could be said as well as sung, one at a time or strung together to create longer sequences. . . . In structured social occasions, especially christenings and weddings, it was desirable to have on hand one or several women who were esteemed as *teicejas*, "singers/reciters." In the spring

---

10. Ibid., 111–12.

and early summer, when groups of youths, especially girls, met in the evenings, there was always one or more who assumed the role of the "singer. . . ." On the other hand, solitary singing was quite common, and singing by men enlisted in a military force or engaged in some celebration is recognized.[11]

The *dainas* are short and for the most part nonnarrative. The quatrain is their favored form. An excellent example of a *daina* is the following, *Ltd* 1148:

Stallī dzima kumeliņis	In the stable a colt is born
No dzeltena auzu salma;	From the yellow oat-straw.
Pirtī dzima arājiņis	In the bathhouse a ploughman is born
No slotiņu lapiņam.	From the whisk's leaves.

The parallelisms between the two distichs are typical of *daina* structure. There is a variant of this *daina*, *Ltd* 1148.1:

Pirtī dzima kaṟavīrs	In the bathhouse a warrior is born
No slotiņas žagariem;	From the besom twigs;
Stallī kaṟa kumeliņš	In the stable his war-steed is born
No dzeltenas auzu skaras.	From the panicles of the yellow oats.

The parallelisms of the distichs tie the quatrain closely together.

As an illustration of a six-line *daina* I have chosen one with many variants. It is usually included in the mythological cycle.

Ltd 33857

Mēnestiņis zvaigznes skaita,	Moon counts the stars
Vai ir visas vakarā.	Whether all are out at nightfall;
Ira visas vakarā,	All the stars are there,
Auseklīša vien nevaid;	All except the morning star;
Auseklītis aiztecēja	For the morning star has gone
Saules meitas lūkoties.	To court the daughters of the sun.

Nos. 33855–59 begin with essentially the same quatrain.

33855

Mēnesnīce zvaigznes skaita,	Moon counts the stars.
Irīg visas vakarā?	Are all there at nightfall?

---

11. Muižniece, 1981, 2.

Visas ira, visas ira,	All are there, all are there,
Auseklīša vien nebij;	Only the morning star was not there.

33856
Mēnesnīca zvaigznes skaita	Moon counts the stars
Vai ir visas vakarā.	Whether all are out at nightfall;
Iraid visas, iraid visas,	All are there, all are there,
Auseklīša vien nevaid;	All except the morning star.

33858
Mēnesitis zvaigznes skaita,	Moon counts the stars
Vai ir visas vakarā.	Whether all are out at nightfall;
Visas zvaigznes vakarā,	All the stars are there at nightfall,
Auseklīša vien nebij;	Only the morning star was not there.

33859
Mēnesniņis zvaigznes skaita,	Moon counts the stars
Vai ir visas vakarā.	Whether all are out at nightfall.
Visas zvaigznes vakarā,	All the stars are there at nightfall,
Ausekliņa vien nevaid;	All except the morning star.

The variations appear in the last couplet of the six-line stanza (or in the last quatrain of No. 33859), a fact that may explain the star's absence. Barons considered these four *dainas* as type-songs, but we would class them as variants of one another, or simply variants.

33855
Auseklītis jūriņā	The morning star is at sea
Baltā putu gabalā.	In a white piece of foam.

33856
Auseklītis Vāczemē	The morning star is in Germany,
Zelta naudu kaldināja.	Minting gold coins.

33858
Auseklītis Vāczemē	The morning star is in Germany,
Zelta svārkus šūdināja.	Sewing a golden skirt.

33859
Auseklīņš Vāczemē	The morning star is in Germany,
Saulītei svārkus šuva,	Sewing the sun a skirt;
Vienu strīpi zelta lika,	One stripe he fashions of gold,
Otru tīra sudrabiņa.	The other of pure silver.

The five *dainas* just cited demonstrate the importance of sound patterns in the Latvian oral traditional songs, a trait they share with all other traditional poetry. Note for example the persistent *v* alliteration, as in lines two and three, "vai ir visas vakarā. / Ira visas vakarā," where it is also coupled with *i* and *a* assonance. The *v* alliteration had begun actually in the first line in *zvaigznes* 'stars', the key word for the *daina*, as does the assonance; and it continues in line four in *vien nevaid*, and in 33856, 33858, and 33859 it appears again in *Vāczemē*, perhaps even having some influence in the choice of that word. In 33859 it is carried along for two additional lines, "Saulītei svārkus šuva [where it combines with the "sun" word *saulītei*] / Vienu strīpi zelta lika."

The *dainas* have been analyzed for formulas, with the help of computers, by Vaira Vīķis-Freibergs and Imants Freibergs.[12] In their analysis they are concerned only with what they call the "syntagmatic" formula, the exact repetition of a string, because this is easiest to treat on the computer. They conclude that their data "reinforce the tentative position that a heavily formulaic structure is typical of oral literature. Furthermore, this characteristic seems independent of the genre of literature in question, since our short, lyrical songs seem to be as formulaic as the long narrative epics analyzed earlier." Looking forward to future research, they wrote: "Ultimately, of course, the study of the verbal formulaic structure of texts should link up with what is known of the poetics of any given literary genre or tradition."

Vīķis-Freibergs has since that writing provided a very succinct description of the *daina* and its structure and the history of its collection and publication. There she treats the distinction between oral and written poetics and discerns that psychologists have the possibility of making valuable contributions in this area, namely, in describing just how the traditional poet creates songs. I take the liberty of quoting her at some length, because what she says is central to the ideas of this book.

> The folk poet differs from the modern poet in several ways. First, she or he had a functional role to play in everyday occurrences and did not cater to a selected elite of the population. In this role, they were expected to exhibit a high degree of skill in performance, but there were no demands from society that they be original or necessarily different from other singers. Second, the skills the poet was expected to acquire were highly technical ones, allowing them to function within a rigorously defined metrical and stylistic framework. This, of course, is something that modern poetry has turned its back on. The folk poet was thus expected to acquire something like a poetic metalanguage, a process

12. Vīķis-Freibergs, V., and I. Freibergs, 1978, 338.

probably not unlike that of learning a second language. . . . Finally, the traditional poet of the Latvian *dainas*, although using the poetic convention of the "lyrical I," is much more intent on expressing folk wisdom and beliefs about various aspects of the human condition than on giving vent to any personalized, individually subjective feelings. The folk poet thus functions within a very regulated and partially redundant system which directs poetic expression in predetermined, well-worn channels. This does not mean, however, that the folk singer has no other choice than to memorize and repeat songs heard from others. This certainly happens, and forms part of the training of a singer, but it need not stop there. The structure of the tradition is open-ended enough so that the mature singer who has mastered the tradition may, if he has enough talent, introduce entirely new elements into the common repertoire of ideas, images and expressions.[13]

One might add that the tradition itself, created as it had been by talented singers in some degree of competition with one another, has an abundance of possibilities of continual combination and recombination of its elements into ever changing mosaics and has little need for the entirely new.

In addition to the work of the Freibergs, Muižniece has analyzed some 593 *dainas* pertaining to death and burial.[14] She did not, however, employ a statistical method nor did she use a computer. There is no doubt whatsoever that the *dainas* are formulaic compositions; they are also clearly oral and traditional. Although they are not long enough to contain much, if any, narrative, they often have a dramatic setting.

Muižniece investigated the formulas in the first distich of Songs 27307–17:

>Vai/ai Dieviņ, galva sāp,
>Es vairs ilgi nedzīvošu.
>
>Oh God, (my) head is aching,
>I shall not live long any more.

"This statement," she writes, "which serves as the introductory formulas to 32 songs, variants, and variations in the *Ld*, plus a few more in the *Ltd*, can be broken down into three simpler formulas, which in turn can fill the appropriate slots in a large number of other songs." She then shows that *Vai/ai Dieviņ* is coupled with a number of other words and clauses in the second colon of the first line to form a large system, for example:

13. Vīķis-Freibergs, 1984, 341.
14. Muižniece, 1981, 224–60.

	vai tētīti	39366
Vai Dieviņ	vai Laimiņ	27304
	galva sāp	27302–12
	grūt' dzīvot	27827
	kur es iešu	27828
	nevar vairs	27131.1[15]

The second line of the distich 27307–17, *Es vairs ilgi nedzīvošu*, "I shall not live long any more," is used in 27307–12, and with *Nu es* (now I) substituted for *Es vairs* in 27313–16, and with *Nu vairs* (now) in 27317. It also has a variant, *Ka es* (that I), which is used in either the second or the fourth line of a quatrain:

> 27348
> Kam, Laimiņa nesacīji
> Ka es ilgi nedzīvošu?
>
> Why, Laima, didn't you tell
> That I shall not live long any more?

and

> 27341
> Grūti pūta līgaviņa
> Uz rociņas gulēdama,
> Vai tā bija paredzējsi,
> Ka es ilgi nedzīvošu?
>
> My bride sighed heavily
> Lying on my arm;
> Alas, did she foresee
> That I shall not live long?

The *dainas* are oral traditional formulaic compositions that exist in many variants. They have their own traditional diction and style, and when someone composes a *daina* not in that style, the resulting song is not felt to be "right."

If one looks at a type-song and its variants, one is struck by the fact that they frequently share a more or less stable core of lines, or even of couplets, which themselves can be varied within given limits and to which other lines and couplets are added. Although Barons recorded the places in which his

---

15. Ibid., 231.

songs were collected and published a list of people who sent them to him, we do not know from whom the individual songs were collected; it is patent that they are not from one individual singer. The variations, therefore, are not in the singing of the same song by the same singer. It is correct to say that the song as we see it in available variants has a more or less stable core, *provided* that we realize that there is no implication that this statement is necessarily true for the song as it exists in the practice of any one singer.

Collectors in this century are meticulous in recording information about the informants, the storytellers and singers, from whose creative minds they have taken down stories and songs. This careful concern for method makes it possible for scholars to investigate the workings of the individual artist as well as of the tradition as a whole. The Milman Parry Collection, like other modern collections, set down such information, and it is to it, and to other collections like it in its rigorous methodology, that we must turn for evidence of the practice of individual singers in varying or not varying the songs they have heard.

The *dainas* belong to an abundantly full and rich tradition. They have already taught us much about the process of composition of short nonnarrative lyric songs, and there is still much more to be learned from them. As the Freibergs have pointed out, formulicity is just as great in the genre represented by the *dainas* as in the long narrative songs. The Latvian tradition has also taught us through its abundance of variants that fixed texts are not characteristic of such a tradition. Individuals seem constantly to have recreated what they heard or, perhaps better, to have remembered what they heard in the context of verbal combinations already existing in their traditionally trained minds and to have responded with an amalgam of what had recently been heard with what had previously been stored in memory. We will find ourselves returning again, I am sure, to the *dainas* and to Latvian scholars for guidance in this significant area.[16] But I turn now to the Serbo-Croatian lyric songs.

In the preface, written in 1823, to the 1824 edition of *Narodne srpske pjesme*, Vuk Karadžić wrote:

All our folk songs are divided into heroic songs, which the men sing to the *gusle*,[17] and women's songs, which not only women and girls sing but also men,

---

16. See further my "Theories of Oral Literature and the Latvian Dainas," A. Lord, 1989. I am much indebted to the Freibergs and to Kristine Konrad for providing me with copies of their work, advising on additional bibliography, and giving valuable assistance in translating Latvian *dainas*. [I am most grateful to Morris Hale of the Linguistics Department of the Massachusetts Institute of Technology for checking the Latvian passages cited in this chapter.]

17. The *gusle* is a one-stringed, pear-shaped, bowed musical instrument.

especially young men, and that for the most part two in unison. Women's songs are sung by one person or by two only for their own entertainment, but heroic songs are sung for the most part for others to listen to. For that reason, in the singing of women's songs one notices the singing rather than the song, but in the singing of heroic songs one notices most the song. (By "song" here Karadžić means "the content of the song.")[18]

He goes on to note that the heroic, gusle songs were found in his day mainly in Bosnia, Herzegovina, Montenegro, and in the "southern, mountainous regions of Serbia." There was a gusle in almost every house. As one goes further north, he observed, around the Sava and the Danube, one sees fewer gusle. In Srem, the Banat, and Bačka only blind singers had them, and they used them for begging. Others were ashamed of the "blind beggar's *gusle* (*slepačke gusle*)." In contrast, according to Karadžić, the women's songs were sung mostly where the heroic songs were sung least, as well as in the towns of Bosnia. In those regions the women and girls live more in society. But in the towns in Srem, Bačka, and Banat not even women's songs are sung but "some sort of new ones, which educated people, school children, and merchants' apprentices compose."[19]

Karadžić also, in this same preface, states that some songs are on the borderline between women's songs and heroic songs, so much that one does not know where to place them. He says that some are more like heroic songs than women's songs, but one would scarcely hear men singing them to the gusle. Yet because of their length they are not sung as women's songs either, "but they are only recited."[20] I have not observed this distinction between sung and recited women's songs in the field in this century, but it is true that some women's songs are ballads rather than lyric songs. In this chapter I am concerned with the latter (in Chapter 7, I look at the problem of the ballad in South Slavic tradition as well as in English).

Nikola Andrić edited the six volumes of women's songs in the Matica Hrvatska's collection. In the preface to the first of those volumes he noted, pointing to the remarks of Antun Rodić concerning his collection of songs, that the young girls "sing only the shorter love songs, which are sung in the *kolo* [ring dance] and in the evening in front of the house when people gather together, but the older women recite the longer ones."[21] Rodić said, as Andrić reports, that "the girls praise their own songs and maintain that they

18. Karadžić, 1824, xvii.
19. Ibid., xvii–xviii; "nego kojekake nove, što prave učeni ljudi i djaci i kalfe trgovačke."
20. Ibid., xviii; "nego se samo kazuju."
21. Andrić, 1909, xii–xiii.

are prettier than those 'old-fashioned' ones that the women tell, but on the other hand the women like their own more, because they are 'better and old.' "[22]

In his high praise for the sensitivity and dynamism of the Croatian girls and women, Andrić paints a lively picture of a singing "event":

> If you have ever stood by at the dancing of a *kolo* and noticed who has the main say, you could be convinced that the girls are more open and keener and more talkative than the men. And at get-togethers! The young men stand by the door and beside the stove with a cane in their hands and a hat on their heads, and they listen to the girls singing (*kako izvijaju*) the love arias, alternating between the old-fashioned narrating (*pričalice*) of the mature women and old grandmothers. The young men stand there—quite passively—and swallow the lines assigned to them by tradition. On the other hand the older men are stronger in their singing of heroic songs to the *gusle*.[23]

The Serbo-Croatian women's songs in Volumes 1 and 5 of Karadžić's collection and in the Mladenović and Nedić supplement are of varying lengths and in a variety of meters.[24] Some of them are narrative and balladic, although unfortunately the conventions of printing have often not provided stanza markings. Some are ritual songs, some love songs, others work songs, and ballads to stanzaic melodies. All these are sung by women and young people, both male and female, except where specialized according to function—for example, certain wedding songs are sung exclusively by women. Although the number of variants may seem somewhat limited compared with the Latvian *dainas*, there is enough material, especially if one includes the lyric texts in the Milman Parry Collection, to make it possible to judge something of the processes of composition and transmission, or at least to note the shape songs have taken in different places and times and in the mouths of different singers. Only rarely, and only in the Parry collection, will we be able to observe the same song text from the same singer more than once.

It is usually assumed that, because they are short, lyric songs are memorized verbatim. But as with the Latvian *dainas*, the number of variants would seem to indicate that the texts are not as fixed as memorization would suggest. I pay particular attention here to the concept of textuality as a means of determining whether the South Slavic songs are fixed textually and hence

---

22. Ibid., xiii.
23. Ibid., xiii–xiv.
24. Mladenović and Nedić, 1973.

memorized, with or without writing, or whether their texts are fluid and the result of composition in performance. I note the degree of verbal correspondence among the variants of the lyric songs, as I have earlier, in *The Singer of Tales*, among the variants of a "theme," or repeated passage, in the investigation of the composition and transmission of the South Slavic epic songs. For we seek to discover whether or not there is a principle of composition and transmission which is to some extent shared by both oral traditional epic and oral traditional lyric songs in the South Slavic poetries.

In some of the songs and variants the first part of the song is comparatively stable and the variants diverge in their endings. Take, for example, Mladenović 155:

"Djevojčice, ružičice,
    Ružo rumena,
Što ti sa mnom ne govoriš,
    Usta medena?"
"Ja bih s tobom govorila,
    Al' mi ne dadu!"
"Ko to ne da, ko l' to smeta?
    Ubio ga Bog!"

"O maiden, little rose,
    Red rose,
Why do you not speak to me,
    Honeyed lips?"
"I would speak with you,
    But they do not let me!"
"Who does not let you, who interferes?
    May God strike him down!"

There are two variants of this song in Karadžić Vol. 1. The first is 1.590:

"Devojčice, ružičice,
    Ružo rumena,
Što ti sa mnom ne <u>besediš</u>,
    Usta medena?"
"Ja bi' s tobom <u>besedila</u>.
    <u>Ne smem od majke</u>."
"A gdi ti je tvoja majka?
    Ne bilo ti je!"
"Eno mi je u gradini,
    Gdi neven bere."
"Uvenulo njeno srce,
    K'o što je moje!"
"A moje je uvenulo.
    Većma ne može."

"O maiden, little rose,
    Red rose,
Why will you not speak with me,
    Honeyed lips?"
"I would speak with you.
    I dare not because of mother."
"Where is your mother?
    May she never be!"
"She is there in the garden,
    Picking a carnation."
"May her heart wither,
    As has mine!"
"And mine has withered.
    It can do no more."

I have underlined the differences in the first six lines between Nos. 590 and 155. After line six they diverge considerably.

The second variant is 1.591:

"Djevojčice, <u>ljubičice</u>, ružo rumena! Što ti sa mnom ne <u>besjediš</u>, usta medena?" "Ja bih s tobom <u>besjedila</u>, al' mi ne daju." "Ko to ne da, ko l' to smeta? Bog <u>nam ga smeo</u>!" "Bogme, tajko, braća moja, i mila majka, Veleći mi da ne ljubim nikog tuđina, Nego moju rodnu braću i roditelje, I onoga koga Bog mi u sreću dadne."	"O maiden, little violet, red rose! Why will you not speak with me, honeyed lips?" "I would speak with you, but they do not let me." "Who does not let you, who interferes? May God take him away!" "Well, daddy, my brothers, and my dear mother, Saying I should love no outsider, But my own brothers and parents, And him who God gave me for my happiness."

The underlinings are of the differences in the first four (or eight, respectively) lines between 591 and 155. The songs diverge greatly after line four (or eight). In the first part of the song the differences between the variants are negligible—*ljubičice* 'violet' in 591 instead of *ružičice* 'rose' in 155 and 590; *besediš* (*besjediš*) and *besedila* (*besjedila*) in 590 and 591 instead of *govoriš* and *govorila*. Song 155 and the first half of song 591 end abruptly with a one-line curse. In 590 and 591 the singer develops the theme of "mother" (590) or (591) elaborates on who the "they" are who are either forbidding or allowing her to speak, as mentioned in 155. There is, then, a stable part of the song which may be continued in different ways. In this case the stable part of the song is the beginning. A sense of textuality belongs to that part but not to the rest of the song.

In the second part of the song, Mladenović 155 and Karadžić 1.591 add to the opening six lines, which end in each case with *al' mi ne daju* 'but they do not let me,' *ko to ne da, ko l' to smeta* 'who does not let you,' 'who interferes,' and they diverge only in the final five-syllable coda: *Bog nam ga smeo!* 'May God take him away!' in 591 and *Ubio ga Bog!* 'May God strike him down!" in 155. That is where Mladenović 155 ends; undoubtedly Karadžić did not publish it for this reason, considering the other two fuller and, hence, better.

Karadžić 591 answers the question who will not allow the girl to speak. Vuk Karadžić 590 does not ask the question at all, because the girl states *ne smem od majke* 'I dare not because of my mother'. The two endings have nothing in common. There is a sense of textuality in the openings, but the second parts are different songs, and one would have to look elsewhere, in some other songs, for their counterparts. One can speak here of the mixing of songs.

In our next example the stable part of the song comprises its middle and final sections, whereas the beginnings exhibit considerable variety, as was the case with the endings in the previous example. Mladenović 143 has four variants—Mladenović 144 and Karadžić 1.285, 1.286, and 5.379. The stable parts consist of a series of questions and the answers to them. The settings of the questions and answers vary from song to song. Here are the questions and answers in Mladenović 143 and 144.

143 (lines 6–18)	144 (lines 6–18)
"O, Bože, moj mili Bože,	"Ustaj, Ano, da te nesto pitam!
Što li je šire od polja?	Šta je šire od sinjega mora?
Što li je dublje od mora?	Šta je dulje od zelena polja?
Što li je brže od konja?	Šta je brže od siva sokola?
Što li je sv'jetlje od mača?	Šta je slađe od đulbe šećera?
Što li je milije od brata?"	Šta je draže od mile matere?"
To junak sluša i gleda.	Progovara plemenita Ana:
"Djevojko, mlada, razumna!	"Lako ti se mogu dosetiti.
Sad da te vadim iz uma.[25]	Šire nebo od sinjega mora.
Šire je more no polje.	Dulje more od zelena polja.
Zmaje je brži od konja.[26]	Draži dragi od mile matere.
Sv'jetlje je sunce od mača.	Brže oči od siva sokola.
Milij' je dragi od brata."	Slađa draga od đulbe šećera."
"O God, my dear God!	"Arise, Ana, that I ask you something!
What is wider than a field?	What is wider than the blue sea?
What is deeper than the sea?	What is longer than a green field?
What is swifter than a horse?	What is swifter than a gray falcon?
What is brighter than a sword?	What is sweeter than rose conserve?
What is dearer than a brother?	What is dearer than a dear mother?"
A hero listens and watches.	Noble Ana spoke:
"O maiden, young, prudent.	"I can easily think of an answer.
. . . .	The sky is wider than the blue sea.
The sea is wider than a field.	The sea is longer than a green field.
A dragon is swifter than a horse.	One's beloved is dearer than a dear mother.
Brighter is the sun than a sword.	Swifter are the eyes than a gray falcon.
Dearer is one's beloved than a brother."	Sweeter is one's beloved than rose conserve."[27]

25. [David E. Bynum offers the opinion that the verse *Sad da te vadim iz uma* is untraditional and is thought to have been interpolated by this text's putative collector, Vuk Vrčević.]

26. The *-e* of *zmaje* is unexpected for the appropriate nominative case, *zmaj*, which is one syllable too short for the octosyllabic line.

27. I am grateful to Richard Janko for pointing out the parallel with the first stanza of Sappho,

One of the differences between these two texts is that Mladenović 143 is in octosyllables (3-2-3) and 144 is in decasyllables (4-6). Of the five questions asked in 143 only four are answered. 'Wider' (*šire*), 'deeper' (*dublje*), and 'swifter' (*brže*), in that order, form three of the five questions in both. 'Dearer' (*milije*) in 143 is represented by *draže* in 144, and it characteristically ends the series. The fourth question is different in each—'brighter' (*sv'jetlje*) in 143 and 'sweeter' (*slađe*) in 144. Of the objects in the questions, only 'field' (*polje*) and 'sea' (*more*) are found in both songs, but in reverse order. The object in the fifth question is always a member of the family—'brother' (*brat*) in 143 and 'mother' (*mater*) in 144. 'Swifter than a horse' (*brže od konja*) in 143 is matched by 'swifter than a gray falcon' (*brže od siva sokola*) in 144. 'Brighter than a sword' (*sv'jetlje od mača*) in 143 and 'sweeter than rose conserve' (*slađe od đulbe šećera*) in 144 have no counterparts in the other song. Some of these differences result from the difference of meters.

The answers vary more than the questions. In the following translations I have underlined the same or similar objects that are wider, deeper, swifter, brighter, sweeter, or dearer than another object.

Mladenović 143	Mladenović 144
The <u>sea</u> is wider than a <u>field</u>.	The sky is wider than the blue sea.
A dragon is faster than a horse.	The <u>sea</u> is longer than a green <u>field</u>.
The sun is brighter than a sword.	One's <u>beloved</u> is dearer than one's dear mother.
One's <u>beloved</u> is dearer than one's brother.	The eyes are swifter than a gray falcon.
	One's <u>beloved</u> is sweeter than rose conserve.

The textuality in the questions and answers sections of these two songs is not as taut as that in the beginning portions of our previous examples. Greater variety is allowed. But the textuality is real nevertheless.

Let us look at the other three variants. First Karadžić 5.379 (lines 19–29):

"Seko moja, tico mekušico!²⁸ "My sister, delicate bird!
Šta je brže od konja viteza? What is swifter than a noble <u>horse</u>?

Fragment 16 (Lobel and Page, 1955): "Some say armies of horsemen are best, some say infantry, some say ships are loveliest, but I say that what one loves is." For an earlier treatment of some of these riddling songs, see A. Lord, 1987a, 68–71.

28. [*Mekušico*, nom. *mekušica*, from the stem *mek* 'soft'. Hirtz, 1941, vol. 2, fasc. 2, p. 274, s.v. *mekušica*, suggests as alternatives *delkuša*, *dilkuša*. On *delkuša*, vol. 2, fasc. 1, p. 84, he comments: "A Turkish word, perhaps from Persian *dilkuša* (adj., meaning 'opening or giving joy to the heart,' 'pleasant,' 'beautiful.')" He offers the possibility that *delkuša* is from the Turkish *dilkuş*, a noun, meaning "bird of the heart or soul." Hirtz, p. 87, defines *dilkuša* as "bird that cheers the heart," "*avis*

Šta je šire od mora sinjega?	What is wider than the blue sea?
Šta je bolje od đuli mehara?[29]	What is better than rose blossoms?
Šta je draže od oca i majke?"	What is dearer than father and mother?"
Njoj govori tica mekušica.	The delicate bird answered her.
"Luda li si, seko lastavice!	"You are daft, sister swallow!
Brže oči od konja viteza.	The <u>eyes</u> are swifter than a noble <u>horse</u>.
Šire nebo od mora sinjega.	The <u>sky</u> is wider than the blue <u>sea</u>.
Bjelji snijeg od đuli mehara.	Snow is whiter than rose blossoms.
Sladji dragi od oca i majke."	One's <u>beloved</u> is dearer than father and mother."

I have underlined the elements found in the previous two variants. The order is different. The horse has an appositive/epithet. There is metathesis of noun and epithet in *mora sinjega* of this version with the more usual *sinjega mora* of Mladenović 144. The family members of the last question are "father and mother" rather than "brother" or "mother." Only one line in the question-and-answer series is different from the other two, and in the question part, 'better' (*bolje*) is inappropriate—a mistake, in fact—as the answer, 'whiter' (*bjelji*) shows. In spite of these differences, the sense of textuality, of certain specific words, is strong in all three variants.

The last two variants in Karadžić are:

1.285 (3–15)	1.286 (10–20)
"Ah, mili Bože i dragi!	"Što je šire od mora sinjega?
Ima l' što šire od mora?	Što l' je brže od konja viteza?
Ima l' što duže od polja?	Što l' milije od brata jedina?"
Ima l' što brže od konja?	Na grančici tica delkušica,
Ima l' što sladje od meda?	Te se ona mlada razgovara.
Ima l' što draže od brata?"	I od derta i od muhaneta.
Govori riba iz vode—	Od srdaha jada velikoga:

---

magnum gaudium afferens, Nachtigall, luscinia." Škaljić, 1966, s.v. *dilkušica*, reports that it is a diminutive of *dilkuša*, Persian, which he translates as "a bird of happiness." He adds: "In our folk poetry probably a nightingale is understood." Professor Sinasi Tekin, of the Harvard Department of Near Eastern Languages, kindly informs me that the form *dilkuşa* cannot mean "nightingale" in Turkish but that Turkish *kuş* means "bird" and that *kuşçuk* is a "tiny or lovely bird." Hony, 1947, 78, defines *dilkuşa*, adj., as "pleasant," "exhilarating." Note that below, in Vuk Karadžić 1.286, line 13, a variant of 5.379, the words *tica delkušica* are actually used, and following Škaljić and Hirtz, I translate this expression as "nightingale." *Tica mekušica*, which Lord originally rendered as "a bird of beauty," is translated as "a delicate bird." The Dictionary of the Yugoslav Academy, Budmani and Maretić, 1904–10, 6.27:596, gives as one of the definitions of *mekušica*, "some kind of imaginary bird."]

29. Mehara, nom. *mehar*, is a variant of Turkish *behar*, in turn from Persian *behar*, meaning "springtime," or "leaf, petal, blossom." See Škaljić, 1966, s.v. *behar*.

"Djevojko, luda budalo!
Šire je nebo od mora,
Duže je more od polja,
Brže su oči od konja,
Sladji je šećer od meda,
Draži je dragi od brata."

"Oh, dear and kind God!
Is anything wider than the sea?
Is anything longer than a field?
Is anything swifter than a horse?
Is anything sweeter than honey?
Is anything dearer than a brother?"
The fish spoke from the water—
"O maiden, innocent fool!
The sky is wider than the sea.
The sea is longer than a field.
The eyes are swifter than a horse.
Sugar is sweeter than honey.
One's beloved is dearer than a brother."

"Bre ne luduj, tico sevdelijo!
Šire nebo od mora sinjega,
Brže oči od konja viteza,
Milij' dragi od brata jedina."

"What is broader than the blue sea?
What is swifter than a noble horse?
What is dearer than an only brother?"
On the branch the nightingale,
The young one spoke
From sorrow and sadness,
From the heart of great sorrow—
"Do not be daft, love-sick bird!
The sky is wider than the blue sea.
The eyes are swifter than a noble horse.
One's beloved is dearer than an only brother."

No. 285, it is to be noted, is octosyllabic and has five questions and answers, whereas 286 is decasyllabic and has only three. In the other texts of this song in Karadžić, there is only one line between the two quotations, but 286 is an exception with four lines. The comparatives and the objects in 286 are, nonetheless, to be found in the other texts, each one of which, however, has some unique element. In 285, that element is "honey."

There can be no doubt about a sense of textuality in these sections of the five variants, although it must be stressed that that does not argue for a fixed text and memorization. What it does exhibit is a remembering of a number of "more or less fixed" texts and a selection, conscious or unconscious—probably the latter—of elements from them.

The variables in the "more or less stable" text in the case of this "theme" (repeated passage) can be stated in the following way. The comparatives 'wider' (*šire*), 'swifter' (*brže*), and 'dearer' (either *draže* or *milije*) are the most likely to appear. 'Sweeter' (*slađe*), 'longer' (*dulje*), 'higher' (*više*), and 'deeper' (*dublje*) may also be found. 'Brighter' (*sv'jetlje*) and 'whiter' (*bjelje*) are used once each in our five texts, a fact that indicates that other less common comparatives are possible. Not only is there a choice of the usual comparatives as they may be known to a given singer, but there is also an opportunity for departing from the trodden path. The only obligatory elements are 'dearer' (*draže*) and one other comparative to introduce it. These comparatives can be used whether the meter is octosyllabic or decasyllabic.

The nouns that follow the comparative are somewhat limited by meter as well as by traditional usage. For example, one cannot say 'swifter than a falcon' (*brže od sokola*) in the octosyllabic line (3-2-3) because *od sokola* has one syllable more than is allowed. *Konj* 'horse' is useful here, because *od konja* fits perfectly into the last position in the 3-2-3 line, whether it be "Što li je brže od konja" or "Ima l' što brže od konja." *Majka* 'mother' is possible in an octosyllabic line (although it is not used in our texts), but *mater* 'mother' is not possible, because its genitive, *matere*, produces an extra syllable. In our two octosyllabic songs, *brat* 'brother' is used for the family member. *Med* 'honey' does not, to the best of my knowledge, have a traditional epithet and cannot be used in the appropriate position, that is, in the second part, of a decasyllable, but it fits perfectly into the octosyllable. There is a rare noun going with 'brighter' (*sv'jetlje*) in the octosyllable, namely, 'sword' (*mač*). These are the "more or less stable" components in the octosyllable.

The variables in the decasyllable overlap with those in the octosyllable, because those found in the octosyllable can be adapted for the decasyllable by the use of an epithet. Thus we have the following:

more 'sea'	*od sinjega mora* 'than the blue sea'
polje 'field'	*od zelena polja* 'than a green field'
konj 'horse'	*od konja viteza* 'than a noble horse'
brat 'brother'	*od brata jedina* 'than an only brother'

There are four nouns in this position which are confined to the decasyllable.

soko 'falcon'	*od siva sokola* 'than a gray falcon'
mater 'mother'	*od mile matere* 'than one's dear mother'
šećer 'sugar'	*od dulbe šećera* 'than rose conserve'
mehar 'blossom'	*od duli mehara* 'than rose blossoms'
	(used once with *b'jelje*, 'whiter')

These are some of the variables in this position in the decasyllable that define a "more or less stable" text.

Finally, what are the variables for the other noun, the object or person better, bigger, whiter, or swifter, for example, than something or somone else? What is needed is a two-syllable noun in the first part of the decasyllable (4-6) or the middle two syllables in the 3-2-3 octosyllable. The same noun will fit either meter. The most common are *more* 'sea', *nebo* 'sky', *oči* 'eyes', and *dragi* 'beloved'. The rare ones are:

zmaje 'dragon'	*zmaje je brži od konja* 'a dragon is swifter than a horse'
sunce 'sun'	*sv'jetlje je sunce od mača* 'the sun is brighter than a sword'
snijeg 'snow'	*b'jelji snijeg od đuli mehara* 'whiter is snow than rose blossoms'
šećer 'sugar'	*slađi je šećer od meda* 'sweeter is sugar than honey'.

The texts that we have seem to be the result of remembering known and used variables rather than of memorization of a fixed text.

If the questions and answers display textuality, that cannot be said for the beginnings of the songs, which describe the characters and the settings of the questioning. I shall review these before commenting on their meaning.

Karadžić 1.285 has the shortest introduction to the questions and answers of the five texts:

> Djevojka sjedi kraj mora.
> Pak sama sebi govori—
>
> A girl is sitting beside the sea
> And says to herself—

Later, in line nine, a fish in the water answers her soliloquy.

Mladenović 143 and 144, the two versions published by Karadžić, both open with five lines. The first has some kinship with Karadžić 1.285, which we have just seen:

Vrela je voda studena,	The water of the spring is cold,
Na nju je mlada rumena.	By it a young pink-cheeked girl.
Rumeno lice umiva,	She washes her pink-cheeked face,
A grozne suze prol'jeva,	And weeps great tears,
A sama sobom govori.	And says to herself.

In this case her questions are answered, not by a fish, but by an unnamed and hitherto unmentioned hero. Except for the last line, there is no verbal correspondence between this opening and that of Karadžić 285, but in both songs a girl is sitting by a body of water, a spring or the sea, and talking to herself. In 143 we do not know why she weeps; we are also puzzled by the sudden appearance of the riddle-answering hero. So also, it seems, was Karadžić, as he chose not to publish it. Mladenović 144 (in decasyllables) gives the girl some companions.

U polju se al-čador viđaše,	On the plain a red tent was seen,
Pod čadorom Ana i Maruša.	Under the tent are Ana and Maruša.
Mara sjedi, a Anuša spava,	Mara is sitting, but Anuša sleeps,
Među njima mlado neženjeno.	Between them an unmarried youth.
Još govori mlado neženjeno.	The unmarried youth spoke further.

In this text it is not a girl who asks the questions but an unmarried youth. His riddles were answered by Ana—who was sleeping! Probably it was this inconsistency that worried Karadžić and caused him not to publish the text. This opening has little in common with the others and seems to have been arbitrarily attached to the questions and answers. One cannot speak of textuality with reference to any of them.

The openings of Karadžić 1.286 and 5.379 are related to one another, but one is fuller than the other, twice as full to be exact. The former has nine lines, the latter eighteen. It turns out that both the riddlers and the answerers in each case are birds:

286 (lines 1–9)	379 (lines 1–18)
Tica i djevojka (*iz Bosne*),	*Plač za dragijem*,
"The Bird and the Girl (from Bosnia)"	"Lament for One Beloved"
Sevdi, bego, tvoje sevdisanje.	Sajvan' vodo, suva žeđo moja!
Ubilo te moje uzdisanje!	Moj dragane, živa željo moja!
Je l' ti druga vezen jagluk dala?	Živom li se željom poželjesmo,
Ja sam ti ga i ljepšega dala,	Kano majka sina u tamnici,
Što na njemu trides't i tri lava,	Sestra brata sa daleka puta!
Na srijedi sofa od merdžana,	Da si mi se uželio dragi,
I na sofi drvce bademovo,	Ti bi mene po kim poručio,
Na grančici tica sevdelija.	Al' po suncu ali po mjesecu,
Turski sjedi, a Turski besjedi.	Al' po onoj danici zvijezdi,
	Po putniku ali namjerniku.
	Ako sam ja drugog pogledala,
	Nijesam ga srcem srdisala.
	Ako sam mu vezen jagluk dala,
	Ja sam tebe ljepši ostavila.
	Na njemu su trides't i tri grane,
	Na srijedi grana bademova,
	Na grančici tica mekušica.
	K njoj dolazi s mora lastavica.
"Pine, o bey, your pining!	"O Sajvan stream, my dry thirst!
May my sighing destroy you!	My beloved, my living desire!

Has another given you an embroidered pillow?	We desired one another with a living desire,
I gave you an even finer one,	As a mother a son in prison,
With thirty-three lions on it,	Or a sister a brother on a distant journey!
In the center a pavilion of coral,	If you really desired me, beloved,
In the pavilion an almond tree,	You would send word by someone,
On a branch a love-sick bird.	By the sun or by the moon,
It sits in Turkish fashion and speaks in Turkish.	By the day-star,
	By a traveler or by a chance encounter
	If I have looked at another,
	I have not loved him in my heart.
	If I have given him an embroidered pillow,
	I have left a finer one for you.
	On it are thirty-three branches,
	In the middle an almond branch,
	On the branch a delicate bird.
	To it comes a swallow from the sea.

The first section of these songs (lines 1–2 of 1.286 and lines 1–12 of 5.379) is a bitter kind of lament, as it were, for a love that has passed, by a girl who has lost her lover. This section is elaborated in 379. In line 11 that variant turns its attention to what was evidently the lover's complaint, that the girl has looked at someone else and embroidered a pillow for him. Even if she has, she says, she did not love him and she had embroidered a finer one for her lover. This is where the two versions meet, although in 286 the girl asks her lover if some other girl has given him an embroidered pillow. If so, she says that she has given him a finer one.

A degree of textuality, that is, of textual or verbal correspondence, actually begins at line 3 of 286 and at line 13 of 379, with the mention in both songs of an embroidered pillow, with the phrase *vezen jagluk dala* 'given an embroidered pillow' and with *ja sam (ti ga) i ljepšega (dala)* 'I (gave) (you) an even finer one' in 286 compared with *ja sam (tebe) ljepši (ostavila)* 'I have (left) a finer one (for you)' in 379. The descriptions of the figures embroidered on the pillows are somewhat different, but there are several elements and words common to both songs. In 286 there are thirty-three lions depicted, in the midst of which is a pavilion of coral, in which is an almond tree; in 379 there are thirty-three branches, in the midst of which is a branch of an almond tree. In both poems a bird is perched on a branch; in 286 it is a *tica sevdelija*, which I have translated as "a love-sick bird"; in 379 it is a *tica mekušica*, which

I have translated "a delicate bird." No. 286 closes this section with the line *Turski sjedi, a turski besjedi,* "It sits in Turkish fashion and speaks in Turkish." In 379 the bird on the branch is joined by a swallow, which comes from the sea and addresses the other bird with the questions that form the core of the song in all its variants.

In sum, then, this song has in the riddle section, as we saw, a more or less stable core, which exhibits a clear sense of textuality, including variables. It is preceded by a section (Karadžić 1.286, lines 3–8; 5.379, lines 13–17) that also has some degree of textuality, but the lines that lead into it vary considerably in the variants. We can speak here of the textuality of certain parts of the song.

With these five variants of a song in mind, let us now look at some other settings for the riddles. There is a group of them in which a lover awakes his beloved and asks the riddles; at least one of these also illustrates another aspect of the South Slavic women's songs. From the appearance on the printed page of the songs in Karadžić's collection (and that of others as well) one can form no idea of stanzaic shape or even whether they had any at all. Fortunately, in the Parry collection we have versions on the phonograph records of some of the songs in Karadžić. Although there is, of course, no way of telling whether the melody to which the songs are now sung was the one used in the nineteenth century, we can see what music the words were sung to in the twentieth. For example, Rabija Zvizdić in Gacko, Herzegovina, in 1935 sang a version of the riddle song in stanzas as follows:

>Parry Text No. 6353, Record No. 3099
>Aj, Dragi dragu alkatmerom budi,
>Aj, alkatmerom budi.
>Aj, "Ustaj, dragi, aman, da te nešto pitam!
>
>Aj, Šta je šire od sinjega mora,
>Aj, od sinjega mora?
>Aj, Šta je draže, aman, od đulbe šećera?
>
>Aj, Šta je draže od oca i majke,
>Aj, od oca i majke?
>Aj, Šta je brže, aman, od sivog sokola?"
>
>Aj, "Draže dragi od oca i majke,
>Aj, od oca i majke.
>Aj, Šire nebo, aman, od sinjega mora.
>
>Aj, Brže oči od sivog sokola,

Aj, od sivog sokola.
Aj, slađe dragi, aman, od oca i majke."

Aj, A lover awoke his beloved with a red carnation,
Aj, awoke with a red carnation.
Aj, "Arise, beloved, that I may ask you something!

Aj, What is wider than the blue sea,
Aj, than the blue sea?
Aj, What is dearer, aman, than rose conserve?

Aj, What is dearer than father and mother,
Aj, than father and mother?
Aj, What is swifter, aman, than a gray falcon?"

Aj, "Dearer is one's beloved than father and mother,
Aj, than father and mother.
Aj, Wider is the sky than the blue sea.

Aj, The eyes are swifter than the gray falcon,
Aj, than the gray falcon.
Aj, Sweeter is one's beloved, aman, than father and mother."

The song is sung in stanzas consisting of couplets with a repetition of the last six syllables of the first line and the use of interjections, such as "Aj" and "aman," at the beginning or the middle of a line. It is worth stressing that we are dealing for the most part, it would seem, with couplets. This is the same building block of composition that we saw in the Latvian *dainas*, and we will note it again and again as we proceed with further lyric material, also notably in English and Scottish ballads and even to some extent in South Slavic epic.

There are two other texts of this song in the Parry collection (Nos. 1577 and 2809) beginning with the same line, *Dragi dragu alkatmerom budi*, "A lover awoke his beloved with a red carnation." They exhibit the same types of variation we have seen in the Karadžić variants. There are four texts in the collection (Nos. 9347, 9819, 10198, and 11176a) that begin with

> Beg Alibeg vjernu ljubu budi.
> "Ustaj, ljubo, da te nešto pitam!"
>
> Ali Bey awoke his true love.
> "Arise, love, that I ask you something!"

and proceed with questions and answers as in the preceding texts. There are sixteen texts in the collection (Nos. 1294, 2264, 4040, 4227, 4645a, 7903,

8641, 8667, 9157, 10289, 10453, 10490, 10511, 10548, 10580, and 12238) that begin with

Dvoje mlado sitno smilje bralo.	Two young people were gathering everlastings.
Đe je bralo, tu je i zaspalo.	Where they gathered them they fell asleep.
Dragi dragu alkatmerom budi.	The lover awoke his beloved with a red carnation.
"Ustaj, drago, da te nešto pitam!"	"Arise, beloved, that I may ask you something!"

and proceed as in other versions.

As an example of the latter opening, I quote one by Šerifa Zvizdić of Gacko. It so happens that we have two versions of the same riddle song from her, Texts Nos. 1577 and 10490. Because they begin with different lines they are listed as separate songs.

1577

Dragi dragu alkatmerom budi.
"Ustaj, draga, da te nešto pitam!"
Šta je šire od sinjeg mora?
Šta je brže od sivog sokola?
Šta je slađe od đulber šećera?
Šta je draže od oca i majke?"
"Kad me pitaš, pravo ću ti kazat'."
Šire nebo od sinjeg mora.
Brže oči od sivog sokola.
Slađe ljuba od đulber šećera.
Mil'i dragi od oca i majke."

10490

Dvoje mlado sitno smilje bralo.
Đe je bralo, onđe je zaspalo.
Dragi dragu alkatmerom budi.
"Ustaj, draga, da te nešto pitam!"
Što je šire od sinjeg mora?
Što je brže od sivoga sokola?
Što je draže od oca i majke?
Što je slađe od đulbeg šećera?"
Šire nebo od sinjega mora.
Brže oko od sivoga sokola.
Drazi dragi od oca i majke.
Slađa draga od đulbehar šećera.
Da sam, Bog dō, kutija šećera,
Ja bi' znala đe bi' se prosulo;
U krevetu đe mi dragi spava.
Kad se prenem, neka šećer jede!
Kad se budi, neka mene ljubi!"

Two young people were gathering everlastings.
Where they gathered them there they fell asleep.

	The lover awoke his beloved with a red carnation.
	"Arise, beloved, that I may ask you something!
	What is wider than the blue sky?
	What is swifter than a gray falcon?
What is sweeter than rose conserve?	What is dearer than father and mother?
What is dearer than father and mother?"	What is sweeter than rose conserve?
	"Since you ask me I shall tell you truly.
	The sky is wider than the blue sea.
The eyes are swifter than the gray falcon.	The eye is swifter than the gray falcon.
One's love is sweeter than rose conserve.	One's beloved is dearer than father and mother.
One's beloved is dearer than father and mother."	One's beloved is sweeter than rose-petal conserve.
	Were I, God grant, a box of sugar,
	I know where I would wish to be strewn;
	In the bed where my beloved sleeps.
	When I start up, let him eat sugar!
	When he awakes, let him love me!"

The core of the riddle section of the song is practically the same in both texts, but—discounting errors such as *sinjeg* for *sinjega*, as the meter would require, and which resulted from the dictation process, errors I have faithfully preserved—they are not identical. There are a few words that are different: *ljuba* instead of *draga*, *mil'i* instead of *draže*, and *đulber* or *đulbeg* instead of *đulbehar*.[30] And there is a typical metathesis of *slađe* and *draže* in the two versions. In spite of the similarities, there are sufficient differences even in the riddle part of the song to make it clear that Šerifa Zvizdić did not have a fixed, memorized text in her mind. It is, rather, a "more or less stable core" that she remembers. Most of the difference, as a matter of fact, is in the beginning and the ending, especially the latter, which is in reality a different song, although it is not written as such in the manuscript. One can surmise that this particular song was suggested by its association with 'sugar\conserve' (*šećer*) in the riddles. It belongs in the tradition of such songs as *Da sam, Bog d'o, studena vodica, Ja bi' znala gdje bi' izvirala* (Parry Texts Nos. 2488, 7638b, 8701, and 9054). Here are two examples:

---

30. *Đulber* and *đulbeg* (*šećer*), more properly *đulbe šećer* 'rose conserve', from Turkish *gül-be-şeker*, are alternatives for *đulbehar* (*šećer*), from Turkish *gül-behar-şeker* 'rose-petal conserve'. *Đulbehar*, however, creates an eleven-syllable line, a fact that probably accounts for the use of *đulber* and *đulbeg*.

48   The Singer Resumes the Tale

8701	7638b
Da sam, Bog d'o, studena vodica,	Da sam, Bog, d'o, studena vodica,
Ja bi' znala gdje bi' izvirala,	Da nijesam Salkova rodica,
Pred bijele draganove dvore.	Ne bi l', Bog d'o, Salke nahodio,
Nek' me nose draganove seke.	Ne bi li se vodu napojio,
Nek me pije draganova majka,	Ne bi l' mene u vodi popio.
Ne bi li me u vodi popila.	Žir zobala, s lista vodu pila,
Ne be li mi sina poklonila!	I u žiru guju sazobala,
	I u vodi stonogu popila!
	Were I, God grant, a cool stream,
	And were I not Salko's relative,
I know where I would flow forth,	That, God grant, Salko might come
Before my beloved's white dwelling.	upon me,
Let my beloved's sisters carry me!	That he might drink the water.
Let my beloved's mother drink me,	That he might drink me in the water.
That she might drink me in the water,	I have eaten mast and drunk water from
That she might give her son to me.	the leaves,
	Amidst the mast I ate a snake,
	I drank a centipede in the water.

It is significant that the differences between versions of the same song by the same singer may be just as great, if not greater, than those between versions by different singers. The principle of composition remains the same in both cases. Further examples of several texts of the same song from the same singer will be found later in this chapter.[31]

In the Parry collection there is yet another set of texts with the same questions and answers but with a different opening and setting than what we have seen so far. They are No. 1497 from Anđa Grubačić and No. 4381 from Derviša Hrustanović, both of Gacko. No. 1497 goes as follows:

Pod onom gorom zelenom	Beneath that green hill
Vrani se konji igrahu,	Black horses were prancing,
Pod sobom zemlju kopahu,	Digging up the ground under them,
A zlatne uzde trgahu,	And tugging at their golden bits.
Na moru curu gledaju,	They were looking at a girl by the sea
Đe bijelo lice umiva,	Washing her white face,
A crne oči ispira.	And rinsing her black eyes.
Sama sobom govori:	She said to herself:
"Ima li šta lepše od mene?"	"Is there anything lovelier than I?"

31. See below at n. 38.

Ima li šta brže od konja?	Is there anything swifter than a horse?
Ima li šta šire od polja?	Is there anything wider than a field?
Ima li šta milije od brata?	Is there anything dearer than a brother?
Ima li šta dublje od mora?	Is there anything deeper than the sea?
Ima li šta slađe od meda?"	Is there anything sweeter than honey?"
Iz gore vila govori:	A vila spoke from the wooded hill:
"I ja sam lepša od tebe.	"I am lovelier than you.
Šire je nebo od polja.	Wider is the sky than a field.
Brže je oko od konja.	Swifter is the eye than a horse.
Dublji je sevdah od mora.	Deeper is longing than the sea.
Mili je drago od brata.	Dearer is one's beloved than a brother.
Slađe je drago od meda."	Sweeter is one's beloved than honey."

No. 4381 uses a present rather than a past tense in the second, third, and fourth lines, and the form of the question is "Ima li išta lepše od mene? / Ima li išta brže od konja?" The version is interesting because once again we find the girl beside a body of water, washing her face and soliloquizing. A new figure, however, appears, the vila.[32] The horses in some other songs are indicative of weddings, being the horses sent to bring the bride to her future husband's house.

It is abundantly clear from the evidence of the various forms the riddle song may take, and from the number of settings in which it is found, that the relationship of any one of these variants to the whole body of variants is extremely complex. And it is even clearer that the scholar or literary critic needs a knowledge of many variants in order to understand properly any given representative of an oral traditional song—or story, for that matter. One must be aware of the tensions of association (like the "tension of essences" of which I wrote when analyzing South Slavic epic song)[33] that cause the singer to go from one group of lines, or formulas, to another. The same opening may lead in several directions, and the same essential riddling core may be concluded in various ways. It is this network of traditional associations that distinguishes oral traditional literature from its written derivative.

32. A *vila* is a supernatural female with wings who inhabits mountain woods and lakes.
33. See A. Lord, 1960, 96–97. Here I have observed that the associations that attract one motif or element to another may be by the force of habit or of tradition. Where the association that is called forth is not necessarily linear or essential, the tension may be "submerged." The association may be caused by the force of elements long existing in tradition and thus brought into the singer's consciousness. Sometimes, as in the case of traditional epic narrative, a particular theme may by this tension of traditional elements automatically call forth a related theme. An example is when in South Slavic epic the theme of a long war or long absence of a hero brings into play the associated theme of deceptive story or recognition. See Alexander, 1995 and forthcoming.

But it is time to consider what these riddle songs are all about. Francis James Child in "Riddles Wisely Expounded" (Child 1) helps to provide the context for the South Slavic riddle songs.[34] Child ballad 1.A tells of a man welcomed by three sisters. The first, the eldest, let him in and bolted the door; the second made his bed; and the third, the youngest, slept with him. The next morning, she asked him to marry her, and he said that he would, if she could answer three questions.

> Sections 13–18
> "O what is longer than the way,
> Or what is deeper than the sea?
>
> Or what is louder than the horn?
> Or what is sharper than a thorn?
>
> Or what is greener than the grass,
> Or what is worse than a woman was?"
>
> "O love is longer than the way,
> And hell is deeper than the sea.
>
> And thunder is louder than the horn,
> And hunger is sharper than a thorn,
>
> And poyson is greener than the grass,
> And the Devil is worse than a woman was. . . ."

Whereupon he married her.

In his introductory note to Child 1, "Riddles Wisely Expounded," Child remarked that 1.A was well known in Germany. He quoted also part of a Russian version translated in Ralston's *Songs of the Russian People* and cited Scottish and Irish versions as well.[35] The opening of the Russian one places the girl in a garden gathering flowers. A merchant's son drives by and salutes her, and she thanks him.

> "Shall I ask thee riddles, beauteous maiden?
> Six wise riddles shall I ask thee?"
> "Ask them, ask them, merchant's son,
> Prithee ask the six wise riddles."
> "Well, then, maiden, what is higher than the forest?

---

34. Child, 1882, 1:4.
35. Ralston, 1872, quoted by Child, 1882, 1:2–3. Ralston's text is taken from Buslaev, 1861, 33–34.

Also, what is brighter than the light?
Also, maiden, what is thicker than the forest?
Also, maiden, what is there that's rootless?
Also, maiden, what is never silent?
Also, what is there past finding out?"
"I will answer, merchant son, will answer,
All the six wise riddles will I answer.
Higher than the forest is the moon;
Brighter than the light the ruddy sun;
Thicker than the forest are the stars;
Rootless is, o merchant's son, a stone;
Never silent, merchant's son, the sea;
And God's will is past all finding out. . . ."

The South Slavic "awaking songs" fall into the same pattern as Child 1, although the beginning is either lacking or different, and there is no mention of marrying; but the analogues make it clear that marriage is what the riddling is about. *Dragi dragu alkatmerom budi*, "The lover awoke his beloved with a red carnation" (Parry Text No. 1577) is the simplest of these. *Dvoje mlado sitno smilje bralo*, "Two young people were gathering everlastings" (Parry Text No. 10490) provides a somewhat fuller setting, and the garden or meadow scene is reminiscent of the Russian songs. *Beg Alibeg vjernu ljubu budi*, "Ali Bey awoke his true love" gives the woman a name and reminds us that *vjerna ljuba* does not always mean "wife."[36] *U polju se al-čador vidjaše*, "On the plain a red tent was seen" (Mladenović 144) places the scene in a field or on a plain, by a tent, and gives the girl a name and a named female companion as well as an unnamed and unmarried youth, and it is he who poses the riddles.

Other South Slavic settings for the riddles are more puzzling. Some of them place the girl by the sea or by a spring, and in them it is she who asks the riddles in a soliloquy. Sometimes she is weeping, and sometimes she is washing her face. In one song she is answered by a man, hitherto unmentioned. It is possible that this song is simply the result of confusion on the part of the singer. But there might perhaps be an implication that the girl is testing him to see what his caliber or intentions may be. Because, as remarked by Child, the Devil or another otherworldly figure sometimes appears in these songs, the testing of the man might not be inappropriate.

Child's remark may help us to understand also *Djevojka sjedi kraj mora*, "A

---

36. See above, after Parry Texts Nos. 9347, 9819, 10198, and 11176a.

girl is sitting beside the sea" (Karadžić 1.285), in which the soliloquy is answered by a fish![37] And *Pod onom gorom zelenom*, "Beneath that green hill" (Parry Text No. 1497) begins with horses impatiently watching a girl by the sea, whose first question is "Is there anyone more beautiful than I?" Her remaining questions, as we saw, were of the more usual kind, such as "Is there anything swifter than a horse?" She is answered, fittingly enough, by a vila, who declares that she is more beautiful than the girl. This latter song would seem to be a mixing of one in which the girl asks the questions about her beauty and is answered by a vila with another song, one that has the usual riddles. In both of these songs it is the girl who poses the riddles and it is a nonhuman who answers them. There is further confusion in the *Pod onom gorom zelenom* song just mentioned in the role of the prancing horses, which are usually waiting upon a weeping maiden. Our maiden does not weep but washes her face and remarks about her beauty. Our Gacko singers in this case have produced an amalgam of parts of variants.

There are a number of separate songs that begin with *Pod onom gorom zelenom*, and it is in their context that we must try to evaluate our text. As we look at some of them, it is immediately apparent that the riddles are not found in them. The group that employ *Vrani se konji igraju*, "Black horses are prancing," in an early line are of most interest to us, because that is the second line of our Gacko text. Karadžić 1.414 is an example:

Pod onom gorom zelenom	Beneath that green hill
I pod najvišom planinom	And beneath the highest mountain
Vrani se konji igraju,	Black horses are prancing,
Pod sobom jame kopaju,	Pawing up pits beneath them,
Srebrna sedla lomljaju,	Breaking their silver saddles,
Zlaćene uzde trgaju;	Tugging at their golden bits;
Dalek' se putu nadaju	They hope for a distant journey
Po lepu Janu devojku,	To fetch the lovely maid Jana,
A Jani sedi, te plače;	But Jana sits and weeps;
Teši je mila snašica:	Her dear sister-in-law comforts her:
"Ne plači, Jano, zaovo!	"Weep not, sister-in-law, Jana!
Kada su mene gledali,	When they came to look upon me,
Onda su višnje sađene;	Then were the cherries planted;
Kada su mene prosili,	When they asked for me,
Onda su višnje cvatile;	Then the cherries blossomed;

37. [David E. Bynum sees an analogue to Karadžić 1.285 in "The Grey Selchie of Sule Skerry," No. 27, in Kinsley, 1969, 91–93.]

Kada su mene vodili,	When they led me away from home as a bride,
Onda su višnje zobane."	Then were the cherries eaten."

Similar to this song are Karadžić 1.415 and 5.39. Except for the impatient horses and the weeping girl, these songs seem to have nothing to do with our riddles. An interesting variant is found in Mladenović 220:

Pod onom gorom zelenom	Beneath that green hill
I pod najvišom planinom,	And beneath the highest mountain
Moja lepa Janjo,	My lovely Janja,
Moja zeferinko,	My zephyr,
Moja čarna oka,	My black eye,
Ubava Janjo devojko!	Pretty maid Janja!
Vrani se konji igraju,	Black horses are prancing,
Pod sobom zemlju kopaju,	Pawing the earth beneath them,
Zlaćene uzde kidaju,	Champing their golden bits,
Srebrna sedla krškaju,	Breaking their silver saddles,
Lepom se putu nadaju	Hoping for a fine journey
Po lepu Janju devojku.	To fetch the lovely maid Janja.
Kada su Janju prosili,	When they asked for Janja,
Redom su dgunje sadili;	They planted the quinces;
Kad su joj prsten davali,	When they gave her the ring,
Redom su dgunje cvetale;	All the quinces blossomed;
Kada su Janju vodili,	When they led Janja away from home as a bride,
Redom se dgunje žutile.	The quinces turned yellow.
Brala ji Janja devojka,	The maid Janja gathered them,
Pa nosi babi na krilo,	And put them in her father's lap,
Babo ji s krila na zemlju:	Her father put them from his lap onto the ground:
"Nit' moja Janja nit' dgunje,	"Neither Janja nor the quinces are mine,
Već moja trava zelena!"	But mine is the green grass!"
Kupi ji Janja devojka,	The maid Janja picked them up,
Pa nosi majci na krilo.	And put them in her mother's lap.
Majka ji s krila na zemlju:	Her mother put them from her lap onto the ground:
"Nit' moja Janja nit' dgunje,	"Neither Janja nor the quinces are mine,
Već moja trava zelena!"	But mine is the green grass!"
Kupi ji Janja devojka,	The maid Janja picked them up,

Pa nosi dragom na krila,	And put them in her beloved's lap.
A dragi s krila u njedra:	And her beloved raised them from his lap into his bosom.
"Moja je Janja i dgunje!"	"Both Janja and the quinces are mine!"

This song adds a new scene to the preceding. Like Karadžić 5.39 it tells what happened to the fruit that was growing to maturity. Although the following song, Karadžić 1.291, does not belong in the *Vrani se konji igraju*, "Black horses are prancing," group of the *Pod onom gorom zelenom* texts, it does have a relationship to the last section of the above.

Pod onom gorom visokom	Beneath that high hill
Crljeno cv'jeće i modro,	Are red and blue flowers,
Brala ga Mare vjerena,	Betrothed Mare gathered them,
Na skut ga babu metala,	Put them in her father's lap,
Babo ga ne će, ter ne će:	Her father did not want them:
"Ni moja Mare, ni cv'jeće."	"Neither Mare nor the flowers are mine."
Pod onom gorom visokom	Beneath that high hill
Crljeno cv'jeće i modro,	Are red and blue flowers,
Brala ga Mare vjerena,	Betrothed Mare gathered them,
Na skut ga majci metala,	Put them in her mother's lap,
Majka ga ne će, ter ne će:	Her mother did not want them:
"Ni moja Mare, ni cv'jeće."	"Neither Mare nor the flowers are mine."
Pod onom gorom visokom	Beneath that high hill
Crljeno cv'jeće i modro,	Are red and blue flowers,
Brala ga Mare vjerena,	Betrothed Mare gathered them,
Na skut ga bratu metala,	Put them in her brother's lap,
A brat ga ne će, ter ne će:	But her brother did not want them:
"Ni moja Mare, ni cv'jeće."	"Neither Mare nor the flowers are mine."
Pod onom gorom visokom	Beneath that high hill
Crljeno cv'jeće i modro,	Are red and blue flowers,
Brala ga Mare vjerena,	Betrothed Mare gathered them,
Na skut ga sestri metala,	Put them in her sister's lap,
Sestra ga ne će, ter ne će:	Her sister did not want them:
"Ni moja Mare, ni cv'jeće."	"Neither Mare nor the flowers are mine."
Pod onom gorom visokom	Beneath that high hill
Crljeno cv'jeće i modro,	Are red and blue flowers,
Brala ga Mare vjerena,	Betrothed Mare gathered them,
Na skut ga dragu metala,	Put them in her beloved's lap,

Dragi ga hoće, ter hoće:	Her beloved wanted them:
"I moja Mare i cv'jeće."	"Both Mare and the flowers are mine."

Only the two Parry songs *Pod onom gorom zelenom* with which we began associate that beginning and the impatient horses with the riddle song. When the horses are described as watching a girl sitting beside the sea, the link is made with such songs as *Đevojka sjedi kraj mora*, "A girl is sitting beside the sea," and we suddenly find her uttering riddles. Her first line, *Ima li išta lepše od mene?* "Is there anyone more beautiful than I?" leads her into a connection with a group of boasting songs, to which the riddles tenuously belong simply by the form of question and comparison. An example of such a song is Parry No. 4457 from Dzemila Pošković of Gacko:

Falijo se žuti limun kraj mora:	The yellow lemon tree beside the sea boasted:
"Ima l' danas išta ljepše od mene?"	"Is there anything today more lovely than I?"
To začula senabija jabuka:	The autumn apple tree heard this,
A govori senabija jabuka:	And the autumn apple tree spoke:
"A i ja sam, bolan, ljepša od tebe.	"My poor fellow, I am lovelier than you.
Tebe pije svaka sorta šerbeta.	All sorts of people drink you in sherbet.
Mene bere sva gospoda pešćeša.	All the gentry choose me for gifts.
Koliko je u Efice avlija,	As large as Efica's courtyard is,
S kraj do na kraj senabija jabuka."	From one end to the other are autumn apple trees."

One could undoubtedly discover links to other songs from this group of boasting songs, and so on from group to group in a seemingly never-ending network of associations. Thus songs modulate from one to another by means of associations of various kinds.

In the case of the *Pod onom gorom zelenom* songs adduced above, we can note not only the variations of the fruit parallel but also the addition to it of an account of what is done with the fruits, a normal progression of narrative. Finally, however, we saw a song in which flowers were treated in the same way as the fruits, but what was only a section of a song in one case is a completely independent song in the other. There is no green hill, there are no impatient horses, simply a girl picking flowers and offering them to father, mother, sister, and brother, all of whom refuse them. At last her lover accepts both the girl and the flowers. Here is a dramatic example of some of the ways in which songs are augmented and interrelated in tradition. The riddles led us from "awaking" songs, to weeping maidens by bodies of water, to impatient horses, all of which are elements associated with marriage: choosing a bride (or bridegroom?) by means of riddles, maidens weeping because they do not wish to leave home, horses eager to set out to fetch the bride from her home. Tradition in the case of the lyric songs, at least, consists of a mass of interrelated and interwoven motifs and their formulaic expressions in discernible themes, or repeated passages, centered in the various stages of wedding ritual.

To return to the riddle songs, finally, in a class very much by themselves are *Tica i djevojka*, "The Bird and the Girl" (Karadžić 1.286) and *Plač za dragijem*, "Lament for One Beloved" (5.379) with their settings of a disappointed, and apparently unfaithful, girl trying to explain to her departed lover that she had always loved him more than the other man. To prove this, she cites the embroidered pillow she gave him, which was finer than the one she had given his rival. The pillow is described elaborately. On it, among other things, is a tree with branches on one of which sits a bird, representing the lover. He asks another bird the riddles, and she answers them, proving that she is worthy to marry him. In the other version the girl bird is sitting on the branch and a swallow from afar asks the riddles. Bird imagery is not uncommon in this poetic tradition, but the elaboration of the setting for the riddles is indeed unusual. The question of marriage is still the point of the riddling test.

We have seen that in some lyric songs in the South Slavic tradition there may be a section of the song at the beginning, in the middle, or at the end, which shows clear signs of a sense of textuality on the part of the singer, whereas other parts of the song may seem independent of textuality. There are some songs, of course, whose textuality embraces the whole song. I turn now to an example of such a song. Mladenović 316 has two variants, Karadžić 1.693 and 5.577. Here are the three texts:

Mladenović 316	
Dok sam bio mlado momče,	While I was a little boy,
Đevojke me bratom zvaše,	The girls called me brother,
Udovice, "Moj brajane!"	Widows, "My big brother!"
A ka' sam se oženio,	But when I was married,
Stare babe, "Drago d'jete!"	Old babas, "Dear child!"
Đevojke me vragom zovu,	The girls called me a devil,
Udovice, "Vragolane!"	Widows, "You joker!"
Stare babe, "Ćut', magare!"	Old babas, "Shut up! ass!"

Karadžić 1.693
Kad sam bio mlado momče,
Đevojke me bracom zvaše,
A nevjeste, "Mlado momče!"
Stare babe, "Majkin sine!"
A kada se ja oženih,
Svakog dobra ja poželih.
Đevojke me vragom zovu,
A nevjeste, "Vragolome!"
Stare babe, "Kurvin sine!"

When I was a little boy,
The girls called me brother,
Brides, "Little boy!"
Old grannies, "Mother's son!"
But when I married,
I lost every good thing.
The girls called me a devil,
Brides, "Devilish one!"
Old grannies, "Son of a bitch!"

Karadžić 5.577
Dokle mene ne oženi majka,
Đevojke me Bogom bratimjahu,
Udovice uzdanicom zvahu,
Desno krilo, sve nevjeste mlade,
Stare bake, "Odi k meni, sinko!"

A od kad se ja oženih, druže,
Đevojke me zovu izdajnikom,
Udovice: "Naš nevjerni druže!"
A nevjeste, "U nevolji druže!"
Stare babe ni "Oklen si, sinko?"

Until my mother married me off,
The girls called me brother-in-God,
Widows called me their trusted friend,
All young brides, their right wing.
Old grannies, "Come and see me, sonny!"

But after I married, friend,
The girls called me traitor,
Widows, "Our faithless friend!"
Brides, "Friend in need!"
Old grannies don't even ask, "Where have you been, sonny?"

Here is a humorous and satiric song, of which the South Slavic tradition has many, a parody, an inversion, of the usual love song. The young man complains that he was much sought for before he married but not desirable afterward.

In spite of the differences among the variants, including the fact that the first two are octosyllabic and the third decasyllabic, this whole song has textuality. Line six in Karadžić 1.693 is unique and breaks up the symmetry of introductory line plus the naming, which is repeated, of three female groups of acquaintances. In Mladenović 316 the singer has reversed lines four and five, also breaking the symmetry. It was probably for this reason that Karadžić did not publish the text. Only Karadžić 5.577 maintains the balanced structure and includes both *udovice* 'widows', otherwise only in 316, and *nevjeste* 'brides', otherwise only in 693.

The structure of this satiric song makes it easy to remember. The "before" and "after" lines are followed by a series of classes of women with a typical comment for each. It is remembered. There is no need to memorize the song, because it can be put together readily enough from ordinary memory, and there is no fixed text to memorize anyway. The lines and half-lines of this song are made up of traditional formulas. The song, or the "theme" (that is, a repeated passage), is not improvised, nor is it memorized. Improvisation would mean that it was made up extempore of mainly nontraditional elements. The materials of the song are traditional, the structure is traditional, and it provides a plan that is easily followed. I believe that one might well say that the song is composed in performance. The stable opening of our first example of South Slavic lyric songs (Mladenović 155, Karadžić 1.590, 591) is also held together by its structure reinforced by such devices of sound as rhyme and alliteration. Its structure is a simple one of vocative plus question and answer. The form is that of a stylized dialogue. The alliteration of *ružičice*, *ružo*, and *rumena* is clear enough, as are the internal rhyme of *djevojčice* and *ružičice* and the end rhyme of *rumena* and *medena*. These are all structural elements that make both remembering and recomposing easy. So do the parallelisms in the riddle song. In the case of some lyric songs, then, composition in performance is the proper descriptive term for the process.

I have given one case above[38] of two versions of a woman's song by the same singer, Šerifa Zvizdić of Gacko. It behooves us to look at more instances of this phenomenon. An instructive example is the short lyric, Karadžić 5.298, under the title *Dođi k mene dragane*, "Come to Me, Beloved":

Puni mi, puni, ladane!	Blow, blow, cold wind!
Dođi mi, dođi, dragane,	Come to me, beloved,
U moju bašču zelenu,	Into my green garden,
Pod moju ružu rumenu!	Beneath my red rose!
Vezem ti zlatnu maramu.	I am embroidering a golden kerchief for you.
Prispjeće tebi Božiću.	It will be ready by Christmas.
Nosi je i ponosi se!	Wear it and be proud!
Spomen' se tvoje dragane!	Remember your beloved!

The Parry collection has forty-four texts of this song. A version of it from Halima Hrvo in Gacko was published in *Serbo-Croatian Folk Songs*:[39]

Puhni mi, puhni, ladane!	Blow, blow, cold wind!
Dođi mi, dođi, dragane.	Come to me, beloved,

38. See above, Parry Texts Nos. 1577 and 10490.
39. Bartók and Lord, 1951, No. 5, 262–63.

U moje dvore bijele!	Into my white dwelling!
Dovedi đoga za sobom!	Bring your white horse with you!
Sveži ga ruži za grane!	Tie him to a branch of the rose tree!
Neka mu ruža miriše!	Let the rose envelop him in its fragrance!
Neka mu duša uzdiše!	Let his spirit sigh with longing!

A transcription by Béla Bartók of the music of this song can be found in the above mentioned publication.[40] In performance, Halima repeats each line. It should be noted in passing that this song text is made up of three couplets, of which the first is extended by one line. The first couplet is identical with the first couplet in the Karadžić text, but the extended lines are different. In one case the beloved is to come to her house, in the other, to her green garden.

We have two versions of this song from Đula Hrustanović of Gacko, Parry Nos. 9467 and 12100:

9467	12100
Puhni mi, puhni, ladane,	Puhni mi, puhni, ladane!
Šalaj, ladane!	Puhni mi, puhni, ladane,
	Šalaj, ladane!
Dođi mi, dođi, dragane,	Dođi mi, dođi, dragane!
Šalaj, dragane,	Dođi mi, dođi, dragane,
	Šalaj, dragane,
U moju bašču zelenu,	U moju bašču zelenu,
Šalaj, zelenu,	U moju bašču zelenu,
	Šalaj, zelenu,
Pod moju ružu rumenu,	Pod moju ružu rumenu,
Šalaj, rumenu!	Pod moju ružu rumenu,
	Šalaj, rumenu,
Majka mi nije kod kuće,	Povedi đoga za sobom!
Šalaj, kod kuće.	Povedi đoga za sobom,
	Šalaj, za sobom!
A dica sitna mala,	Sveži ga ruži za grane!
Šalaj, pospala.	Sveži ga ruži za grane,
	Šalaj, za grane!
A dedo stari ne mari,	Neka mu ruža miriše!
Šalaj, ne mari.	Neka mu ruža miriše,
	Šalaj, miriše!
	Neka mu duša uzdiše!
	Neka mu duša uzdiše,
	Šalaj, uzdiše!

40. Ibid., 100–101.

	Ti dođi meni pod pendžer!
	Ti dođi meni pod pendžer,
	Šalaj, pod pendžer!
	Ja ću te mlada ljubiti,
	Ja ću te mlada ljubiti,
	Šalaj, ljubiti,
	A ti ćeš mene uzeti,
	A ti ćeš mene uzeti,
	Šalaj, uzeti.
	Blow, blow, cold wind!
	Come to me, beloved,
	Into my green garden,
	Beneath my red rose-tree!
My mother is not at home,	Bring your white horse with you!
And the little children have fallen asleep,	Tie him to the branches of the rose-tree!
And old grandfather does not care.	Let the rose envelop him in its fragrance,
	And let his spirit sigh with longing!
	Come beneath my window!
	I shall love you, young as I am.
	And you will take me!

Hrustanović's first four lines are alike in both of her texts and they agree with the first four lines of Karadžić 298, although only the first couplet is shared with Hrvo's text from the Bartók book. Beginning with line five, these three dictated versions tell different stories. In 298 the girl is embroidering a golden kerchief, to be finished by Christmas, which the lover may wear to remember his beloved. In 9467 the girl adds that her mother is not at home, the children are asleep, and old grandfather does not care. Đula's other version, beginning with line 5, agrees with lines 4–7 of Halima's Bartók text but continues the story to its culmination.

The Parry collection also has two dictated texts of this song from Đulsa Čampara (Nos. 4029 and 7323). They agree with Đula Hrustanović's No. 12100 through the line *Neka mu duša uzdiše!* "Let his spirit sigh with longing!" No. 4029 ends there, but 7323 adds, in a different meter(!), lines suggested by the horse and obviously taken from another song:

Podajte mi đogi jedno kilo soli!	Give my white horse a kilo of salt!
Podajte mi đogi jedno kilo soli!	
Nek moj đogo znade, da mene imade!	Let my white horse know that he has
Nek moj đogo znade, da mene imade!	me!

In the case of both of these singers there is a stable core of the song and a tendency to go beyond that core by adding several more lines.

Đula Dizdarević dictated three versions of this little song to Čedika Šaković (No. 10528) and to Halid Dizdarević (Nos. 11740 and 11752). The first of these is like the first of Đula Hrustanović's texts, ending with

Majka mi nije kod kuće,	Mother is not at home,
A deca sitna malena	And the little children
Jesu mi sada zaspala,	Have now fallen asleep,
A dedo stari ne mari.	And old grandfather does not care.

No. 11740 begins with the two unexpected lines, then uses several familiar ones, and ends with new material, though an old subject:

"Puhni, vjetre, ne deri mi derte!	"Blow, wind, do not tear my grief!
Puhni mi, hlade, razderi mi jade!	Blow, cold one, tear apart my sorrows!
Puhni mi, puhni, hladane!	Blow, blow, cold wind!
Dođi mi, dođi, dragane,	Come to me, beloved,
U moju bašču zelenu,	Into my green garden,
Pod moje dvore bijele!	To my white dwelling!
Dođi mi, dragi, u bašču,	Come, beloved to the garden,
Pod moju ružu rumenu,	Beneath my red rose-tree,
Pod moje dvore bijele!"	To my white dwelling!"
Zove ga cura na konak.	The girl invited him in to spend the night.
Lijepo ga cura dočekala.	The girl received him well.
Mehku mu stere postelju,	She spread a soft bed for him,
I gosposku večeru.	And a lordly supper.

Once again we have a more or less stable core with surrounding variations. No. 11752 has more surprises:

Puhni mi, puhni, hladane!	Blow, blow, cold wind!
Dođi mi, dođi, dragane,	Come to me, beloved,
U moju bašču zelenu,	Into my green garden,
Pod moju ružu rumenu,	Beneath my red rose-tree,
Pod moj pendžer bijeli!	Beneath my white window!
Ja ću tebe čekati,	I shall await you,
Slatko šerbe mutit'.	And mix sweet sherbet.
Vrata ću ti otvorit'.	I shall open the door for you.
Kad ti bideš na vratima,	When you are at the door,

Nemoj plaho trupati!	Do not knock loudly!
Moj je tata mučna tabijata.	My daddy has a bad temper.

Although for the analysis of variants I have chosen songs I knew and liked and of which, from my work on the Bartók book, I was aware that there were a number of texts available, I believe that they are typical of their genre. In working with traditional songs and stories, it does not matter where one begins, because all songs and stories of a given traditional genre are interconnected.

An oral traditional song, no matter what its length or "genre," textually, consists of one or more groups, large or small, of lines forming a more or less stable core adapted to context. Both the core and the lines used to adapt it consist typically of blocks of lines of varying size, but normally between two and four lines, linked in various ways that result (although probably not consciously conceived of for this purpose) in their being "memorable" and easily recalled when needed—or, more properly, when association brings them to mind. "Tension of essences" is close to "free association." There seems, then, to be a principle operative in the oral traditional material considered which says that, no matter what the size of the composition, the traditional singers work with comparatively small blocks of lines intermediate between the formula and the theme.

Whether dealing with versions from a single singer or from several, one thus frequently encounters the more or less stable core of lines to which new elements are added. Sometimes they are added at the beginning. When they are placed after the "core," it is almost as if after a given point in the song the singer were filling out the song with familiar traditional ideas and formulas. It can truly be said that even with short lyric songs, which are erroneously thought to have a fixed text kept verbatim in the memory, the concept of a memorized text needs to be modified. The larger the sample with which one works, the less adequate is the concept of word-for-word memorization as a means of song transmission.

Editor's Addendum

Lord has demonstrated the oral composition of two large bodies of lyric poetry, Latvian *dainas* and Serbo-Croatian women's songs. His method was to show that these short, nonnarrative poems were not memorized but were composed in performance by combining familiar, oft repeated blocks of lines (a stable, but not fixed, core of wording) with new or additional poetic material. Although formulas abound in such poems, his method depended not so much on showing the proliferation of formulas as on demonstrating the persistence of blocks of lines, belonging to or leading to the compositional device of the "theme," or repeated passage. He thus advanced from an analysis of short repeated phrases to larger units of thought.

The question naturally arises whether Parry and Lord's methods can be applied to ancient Greek lyric and elegiac poetry in an effort to determine whether such poetry could have been composed orally. Milman Parry had indeed considered the question. In this "excursus" I gather together the pertinent remarks of Parry and other scholars. I quote them at some length in order to present their views as precisely as possible.

In "Studies in the Epic Technique of Oral Verse-Making, II. The Homeric Language as the Language of an Oral Poetry," under the heading of "The Traditional Language of Lesbian Lyric Poetry," Parry made the following statement:

> The same forces which created the poetic epic language of Homer created the poetic lyric language of Sappho and Alcaeus. The scant remains of these two poets do not allow us to show, as we can do for Homer, that their diction is formulaic and so oral and traditional. We do know, however, that Solon and Theognis were still following an oral tradition of . . . poetry, and that they lived at that time, always so precious for our own knowledge of oral poetries of the past and present, when verse-making was oral but writing known and used as a means of recording and keeping. All that we know of the use of writing in Greece at the beginning of the sixth century points to the same thing for Sappho and Alcaeus. Yet while we may still feel some doubt as to the way in which they made their verse, there is not the least doubt that their poetic language was drawn from an oral tradition; only in an oral poetry does one ever find such a variety of forms that have each one its own metrical value.[41]

He then proceeded to illustrate Sappho and Alcaeus's use of "the endings of the spoken language, that is of the inscriptions," and of archaic and artificial forms, found in dialects other than Lesbian.

In a letter to Albert Lord, dated May 19, 1971, Jesper Svenbro wrote to query the relationship between orality and lyric poetry and between epic and lyric poetry. He remarked:

> Without any systematic investigation ready at the moment I have noticed some formulaic lines in the Lesbian poets:

41. Parry, 1971, 347.

Sappho 1.17   Lobel-Page   κ]ὤττι μοι μάλιστα θέλω γένεσθαι
Sappho 5.3   "   κὤσσα ϝ]οι θύμωι κε θέληι γένεσθαι
and
Sappho 31.6   "   καρδίαν ἐν στήθεσιν ἐπτόαισεν
Alcaeus 283.3   "   κἀλένας ἐν στήθ[ε]σιν [ἐ]πτ[όαισας
and formulaic phrases like
Sappho 1.10   περὶ γᾶς μελαίνας
Sappho 16.2   ἐπ[ὶ] γᾶν μέλαι[ν]αν
Sappho 20.6   γ]ᾶς μελαίνας

(all in the same metrical position) which along with the 'variety of forms that have each one its own metrical value' in the Lesbian poets could indicate that Parry was quite right. We have to remember that some ten thousand lines of Sappho survived until late antiquity, so if we are able to find formulas in the scant remains, we would certainly find much more if we had all of it before our eyes.[42]

Svenbro's observations on formulas in Sappho are substantiated by the research of Gregory Nagy: "There are rigid correspondences between the Sapphic pentameter and the Homeric hexameter not only in meter and phraseology but also in the placement of this phraseology.... Sappho had at her disposal a tradition of inherited formulas which were parallel to the inherited meter of her verses. The rigid phraseological correspondences between her pentameter and the epic hexameter are due to parallel inheritance of related formulas from related meters."[43]

In "Studies in the Epic Technique of Oral Verse-Making, I. Homer and Homeric Style," under the heading "The Formula Outside Homer," Parry cited studies dealing with elegiac poetry:

> N. Riedy found in Solon 48 phrases repeated without change from the *Iliad* or the *Odyssey* or the Hymns; of these all but one are found in the 221 elegiac verses of this poet. There are none in his iambics. This makes about 21 epic phrases to a hundred verses, a figure fairly near that found for the gnomic part of the *Works and Days*. In the 932 verses of Theognis which Bergk thought genuine R. Küllenberg found 144 phrases repeated from Homer, Hesiod, or the Hymns, which would be about fifteen epic phrases to a hundred verses. No one has studied the shorter repetitions within elegiac poetry, but Küllenberg remarks that in the hexameter the elegy follows the epic. So here too the

---

42. See Svenbro, 1984, 65 and nn. 58 and 59; also Svenbro, 1988, 163 and n. 7; and 1993, 146–52 and nn. 7, 10.
43. Nagy, 1974, 131–34; see also pp. 120–35.

formulaic element must be studied as a part of the traditional diction of the early verse in hexameters. But Küllenberg also states that the elegy follows itself in the pentameter. He quotes in proof 18 phrases, all found in the last half of the pentameter, which appear in the work of the elegiac poets a total of 99 times. Moreover, certain of the systems into which these phrases fall are long enough to show the traditional character of the greater part of the expressions which make them up. . . . The example of Serbian poetry shows that traditional dictions can exist side by side for different verse-forms and for different types of poetry, and the doubt which hangs over the sources of Theognis's poem would point to anything but an originally written text.[44]

In a volume of essays edited by Thomas J. Figueira and Gregory Nagy, one finds frequent allusion to the elements of oral composition in the *Theognidea*, "about fourteen hundred verses in all," representing "something more than the life's work—however long that life may have been—of a single poet."[45] Nagy discusses the Homeric poems in the context of pan-Hellenism, a process he applies also to Hesiod and to the Theognidean poetry.[46] In considering, moreover, the passages in the Theognidea which are believed to be excerpts from Solon and other writers of elegiac poetry, Nagy demonstrates that

> the sharing of doublets in the textual traditions of two distinct poets, as also in that of a single elegiac poet such as Theognis, cannot be dismissed as merely a matter of textual transposition. As the evidence collected by Pietro Giannini and others strongly suggests, formulaic behavior characterizes the diction of not only Theognis but also of Solon, Tyrtaeus, Mimnermus, and all the other poets of archaic elegiac. Moreover, the formulas of elegiac pentameter are independent from, though cognate with, those of Homeric and Hesiodic hexameter. Any given sharing of doublets in Theognis, or in Theognis and

---

44. Parry, 1971, 280–81. See Riedy, 1903; Küllenberg, 1877. See Harrison, 1902, 100–134, with reference to "the many verses and passages in Theognis which some editors have given to Tyrtaeus, Mimnermus and Solon because they are found, in more or less the same form, in their work as well. . . . If the small amount of poetry we have is typical, the common element in the elegy was very large" (cited by Parry, 1971, 281). For the view that much of the poetry of Archilochus is oral and largely Homeric in diction, whereas some of his poems exhibit transitional characteristics, see Page, 1963; also Notopoulos, 1966.
45. Figueira and Nagy, 1985, 1. The editors date the *Theognidea* to the period 640–479 B.C.
46. Nagy, 1985, 35, n. 17.3. See also Nagy, 1982, 52, 60–62; and Parry, 1971, 279–80. For the orality of Hesiod, see Hoekstra, 1957; G. Edwards, 1971; Pavese, 1972, 111–96; Peabody, 1975; Hainsworth, 1981; Janko, 1982; and Thomas, 1992, 102 n. 1. For orality in the Homeric Hymns, see Brillante, Cantilena, and Pavese, 1981, esp. the following articles: Segal, on the *Hymn to Demeter*, 107–62; Kirk, on the *Hymn to Apollo*, 163–82; and Herter, on the *Hymn to Hermes*, 183–201. See also Janko, 1982, chap. 2, 18–41. On the *Hymn to Aphrodite*, see Preziosi, 1966.

another given elegiac poet—even when the match is several verses in length—can be ascribed to the workings of oral poetry, where we can expect parallel topics to be handled with parallel sequences of thematic development, which in turn will be expressed with remarkably parallel formulaic patterns.[47]

Nagy gives an example of doublets in the elegiac corpus where slightly different wording (for example, between Solon and Theognis) illustrates not only the formulaic system but likewise the lack of a fixed text, important signs of oral composition.[48] These qualities of fluidity within a stable core of lines, as we have seen, are found abundantly in Lord's citations from Latvian and South Slavic lyrics, composed in performance.

Andrew L. Ford questions the interpretation that explains the σφρηγίς, the seal that Theognis places upon his utterances, as his assertion of authorship. Instead Ford shows that "the seal can have had little practical value as the claim of authorship in the archaic period when poetry was circulated freely in oral performances rather than in books."[49] One might add that Theognis himself says that he learned as a boy from the nobles, "the good," what he will pass on to Cyrnus. This traditional process is essentially the way the oral singer learns and transmits poetry.

Nathan A. Greenberg examines the question whether the language of archaic Greek elegiac is formulaic. He is not entirely happy with Pietro Giannini's conclusion that there are formulaic expressions not only in the hexameter lines of the elegiac couplet but also in the pentameter line. In his examination of elegiac usage of *agathos*, Greenberg does not find many formulas of the noun-epithet type. His view that this is almost the only type of the Homeric formula is unjustified. Lord has urged that the concept of the formula and the unit of thought (including subject and predicate) be extended to the half-line and from the half-line to the full line and beyond that to the couplet or block of lines. In the analysis of shorter lyrics as well as of epic verse, Lord was able to demonstrate that the repetition of blocks of lines is a vital aspect of oral composition. Greenberg experiments successfully with this larger concept by applying to elegiac poetry the idea of an interplay between the hexameter and pentameter lines of the couplet: "Rather than end the thought with the hexameter, the hexameter line is used, often to set the stage, to induce a set of expectations, which the pentameter line is designed to satisfy with closure of sense, with rhetorical point, wit, and contrast. Often the pentameter plays one hemistich against the other."[50]

47. Nagy, 1985, 48. See Giannini, 1973; and Nagy, 1979b.
48. Nagy, 1985, 49–50.
49. Ford, 1985, 83.
50. In Figueira and Nagy, 1985, 256; for examples entailing contrasts of *agathos* and *kakos*, see 256–57. See Giannini, 1973.

Greenberg generously allows for a larger vision of oral poetry in its application to elegiac verse:

> The processes of oral composition are more varied than at first supposed. There is room for poetic ingenuity under any hypothesis, and room for ongoing development and improvement of oral traditional poetry. Even if we look in vain elsewhere for the sort of fixed phrases embodied in the epic epithet, however, there is no need to jettison Parry's insights on the social and cultural settings out of which oral traditional poetry arises. It has become clear that we do not need literacy to produce epic poetry and *a fortiori* the shorter pieces of elegiac poetry.[51]

Nagy's study of convergent and divergent wording of doublets in the extant corpus of elegiac poetry and Albert Lord's exploration of stable but flexible blocks of lines in Latvian *dainas* and South Slavic lyrics are compelling examples of the expanding horizons of traditional oral poetry inherent in Greenberg's statement.

I can find no mention of elegiac poetry in Eric Havelock's *The Muse Learns to Write*.[52] He argues, however, that the resistance to the use of the Greek alphabet lasted to the time of Euripides and that the "partnership between orality and proto-literacy molded the unique character of classic Greek literature." He maintained that "surviving orality also explains why Greek literature to Euripides is composed as a performance, and in the language of performance."[53] He illustrates what he calls "the dynamics of the oral tongue" by citing from Sophocles' *Oedipus* striking passages that are "concrete, dynamic, and particular in their expression." Yet objections arise. One must not confuse the dramatists' composition *for* performance with the oral poet's composition *in* performance. Performance by itself does not necessarily constitute oral literature, *pace* Ruth Finnegan,[54] except in the most literal sense of the word *oral*.

It is appropriate here to recall Parry's remarks about Greek choral poetry and Attic tragedy.[55] With respect to choral poetry, he said:

> There is no need of pointing out that so few formulas in the work of Pindar and Bacchylides could have no measurable effect on the way in which they made their verses; but besides that it is only too clear that these repeated

---

51. Figueira and Nagy, 252.
52. Havelock, 1986; but see Havelock, 1982, 19: "Elegiac, like lyric, was a functional component of orally preservable communication."
53. Havelock, 1986, 93.
54. See A. Lord, 1987b, 324–37, esp. 326–27; Finnegan, 1976, 137.
55. Parry, 1971, 281–98.

phrases are not formulas. They are all of them high-sounding expressions which the poet has been able to work into his verse. . . . Far from being formulas by which he would regularly express his idea under certain metrical conditions, these phrases were to him fine expressions which his mind kept solely for their beauty, and which the chance of his verse now let him use. One would not deny all usefulness to them, since they did after all fit into his verse, but that is exactly the usefulness of any phrase which goes to make up any poem.[56]

With regard to the Attic dramatists, Parry concludes:

We took care [pages 285–98] to see just how many repetitions there were in tragedy, supposing that the exact difference in number between those in Attic poetry and those in Homer would have some bearing upon the problem of the formulas in the *Iliad* and in the *Odyssey*. But the truth is that only the absolute difference thus proved has any bearing on Homer's practice. The contrast between a vast number of repetitions in Homer and a comparatively very small number in the work of the tragic poets at once suggested that repetition could not be due to the same causes in both cases. Then a study of the nature of the repetitions in tragedy showed that almost none of them, or even none of them at all, are true formulas, and so we reached that important point where we know surely that Homer's poetry is governed by factors unknown to later Greek poetry.[57]

---

56. Ibid., 283. Havelock, 1982, 16 and n. 27, however, maintains, following Fennell, that "it is probable that [Pindar] did not write his odes." He cites Fennell, 1893,: "Metrical literature was not committed to writing for nearly a generation after the Persian Wars, i.e., not until Pindar was an old man" (xvii). See the remainder of Havelock's note: "Internal evidence of the odes we have could support the view that the poet occasionally sent either a papyrus of the poem for performance overseas, or one or more musicians who had memorized the poem, or did both."

57. Parry, 1971, 299.

CHAPTER 3

Homer and the Muses: Oral Traditional Poetics, a Mythic Episode, and Arming Scenes in the Iliad

Some critics have questioned whether the work of Milman Parry leaves room for an appreciation of the aesthetics of the Homeric epics. There must, of course, always be a place in any approach to Homer for such an appreciation. But an analysis of Homer's style and aesthetics must also be based, in my opinion, on an understanding of the traditional nature of the composition of the *Iliad* and the *Odyssey*. Paolo Vivante in his book *The Epithets of Homer* assumes, rather grudgingly, that Homer was an oral poet in Parry's sense of the term.[1] Yet when he proceeds to discuss Homeric aesthetics, he ignores entirely the oral traditional qualities and aesthetic values of Homer's poetry, even denying, it would seem, its place in tradition.

For Vivante, poetics is existential; the poetic moment is single and timeless; there can, in his view, be no such thing as tradition. Every moment, every word, every thought, every scene in the more than 27,800 lines of the Homeric poems, must according to him be a vibrant expression of its nature and identity, of its own here and now, because it is poetry, and all poetry, as poetry, is alike. Meter is almost completely absent from his book—he might just as well have been writing about prose. I find it hard to conceive of poetry without some form of rhythmic or acoustic structure. Come to think of it, Vivante seems not to be much interested in structure either. I find that his denial of tradition divorces him from the facts. Often what he has to say lacks focus and is ambiguous. In his preface, for example, he writes:

---

1. Vivante, 1982, chap. 22, n. 1: "I grant for the argument's sake that Homer was an 'oral poet,' as supposed by Parry. Whether he wrote or not is not relevant to my thesis."

> We must recognize that there *was* a poetic intelligence at work, that there *was* a point of intensified activity and a full consciousness of what was being achieved. This is to say that we must reckon with the intellectual climate of the age. The poet and his listener were at one in a moment of poetic awareness, and this relation was not the mere interplay which exists between a performer and his audience. The interest lay in the mode of delivery, quite apart from any particular subject matter.[2]

If you consider carefully what he has said, you may have some questions. What was the intellectual climate of the poet's age? What is actually meant by the poet and his audience being at one in a moment of poetic awareness? Why should that not be part of the interplay between poet and audience? Is "mere" necessary? Finally, what does he mean by "mode of delivery?" His book does not answer these questions. He continues:

> Here was a breaking point in the tradition, an intellectual and artistic movement reaching its acme. Such an intense experience could not be drawn out at length; a long elaboration would have weakened it. I thus imagine that the creative period was much shorter than is commonly assumed, not necessarily longer than three generations. . . . See how the repetitions of the same phrase or typical scene are but literal instances of an intuited measure which is rehearsed on a variety of matter—from the battle scenes, say, to the encounters in Hades. Rather than inveterate craft we have here a touch so firm and so pliant as to become a mode of thought. Can such a sense of things be traditional?[3]

If Vivante means that for three generations, including Homer's probably as the last, the ancient Greek tradition of epic song was at its height, expressing its thoughts and feelings in a superbly apt poetic style fully participated in and appreciated by those who listened to it, I could not find great cause to disagree. It is true that I do not know why he chose to limit the acme to three generations, except that—as Vivante probably does not know—that span is a common folk idea, which happens to be false. We in the Parry collection have documentary evidence of song traditions covering more than four hundred years. If Vivante meant to say what I have indicated, why did he not do so and omit the questioning of the existence of tradition?

Vivante's romantic and unreal world is essentially synchronic or, as he likes to express it, existential. This concept is applicable to the nontraditional modern poet, or to a nontraditional poet at any period the intellectual

2. Ibid., ix.
3. Ibid.

climate of which fosters nontraditional poetry. To apply that concept without modification to a traditional poet whose work is, at one and the same time, both synchronic and, by definition, diachronic, and must be read, or listened to, and appreciated by the literary critic as such on pain of not understanding the poet at all, is to be gravely mistaken. When one has taken away metrics, mythology, subject matter, mere description, mere narration, mere whatever, as does Vivante, the ultimate reality is a moment of poetic awareness, perhaps of a continuous series of moments of ecstasy, lasting for 27,800 lines and more—or should I say for three generations?—which might give even Zeus pause.[4]

The Homeric critic cannot afford to ignore the mythological themes latent in the Homeric poems, nor the discipline of the comparatist. The listener's (or reader's) pleasure is all the keener for the recognition of mythic patterns underlying Homeric episodes. A striking example of cosmic proportions is found in Achilles' fight, in Book 21 of the *Iliad*, with the river-god Xanthus, called Scamander by men. Why does Achilles fight with a river? No other hero in the poem fights with a natural phenomenon. One answer to the question is that the river has been glutted with corpses and is angry. That is, indeed, what the river himself says, but rivers do not speak. Talking horses are one thing; they are a hero's alter ego; but rivers?—not except in their capacity as gods.[5]

Clearly with the fight with the river the *Iliad* has entered into a different phase from its earlier books, although it was close to it in Diomedes' exploits with the gods and goddesses in Book 5 and again in Book 8, when Zeus, having threatened the gods with a tug of war should they help the Trojans or the Danaans in battle, frightens Diomedes from the fighting.[6]

---

4. For the denigration of mythological analysis and of attempts to fathom the layers of meaning latent in the Homeric poems, see ibid.: "What the theorists of oral composition have done is to transform this concrete inevitable relation between speaker and hearer into a grand abstraction. Anthropology and history are now brought into the picture. The audience becomes the tradition, the depositary of myth and folklore, the spirit of the age; and the poet is made into the spokesman of the tribe; he embodies in his work the rich threads of a tradition which is the common property of his milieu" (176).

5. In the context of the fight with the river, compare Baal's fight with Judge River in the Baal epic; see Cross, 1977, chap. 6, "The Song of the Sea and Canaanite Myth," esp. 112–15. Achilles' fight with the river may possibly find an echo in the story of Gen. 32:24–30 of Jacob's wrestling with an angel (man) at the ford of the river Jabbok. There is some evidence that Jacob's supposed adversary was a river-god; for the word *wrestled* in Hebrew is a verbal play on the name of the river "Jabbok"; see *The New Jerome Biblical Commentary*, sec. 2.54, pp. 33–34. His adversary was indeed divine, (Gen. 32:28); for the angel said to him, "Your name shall no more be called Jacob, but Israel, for you have striven with God and with men, and have prevailed" (Revised Standard Version).

6. See *Iliad* 8.133–36: "He thundered horribly and let loose the shimmering lightning / and dashed it to the ground in front of the horses of Diomedes / and a ghastly blaze of flaming sulphur shot up, and the horses / terrified both cringed away against the chariot." The translations of the

When Achilles has put on his divine armor, he becomes 'like a god' (δαίμονι ἶσος),[7] and the poem shifts easily enough to a duel between Achilles as god with another god, namely, the river Xanthus. The change is perfectly in harmony with the surroundings, because in the scene in Book 21, a host of gods is on the field, sometimes fighting, and listed among them is Xanthus, or Scamander. Homer, as usual, has the situation on the stage well in hand. Achilles as *god* has entered a miniature "war of the gods." Immediately after the fight with the river, a veritable war among the gods ensues, albeit of comic proportions, with Poseidon unsuccessfully urging Apollo into the fray. Artemis scolds her brother, and Hera boxes Artemis's ears, while Hermes fears to attack Leto.

In ancient Greece there was a myth of the "war of the gods," best known to us in Hesiod's *Theogony*, a pattern of "power politics." The *Theogony*, although perhaps later than the Homeric poems, can serve as an excellent background for the approach to this mythic pattern in the *Iliad*; one sees it constantly in Zeus's relations with the other gods. In the *Iliad* we find him concerned with maintaining his role as most powerful of the gods. His will must prevail, but he has some trouble keeping the control of affairs in his hands. The most ancient analogue of the "war of the gods" is found in the Babylonian creation epic, *Enuma Elish*, depicting the struggle between cosmic order and chaos and the rise to power of the god, Marduk.[8] This pattern appears operative also in the narrative of Achilles' fight with the river, in which the hero struggles with cosmic forces. Here it may be that two patterns meet, that of the partly human hero fighting supernatural forces and that of the war of the gods.

In *Iliad* 21, in Achilles' fight with the river, the pattern of the war of the gods shades into still another pattern, that of the almost-death of the hero. Achilles almost dies in his fight with the river, but he is saved by Hera, who sends Hephaestus with fire to subdue the waters. This is one of the most dramatic scenes in the poem:

> And every time swift-footed brilliant Achilleus would begin
> to turn and stand and fight the river, and try to discover
> if all the gods who hold the wide heaven were after him, every

---

Iliad and the *Odyssey* used throughout this book, apart from occasional exceptions, are those of Richmond Lattimore: *The Iliad of Homer*, 1951, and *The Odyssey of Homer*, 1967.

7. *Iliad* 21:227; cf. 21.17–18: "But heaven-descended Achilleus left his spear on the bank / leaning against the tamarisks, and leapt in like some immortal" (... ὁ δ' ἔσθορε δαίμονι ἶσος).

8. See E. A. Speiser, in Pritchard, 1950, 60–72; Heidel, 1951; and Hesiod, 1966, 22–24 and index s.v. "Babylonian texts."

time again the enormous wave of the sky-fed river
would strike his shoulders from above. He tried, in his desperation,
to keep a high spring with his feet, but the river was wearing his knees out
as it ran fiercely beneath him and cut the ground from under
his feet. Peleides groaned aloud, gazing into the wide sky:
"Father Zeus, no god could endure to save me from the river
who am so pitiful. And what then shall become of me?
It is not so much any other Uranian god who has done this
but my own mother who beguiled me with falsehood, who told me
that underneath the battlements of the armoured Trojans
I should be destroyed by the flying shafts of Apollo.
I wish now Hektor had killed me, the greatest man grown in this place.
A brave man would have been the slayer, as the slain was a brave man.
But now this is a dismal death I am doomed to be caught in,
trapped in a big river as if I were a boy and a swineherd
swept away by a torrent when he tries to cross in a rainstorm."[9]

I can cite an example of the almost-death of the hero from South Slavic epic. In one of the most famous of the songs of Marko Kraljević, the hero meets with the formidable roadblocker, Musa the Highwayman, who turns out to have three hearts, one of them a serpent. In this combat, Marko was saved by the aid of the vila, the winged mountain spirit who was his blood sister. Other examples of the theme of the near death of the hero come to mind in the almost-death of Beowulf in his fight with Grendel and his dam, also of Charlemagne in his combat with Baligant.

Achilles' fight with the river is a superb episode in and of itself, a powerful departure, in its struggle with the forces of nature, from the abundant battle scenes between one hero and another. The realization that Achilles' combat with the river Xanthus has reverberations with mythic themes in other epics in world literature adds depth to one's appreciation of Homer's mastery of the material of his song.[10]

To return to the subject of poetic language, Homer's had been forged by generations of singers before him, just as the average speaker of any language has inherited his nonpoetic language, which has been forged by generations of speakers before him and indeed by the same process of assimilation. In both cases not only are words inherited but also clusters of words in a variety

---

9. *Iliad* 21.265–83.
10. For Achilles' fight with the river Xanthus as an instance of mythological exemplum in Homer, see Nagy, 1992b, 325. He sees a partial comparison with Heracles' fight with the divine ruler Acheloos in Archilochus F 286–87 West.

of combinations, together with the flexibility to create new combinations. But, although the basic process is the same, effected by singing or speaking rather than in writing, Homer's composing of epic songs is different from the average speaker's utterances, a vital difference being, of course, that Homer is singing in dactylic hexameters, whereas the average speaker is speaking in ordinary prose.

Homer, I maintain, inherited a poetic language adapted to metrical utterance, including words to express the most needed ideas and feelings in the epic songs and providing models for creating means to express any other ideas he may have wished to convey to his listeners. The modern poet seeks, rather, to create an individual, even individualistic, language of his own with its own diction and poetics. He can and is expected to seek new modes of thought and of language. The poetic moment is that of composition, a moment ideally relived by the listener or reader.

Homer, like other traditional singers of epic, does not eschew his inherited language, because it is an ideal language created to serve a particular purpose and serving it very well; it is necessary for him. The intellectual climate of Homer's age expressed itself fully and satisfactorily in that poetic language; it sought no other. Instead, the intellectual climate of the modern poet consciously seeks individual creation, a new and individual poetic language. It is on this basis that the difference in poetics between oral traditional epic and written nontraditional epic is predicated.

Yet—and here is a crucial paradox the literary critic, the aesthetician, and the scholar *must* fully understand—the traditional poet is still a creator, not of a new poetic language but of an ever new *song* at each retelling. He even to some varying extent may create not only a new *song* but also a new *text* at a retelling. But though the text or the song may be new, the language is not. Most of the words and combinations of words, ideas and combinations of ideas, belong in the poet's inherited traditional poetic language and song. This is not to say that traditional art is created by a "collective" and that it is collective poetics;[11] for that is like saying that *language* was created by a collective. The traditional poet's language is diachronic, as, indeed, is all language, except when the nontraditional poet consciously breaks it. Its poetics consist of much more than meter, or its equivalent—important

---

11. [Lord's denial that oral traditional art is produced by a "collective" should lay to rest Rosalind Thomas's interpretation of Parry's and Lord's views whereby "Homer's *Iliad* and *Odyssey* were not the creation of one poetic genius" (Thomas, 1992, 29) or that they were the product "of more than one poet" (31). The formative influence of tradition in oral poetry, as affirmed by Parry and Lord, does not imply multiple authorship and does not exclude the possibility of individual talent or genius in a particular oral poet, such as a Homer or an Avdo Međedović. On this point, see Janko, 1990, 326.]

though that be—which is but the frame and rhythm of an idea, one of the contributing factors in poetics without which poetry would not be poetry.

When I spoke about words and combinations of words, I, of course, had formulas and themes in mind. But it must be understood that these formulas are not necessarily fixed entities although they may attain a kind of stability in a singer's usage which is not by any means the same as permanent fixity. They are not dead phrases floating vaguely about as stock in trade for the poet singer. They are a living part of dynamic, traditional poetic language.

Moreover, as Cecil Bowra pointed out years ago, the epithets and other traditional elements have their own history.[12] Some are older than others; some are more "intense," if that is the word, than others; some are particularized; and so on. They cannot be treated en masse by the discerning critic, nor can even the undiscerning afford to dismiss them en masse and still understand the poetics of a Homer. There was a time when they were bright and shiny, brand new. There were some that, once created, never survived on the lips of the singer who brought them forth or were never repeated or recreated by any other singer. Some lasted a short time only. But some were experienced anew many times. They were useful, of course, and it is that usefulness of which Milman Parry wrote; but they were more than useful. As Parry himself has said, they were also "right."[13] Some of them aged gracefully, some not. But live they did, and do; for when they are dead, traditional singers discard them and consign them to oblivion because they are no longer pertinent or worthy of being remembered.

To treat the traditional formulas and themes as if they were vibrantly brand new each time they appear is, however, to miss their peculiar quality of traditionality, a kind of patina that is theirs alone. The literary critic should strive to see and appreciate the value of that patina. To try to refurbish the objet d'art by trying to make it look brand new is to falsify it. A patina is not the same as tarnish or grime.

I want now to turn again to a specific aspect of Homer's *Iliad* and to comment on the arming scenes.[14] I have chosen the arming scenes because

---

12. Bowra, 1930, 81–84.
13. Parry, 1971: "For the ornamental epithet does not have an independent existence. It is one with its noun, with which it has become fused by repeated use, and the resulting noun-epithet formula constitutes a thought unit differing from that of the simple noun only by an added quality of epic nobility" (249); "But if it [the phrase] does not suit in every way, or if a better way of fitting the idea to the verse and the sentence is found, it is straightway forgotten or lives only for a short time, since with each new poet and with each new generation of poets it must undergo the twofold test of being found pleasing and useful" (330).
14. [A. Lord, 1991, 89–93, discussed arming scenes in the *Iliad*. In spite of the repetition, it seemed best to include the previous remarks for the sake of the continuity and cohesion of the present discussion, which adds extensively to what was said in the earlier treatment of the subject.]

Paolo Vivante has written, "Consider again the existential importance of the instances. . . . They have their own self-contained nature, they have their own inevitable way of taking place irrespectively of any specific occasion or purpose. . . . Insofar as he arms himself, Achilleus is not different from Paris."[15] I wonder if Vivante has compared the arming scenes.

There are four arming scenes in the *Iliad* that share a central group of lines, but Homer clearly and carefully distinguishes one arming and hence one person from another; for the arms fit the hero.[16]

The arming of Paris in 3.330–38 begins with the lines

> κνημῖδας μὲν πρῶτα περὶ κνήμῃσιν ἔθηκε
> καλάς, ἀργυρέοισιν ἐπισφυρίοις ἀραρυίας·
> δεύτερον αὖ θώρηκα περὶ στήθεσσιν ἔδυνεν.
>
> First he placed along his legs the fair greaves linked with
> silver fastenings to hold the greaves at the ankles.
> Afterwards he girt on about his chest the corselet.

The arming of Agamemnon in 11.17–45, that of Patroclus in 16.131–39, and finally the arming of Achilles himself in 19.369–74 and 380–83, all begin with the same three lines. These are the only times when any of these lines, alone or in combination, is used in the Homeric corpus as it has come down to us. That sets those four arming scenes in a place by themselves.

The first epithet in these three lines is καλάς 'fair', and I suggest that one of the elements in its choice was the fact that it alliterates with the *k*s of the preceding line. The only other epithet in these lines immediately follows καλάς, namely, ἀργυρέοισιν 'silver', and I suggest that one of the factors in its choice also was its assonance with the last word in its line, ἀραρυίας 'linked', although it is to be noted that it does not qualify that word.

Note the structure of the first two lines above:

noun acc.	adverb	prep. phrase	verb
κνημῖδας	πρῶτα	περὶ κνήμῃσιν	ἔθηκε
epithet	epithet	noun	participle
καλάς	ἀργυρέοισιν	ἐπισφυρίοις	ἀραρυίας

---

15. Vivante, 1982, 50.
16. For a perceptive treatment of these four arming scenes, see Armstrong, 1958: "A reading of these four passages leads me to the conclusion that there is a real difference between the arming of Paris and the arming of Achilles, that Homer, as an oral poet, may so arrange his formulaic diction and his formula by variation, expansion, even by invention that he thereby enriches both the texture of his verse and the meaning of his poem" (353–54). In what follows I hope to add to and corroborate his conclusion. See also Lorimer, 1950, 188–92; and Kirk, 1985, 313–16.

and the third line:

adverb	noun acc.	prep. phrase	verb
δεύτερον	θώρηκα	περὶ στήθεσσιν	ἔδυνεν

The clasps are used only in these four passages in the *Iliad* and in the related 18.459, when Thetis asks Hephaestus for armor for Achilles:

καὶ καλὰς κνημῖδας ἐπισφυρίοις ἀραρυίας.
and beautiful greaves fitted with clasps.

Here the epithet for clasps (fastenings) is not used because the greaves are simply enumerated in a list of the items of armor to be prepared; they are not being donned. Hence only one line is used, not two. When the donning is described, two lines are needed in order to include the verb.

The same principle of alliteration that we saw above seems to influence the other words used in lines having κνημῖδας 'greaves' in them. So in 18.613 we find:

τεῦξε δέ οἱ κνημῖδας ἑανοῦ κασσιτέροιο.
He made for him greaves of light tin.

I cannot refrain from quoting the entire passage of which this is the last line, partly for the alliterations, partly for the repetitions of τεῦξε 'made, wrought', and partly for the cumulative effect of the lines themselves:

609 Αὐτὰρ ἐπεὶ δὴ τεῦξε σάκος μέγα τε στιβαρόν τε,
τεῦξ' ἄρα οἱ θώρηκα φαεινότερον πυρὸς αὐγῆς,
τεῦξε δέ οἱ κόρυθα βριαρὴν κροτάφοις ἀραρυῖαν,
καλὴν δαιδαλέην, ἐπὶ δὲ χρύσεον λόφον ἧκε,
τεῦξε δέ οἱ κνημῖδας ἑανοῦ κασσιτέροιο.

Then after he had wrought this shield, which was huge and heavy,
he wrought for him a corselet brighter than fire in its shining,
and wrought him a helmet massive and fitting close to his temples,
lovely and intricate work, and laid a gold top-ridge along it,
and out of pliable tin wrought him leg-armour. . . .

The greaves are of tin partly at least because 'tin' (κασσίτερος), alliterates with κνημῖδας. We find also the same descriptive genitive κασσιτέροιο with the singular κνημίς in 21.592:

ἀμφὶ δέ οἱ κνημὶς νεοτεύκτου κασσιτέροιο
σμερδαλέον κονάβησε. . . .

Round about it the greave of newly made tin
clanged terribly. . . .

'Newly made' (νεοτεύκτου) is clearly a very apposite epithet in this passage; for the greave in question is that in the new armor made by Hephaestus for Achilles. It is not actually, then, a "fixed epithet" for κασσίτερος, although the epithet νεοτευχής is used again in the *Iliad* in 5.194:

193 ἀλλά που ἐν μεγάροισι Λυκάονος ἕνδεκα δίφροι
καλοὶ πρωτοπαγεῖς νεοτευχέες· ἀμφὶ δὲ πέπλοι

somewhere in the great house of Lykaon are eleven chariots,
beauties, all new made, just finished, and over them blankets.

At line 3.333, Homer continues the arming of Paris, with an idea peculiar to that hero's corselet:

οἷο κασιγνήτοιο Λυκάονος· ἥρμοσε δ' αὐτῷ.
of Lykaon his brother since this fitted him also.

which picks up the *k* alliteration again. After the description of the greaves, the donning of the armor is resumed in lines 334–38:

ἀμφὶ δ' ἄρ' ὤμοισιν βάλετο ξίφος ἀργυρόηλον
χάλκεον, αὐτὰρ ἔπειτα σάκος μέγα τε στιβαρόν τε·
κρατὶ δ' ἐπ' ἰφθίμῳ κυνέην εὔτυκτον ἔθηκεν
ἵππουριν· δεινὸν δὲ λόφος καθύπερθεν ἔνευεν·
εἵλετο δ' ἄλκιμον ἔγχος, ὅ οἱ παλάμηφιν ἀρήρει.

Across his shoulders he slung the sword with the nails of silver,
a bronze sword, and above it the great shield, huge and heavy.
Over his powerful head he set the well-fashioned helmet
with the horse-hair crest, and the plumes nodded terribly above it.
He took up a strong-shafted spear that fitted his hand's grip.

The same lines are used in the arming of Patroclus in 16.135–39, and there too they are preceded by a line peculiar to Patroclus, referring to the breastplate, or corselet. Actually, of course, it is Achilles' armor, borrowed by Patroclus:[17]

17. [For a discussion of the arming of Patroclus, see Janko, 1992, 333–36.]

134 ποικίλον ἀστερόεντα ποδώκεος Αἰακίδαο.
    elaborate, and starry, of swift-footed Aiakides.

The last line of the run, which mentions the spears, is changed from one spear taken up by Paris to two taken up by Patroclus:

3.338   εἵλετο δ' ἄλκιμον ἔγχος, ὅ οἱ παλάμηφιν ἀρήρει.
        He took up *a* powerful spear that fitted his hand's grip.

16.139 εἵλετο δ' ἄλκιμα δοῦρε, τά οἱ παλάμηφιν ἀρήρει.
        He took up *two* powerful spears that fitted his hand's grip.

The arming of Paris ends with that line, but that of Patroclus continues with what he did *not* take, Achilles' Pelian ash spear.[18] In other words, the basic lines in each case have been adapted to the hero of the moment, Paris or Patroclus.

But the first three lines we considered were used to introduce the arming of Agamemnon and of Achilles as well. In the case of Agamemnon, lines 11.20–28 describe the special corselet Agamemnon put on:

20 τόν ποτέ οἱ Κινύρης δῶκε ξεινήϊον εἶναι.
    πεύθετο γὰρ Κύπρονδε μέγα κλέος, οὕνεκ' Ἀχαιοὶ
    ἐς Τροίην νήεσσιν ἀναπλεύσεσθαι ἔμελλον·
    τοὔνεκά οἱ τὸν δῶκε χαριζόμενος βασιλῆϊ.
    τοῦ δ' ἤτοι δέκα οἶμοι ἔσαν μέλανος κυάνοιο,
25 δώδεκα δὲ χρυσοῖο καὶ εἴκοσι κασσιτέροιο·
    κυάνεοι δὲ δράκοντες ὀρωρέχατο προτὶ δειρὴν
    τρεῖς ἑκάτερθ', ἴρισσιν ἐοικότες, ἅς τε Κρονίων
    ἐν νέφεϊ στήριξε, τέρας μερόπων ἀνθρώπων.

> [First he placed along his legs the beautiful greaves linked
> with silver fastenings to hold the greaves at the ankles.
> Afterwards he girt on about his chest the corselet]
> that Kinyras had given him once, to be a guest present.
> For the great fame and rumour of war had carried to Kypros
> how the Achaians were to sail against Troy in their vessels.
> Therefore he gave the king as a gift of grace this corselet.
> Now there were ten circles of deep cobalt upon it,
> and twelve of gold and twenty of tin. And toward the opening
> at the throat there were rearing up three serpents of cobalt
> on either side, like rainbows, which the son of Kronos
> has marked upon the clouds, to be a portent to mortals.

18. [Shannon, 1975, 31–86, has an extensive discussion of Achilles' ash spear.]

After this special passage the lines in the two other armings (those of Paris and Patroclus) reappear in that of Agamemnon slightly changed in 11.29–31:

> ἀμφὶ δ' ἄρ' ὤμοισιν βάλετο ξίφος· ἐν δέ οἱ ἧλοι
> χρύσειοι πάμφαινον, ἀτὰρ περὶ κουλεὸν ἦεν
> ἀργύρεον, χρυσέοισιν ἀορτήρεσσιν ἀρηρός.
>
> Across his shoulders he slung the sword, and the nails upon it
> were golden and glittered, and closing about it the scabbard
> was silver, and gold was upon the swordstraps that held it.

Before the first line has ended, the sword's description has begun. That description is followed immediately by that of the shield (32–40), a special and ornate passage that is unparalleled in the other passages.

> ἂν δ' ἕλετ' ἀμφιβρότην πολυδαίδαλον ἀσπίδα θοῦριν,
> καλήν, ἣν πέρι μὲν κύκλοι δέκα χάλκεοι ἦσαν,
> ἐν δέ οἱ ὀμφαλοὶ ἦσαν ἐείκοσι κασσιτέροιο
> 35 λευκοί, ἐν δὲ μέσοισιν ἔην μέλανος κυάνοιο.
> τῇ δ' ἐπὶ μὲν Γοργὼ βλοσυρῶπις ἐστεφάνωτο
> δεινὸν δερκομένη, περὶ δὲ Δεῖμός τε Φόβος τε·
> τῆς δ' ἐξ ἀργύρεος τελαμὼν ἦν· αὐτὰρ ἐπ' αὐτοῦ
> κυάνεος ἐλέλικτο δράκων, κεφαλαὶ δέ οἱ ἦσαν
> 40 τρεῖς ἀμφιστρεφέες, ἑνὸς αὐχένος ἐκπεφυυῖαι.
>
> And he took up the man-enclosing elaborate stark shield,
> a thing of splendour. There were ten circles of bronze upon it,
> and set about it were twenty knobs of tin, pale-shining,
> and in the very centre another knob of dark cobalt.
> And circled in the midst of all was the blank-eyed face of the Gorgon
> with her stare of horror, and Fear was inscribed upon it, and Terror.
> The strap of the shield had silver upon it, and there also on it
> was coiled a cobalt snake, and there were three heads upon him
> twisted to look backward and grown from a single neck, all three.

The basic lines then reappear for another brief spell, also somewhat modified, in lines 41–45:

> κρατὶ δ' ἐπ' <u>ἀμφίφαλον</u> κυνέην θέτο <u>τετραφάληρον</u>
> ἵππουριν· δεινὸν δὲ λόφος καθύπερθεν ἔνευεν.
> εἵλετο δ' ἄλκιμα δοῦρε <u>δύω, κεκορυθμένα χαλκῷ,</u>
> <u>ὀξέα</u>· τῆλε δὲ χαλκὸς ἀπ' αὐτόφιν οὐρανὸν εἴσω
> λάμπ'. . . .

Upon his head he set the helmet, two-horned, four-sheeted,
with the horse-hair crest, and the plumes nodding terribly above it.
Then he caught up two strong spears edged with sharp bronze
and the brazen heads flashed far from him deep into heaven.

I have underlined the changes from the "basic lines" of the theme—for that is what it is—although one should also note that line 43 has the ἄλκιμα δοῦρε 'strong spears' found in the arming of Patroclus in 16.139. The arming of Agamemnon ends with line 44 above, or, more strictly, after the first word of line 45. Thus the arming of Agamemnon is completed, a combination of modified basic lines and special passages pertaining to it alone.

As one might expect, the arming of Achilles in his newly made armor is also special,[19] although the "basic lines" reappear, and we feel their steadying effect. In fact, unlike the other three cases, including that of Paris, which have one line or more special to the hero after the first three introductory lines, in Achilles' arming the basic lines continue immediately after the three introductory lines:

> 19.372 ἀμφὶ δ' ἄρ' ὤμοισιν βάλετο ξίφος ἀργυρόηλον
> χάλκεον· αὐτὰρ ἔπειτα σάκος μέγα τε στιβαρόν τε
> εἵλετο, τοῦ δ' ἀπάνευθε σέλας γένετ' ἠΰτε μήνης.
>
> and across his shoulders [he] slung the sword with the nails of silver
> a bronze sword, and caught up the great shield, huge and heavy
> next, and from it the light glimmered far, as from the moon.

The last line, of course, is not one of the basic lines but had to be introduced here because of the grammatical role of εἵλετο 'caught up' as verb whose direct object, σάκος 'shield', is in the preceding line.

The arming continues after an extended simile (lines 375–380a, the only extended simile in the four armings) comparing the way in which the light shone from Achilles' shield with that from a blazing fire set for mariners across the sea:

> ὡς δ' ὅτ' ἄν ἐκ πόντοιο σέλας ναύτῃσι φανήῃ
> καιομένοιο πυρός, τό τε καίεται ὑψόθ' ὄρεσφι
> σταθμῷ ἐν οἰοπόλῳ· τοὺς δ' οὐκ ἐθέλοντας ἄελλαι
> πόντον ἐπ' ἰχθυόεντα φίλων ἀπάνευθε φέρουσιν·

---

19. For the arming of Achilles and particularly for his shield, see M. Edwards, 1987, index s.v. "Armor of Achilles."

> ὡς ἀπ' Ἀχιλλῆος σάκεος σέλας αἰθέρ' ἵκανε
> καλοῦ δαιδαλέου. . . .
>
> And as when from across water a light shines to mariners
> from a blazing fire, when the fire is burning high in the mountains
> in a desolate steading, as the mariners are carried unwilling
> by storm winds over the fish-swarming sea, far away from their loved ones;
> so the light from the fair elaborate shield of Achilleus
> shot into the high air. . . .

Fire and blazing light are associated especially with Achilles and his armor. The most memorable instance occurs in 18.205–14 as Achilles returns to the fight and, before the gift of his armor, appears at the trench, in an "epiphany" when Athena causes a golden cloud to circle about his head and kindles from it a blazing flame.[20]

Then for a moment there is an echo of the basic lines as Achilles puts on his helmet in lines 19.380b–83, lines in which the poet says that the helmet "shone like a star":[21]

> περὶ δὲ τρυφάλειαν ἀείρας
> κρατὶ θέτο βριαρήν· ἡ δ' ἀστὴρ ὣς ἀπέλαμπεν
> ἵππουρις τρυφάλεια, περισσείοντο δ' ἔθειραι
> χρύσεαι, ἃς Ἥφαιστος ἵει λόφον ἀμφὶ θαμειάς.
>
> And lifting the helm he set it
> massive upon his head, and the helmet crested with horse-hair
> shone like a star, the golden fringes were shaken about it
> which Hephaistos had driven close along the horn of the helmet.

Achilles then tries himself in his armor in lines 384–86, "and the armour became as wings and upheld the shepherd of the people." Finally he takes up his Pelian ash spear, his "special weapon." With this his arming ends. It covers twenty-three lines—the next to the longest of the four passages involved.

---

20. For the importance of fire and flaming light for the *Iliad* and particularly for Achilles, see Whitman, 1958, chap. 7, "Fire and Other Elements," esp. 137–39. Whitman points out that in Book 18, "we meet the god of fire himself, Hephaestus. The forging scene opens with twenty bellows blowing up the coals for the work to begin. The *thorax* is brighter than the gleam of fire. The great shield is too transcendent an image to be wholly dominated by fire images, but it includes them; sun, moon, and stars, the fiery bodies of heaven (to all of which Achilles, dressed in these arms, is later compared) occupy a prominent position together with the other three elements, earth, sky, and sea" (138).

21. Contrast how Hector in *Iliad* 11.61–63 with his shield is compared to a baneful star: "And Hektor carried the perfect circle of his shield in the foremost, / as among the darkened clouds the bale star shows forth / in all shining, then merges again in the clouds and the darkness."

The arming of Agamemnon with its twenty-eight lines surpasses it by five lines. Paris's arming takes nine lines and Patroclus's fourteen.

It is not surprising to find that the lines about Achilles' Pelian ash spear (388–91) are alike in the arming of Patroclus, who does *not* take it (16.139–44), and of Achilles, who does.

> 139 εἵλετο δ' ἄλκιμα δοῦρε, τά οἱ παλάμηφιν ἀρήρει.
> ἔγχος δ' οὐχ ἕλετ' οἶον ἀμύμονος Αἰακίδαο,
> βριθὺ μέγα στιβαρόν· τὸ μὲν οὐ δύνατ' ἄλλος Ἀχαιῶν
> πάλλειν, ἀλλά μιν οἶος ἐπίστατο πῆλαι Ἀχιλλεύς,
> Πηλιάδα μελίην, τὴν πατρὶ φίλῳ πόρε Χείρων
> Πηλίου ἐκ κορυφῆς, φόνον ἔμμεναι ἡρώσσιν....
>
> He took up two powerful spears that fitted his hand's grip,
> only he did not take the spear of blameless Aiakides,
> huge, heavy, thick, which no one else of all the Achaians
> could handle, but Achilleus alone knew how to wield it;
> the Pelian ash spear which Cheiron had brought to his father
> from high on Pelion to be death for fighters....

Achilles takes up the spear in 19.387:

> ἐκ δ' ἄρα σύριγγος πατρώϊον ἐσπάσατ' ἔγχος
> Next he pulled out from its standing place the spear of his father.

Then the description of the spear follows as in 16.141–44. The alliteration in the Greek in these passages about the Pelian ash spear echoes around three ideas, Πηλιάδα 'the Pelian one' (143, and Πηλίου 144 and 19.390 and 391); πάλλειν 'to brandish' (142 and 19.389, ἐπίστατο Πῆλαι, also 142 and 19.389); and πατρώϊον 'of his father' (ἐσπάσατ' 19.387 [and πατρὶ 143 and 19.390]).

The epithets for the spear in these passages, in addition to Πηλιάδα, which together with πάλλειν establishes the alliteration, are worthy of our attention: βριθὺ, μέγα, στιβαρόν 'heavy, huge, thick'. They are found in the same position three more times, always qualifying ἔγχος 'spear' at the end of the preceding line (the sole exception is in the arming of Patroclus, 16.140, where ἔγχος is at the beginning of the line). Twice they are used, interestingly enough, to describe Athena's preparing to depart from Olympus:

> 5.745–47 and 8.389–91
> ἐς δ' ὄχεα φλόγεα ποσὶ βήσετο, λάζετο δ' ἔγχος
> βριθὺ μέγα στιβαρόν, τῷ δάμνησι στίχας ἀνδρῶν

ἡρώων, οἷσίν τε κοτέσσεται ὀβριμοπάτρη.
(391 reads: ἡρώων, τοῖσίν τε κοτέσσεται ὀβριμοπάτρη.)

She set her feet in the blazing chariot and took up a spear
heavy, huge, thick, wherewith she beats down the battalions of fighting
men, against whom she of mighty father is angered.

The passages continue to lines 752 and 396 respectively without change of wording.

The third passage, 16.802, is in the killing of Patroclus and refers, of course, to the spear carried by him, not the Pelian ash spear of Achilles, it is to be noted, but, significantly, its substitute:[22]

801 πᾶν δέ οἱ ἐν χείρεσσιν ἄγη δολιχόσκιον ἔγχος,
βριθὺ μέγα στιβαρὸν κεκορυθμένον· αὐτὰρ ἀπ' ὤμων
ἀσπὶς σὺν τελαμῶνι χαμαὶ πέσε τερμιόεσσα.

And in his hands was splintered all the huge, great, heavy,
iron-shod, far-shadowing spear, and away from his shoulders
dropped to the ground the shield with its shield sling and its tassels.

In this passage of "unarming" Patroclus we find the helmet knocked to the dust in line 793:

τοῦ δ' ἀπὸ μὲν κρατὸς κυνέην βάλε Φοῖβος Ἀπόλλων.
Apollo now struck away from his head the helmet.

The shield, as we have just seen, dropped from his shoulders, and finally in line 804 the corselet is broken:

λῦσε δέ οἱ θώρηκα ἄναξ Διὸς υἱὸς Ἀπόλλων.
The lord Apollo, son of Zeus, broke the corselet upon him.

We see, therefore, that the epithets βριθὺ, μέγα, στιβαρόν are used together only for the spears of Athena and Achilles and for the substitute spear of Patroclus. In fact, in the *Odyssey* the only line in which βριθύ is found also describes Athena's departure from Olympus, the same one with which we are now familiar:

22. [The spear at 16.802 has been discussed by Bannert, 1984, and 1988, 159–67. See also Janko, 1992, on 16.141–44 and 801–2.]

Odyssey 1.99–101
εἵλετο δ' ἄλκιμον ἔγχος, ἀκαχμένον ὀξέϊ χαλκῷ,
βριθὺ μέγα στιβαρόν, τῷ δάμνησι στίχας ἀνδρῶν
ἡρώων, τοῖσίν τε κοτέσσεται ὀβριμοπάτρη.

Then she caught up a powerful spear, edged with sharp bronze,
heavy, huge, thick, wherewith she beats down the battalions of fighting
men, against whom she of the mighty father is angered.

This combination of epithets is clearly special and not used for any ἔγχος 'spear' among the many in the *Iliad* and *Odyssey* but only for the one Athena picks up on Olympus when she comes down to Ithaca or Troy, one that is fatal for the ranks of men, or otherwise only for Achilles' ἔγχος, the Pelian ash spear (or its substitute, which, as substitute, is shattered), which is also fatal to the ranks of men.

The epithets μέγα and στιβαρόν are also common with σάκος 'shield' in the arming of Paris, Patroclus, and Achilles and in the ordering and making of the great shield in 18.478 and 609. The other specific instances are 3.335 (Paris), 16.136 (Patroclus), and 19.373 (Achilles):

χάλκεον· αὐτὰρ ἔπειτα σάκος μέγα τε στιβαρόν τε
a bronze sword, and above it the great shield, huge and heavy.

The two instances in Book 18 are:

478 ποίει δὲ πρώτιστα σάκος μέγα τε στιβαρόν τε
First of all he forged a shield that was huge and heavy.

and:

609 αὐτὰρ ἐπεὶ δὴ τεῦξε σάκος μέγα τε στιβαρόν τε,
Then after he had wrought this shield, which was huge and heavy,

It is curious to find Paris's arming included in what is otherwise an all-Achilles phenomenon. It is also curious to find that the most elaborate arming, that of Agamemnon, is excluded. Put in other words, why does Paris have a σάκος μέγα τε στιβαρόν τε 'a shield huge and heavy', and why does Agamemnon have an ἀμφιβρότην πολυδαίδαλον ἀσπίδα θοῦριν 'man-enclosing elaborate stark shield'? The answer to the latter question is easier than that to the former. Agamemnon's shield is also very special with its four epithets, 11.32–33:

> ἂν δ' ἕλετ' ἀμφιβρότην πολυδαίδαλον ἀσπίδα θοῦριν,
> καλήν, ἣν πέρι μὲν κύκλοι δέκα χάλκεοι ἦσαν,
>
> And he took up the man-enclosing elaborate stark shield,
> a thing of splendour. There were ten circles of bronze upon it.

The last epithet, καλήν 'splendid', may be explained by the alliteration of the line, recalling a similar case with the greaves, although in this case the alliteration is anticipatory.

The epithet θοῦριν is usually associated in penultimate position with the genitive θούριδος ἀλκῆς 'impetuous might' (twenty times in the *Iliad*) or with the accusative of Ares, θοῦρον Ἄρηα 'violent Ares' (nine times in the *Iliad*, of which seven are in penultimate position and two in the second foot). It is used twice in the nominative with Ares; it is used three times in the feminine accusative with ἀλκήν:

> 5.507   θοῦρος Ἄρης ἐκάλυψε μάχῃ Τρώεσσιν ἀρήγων,
> As violent Ares defending the Trojans mantled in dark night the battle,
>
> 24.498 τῶν μὲν πολλῶν θοῦρος Ἄρης ὑπὸ γούνατ' ἔλυσεν.
> Violent Ares broke the strength in the knees of most of them.
>
> 7.164   τοῖσι δ' ἐπ' Αἴαντες, θοῦριν ἐπιειμένοι ἀλκήν,
> and next the two Aiantes rose, their fierce strength upon them,
>
> 18.157 τρὶς δὲ δύ' Αἴαντες, θοῦριν ἐπιειμένοι ἀλκήν,
> Three times the two Aiantes with their battle-fury upon them,

The epithet θοῦρος 'fierce' seems to be comfortable with words beginning with alpha. It is used once of the aegis, 15.308!

> 306 Τρῶες δὲ προὔτυψαν ἀολλέες, ἦρχε δ' ἄρ' Ἕκτωρ
> μακρὰ βιβάς· πρόσθεν δὲ κί' αὐτοῦ Φοῖβος Ἀπόλλων
> εἱμένος ὤμοιιν νεφέλην, ἔχε δ' αἰγίδα θοῦριν,
> δεινὴν ἀμφιδάσειαν ἀριπρεπέ', ἣν ἄρα χαλκεὺς
> Ἥφαιστος Διὶ δῶκε φορήμεναι ἐς φόβον ἀνδρῶν.
>
> The Trojans came down on them in a pack, and Hektor led them
> in long strides, and in front of him went Phoibos Apollo
> wearing a mist about his shoulders, and held the tempestuous
> terrible aegis, shaggy, conspicuous, that the bronze-smith
> Hephaistos had given Zeus to wear to the terror of mortals.

The epithet θοῦριν is used once more with ἀσπίδα, in 20.162, when Aeneas goes forth to meet Achilles, and it is Aeneas's shield to which it is applied:

> 161 Αἰνείας δὲ πρῶτος ἀπειλήσας ἐβεβήκει,
> νευστάζων κόρυθι βριαρῇ· ἀτὰρ ἀσπίδα θοῦριν
> πρόσθεν ἔχε στέρνοιο, τίνασσε δὲ χάλκεον ἔγχος.
>
> First of the two Aineias had strode forth in menace, tossing
> his head beneath the heavy helm, and he held the stark shield
> in front of his chest, and shook the brazen spear.

The associations of θοῦρος with ἀλκή, with Ares, and with the aegis suggest a fearsome characteristic of Agamemnon's shield with its Gorgon's head, reminding one of the shield of Heracles rather than that of Achilles. I note, however, in the *Shield of Heracles* itself (line 319), that one finds the shield referred to thus:

> Ἥφαιστος ποίησε σάκος μέγα τε στιβαρόν τε
> Hephaestus made the shield great and strong.

A few lines earlier in the *Shield* (line 315) we find another epithet for Heracles' shield which is also among those used for Agamemnon's:

> πᾶν δὲ συνεῖχε σάκος πολυδαίδαλον....
> and enclosed all the cunning work of the shield.[23]

It is time to look at the last two of the epithets applied to Agamemnon's great shield, πολυδαίδαλον 'intricately worked' and ἀμφιβρότην 'man-enclosing'; πολυδαίδαλον is used six more times in the *Iliad* in addition to 11.32 in the arming of Agamemnon. We find it four times (3.358, 4.136, 7.252, and 11.436). in the line

> καὶ διὰ θώρηκος πολυδαιδάλου ἠρήρειστο.
> and smashed its way through the intricately worked corselet.

The first instance is in the duel between Menelaus and Paris. The latter has thrown his spear, which was caught by Menelaus on his shield. After a prayer

---

23. Trans. by Evelyn-White, 1943, 243.

to Zeus, Menelaus casts his spear and strikes "the shield of Priam's son on its perfect circle":

> 355 ἦ ῥα καὶ ἀμπεπαλὼν προΐει δολιχόσκιον ἔγχος,
> καὶ βάλε Πριαμίδαο κατ' ἀσπίδα πάντοσ' ἐΐσην·
> διὰ μὲν ἀσπίδος ἦλθε φαεινῆς ὄβριμον ἔγχος,
> καὶ διὰ θώρηκος πολυδαιδάλου ἠρήρειστο·
> ἀντικρὺ δὲ παραὶ λαπάρην διάμησε χιτῶνα
> ἔγχος· ὁ δ' ἐκλίνθη καὶ ἀλεύατο κῆρα μέλαιναν.

> So he spoke, and balanced the spear far-shadowed, and threw it
> and struck the shield of Priam's son on its perfect circle.
> All the way through the glittering shield went the heavy spearhead
> and smashed its way through the intricately worked corselet;
> straight ahead by the flank the spearhead shore through his tunic,
> yet he bent away to one side and avoided the dark death.

The second instance of the line is in another famous passage involving Menelaus, that of his being wounded by the arrow of Pandarus, 4.134–38:

> ἐν δ' ἔπεσε ζωστῆρι ἀρηρότι πικρὸς ὀϊστός·
> διὰ μὲν ἂρ ζωστῆρος ἐλήλατο δαιδαλέοιο,
> καὶ διὰ θώρηκος πολυδαιδάλου ἠρήρειστο
> μίτρης θ', ἣν ἐφόρει ἔρυμα χροός, ἕρκος ἀκόντων,
> ἥ οἱ πλεῖστον ἔρυτο· διαπρὸ δὲ εἴσατο καὶ τῆς.

> The bitter arrow was driven against the joining of the war belt
> and passed clean through the war belt elaborately woven;
> into the elaborately wrought corselet the shaft was driven
> and the guard which he wore to protect his skin and keep the spears off,
> which guarded him best, yet the arrow plunged even through this also.

It is not, of course, surprising that there should be a correlation between the lexicon of arming scenes and that of wounding scenes in which the armor is penetrated or broken, as we have seen in the "unarming" of Patroclus.

The aborted duel between Ajax and Hector is the scene in which πολυδαιδάλου is used a third time in the *Iliad*, and it is also not surprising, because another son of Priam is involved, to find some of the same lines (7.248–54):

> ἐν τῇ δ' ἑβδομάτῃ ῥινῷ σχέτο· δεύτερος αὖτε
> Αἴας διογενὴς προΐει δολιχόσκιον ἔγχος,

> καὶ βάλε Πριαμίδαο κατ' ἀσπίδα πάντοσ' ἐΐσην.
> διὰ μὲν ἀσπίδος ἦλθε φαεινῆς ὄβριμον ἔγχος,
> καὶ διὰ θώρηκος πολυδαιδάλου ἠρήρειστο·
> ἀντικρὺ δὲ παραὶ λαπάρην διάμησε χιτῶνα
> ἔγχος· ὁ δ' ἐκλίνθη καὶ ἀλεύατο κῆρα μέλαιναν.
>
> but was stopped in the seventh ox-hide. Then after him Ajax
> the illustrious in turn cast with his spear far-shadowing
> and struck the shield of Priam's son on its perfect circle.
> All the way through the glittering shield went the heavy spearhead,
> and crashed its way through the intricately worked corselet;
> straight ahead by the flank the spearhead shore through his tunic,
> yet he bent away to one side and avoided the dark death.

The fourth and final instance of this line in the *Iliad* is in the scene of the wounding of Odysseus in 11.434–36:

> ὣς εἰπὼν οὔτησε κατ' ἀσπίδα πάντοσ' ἐΐσην.
> διὰ μὲν ἀσπίδος ἦλθε φαεινῆς ὄβριμον ἔγχος,
> καὶ διὰ θώρηκος πολυδαιδάλου ἠρήρειστο.
>
> He spoke, and stabbed Odysseus' shield in its perfect circle,
> All the way through the glittering shield went the heavy spearhead
> and crashed its way through the intricately wrought corselet.

In the two duels the spear does not do as great damage as it might have, because the wounded man leans to the side and it does not hit a vital spot. In the woundings of Menelaus and of Odysseus, Athena saves the heroes. In 4.127–29 she saves Menelaus:

> Still the blessed gods immortal did not forget you,
> Menelaos, and first among them Zeus' daughter, the spoiler,
> who standing in front of you fended aside the tearing arrow.

and in 11.437–38 she keeps the point of the spear from penetrating too far:

> and all the skin was torn away from his ribs, yet Pallas
> Athene would not let the point penetrate the man's vitals.

Note that the epithet πολυδαίδαλος is used only once to describe a shield—that of Agamemnon—but four times for the corselet, to which it seems to belong more commonly. Yet it marks the significant wounding of significant figures at significant junctures in the epic: namely, the two duels that might have ended the war; the breaking of the truce; and in Book 11, the wounding of Odysseus, the last of the three chiefs (the other two were Agamemnon and Diomedes) who were taken from the field, in Odysseus's case by Menelaus and Ajax. This action clears the arena eventually for Hector. It is followed immediately, however, by Paris's wounding of Machaon, whom Nestor takes from the field; by Ajax's stunning retreat; and by Paris's wounding of Eurypylus, whom Ajax joins. These events set the stage for Achilles' sending of Patroclus to Nestor to learn whom he was taking off the field. Patroclus is delayed in his mission as he stops to help Eurypylus, whom he meets as he passes the ships of Odysseus on his way back with Nestor's entreaty to Achilles to send Patroclus into the battle in his, Achilles', armor. Thus all four of the scenes in which this line appears are decisive for the outcome of the epic. Truly, ornamentation underlines important action, points to it, as it were; it is not "mere ornamentation" in oral traditional epic.

The description of Agamemnon's shield and the four woundings leave two other instances of πολυδαίδαλος in the *Iliad* yet to be discussed. They are found in the last two books of the epic. In 23.743 the epithet is used, this time in the sense of "skillful," to describe the Sidonian craftsmen who made a mixing bowl of silver offered as a prize in the foot race in the funeral games for Patroclus. I quote the passage at some length:

> 740 Πηλεΐδης δ' αἶψ' ἄλλα τίθει ταχυτῆτος ἄεθλα,
> ἀργύρεον κρητῆρα, τετυγμένον· ἓξ δ' ἄρα μέτρα
> χάνδανεν, αὐτὰρ κάλλει ἐνίκα πᾶσαν ἐπ' αἶαν
> πολλόν, ἐπεὶ Σιδόνες πολυδαίδαλοι εὖ ἤσκησαν,
> Φοίνικες δ' ἄγον ἄνδρες ἐπ' ἠεροειδέα πόντον,
> 745 στῆσαν δ'ἐν λιμένεσσι, Θόαντι δὲ δῶρον ἔδωκαν·
> υἱὸς δὲ Πριάμοιο Λυκάονος ὦνον ἔδωκε
> Πατρόκλῳ ἥρωϊ Ἰησονίδης Εὔνηος.
> καὶ τὸν Ἀχιλλεὺς θῆκεν ἀέθλιον οὗ ἑτάροιο,
> ὅς τις ἐλαφρότατος ποσσὶ κραιπνοῖσι πέλοιτο.

> At once the son of Peleus set out prizes for the foot-race:
> a mixing-bowl of silver, a work of art, which held only
> six measures, but for its loveliness it surpassed all others
> on earth by far, since skilled Sidonian craftsmen had wrought it
> well, and Phoenicians carried it over the misty face of the water
> and set it in the harbour, and gave it for a present to Thoas.
> Euneos, son of Jason, gave it to the hero Patroklos
> to buy Lykaon, Priam's son, out of slavery, and now

> Achilleus made it a prize in memory of his companion,
> for that man who should prove in the speed of his feet to run lightest.

This history of the mixing-bowl reminds one of the earlier scenes, especially that of Lykaon's death in Book 21 at the hands of a ruthless Achilles maddened at the loss of Patroclus. But that scene has nothing to do, of course, with the epithet, which is not in the earlier passage. We have now moved instead to a different context for the epithet's use, that of the makers of beautiful objects for the house or for personal adornment rather than intricately wrought armor. The scenes in this group of contexts are of peace, not of war.

This point is illustrated also by the final case of πολυδαίδαλος 'ornate', where it is used to describe the couch to which Achilles returned after putting Hector's body on a litter for Priam to take back to Troy (24.596–98):

> ἦ ῥα, καὶ ἐς κλισίην πάλιν ἤϊε δῖος Ἀχιλλεύς,
> ἕζετο δ' ἐν κλισμῷ πολυδαιδάλῳ, ἔνθεν ἀνέστη,
> τοίχου τοῦ ἑτέρου, ποτὶ δὲ Πρίαμον φάτο μῦθον.

> So spoke great Achilleus and went back into the shelter
> and sat down on the elaborate couch from which he had risen,
> against the inward wall, and now spoke his word to Priam.

The form πολυδαίδαλον is used twice in the *Odyssey* (6.15 and 18.295) and once in the *Homeric Hymn to Apollo*, and πολυδαίδαλος is used once in the *Odyssey* (13.11). In 6.15 it refers to Nausikaa's bedchamber, which Athena visits:

> βῆ δ' ἴμεν ἐς θάλαμον πολυδαίδαλον, ᾧ ἔνι κούρη
> κοιμᾶτ' ἀθανάτῃσι φυὴν καὶ εἶδος ὁμοίη,
> Ναυσικάα, θυγάτηρ μεγαλήτορος Ἀλκινόοιο.

> and she went into the ornate chamber, in which a girl
> was sleeping, like the immortal goddesses for stature and beauty,
> Nausikaa, the daughter of great-hearted Alkinoös.

In 18.295, Eurymachus sends his herald for a gift for Penelope, a lovely necklace:

> ὅρμον δ' Εὐρυμάχῳ πολυδαίδαλον αὐτίκ' ἔνεικε,
> χρύσεον, ἠλέκτροισιν ἐερμένον, ἠέλιον ὥς.

Eurymachos' man came back with an elaborate necklace
of gold, strung with bits of amber, and bright as sunshine.

The epithet describes a gift also in 13.11, a gift of gold from Alcinous for Odysseus:

10   εἵματα μὲν δὴ ξείνῳ ἐϋξέστῃ ἐνὶ χηλῷ
κεῖται καὶ χρυσὸς πολυδαίδαλος ἄλλα τε πάντα
δῶρ', ὅσα Φαιήκων βουληφόροι ἐνθάδ' ἔνεικαν.

Clothing for our guest is stored away in the polished
chest, and intricately wrought gold, and all those other
gifts the Phaiakian men of counsel brought here to give him.

Finally, to round out the picture, πολυδαίδαλον 'carved' is used in the *Homeric Hymn to Apollo*, line 345, to describe Hera's chair on Olympus:

344   οὔτε πότ' εἰς εὐνὴν Διὸς ἤλυθε μητιόεντος,
οὔτε πότ' εἰς θῶκον πολυδαίδαλον ὡς τὸ πάρος περ
αὐτῷ ἐφεζομένη πυκινὰς φραζέσκετο βουλάς.

And thereafter she never came to the bed of wise Zeus for a full year, nor to sit in her carved chair as aforetime to plan wise counsel for him.[24]

None of this has anything to do with the shield of Agamemnon, but in searching out the uses of the epithet in the Homeric poems we have learned that πολυδαίδαλος 'intricately wrought' is found in two main contexts. The shield belongs in the war context, where, however, the epithet is applied most frequently to a corselet, but only in this context to a shield, Agamemnon's. In the peace setting it is applied often to gifts or to a prize. In the arming of Agamemnon, one may recall, the second piece of armor he dons, after the greaves, is the corselet, which had been a guest present to him. Could it be that the corselet and its history had, by association of ideas, brought πολυδαίδαλος to Homer's mind, which he applied a few lines later to the shield?

Finally there is the epithet ἀμφιβρότην for Agamemnon's shield, "covering the whole man, man-enclosing," which is found, in the genitive, three more times in the *Iliad* (2.389, 12.402, and 20.281).[25] It is not used in the

---

24. Ibid., 348–49.
25. See Lorimer, 1950: "It [Agamemnon's shield] is described as ἀμφιβρότη, 'coming around both sides of a man', an epithet originally designed for the body-shield, both forms of which are seen on the monuments to have a deep curvature within which the figure of the warrior disappears.

Odyssey. This is an epithet that cannot ordinarily be used with anything except a shield. In 2.388–89, Agamemnon is urging the Argives back to have dinner and to prepare their weapons for fighting; for they will fight all day without respite until darkness comes:

> ἱδρώσει μέν τευ τελαμὼν ἀμφὶ στήθεσφιν
> ἀσπίδος ἀμφιβρότης, περὶ δ' ἔγχεϊ χεῖρα καμεῖται.
>
> There will be a man's sweat on the shield-strap binding the breast to
> the shield hiding the man's shape, and the hand on the spear grow weary.

Agamemnon's speech ends the assembly in which the Argives are turned back from returning home after the incident of the baneful Dream, a noteworthy speech in an important, if puzzling, episode of the epic.

Where the words ἀσπίδος ἀμφιβρότης 'man-enclosing shield' occur in 12.402, we also find a significant episode. Sarpedon has just pulled down part of the battlements:

> And Sarpedon, grabbing in both ponderous hands the battlements,
> pulled, and the whole thing came away in his hands, and the rampart
> was stripped defenceless above. He had opened a pathway for many.

At this point, Ajax and Teucer attack him:

> 400 Τὸν δ' Αἴας καὶ Τεῦκρος ὁμαρτήσανθ' ὁ μὲν ἰῷ
> βεβλήκει τελαμῶνα περὶ στήθεσσι φαεινὸν
> ἀσπίδος ἀμφιβρότης· ἀλλὰ Ζεὺς κῆρας ἄμυνε
> παιδὸς ἑοῦ, μὴ νηυσὶν ἔπι πρύμνῃσι δαμείη.
>
> Aias and Teukros aimed at him together, and Teukros
> hit him with an arrow in the shining belt that encircled
> his chest to hold the man-covering shield, but Zeus brushed the death spirits
> from his son, and would not let him be killed there beside the ships' sterns.

So Sarpedon is spared for the time being.

The final instance of ἀσπίδος ἀμφιβρότης (20.281) is in another striking scene, the encounter of Achilles with Aeneas. The role of the shield is

---

"The adjective is inappropriate to the round shield, which is sometimes quite flat and which, because its rim lies on one plane, cannot envelop the bearer even when it is convex. ἀμφιβρότη, which is used only with ἀσπίς and, apart from B 389, only in contexts which show that the shield in question is round . . . must have acquired in epic the general meaning of 'man-protecting'; the fact that it occurs only four times in the vulgate suggests that in Homer's day it was almost obsolete" (189).

dramatic. Achilles has cast the Pelian ash spear, which struck the outer rim of the shield where it was thinnest:

276   ... ἡ δὲ διαπρὸ
    Πηλιὰς ἤϊξεν μελίη, λάκε δ' ἀσπὶς ὑπ' αὐτῆς.

> The Pelian ash spear
> crashed clean through it there, and the shield cried out as it went through.

The reaction of Aeneas involves the shield:

278   Αἰνείας δ' ἐάλη καὶ ἀπὸ ἕθεν ἀσπίδ' ἀνέσχε
      δείσας· ἐγχείη δ' ἄρ' ὑπὲρ νώτου ἐνὶ γαίῃ
      ἔστη ἱεμένη, διὰ δ' ἀμφοτέρους ἕλε κύκλους
      ἀσπίδος ἀμφιβρότης.

> Aineias shrank down and held the shield away and above him
> in fright, and the spear went over his back and crashed its way
> to the ground, and fixed there, after tearing apart two circles
> of the man-covering shield.

Aeneas stands stock still and is overcome with emotion when he sees how close the spear came to him. He picks up a huge stone "which no two men could carry / such as men are now, but by himself he lightly hefted it." Achilles would have fended it off with his shield and dispatched Aeneas with his sword, but Poseidon intervenes with the gods to save Aeneas. Poseidon's ensuing conversation with Athena and Hera is reminiscent of Zeus's with the same worthies over the case of his son Sarpedon. As a result, Poseidon goes to the field of action (20.321–27):

> There quickly he drifted a mist across the eyes of one fighter,
> Achilleus, Peleus' son, and from the shield of Aineias
> of the great heart pulled loose the strong bronze-headed ash spear
> and laid it down again before the feet of Achilleus;
> but Aineias he lifted high from the ground, and slung him through the air
> so that many ranks of fighting men, many ranks of horses,
> were overvaulted by Aineias, hurled by the god's hand.

Although the sparing of Aeneas by Poseidon, playing Aphrodite's role, reminds one, and quite rightly, of the scene in which Sarpedon is spared and inevitably, and more cogently, of course, also of the major scene in which he is not spared, it is not the noun-epithet combination ἀσπίδος ἀμφιβρότης that makes the association. Yet, as was the case with θώρηκος πολυδαι-δάλου 'intricately worked corselet', these noun-epithet combinations tend to occur in significant passages, some of which are multiforms of the same thematic material. How many of the scenes to which these epithets have led us involved sparing the life of an important figure in the heroic world!

We could continue in this vein and broaden our experience of arms and arming, investigating the epithets and other key words, observing them in their several and varied contexts, but we have examined enough to illustrate Homer's technique. Sound patterns have been shown to play a large role in the choice of the epithets and in the phrasing of the lines. We have seen that Homer has a group of basic lines for arming, which he supplements and modifies as the scene and action require. We saw also that there are apparently only four armings in which this basic group forms the nucleus: that of Agamemnon, the longest and most special (in which the shield finds its closest parallel in the *Shield of Heracles*, not in Achilles' shield); those of Achilles and Patroclus; and finally, and perhaps somewhat strangely, that of Paris. Notable are the otherworldly or divine connections in the major three, excluding Paris's. In spite of the basic lines, the armings of Achilles and Paris are distinct and reflect the character of their heroes. It is clear that epithets are not used mechanically; rather, particular noun-epithet combinations recur in observable patterns in passages crucial for the action of the poem. A study of the ambiance of these phrases reveals their discriminating use in related passages important for their human and often divine associations. Their repetition is not accidental but helps to emphasize key ideas. Repetition and ornamentation are surely meaningful elements in oral epic tradition.

CHAPTER 4

Beowulf *and Oral Epic Tradition*

The Germanic peoples told stories in song from very ancient times. When some of these became known in the Middle Ages the tradition was already very old and in a state of transition from a purely oral to a fully written poetry. One can speak of at least three influences on the oral traditional matrix. One was that of writing itself; another was the effect of the meeting of Germanic vernacular songs such as *Elene* or *Christ* with Latin; a third, later, was that of the medieval French tradition of narrative, itself in origin an oral tradition.

One branch of Germanic sung narrative appeared in continental Germany in Old and Middle High German in the shape of such songs as the *Hildebrandslied*, *Gudrun,* and the *Nibelungenlied*. A second branch is represented by the *Poetic Edda* in Iceland. And a third was the Old English (Anglo-Saxon) and Middle English tradition, or traditions, as the case may be.

It is clear that the basic metrical system common to all Germanic peoples was formed in the oral period and was related to Indo-European metrics. It is tonic rather than syllabic, consisting of from two to four stressed syllables in each hemistich with a varying number of unstressed syllables. In Old High German, Old Norse, and Anglo-Saxon the two hemistichs are bound together by alliteration. Thus the beginning of the Old High German *Hildebrandslied* in the manuscript:

       Ik gihôrta ðat seggen, ðat sih urhêttun   ænon muotîn
       Hiltibra(n)t enti Haðubrant   untar heriun tuêm.

This chapter, in slightly different form, was delivered as the Schick lecture in March 1990, at Indiana State University, Terre Haute.

sunufatarungo.   Iro saro rihtun,
garutun sê iro gûdhamun,   gurtun sih iro suert ana
helidos ubar (h)ringâ.   Dô sie tô dero hiltiu ritun.¹

I have heard this said,
that single warriors, Hildebrand and Hadubrand,
contended between two armies
of the people of the father and son. They prepared their armor,
they fixed their warshirts, they girded their swords
over the ring-mail, the heroes, as they rode to the fight.²

And the opening stanzas of "Vǫlospá," the first poem in the Codex Regius of the Old Norse *Poetic Edda*:

> Hlióðs bið ec allar   helgar kindir,
> meiri oc minni,   mogo Heimdalar;
> vildo, at ec, Valfǫðr,   vel fyrtelia
> forn spioll fira,   þau er fremst um man.
>
> Ec man iotna,   ár um borna,
> þá er forðom mic   fœdda hǫfðo;
> nío man ec heima,   nío íviði,
> miotvið mœran   fyr mold neðan.³
>
> Hearing I ask   from the holy races,
> From Heimdall's sons,   both high and low;
> Thou wilt, Valfather,   that well I relate
> Old tales I remember   of men long ago.
>
> I remember yet   the giants of yore,
> Who gave me bread   in the days gone by;
> Nine worlds I knew,   the nine in the tree
> With mighty roots   beneath the mold.⁴

And, finally, the opening lines of *Beowulf*:

> Hwæt! We Gardena   in geardagum,

---

1. Text from Wadstein, 1903, "Berichtigter Text."
2. [Trans. by Stephen A. Mitchell, kindly supplied by him in a letter dated August 10, 1993.]
3. Text from Neckel, 1983, 1.
4. Bellows, 1969, 3.

þeodcyninga, þrym gefrunon,
hu ða æþelingas ellen fremedon.[5]

Lo! We have heard of the glory of the kings of the people of the Spear-Danes in days of yore—how those princes did valorous deeds![6]

The hemistichs of the stanzas of the *Nibelungenlied* and *Gudrun* are longer and lack the alliteration. The pairs of lines rhyme, however, and the last hemistich of the fourth line is longer than the others. This, too, although emerging later, appears to have been a traditional meter. Thus begins the *Nibelungenlied*:

Uns ist in alten mæren wunders vil geseit
von heleden lobebæren von grôzer arebeit,
von fröuden, hôchgezîten, von weinen und von klagen,
von küener recken strîten muget ir nu wunder hœren sagen.[7]

We have been told in ancient tales many marvels of famous heroes, of mighty toil, joys, and high festivities, of weeping and wailing, and the fighting of bold warriors—of such things you can now hear wonders unending![8]

If the first element in the oral traditional character of the Medieval English epic is its metrical base, the second is the formulaic language, with its tendency to an appositive style (of which Fred C. Robinson has written so perceptively) which shapes ideas into the forms provided by the meters.[9] In studying the repeated noun-adjective phrases for gods and heroes, the noun-epithet formulas, in the Homeric poems, Milman Parry came to realize that the formulas, and the systems they formed, were characteristic not only of traditional but also of *oral* traditional poetry. Rapid composition of lines in performance was made possible by the formulas, and therefore the presence of a large number of them in any given poem was an indication that its style was of oral traditional provenance.

The basic unit larger than a line is a block of lines varying in number from

---

5. Citations from *Beowulf* follow the text of Dobbie, 1953.
6. Translations from *Beowulf* are from Clark Hall, 1950, with occasional modifications.
7. Bartsch, 1886, 1.
8. Hatto, 1969, 17. [It is notable that the opening lines quoted above of the *Hildebrandslied*, "Vǫlospá," *Beowulf*, and *Nibelungenlied* stress what the poet *heard* as the source of his tale, thus emphasizing the role of oral tradition. On this point, see Haymes, 1987. For the traditional nature of Old English opening lines, see Foley, 1991, 214–23.]
9. Robinson, 1985.

two to perhaps six. They follow regularly repeated syntactic and semantic patterns, often with similar wording, although it is necessary to remember that, in Old English poetry, verbal correspondence is not so marked as in other traditions because of the paratactic style and the requirements of alliteration. The lines that make up the block are not consistently memorized but are remembered.[10]

A study of the introductions to speeches in *Beowulf* and *Elene* revealed several such blocks, for example:

Beowulf 258–59
Him se yldesta   ondswarode,
werodes wisa,   wordhord onleac:

To him answered the leader of the band, the chieftain of the troop unlocked his store of words:

340–42a
Him þa ellenrof   andswarode,
wlanc Wedera leod, word æfter spræc,
heard under helme:

Then the man renowned in strength answered him; the proud leader of the Geats, hardy under his helmet, rejoined in speech:

Elene 454–55
Þa ic fromlice   fæder minum,
ealdum æwitan,   ageaf ondsware:

Then I boldly gave reply to my father, the old man learned in the law:

462–63
Ða me yldra min   ageaf ondsware,
frod on fyrhðe   fæder reordode:

Then my parent replied to me, my wise-minded father declared:[11]

I noticed an excellent example of such a couplet also in the description of King Arthur's arming in the Middle English *Alliterative Morte Arthure*. The

---

10. For the difference between rote memorization and "remembering," see Chapter 1, after n. 26.
11. See A. Lord, 1991, 147–69, esp. 164. Text of *Elene* from Krapp, 1932; trans. by Bradley, 1982.

first line of the couplet is the same in both occurrences of the theme, but the second line is somewhat variable:

> 912–13
> His gloues gaylyche gilte and grauen at þe hemmez
> With graynez and goblets, glorious of hewe.[12]
>
> His gauntlet brightly gilded and trimmed at the edge
> With seed-pearls and gems of a glorious hue.
>
> 3462–63
> His gloucs gayliche gilte and grauen by þe hemmys
> With graynes of rubyes full gracious to schewe.
>
> His gloves gloriously gilded and engraved at the edge
> With beads of ruby, bright to behold.[13]

Such a block has not been memorized, but the alliteration serves not only to knit separate parts of the first line together but also, by carrying over to the beginning of the second line, to link the two lines into a memorable couplet. I do not intend to imply that the *Alliterative Morte Arthure* is an oral traditional poem. Such constructions, however, do point to the fact that many of the characteristics of oral poetry can be found in it. This fact has already been abundantly documented by scholars from Ronald A. Waldron to Jean Ritzke-Rutherford and Valerie Krishna.[14]

The style of oral traditional epic poetry is far too complex to have been invented by a single person and must have been developed over the centuries by generations of poet/singers. All this has been expounded with diligence and grace by Alain Renoir.[15] The meter and the style of Anglo-Saxon narrative verse were inheritances from the oral tradition in which they originated. We might use Walter Ong's convenient term and call them "oral residue."

Oral tradition is naturally subject to changes in the community.[16] Some social changes are rapid and some gradual. The changes are usually brought about by "outsiders," or by "outside influences." There may be massive transformations such as the religious conversions that took place in late

---

12. Text follows Hamel, 1984.
13. Trans. by Krishna, 1983.
14. Waldron, 1957; Ritzke-Rutherford, 1981; Krishna, 1976, 27–34, 37–38, and 1982. For a convenient summary, see Parks, 1986.
15. Renoir, 1988.
16. For my definition of tradition, see Chapter 1.

antiquity and the Middle Ages. Historical events such as war may decimate a community and alter the tempo of change. One more gradual change that may come about is the spread of literacy and the introduction of new types of entertainment.

The singing of epic songs is very ancient. It is clear that it began in an "oral" period. Tradition, that is to say, all the singers before and contemporaneous with each singer/performer, bequeathed to him a technique of composing songs in performance. This technique is not improvisation, if by improvisation we mean that which is impromptu, without premeditation or preparation. What I am talking about is a very special type of composition. Each performance results in a "new" text, to be sure, but that "new" text is made up of formulas, blocks of lines, and themes of preceding performances. Such a method of composition produces a recognizable style.

Milman Parry's fundamental insight about oral tradition is in essence that there are elements of style that arise from the necessity of composing and recomposing songs rapidly in performance. The presence of these elements in any given text is an indication that it belongs in the category of oral traditional songs. In the fifties this insight was applied to *Beowulf* by Francis Peabody Magoun, Jr., who concluded that *Beowulf* was an oral traditional poem.[17] In *The Singer of Tales* in 1960, a revised version of my 1949 doctoral dissertation, I came to the same conclusion about *Beowulf*, among other medieval works. These conclusions were based on a study of the number of formulas and formulaic expressions in the text.

In 1966, Larry Benson argued that there were as many formulas in the Anglo-Saxon translation of Boethius as in *Beowulf*. He showed that all Old English poetry, even that which was "written" on the basis of Latin sources, used a formulaic style. The controversy has continued since then. Ann Chalmers Watts in 1969 reviewed the whole problem very even handedly and thoroughly. She concluded that we would probably never be able to arrive at a final, satisfactory solution. But the research has continued and has generated some fine scholarship for and against oral provenance. We now know a great deal more about formulaic and thematic composition in other parts of the world where there are living traditions, and the analyses of stylistic features in the Anglo-Saxon texts themselves have been improved and fine-tuned.[18]

Before going further, I want to dispel, if I can, some of the misunderstandings that have arisen about the art of oral composition and its relationship to

17. Magoun, 1953.
18. See Chapters 5 and 6.

Old English epic poetry. In discussing the relationship of oral style to the Old English *Beowulf*, Derek Pearsall wrote, "Lord himself points out that literacy is the death-blow to oral tradition, and that the writing down of orally composed verse is impossible (before the invention of the phonograph) or at least artistically disastrous, as with the method of 'oral dictation;' yet this, it is presumed, is how all existing Old English poetry came to be written down."[19]

The first statement, that "literacy is the death-blow to oral tradition,"—those are his words, not mine—has some truth in it, but it would be more accurate to say that literacy carries the seeds of the eventual demise of oral traditional composition. In time, literacy usually means or can mean the end of the practice of oral traditional sung narrative. It is not, however, writing per se that brings about the change; oral traditional epic flourished in the Slavic Balkans for centuries in communities where significant portions of the population were literate. But gradually the epic began to be written down, and the concept of a *fixed text*, and of *the* text, of a song came to be current. With that concept arose the need for memorization rather than recomposition as a means of transmission. Literacy also often brought with it, as it came from outside of the community, changes in the society itself. In the Middle Ages, for example, the institution of the church introduced a new establishment that was often antagonistic to the old. The function of the oral traditional epic, namely, to express and maintain a system of values, including a developed sense of the heroic, was in danger of being usurped by a different hierarchy. In this way also, literacy, or what it imported, meant the eventual fading away or reinterpretation of the heroic society.

I am puzzled when Pearsall says that, according to me, writing down oral traditional poetry is impossible or artistically disastrous, "as with the method of dictation," before the invention of the phonograph. He seems to have misunderstood completely and misconstrued the facts. There is nothing wrong with the method of dictation; it is not by any means "artistically disastrous." I have seen and heard thousands of lines dictated very successfully by singers. I have even demonstrated that dictated texts are sometimes better than sung texts. It is true that there are singers who have difficulty in dictating, but that is the exception rather than the rule. As noted, the Old English poetry, insofar as it *is* oral traditional poetry, was very probably dictated.

Pearsall also wrote, "The further proposition, that Old English poetry, in its existing form, was composed extempore, is untenable."[20] This has been

19. Pearsall, 1977, 17.
20. Ibid.

the most pervasive misunderstanding of all. I have already addressed this objection,[21] but I want to stress once again that neither Parry nor I have ever said that Old English, or Homeric, or South Slavic oral traditional epic was composed "extempore." To say that a poetry is composed in performance, from traditional elements, is not the same as saying that it was composed extempore.

Pearsall's concluding comments on the views of Parry demonstrate a widely held belief in the general inferiority of oral traditional literature: "But the theory is irrelevant to most of the important questions about the poetry, and, by substituting the crude notion of improvisation for the many more varied and subtle kinds of *composition*, has distracted attention from the quality of Anglo-Saxon poetry that most needs stressing, its learned and lettered provenance."[22] I have already indicated that oral traditional epic poetry cannot be grasped in terms of a vague and overly generalized usage of the word *improvisation*. But I also suggest that what in Anglo-Saxon poetry is sometimes thought of as being of "learned and lettered provenance" is actually comfortably within the range of the compositional techniques of oral traditional literature.

After dismissing what he calls the oral theory, Pearsall turned, naturally enough, to a consideration of the role of Latin in the development of Anglo-Saxon poetry, specifically *Beowulf*. He felt sure that there was Virgilian influence in that poem. He was convinced that the *Beowulf* poet received the idea of writing an epic from his knowledge of Virgil's *Aeneid*. This is, of course, not by any means a new claim, but it is surprising to me how it continues to be held so adamantly by a few scholars, notably Theodore Andersson.[23]

Although it appears that Virgil was used in monastery schools and, depending on when one dates *Beowulf* and when and how the poet learned to write, if he did, he may have read some Virgil. I do not know of any evidence that schoolboys read the whole of the *Aeneid* with all the care that the critic implies. Actually, the Anglo-Saxon bard did not need to seek inspiration from abroad. Oral traditional narrative verse holds within itself not only the potential for epic but also an ongoing mixing and combining of songs and stories. It has been the dictum for a long time that the Germanic peoples had a tradition of short heroic lays, of which the Finnsburh fragment, *Waldere*, and the *Hildebrandslied* are held up as examples. The Christian South Slavic oral epic tradition is also made up of short songs, and there is a

21. See above; also Chapter 1 at n. 12, and A. Lord, 1991, 76–77.
22. Pearsall, 1977, 18.
23. See Andersson, 1976, esp. chap. 4.

large body of songs of local raids and feuding, some Christian and some Moslem, which are short. But some of the South Slavic epics—again, both Christian and Moslem—can reach considerable length; for example, in the Christian tradition, the *Ženidba Dušanova*, "The Wedding of Dushan," has 690 lines; the *Ženidba Maksima Crnojevića*, "The Wedding of Maksim Crnojević," has 1,226 lines; and in the Moslem tradition, there are songs of more than 10,000 lines. A person brought up in the singing tradition, as I believe the poet of *Beowulf* was, who found himself in a monastery and with the ability to write, might well have been moved to set down a "mingling" of songs. Such "minglings" take place quite naturally in oral traditional literature. The epic can "grow from within," without outside models.

Beowulf's recounting to Hygelac of his adventures at Heorot has been pointed to by Pearsall as a technique that the poet learned from Virgil. There is irony here, of course, as Virgil's model was Homer, and Homer was clearly an oral traditional poet. Such recounting is common in oral traditional poetry, and we find it also in records of poetic traditions from the earliest times, including striking examples in the *Gilgamesh Epic*, down to the present. In editing one of Avdo Međedović's dictated songs (Parry No. 6802, 7,621 lines) I found that it contains portions of events recapitulated not once but two or three times by different participants to different persons. The *Beowulf* poet did not need to go to Virgil to learn a device shared by all Indo-European oral poetic traditions. It would seem very strange, indeed, if the Germanic tradition alone were ignorant of that technique, even if we do not find any instances in the very scanty surviving materials older than *Beowulf*.

The style of the *Aeneid* is so different from that of *Beowulf* that it seems to a classicist as an extraordinary case of wishful thinking to believe that the one influenced the other. For one thing, the complex style of Virgil with its intricate word order makes no use of true formulas, as Parry proved in detail years ago.[24] *Beowulf* also has intricate word order necessitated in part by the exigency of the Germanic line, but its intricacies are not like those of Virgil and are inheritances from a long tradition. Nothing could be more different in tone and method of composition than *Beowulf* is from the *Aeneid*. The style of the *Aeneid* is allusive; it cannot be read and fully understood without reference to the specific wording of Virgil's literary sources; his epic must be perceived through a web of learned allusions. He quoted or adapted the words of other authors, not only Homer but erudite Hellenistic poets such as Apollonius and Callimachus. Moreover, present-day Virgilian scholarship

---

24. Parry, 1971, 29–36, "The Traditional Epithet in Homer" (L'épithète traditionnelle dans Homère: Essai sur un problème de style homérique).

even questions whether Aeneas should be thought of as a hero in the Homeric, or in the Germanic, sense. He is full of self-doubt and misgivings. If the *Beowulf* poet ever read the *Aeneid*—which I very seriously doubt—it seems to have had no effect on him.

I venture to suggest that the complexity of Anglo-Saxon poetics, a complexity which is that of an oral traditional poetics, has led scholars ignorant of the latter to suppose that only a literate society could produce such complexity. They assume that oral traditional poetics must be simple and unsophisticated. This is in reality not the case. We should rather be seeking to understand fully the richness of oral traditional style. When we do understand that, we will stop looking elsewhere for the source of at least some of the elements that contribute to its excellence.

There are those who would say that *Beowulf* is a transitional text. In *The Singer of Tales*, I said that there was no such thing as a transitional text, but I now see the usefulness of the term, provided that we formulate it to be applicable in more precise contexts. What is needed is an exact description of a "transitional" text, so that we will not use the category merely as a resting place for compositions we do not understand. One cannot designate a literary work as transitional between oral and written unless one knows the characteristics of both forms of composition.[25]

Most of us know something about the style of written composition. We learned about it in school, we practice it in varying degrees, we almost take it for granted assuming that, if there is anything else, it must be inferior. This is an ironic situation.[26] Literary style was formed and reached high complexity before the invention of writing. That it did so in Greece is proved by the tradition that led to the Homeric poems. The magnificence of Homeric style was a product of the generations of singer/poets before and including Homer. There was no period of written literature before the Homeric poems were *written down*. They needed writing to be recorded but not to be composed, except insofar as the dictating process allowed time for a longer "performance" than was usual.

One should be able to point to something that is definitely a "written" characteristic in order to prove that a text is transitional. I can find oral traditional characteristics in the style of *Beowulf*. I am not sure if I can say of

---

25. See Chapter 10 for a treatment of the transitional text.
26. In linguistic terms, as Gregory Nagy has pointed out (1990b), oral traditional literary style is "unmarked," that is to say that it is the norm from time immemorial; whereas written literary style is "marked," which is to say that it is a later development from the established "norm." "Written is not something that is not *oral*; rather it is something in addition to being oral, and that additional something varies from society to society" (8).

anything in the style of *Beowulf* that it *must* be from a written tradition. For that reason, I still tend to say that it is an oral traditional poem, possibly literally written down by an oral traditional poet who was in a monastery or close to one. Neither the writing nor the monastery frightens me away from this opinion, although both the writing and the monastery hold the *potential* of transition.

The subject matter of *Beowulf*, put most simply—the encounter of a hero with three terrifying monsters—certainly belongs to the lore of a people, and the analogues in Old Norse and other Germanic narratives bear that out. Even if the attitude of the poet is Christian—and there seems to be no doubt of that—the fundamental story is a pagan one. It is basically a traditional tale. Generally speaking it is a mythic tale. I do not mean that it concerns itself with gods such as those we know from Norse mythology. The pattern is that of a story in what Eliade would call the "sacred," as opposed to the "profane" world. The monsters at least inhabit an "other world."

To determine what the first, the oldest, perhaps even the primordial meaning of such an oral traditional epic as *Beowulf* may be, we must begin by seeking out the mythic pattern that constitutes what Noam Chomsky might call its "deep structure."[27] One must not be surprised to discover that there may be more than one such pattern. I have elsewhere written of "interlocking mythic patterns" in *Beowulf*.[28] One that involved the episode with Unferth in which Beowulf is mocked on his arrival at Heorot was a "return" pattern, and the other, which mingled with it, concerned monsters, death, and a journey. Although we shall probably never know the details of the origin of any complex of traditional narratives, it may be that we can have a glimpse of the meaningful shapes of its embryo.

Both the style and the myth point to a ritual or religious origin and function for epic. Oral traditional epic is not merely entertainment, as it tends to become in the course of time and social change, but has a serious function in its society. It contains the ideals and values of the society, as well as a regard for the fundamental problems of both the community and the individual and for how they may be met and accepted if they cannot be solved.[29]

Delving under plots to mythic patterns, and even at times below the Germanic to Indo-European, we easily reach the generic narrative of the "monster-slayer."[30] The sequence of elements in that large group of stories

27. Ducrot and Todorov, 1979, s.v. "Surface Structures and Deep Structures," 242–47.
28. A. Lord, 1991, 140–46.
29. See Chapter 1 at n. 15; also Chapter 8 at n. 28.
30. I am not referring to the Aarne-Thompson tale type of the monster-slayer but constructing a simpler one of my own for the present purposes. Calvert Watkins (1987), in a well-argued paper,

would begin with (1) an unusual, or special, kind of hero, who (2) has a special weapon, or weapons, (3) to encounter a monster, that is, by definition, a special kind of opponent, usually what we would call "supernatural." In the course of that encounter the hero (4) is almost killed but is saved by (5) divine intervention, to (6) kill the monster, thus restoring order and normality to the world of humankind. My models for this pattern are Marduk, Gilgamesh, Zeus in Hesiod's *Theogony*, Heracles, Achilles in Homer's *Iliad*, and others.

Beowulf fits the pattern very well: (1) There is something unusual about Beowulf's younger years, as the poem itself tells us. Some of the other heroes in this narrative pattern also have unusual childhoods. Beowulf's name, "Bee-wolf," or "bear," may indicate an affinity with animals (compare Heracles), and the fact that he possesses the special weapons needed indicates that he is the sort of person who is qualified to use them. (2) Beowulf uses two special weapons for his first two encounters: he has his innate "grip" with which to meet Grendel and a special sword with which to fight Grendel's mother in the mere. For his third encounter, that with the dragon, Beowulf no longer has a special sword nor a special grip. He does have, however, an unusual iron shield, which, in lines 2335–41, he ordered to be made, in place of the ordinary wooden shield, to protect him from the dragon's fire.[31] Beowulf has at last passed into the realm of mortal men, and the honorable death of a hero is his destiny. I do not need to dwell on (3) the monsters, tempting though it may be, because it is enough that they be recognized as bona fide monsters. (4) Beowulf in his first victorious meeting with Grendel was killed by proxy in the person of Hondscio, who died a grim death in his stead; but Beowulf was almost killed by Grendel's mother and saved miraculously (5) by the appearance of an ancient sword. In the third encounter there is neither special weapon nor divine intervener. (6) He kills his opponents (and meets his own death).[32]

I have recited these elements for several reasons. First to remind ourselves of them; second to show that the action of *Beowulf* is at base an Indo-European myth—it may even be broader than that—found in other oral traditional epics; and third to point to the special character of the third encounter. Beowulf's fundamental story, as well as its basic style, belongs to oral traditional literature. Its mythic pattern gives a "deep structure" and layers of meaning stretching back to very ancient times. Both the style and

---

demonstrates the longevity and widespread occurrence of the theme Hero-Slay-Serpent and its formulaic expression. [He continues this study in a forthcoming book, particularly in pt. 2, "A Contribution to the Theory of the Formula."]

31. [This last point has been contributed by Daniel Donoghue.]
32. [For the monster-fight pattern, cf. Foley, 1991, 231–42.]

the story have, in the manner of live traditions, adapted themselves to the times during which they took the shapes in which we have them.

We might discern in *Beowulf* at least three general *areas*—I almost said "levels" or "layers," but that might indicate differences of date, and I want to avoid that implication. The first, oldest, and largest is the mythic story, as I have briefly and rather simplistically outlined it. I believe that the narrative pattern has Indo-European roots and that it has undergone many sea changes as it has found its way from Germanic singer to Germanic singer.

The second area came into play comparatively recently when the singers and their society came under the influence of Judaeo-Christianity. This area includes, of course, the song of creation that became attached to the tale. It is reasonable to suppose that some of the medieval monks were traditional singers, brought up in the tradition of singing before they entered the monastery; such brothers—or, if not a monk, a singer who was close enough to the monastery to have known the biblical stories—could have made this adaptation of the monster-slaying myth at any time after the biblical stories became known in a Germanic, most probably Anglo-Saxon community. It might have come into the ken of the singer/monks from their own reading of the Scriptures; but it may equally well, I believe, have arrived at the singers, whether monks or not, through the reading of the Scriptures by the clerics in the refectories or by way of the accounts of creation told or read in the pulpit. This area includes also the genealogy of Grendel as a descendant of Cain. One might speculate—and it is just that—that the singer may have substituted a biblical story he had heard for some other subject sung by the bard at Heorot.

The tradition to which *Beowulf* belonged carried in the form of its stories the meaning of the myth that a divinely endowed hero brings order to primordial chaos or, in a later stage, restores divinely created order when it has been disturbed by a resurgent chaos. When that tradition met the Judaeo-Christian accounts of the earliest establishing of order in the universe, as recounted in the story of creation, it sensed an affinity between its version and the biblical story. Tradition is fond of emphasizing basic meanings by expressing them in multiforms. Duplication is one of the most important principles of structure in oral traditional literature. An oral traditional form of *Beowulf* may have assimilated the biblical account of creation some time before our text was composed, but it could also have been placed where it is by the *Beowulf* poet himself, if he were an oral traditional poet, as I believe. It was inserted early on in the narrative, lines 90–98, where it belongs, because it states in mythic, or "sacred," terms one of the fundamental messages of the poem. At the same time, it also naturally identifies resurgent chaos, namely, Grendel and his tribe, with the fratricidal Cain from the same biblical story, line 107; later, line 1261.

Oral tradition frequently duplicates meaningful elements as a subconscious means of making the magic of the tale more powerful, and the adding of an ancient story of power to a more "modern" one, if I have the chronology correct, is a way of reinforcing the strength of the basic narrative. As God established order in the universe, so Beowulf reestablished order when it had been upset by the chaos introduced, or reintroduced, by Grendel. This is a good example of oral traditional literary thinking and compositional technique. The biblical elements were properly assimilated into the oral traditional monster-slaying myth near the beginning of the story to set its tone and significance, which will permeate the whole poem.

To me, the background of Grendel and his like as it is told in our poem after the mother's ravages in which she killed Æschere, smacks of oral traditional tales more than of a learned tract. King Hrothgar explains (1345–61):

> "I have heard dwellers in the country, subjects of mine, counsellors in hall, say this:—that they have seen two such huge wanderers of the marches guarding the moors, alien spirits, of whom one was, so far as they could most clearly tell, the semblance of a woman. The other wretched one whom, in past days, dwellers in the land named Grendel, trod exile-paths in human form, howbeit he was greater than any other man. They have no knowledge of a father, whether any such had been begotten for them in times past among the mysterious demons. They dwell in a land unknown, wolf-haunted slopes, wind-swept headlands, perilous marsh-paths, where the mountain stream goes down under the mists of the cliffs,—a flood upon the earth...."

A third area discernible in *Beowulf* is made up of the allusions to Germanic history and legend. Insofar as the events and personages come from tales and songs in oral tradition, these allusions are easily accepted as part of the oral traditional poem. They point to a poet who was conversant with Germanic legend and history or, put another way, a poet in a rich tradition that contained many songs and stories from the Teutonic past. In one of these, when the scop sang the lay of Finn, we may have a picture of how and when the *Beowulf* poem itself was sung. After the victory over Grendel there was rejoicing in the Hall of Heorot: "There was singing and music together in accompaniment in presence of Healfdene's warlike chieftain; the harp was played, and many a lay rehearsed, when Hrothgar's bard was to provide entertainment in hall along the mead-bench,—about the sons of Finn, and how disaster came on them" (1063–68).

Strangely enough, these historical references, or allusions, were at one time somewhat more of a problem for me in understanding the composition of *Beowulf* than the biblical stories were. But I wonder if that is not because I was using the South Slavic songs as my main comparative model; so far as I can see now, very seldom does one South Slavic poem make overt references to events in another, or in general to events outside of the poem itself. When we turn, however, to the Homeric poems as comparative model, then the difficulty is removed because Homer refers to other myths and legends that exist in the oral traditional repertory of ancient Greek bards. For example, he knew and made reference to the story of the Argonauts. In the *Odyssey* (12.66–72), Circe tells Odysseus that he and his men will have to pass through the Clashing Rocks:

> ". . . No ship of men that came here ever has fled through,
> but the waves of the sea and storms of ravening fire carry
> away together the ship's timbers and the men's bodies.
> That way the only seagoing ship to get through was Argo,
> who is in all men's minds, on her way home from Aietes;
> and even she would have been driven on the great rocks that time,
> but Hera saw her through, out of her great love for Jason."

And again, another famous example, when Agamemnon finally admits to Achilles that he was wrong in taking Briseis from him, he blames Atê, 'Delusion':

> *Iliad* 19.91–99
> "Delusion is the elder daughter of Zeus, the accursed
> who deludes all; her feet are delicate and they step not
> on the firm earth, but she walks on the air above men's heads
> and leads them astray. She has entangled others before me.
> Yes, for once Zeus even was deluded, though men say
> he is the highest one of the gods and mortals. Yet Hera
> who is female deluded even Zeus in her craftiness
> on that day when in strong wall-circled Thebe Alkmene
> was at her time to bring forth the strength of Herakles."

And Homer goes on (19.100–133) to tell the story at some length of the way in which Hera deceived her husband so that Eurystheus was born before Heracles, who thus became subject to him.

In Homer we have an oral traditional poet who found no difficulty in staying the forward action of his song, even at such a significant point as that when Agamemnon admits his fault and offers recompense to Achilles, in order to tell at some length another pertinent tale, another well-known myth. Telling a story within a story as above and as with the Finnsburh episode in *Beowulf* is common in oral traditional epic.

A fourth area drawn most naturally into the orbit of the myth in its elaboration in Anglo-Saxon tradition was the use of other poetic genres. Joseph Harris has enumerated them and they require further study.[33] Just to mention a few, they include a praise poem, elegies, boasts, laments, and finally a "death song."[34] These, in my opinion, are not assembled mechanically but integrated into the narrative in such a natural way that I feel sure the process was not self-conscious. As with the other three areas, they too, I believe, were living in oral tradition in the poet's day, an oral tradition of which he was a distinguished and talented representative.

Beowulf is a complex and magnificent poem setting forth an ancient theme of the establishing and maintaining of order on earth by the action of gods and heroes. As its story was told over generations, it attracted multiforms from the Bible, from other myths, history, and legend, and from other oral traditional genres, all of which served to strengthen the inherited meaning. The grandeur of its traditional style contributed also to the enhancement of the subject of the epic. Miraculously the traditional poet succeeded in telling once again an old, old story, in that telling gave it relevance to contemporary spiritual and historical realities, at the same time focused on the individual hero, in whose triumphs the listener can, even in our day, share and thereby be enlarged.

I envisage the poet of *Beowulf* as an oral traditional poet/singer who had come under the influence of biblical stories, at least the early parts of Genesis, probably from hearing them in a church or monastery. Those stories entered into his inherited Germanic monster-slaying mythic tales. Not only does the scop in Heorot sing of the creation, but the race of monsters is depicted as descendants of Cain. The creatures themselves are like their analogues in Scandinavian lore. But there is another ingredient that has to be accounted for. Whereas references to Germanic lore, such as the dragon-slaying Sigmund, would be part of the poet's traditional store of narrative, the historical events mentioned seem to me to point to a man who was in a community where that kind of knowledge would be available, where he would have heard history as well as Scripture. And that argues for a traditional singer/poet who was, presumably in later years—this is a guess,

---

33. Harris, 1981b.
34. See Martin, 1989, chap. 2, "Heroic Genres of Speaking."

but a good one—living in a monastery. I do not believe that he needed to read in order to have acquired the knowledge that he seems to have had. He could have gained it all by hearing, a not uncommon method in the Middle Ages.

The *Beowulf* poet's style is consistently oral traditional, but elements in his subject matter were new, and they required adaptation of ancient formulas and creation of some new ones, either on his own part or on the part of other singers in his tradition before or around him. We might legitimately think of his style as transitional in the sense that the poet wrote down his poem; perhaps we might think of his technique as that of a latter-day Cædmon.[35] It is clear to me that *Beowulf* is not an imitation of anything. I feel sure that the poet is not looking at oral traditional poetry as something apart from himself that he is going to "imitate." The style is natural to him. If his style is transitional, he has not gone so far away from the tradition that his poem is without traditional characteristics or that he has reached the written style of Virgil.

What I have discussed so far seems to account fairly well for the style and the subject matter. I am still haunted by the inconsistencies between the narrative in the early part of the poem depicting Beowulf's fight with Grendel and that in the retelling by Beowulf at the court of Hygelac. The *glof* 'glove,' 'pouch' still troubles me. Why did the poet of *Beowulf* not mention the *glof* in the account of the hero's fight with Grendel, when all eyes were on the contest, when ears were about to echo with the breaking of benches, when dramatic tension was at its height? He missed a significant detail! Why also did he not mention the name of Hondscio when the companion of Beowulf was so gruesomely being consumed? If he were a literary author using writing, why did he not go back and correct his text as all authors with writing can do? Why leave the inconsistency? An answer might be that he was an oral traditional singer who dictated the poem, and we all know that such inconsistencies can arise in that poetry.

The inconsistencies can be accounted for, I think, if we have a truly oral traditional poet with a knowledge of other versions of monster or troll stories in which the *glof* appears. I have to insist on that or else go to the idea of more than one poet, an idea that I find repugnant. By the time Beowulf arrived home the poet, operating in a perfectly good oral traditional manner, slipped the *glof* into Grendel's hand even as he named Hondscio. Perhaps he thought he had mentioned them before. Perhaps he usually did, but in singing,

35. [A. Lord, 1993.]

writing, or dictation—I like to keep all these possibilities—he neglected to mention them. At any rate, that is a way of accounting for those inconsistencies which is compatible with the oral traditional style.

The poet was a sensitive narrator, taking full advantage of the tradition in which he belonged as well as of the new elements appearing in the community or communities in which he lived and sang. There are many questions to be asked and pondered, but I believe that the foregoing view of this magnificent poem, profound and moving, artistically and traditionally subtle, is not an impossible one.

Editor's Addendum

In endeavoring to determine whether *Beowulf* is an oral traditional poem or, rather, reflects a transitional stage between oral and written, one is tempted to look for guidance to Katherine O'Brien O'Keeffe's discerning and meticulously crafted book, *Visible Song: Transitional Literacy in Old English Verse*.[36] In her preface she expresses the belief that "at some early point, verse in Old English was oral. From the time that Old English was first written, however, composition of verse in writing may be defined as "literate" but only in a seriously restricted sense." She adds:

> Further, my argument assumes the possibility of one or more transitional states between pure "orality" and pure "literacy" and seeks to describe some of the features of an early transitional state characterized by what I shall call "residual orality." By this term I mean a state after the introduction of writing in a culture which nonetheless exhibits many features characteristic of "pure" orality. And finally, I make the assumption that the special character of developing literacy before the Conquest may be described from the manuscripts of Old English and Latin verse. (ix–x)

O'Keeffe discounts both the analysis of style and the use of information based on study of sources in attempts to determine the orality of Old English texts. She questions some of Larry Benson's methods of formulaic analysis, although she is greatly influenced by his 1966 article, which indicated that several "literary" works have a high percentage of formulas. Instead she turns to a scrupulous examination of the physical characteristics of Old English

---

36. O'Keeffe, 1990.

manuscripts, such as mise-en-page, spacing, capitalization, and punctuation, which "provide strong evidence of persisting residual orality in the *reading and copying* of poetry in Old English" (6; the italics are mine).

We may illustrate her methods by considering her conclusions about two Anglo-Saxon poems, Cædmon's *Hymn* and *Solomon and Saturn I*. In her study of Cædmon's *Hymn* she distinguishes between the Latin and the Old English environment of the *Hymn*: "When the *Hymn* travels as 'gloss' to the *Historia ecclesiastica*, the text is subject to little variation, while those records of the *Hymn* which are integrated in the West Saxon translation of the *History* show a high degree of freedom in transmission" (46).

O'Keeffe readily accepts Cædmon's *Hymn* as the product of oral composition, whereas she defines *Solomon and Saturn I*, "precisely the obverse of Cædmon's *Hymn*," in the following manner:

> Its origin and date are obscure (though quite probably late and almost surely a product of writing) and its subject arcane. One version of the poem is twenty times the length of Cædmon's *Hymn*. . . . Despite the important differences between them, both Old English poems preserve in their transmission evidence of transitional literacy in the formulaic reading which their variants imply and in the conventions of formatting the manuscripts display. (48)

She concludes:

> Cædmon's *Hymn* and *Solomon and Saturn I* could not be farther apart in their origins, histories, intellectual presuppositions or circumstances of transmission. They do, however, share one important characteristic: the writing of their verses, reflected both in numerous appropriate variants and in minimal graphic aids for decoding, demonstrates strongly that the poems called forth "formulaic" guesses as an essential part of reading activity.[37] (76)

Here we are faced with a problem. The physical qualities that O'Keeffe has so carefully detected in the manuscript transmission of Cædmon's *Hymn* and of *Solomon and Saturn I* are very much alike—in the nature of their variants, in mise-en-page, spacing, and punctuation. These are the qualities by which she defines the transitional role of the reader and the scribe, who are all-important to her, and by which she plots the place of a particular Anglo-Saxon text in the continuum of orality to literacy. As she says in her preface,

---

[37]. By "formulaic guesses" or "formulaic reading" O'Keeffe means textual variants that are metrically, syntactically, and semantically appropriate.

"the copyists get all the lines." She stresses the participatory role of the scribes and at times compares them with the performer of a poem.[38] Yet, in spite of the similarity in their manuscript transmission, Cædmon's *Hymn* and *Solomon and Saturn I* have quite different places on the spectrum ranging from oral to written. One is oral and the other "almost surely a product of writing." Thus though O'Keeffe's methods of analyzing Anglo-Saxon manuscripts bring us closer to what she would call "the textual reality" of a poem and to the transitional literacy of the scribes and their contemporary readers than do the editions of modern scholarship, these methods cannot in the final analysis define whether a given poem is oral or written. For that information we have to look again at the poem's style and whatever data are available concerning sources and circumstances of composition, elements she wishes to discount.

In succeeding chapters of her book, O'Keeffe makes valuable observations about the relative literacy of the Metrical Preface to Alfred's *Pastoral Care* and the poems of the Anglo-Saxon *Chronicle* on the basis of graphic cues and the reading of the manuscript text. Especially in the chapter where she rigorously examines the punctuation or "pointing" of important codices, she is able to conclude that a "scarcity of points in a realized text represents an early state in the conceptualizing of visual information, and a higher number of points arranged in a coherent pattern indicates a later stage."[39] This dictum has bearing on the state of MS BL, Cotton Vitellius A. XV, which contains the text of *Beowulf*. This poem could not figure in O'Keeffe's analyses because there is only this single witness to its text, and thus a study of variants is not possible. She is able to show, however, that because of its "relatively underdeveloped punctuation" and the "division of the text into long statements" (178–79), the *Beowulf* manuscript's scribal practice accords with its accepted, relatively early dating, that is, the late tenth century.

Certainty regarding the "orality" of *Beowulf* or its possible "transitional literacy" may not be within reach. Yet some progress toward an answer to this question may be attainable. Despite Benson's article and O'Keeffe's forsaking of stylistic analyses and "source" study in favor of paleographic observation,[40] one can show that not all formulaic poetic styles are alike. Refinement of formulaic analysis still holds out promise, as Lord's comparative study of the formulaic structure of introductions to direct discourse in

---

38. Moffat, 1992, does not share O'Keeffe's confidence in the ability of scribes, but he calls into question "the general applicability of the idea of the sensitive and competent Anglo-Saxon scribe" (823).
39. O'Keeffe, 1990, 172.
40. See also Doane, 1991.

Beowulf and *Elene* has demonstrated.[41] One should not automatically assume for *Beowulf* the same place on the continuum from orality to literacy which the various Old English religious poems hold. The heroic traditionality of *Beowulf* demands its own special scrutiny. Our focus is first on the performing poet and then on his reader or scribe.

41. A. Lord, 1991, 147–69. For further reference to Benson's article, see Chapter 5 below.

CHAPTER 5

The Formula in Anglo-Saxon Poetry

In this chapter I explore the degree to which oral traditional style informs, that is to say, manifests itself in, *Beowulf* and other Anglo-Saxon poetry. The adaptation to Anglo-Saxon poetics of Milman Parry's definition of the formula and the formulaic system, as well as the concept of the "theme" (the latter treated in Chapter 6) have received considerable attention. Much has been written on the formula in Old English, and there have been excellent summaries. One thinks especially of Ann Chalmers Watts's *The Lyre and the Harp*.[1] We come back to Larry Benson's assertion that written Old English is as formulaic as what might well be oral traditional poetic texts.[2] He was criticizing my application, in *The Singer of Tales*, of Parry's view of the formula to *Beowulf*. John D. Niles in a 1981 article and in his 1983 book *Beowulf* has responded both to Watts and to Benson. He comments on Watts's work as follows:

> In particular, the main contention of Ann Chalmers Watts in her study *The Lyre and the Harp*—that when closely scrutinized, Anglo-Saxon narrative poetry is not highly formulaic and therefore has no claim to be called oral—is unjustified because it is based on a concept of the formula as a fixed phrase. . . .
> To Watts, a formula in Old English is "a repeated sequence that fills one of

---

Portions of this chapter were presented at a lecture, "Recent Comparative Perspectives on Oral Traditional Poetry," sponsored by the Center for the Study of Comparative Folklore and Mythology, the Folklore and Mythology Program, and the English Department, at the University of California at Los Angeles, February 20, 1986.
  1. Watts, 1969; see Chapter 4 at n. 18.
  2. Benson, 1966.

Sievers' five basic rhythmical types" (p. 90), or in other words, a repeated verse. Watts correctly concludes that the formula *thus defined* is not of outstanding importance in *Beowulf*, but since her definition is ill chosen, her conclusion has no bearing on the question of the validity of the oral-formulaic theory.[3]

Niles analyzes the systems of the first fifty verses of *Beowulf* and then gives the results of a similar analysis of the first five hundred verses. He concludes:

> Close to *two out of three* verses in the poem are members of one or another identifiable formulaic system. In creating these phrases, the poet not only was working within the linguistic patterns afforded him by the natural language, he was using more highly specialized patterns which enabled him to compose fluently in the alliterative form. On the other hand, only about *one verse in six* recurs elsewhere in substantially the same form. To call these verses "fixed formulas" would be misleading, for most of them (almost 80%) are members of one or another flexible formulaic system. In other words, the diction of *Beowulf* is indeed highly formulaic, but far more important than the repetition of fixed phrases is the substitution of one verbal element for another within flexible formulaic systems one half-line in length.[4]

Niles carefully restricts himself to *Beowulf* rather than considering all the poetry in the *Anglo-Saxon Poetic Records* (*ASPR*). He criticized certain of Benson's conclusions as follows:

> By comparing a number of passages of Anglo-Saxon poetry, Benson shows that formulas occur in the work of authors known to have been composing pen in hand. He concludes that since all Old English poetry is formulaic, there can be no way of determining the oral vs. written nature of a given text. Benson has well shown that blind formulaic analysis of a particular passage of Old English poetry is no sure proof of its mode of creation. Many a learned author has been known to use formulas, whether for rhetorical effect, for atmosphere, or because the poetic language itself is steeped in them. In the absence of definite information indicating the mode of creation of a text, one must use great caution in attributing it to a singer. All the same, like Watts, Benson fails to make a distinction between living formulaic language and the parroting of formulaic tags. In seeking evidence for the mode of composition of a text, one must not only count the number of fixed formulas in the work, for these are easily imitated by a lettered author. One must look for evidence that the poet in question made formulaic language his *habitual mode of thought*.[5]

3. Niles, 1981, 410.
4. Ibid., 409.
5. Ibid., 410–11.

My reply to Benson's article was "The Formulaic Structure of Introductions to Direct Discourse in *Beowulf* and *Elene*,"[6] in which I was able to show that the formulas used in introductions to speech are handled by the *Beowulf* poet in a way different from that of any other Anglo-Saxon poet whose works we have. The *maþelode* '(he) spoke' formula systems belong to *Beowulf* par excellence; in fact "they are used twenty-six times in *Beowulf* compared with nine in *Elene* and four in *Genesis*—twice as many in *Beowulf* as in the other two combined."[7] But that is not all, as I pointed out:

> It is not, however, merely that the formula systems on *maþelode* are used more frequently than in any other system in *Beowulf* or than elsewhere in Anglo-Saxon poetry. What is more significant is that they are used differently. The poet of *Beowulf* does not hesitate to employ these formulas over and over again, even in long sequences, without striving for variety, although we can see from the list just given [of other words to introduce speech] that he had alternatives in his repertory, if he chose to use them. . . . It is especially significant to observe the two "runs" of eight or nine *maþelodes* [between lines 348 and 631 and between lines 1215 and 1999]. They, as well as the word itself, differentiate *Beowulf* from the other Anglo-Saxon poems. Within the poem they also appear to distinguish the scenes in Heorot from that in Hygelac's hall and to show a continuity with the dragon episode, marking significantly the generational succession from Beowulf to his kinsman Wiglaf.[8]

In Cynewulf's *Elene*, however, in long series of introductions to direct discourse such as between lines 78 and 537 and between lines 604 and 685, with a number of *maþelodes*, the use of this verb is interrupted by other words for introducing speech. A noteworthy example of how the series of words for speech is broken occurs in the second major group of exchanges of speeches in *Elene*, beginning in line 573 with Elene's address to the assembled people. As I have written,

> this fact is the more amazing because in the passage in question Cynewulf is following the Latin source very closely, and the Latin speeches are all, without exception, introduced by *dixit*. Cynewulf varies the verbs of speaking more than either the *Beowulf* poet or the Latin does. In addition Cynewulf in this passage employs the epithet for Elene used regularly in the Latin text, *beata*, which becomes *eadige* in Anglo-Saxon, only *once* (619) in *Elene*. Cynewulf also

---

6. A. Lord, 1991, 147–69.
7. *Beowulf* contains 3,182 lines; *Elene* has 1,321; *Genesis*, 2,936. The total of *Elene* and *Genesis* is 4,257 lines.
8. A. Lord, 1991, 151–52, 161.

uses *tireadig* (605) and *ædele* (662). In short, here too as in the sequences of words introducing speech, Cynewulf prefers variety.[9]

It is not enough to say, as Benson does, that Old English poetry is "both formulaic and lettered."[10] It is essential to realize that one can distinguish in number and usage the formulas in *Beowulf* from those in the Old English poems that stem from religious and from learned secular sources. A formulaic "residue" carried over from a previous oral practice is different from the formulaic systems in a poem that belongs to a still-living heroic tradition.

In his book on *Beowulf*, Niles adds a consideration of "compound diction" as a mark of the poet's oral style:

> One striking feature of *Beowulf* is its extraordinary wealth of compound diction. To a large extent this vocabulary appears to be formal and inherited rather than idiosyncratic, and it seems a particular adjunct to the heroic style. . . . These compounds have long attracted attention. They have been counted and catalogued, and their aesthetic effect has been described. All I need to stress is that they are not merely ornamental; they are not used merely for poetic effect. They are functional, and this is their prime reason for being. The unusually rich and varied compound diction in *Beowulf* is the product of a centuries-old tradition of alliterative verse-making, and the poet used it not only because he loved it but because it helped him compose.[11]

In his study of *Beowulf*, Niles is indebted to Donald K. Fry's definition of the formula, which is the one most commonly accepted by Old English scholars. Fry's most noteworthy and important articles are "Old English Formulas and Systems," and "Some Aesthetic Implications of a New Definition of the Formula."[12] He defines an Old English formula as a "group of words, one-half line in length, which shows evidence of being the direct product of a formulaic system." In Milman Parry's view, groups of related formulas made up "systems" from which Homer chose his diction, but Fry proposed, rather, that "a formula is *generated from* a system," which he defines as "a group of half-lines, usually loosely related metrically and semantically, which are related in form by the identical relative placement of two elements, one a variable word or element of a compound usually supplying the alliteration, and the other a constant word or element of a compound, with approximately the same distribution of non-stressed elements."[13]

9. Ibid., 165.
10. Benson, 1966, 340–41.
11. Niles, 1983, 138.
12. Fry, 1967b, 1968c.
13. Fry, 1967b, 204.

Fry summed up his conclusions on formulas and on oral versus written texts in Old English in a 1977 paper published in 1981, and I can do no better than quote parts of its last three paragraphs:

> The basic building block of this poetry and of any oral poetry is the formula. But formulas work differently in different traditions. Parry's classic definition of a formula as "a group of words which is regularly employed under the same metrical conditions to express a given essential idea" fits Homeric Greek rather well, but Old English poorly. An Old English formula may consist of one long compound word rather than "a group of words." The formula may appear only once, not "regularly employed," but be closely related to other formulas from the same system. Since all Old English half-lines are metrically equivalent, "under the same metrical conditions" proves meaningless. And finally, Old English formulas seem to be related only in form, not in content, i.e., they do not "express a given essential idea." The first step in determining the formula in any given corpus requires identification of the basic unit of composition. In Greek, dactylic feet in various combinations comprise the units. For Old English, the unit is the half-line. The Middle English unit seems to be stressed pairs of words occurring together.[14]

I do not wish to detract from Fry's important contributions in this field; for they moved the study of Anglo-Saxon formulas forward on their own path, and they also broadened and deepened our sense of the intricacy of structure characteristic of oral traditional narrative style. I find it necessary, however, to comment on several aspects of his definitions of formula and system vis-à-vis Parry's.

One, Fry's 1967 definition of the formula, as quoted above, began with "a group of words," but in 1977 he stated that Parry's definition was inadequate for Old English, because "an Old English formula may consist of one long compound word rather than 'a group of words.' " Parry's first definition of the formula was "in the diction of bardic poetry, the formula can be defined as an expression regularly used, under the same metrical conditions, to express an essential idea."[15] The form of the definition I generally use begins "a word, or group of words." The debate as to whether a one-word formula is legitimate or not is of long standing and will probably continue.

Two, Fry's definition of the formula in Old English seems to eliminate two elements in Parry's definition, namely, "regular use," and "essential idea," which I believe are vital to an understanding of the nature of a formula. Fry's definition is mercifully simple, but after placing the formula,

14. Fry, 1981, 172–73.
15. Parry, 1971, 13.

quite properly, in a system, he then presents us with a definition of a system, which is more complex. Actually, Parry stated that it is not necessary to find a phrase more than once in any text for it to be a formula. He clearly stated, as we saw above, that he was approaching the formula from the side of repetition because it was easier to see that it was used regularly if it was repeated but that its repetition in any given text depended on whether the idea embodied in it was needed again under the given metrical conditions—including "placement in the line," to use Fry's phrase—and not on the nature of the formula itself.[16] There is a crucial difference between a formula in an oral poem and a repetition used by a writer in a literary milieu. Formulas are vital for the oral poet; for they help in verse making. A poet in a written tradition employs repetition for aesthetic effect or for referential reasons. Formulas embody all previous occurrences and not any particular one; in an oral poem they do not point to other uses of the same formula.

"Regular use," however, is important in the definition of the formula, be it in Old English or in any other tradition, no matter how one chooses to word it. If one wishes to interpret Fry's definition of a system as implying "regular use," and as including, under "semantic," the concept of "essential idea," then his definition may not be so radical as it may seem but may be the same thing in disguise, except for the restricting of Parry's "metrical conditions" to a half-line in the case of Old English. Be that as it may, Fry's discussion of his definition in his 1967 article admirably analyzes what I have later termed the "weaving style," namely, the intricate pattern of interrelationships of formulas and of formulaic expressions which is typical of oral traditional style.

Three, in limiting the formula to a half-line in the case of Anglo-Saxon poetry, Fry has, I believe, been too conservative. Recent work seems to indicate that we should extend the boundaries of the formula because, like everyone else, the singers do not think, or compose, in terms of half-lines. They think in whole lines or, even better, in terms of clauses, or perhaps of whole sentences, which may well be of greater length than a whole line, to say nothing of a half-line. In other words, they do not compose in terms of subjects *or* of verbs but of subjects-plus-verbs, that is, in terms of larger syntactic and semantic units. If we leave untouched Fry's restriction on length for the Old English formula, we will have to invent another simple term for the longer units.

Fry also expressed his opinion on oral versus written Old English poetry:

---

16. For the conviction that an expression need not be used more than once by a singer for it to be considered a formula, see Bynum, 1987, 103–6.

> For Old English the hardest problem turned on identifying oral versus written texts. . . . Recently most scholars believe that oral and written texts are indistinguishable anyway, since Old English writers inherited and imitated the formulaic style, indeed the only poetic they knew. We can distinguish oral texts only when some contemporary, such as Bede, labels them for us; unfortunately, for Old English, that includes only *Cædmon's Hymn*. Certain factors in medieval authorship complicate this picture further. Anglo-Saxon poetry lacks a chronology. Fewer than ten Old English poems can be dated at all, and we think *Beowulf* was composed sometime between 658 and 1025! Only six poems have known authors; indeed the whole idea of authorship or literary property was different or perhaps non-existent in the vernacular. Poets simply recomposed each other's works without attribution or guilt.[17]

Fry thus states that the method of composition is the same whether it be done orally or in writing. There is merit in that suggestion, I believe, but only for the earliest period of written Old English poetry, the first stage of transition, as it were, or the last of oral traditional poetry, depending on the direction of one's approach. It should be our task to determine how the oral formulaic style changes in time as the method of composition changes; for change it must, and does, through the increased influence of reading and writing and, more particularly, through the eventual imitation of new poetic models, for example, Latin poetry. Those changes in style are visible and measurable.

Fry's final paragraph deals with aesthetics:

> Finally and paradoxically, although we cannot distinguish oral from written texts, oral aesthetics are different, understandable only on their own terms. For example, repetition in a writing poet is a flaw, but for an oral poet repetition is a badge of loyalty to inherited poetic traditions and values. Oral poems "sound alike" internally and externally because their poets wanted them to, to please an audience appreciative of traditional verse.[18]

Fry is aware of the inconsistency, as he notes the paradox, but he makes no attempt to explain it. Yet it cries out for explanation. Would not the loss of repetitions of which he speaks as distinguishing marks of oral aesthetics be visible and measurable when the aesthetics change, when the repetitions begin to be less and less acceptable, thus modifying the method of composi-

---

17. Fry, 1981, 173.
18. Ibid.

tion? When does that begin to be perceptible? There are many questions still to be investigated.

Anita Riedinger's article "The Old English Formula in Context" builds on the work of Fry.[19] She redefines for Old English the terms *formula* and *system*, which have been current in scholarship since the days of Milman Parry, and gives a definition for a "set," a word used by Valerie Krishna and by John Niles for a "system."[20]

Riedinger's idea of content is explained simply by observing the situations in which a formula such as *nihtlangne fyrst* 'the space of a whole night' is used. It occurs five times in four different poems: once each in *Beowulf*, *Exodus*, and *Elene*, and twice in *Andreas*. In all five cases it "signifies a terrifying period of time prior to a battle." To substantiate this statement she notes that "Unferth dares Beowulf to wait that long near Grendel (Bwf 528a)"; "the terrified Israelites . . . wait *nihtlangne fyrst* for battle with the Egyptians (Exo 208b)"; "the fearful Constantine and his Romans . . . do the same before battle with the Goths and Huns (Ele 67b)"; the angels who transported Andreas to the land of Mermedonians leave him asleep "*nihtlangne fyrst* outside the gates of his enemies (And 834b)"; and he waits in prison that period of time before being returned for torture.[21] "In each instance," she says, "the context reveals ominous connotations not explicitly suggested by the formula." To her, this formula always carries with it such "ominous connotations." Such formulas "may be said to signify themes rather than to express them, because they are dependent for their full meaning upon a context external to the semantics of the formulas themselves; that is, the words themselves do not mean 'impending disaster,' yet this is their invariable context."[22] I agree with her that, if this is true, such a meaning would be traditional, because it is shared by more than one poet. I would add that it is likely that considerable time would be required for such a meaning to become traditional. It follows, then, that traditional "thematic formulas" must be of some age. I suggest that they, like the basic formulaic style itself,

---

19. Riedinger, 1985. An important article by Fry not mentioned in the preceding survey is Fry, 1968a. It stems from Benson, 1966, and continues the discussion of thrift in *Beowulf* as set forth in Whallon, 1961, 1965a, and 1965b.

20. Riedinger, 1985, 306 no. 30; Krishna, 1982: "A true formula therefore is not simply a repeated phrase but a phrase that fits into a system or set that exhibits extension and, most important, thrift" (77); Niles, 1983, characterizes a system as "a set of verses of a similar metrical type in which one main verbal element is constant" (126).

21. The abbreviations of Old English texts are those listed in Bessinger with Smith, 1978. See Riedinger, 1985, 294 no. 4. The Old English texts are from the *ASPR*, and the translations of the passages cited by Riedinger are hers, with slight modifications.

22. Riedinger, 1985, 297.

must also have originated in the period when the poetry was oral rather than written.

Riedinger expands the context of the thematic formula by noting that some formulas of that type "stand . . . at the center of a cluster of recurrent motifs that are not themselves usually expressed by the same formulas."[23] Thus *wan under wolcnum* 'dark beneath the clouds' is used four times, once each in *Beowulf*, *The Dream of the Rood*, *Guthlac B*, and *Andreas*. "The cluster of recurrent motifs" in this case are "death or sleep, a shining light, and shadows." In *The Dream of the Rood* the words of the Cross, speaking of the crucifixion, make use of these motifs. (The underlinings are mine.)

> DrR 52b–56
>   þystro hæfdon
> bewrigen mid <u>wolcnum</u>   wealdendes hræw,
> <u>scirne sciman</u>,   sceadu forðeode,
> <u>wann under wolcnum</u>.   Weop eal gesceaft,
> cwiðdon cyninges <u>fyll</u>.   Crist wæs on rode.

Darkness had covered the Ruler's corpse, <u>shining radiance, with clouds</u>; a <u>shadow</u> went forth, <u>dark beneath the clouds</u>. All creation wept, mourned the King's <u>death</u>. Christ was on the cross.

We find the formula in *Guthlac B* in the description of the night when the saint is dying:

> Glc 1278b–86a
>   Þa se æþela glæm
> setlgong sohte.   swearc norðrodor
> <u>won under wolcnum</u>,   woruld miste oferteah
> þystrum biþeahte,   þrong niht ofer tiht
> londes frætwa.   Ða cwom <u>leohta mæst</u>,
> halig of heofonum   hædre <u>scinan</u>,
> beorhte ofer burgsalu.   Bad se þe sceolde
> eadig on elne   endedogor,
> awrecen <u>wælstrælum</u>.

Then the <u>glorious radiance</u> reached its setting; the northern sky dimmed, <u>dark beneath the clouds</u>, covered the world with mist, wrapped it in darkness; night rushed across the expanse of the land's adornments. Then, holy from the heavens,

---

23. Ibid., 300.

the greatest of lights came shining clearly, bright above the city's dwellings. He who had to do so awaited his last day, blessed with courage, pierced by death's arrows.

Riedinger continues: "The next ten verses describe the miraculous light that illuminates the darkness and include the phrase *scadu sweþredon* 'shadows disappeared' " (300).

The example from *Beowulf* occurs when Hrothgar, aware that Grendel will visit Heorot, departs from the hall to go to bed:

> Bwf 644b–51a
> oþþæt semninga
> sunu Healfdenes   secean wolde
> æfenræste;   wiste þæm ahlæcan
> to þæm heahsele   hilde geþinged,
> siddan hie sunnan leoht   geseon ne meahton,
> oþðe nipende   niht ofer ealle,
> scaduhelma gesceapu   scriðan cwoman,
> wan under wolcnum.

. . . until presently the son of Healfdene wished to seek his evening rest. He knew the battle planned by the terrible one for that high-hall after they could not see the sun's light and night, obscuring all, the shapes of covering shadows, came gliding, dark beneath the clouds.

Neither the word *sleep* nor the word *death* is used specifically in the *Beowulf* passage; sleep, at least, is implied in *æfenræste* 'evening rest'. Moreover, a little later in the poem, when Grendel approaches Heorot, the poet uses some of the words belonging to the thematic cluster:

> Bwf 702b–3
>   Com on wanre niht
> scriðan sceadugenga.   Sceotend swæfon

In the dark night the walker-in-shadows came gliding. The warriors slept. . . .

Twelve lines later, a variant of *wan under wolcnum* is found with the shining brightness of gold, a "light" not noted by Reidinger, but which I deem may be pertinent to the theme in this part of *Beowulf*:

> Bwf 714–16a
> Wod under wolcnum   to þæs þe he winreced,

<blockquote>
goldsele gumena,   gearwost wisse,
fættum fahne.
</blockquote>

He strode <u>beneath the clouds</u>, until he might most clearly perceive the <u>gold-hall</u> of men, the wine-hall shining with gold plate.

I see no reason why Riedinger should feel that *wod under wolcnum* is "non-traditional," purely on the grounds that it is not found again in the corpus. I prefer to view it simply as a formulaic expression, possibly a formula, that is an apt variant of *wan under wolcnum*.

Finally, *wan under wolcnum* is found in *Andreas* in the same context where we previously noted the thematic formula *nihtlangne fyrst*, namely, after the angels have carried Andreas miraculously during a sleep to Mermedonia and left him still asleep for the remainder of the night outside the walls of the city where his enemies dwell. Here is the passage, including the coming of dawn:

<blockquote>
And 831–37a
Leton þone halgan   be herestræte
swefan on sybbe   under swegles hleo,
bliðne bidan   burhwealle neh,
his niðhetum,   <u>nihtlangne fyrst</u>,
oðþæt dryhten forlet   <u>dægcandelle</u>
<u>scire scinan.</u>   Sceadu sweðerodon,
<u>wonn under wolcnum.</u>
</blockquote>

They let the holy one sleep in peace by the army road under the protection of the sky happily to await near the city wall of his enemies, <u>for the space of a night</u>, until the Lord allowed <u>the day-candle to shine brightly</u>; <u>the shadows</u> disappeared, <u>dark beneath the clouds</u>.

Riedinger interprets this passage according to the other contexts in which *nihtlangne fyrst*, on the one hand, and *wan under wolcnum* on the other, appear in the corpus. I am sorry to say that I do not entirely agree with her, tempting as it may be to see these thematic formulas casting an ominous gloom on this passage. There just are not enough cases in Anglo-Saxon poetry to prove that the context is *always* ominous. She has, indeed, indicated that it is not. She *has* demonstrated, however, that a cluster of formulas joins these four or five scenes in these poems, and she has noted that in all but one of them, the context is gloomy and ominous. That is interesting and valuable. When she stretches the evidence to create an absolute, she does disservice to her cause. One must be careful about such generalizations; for the body of extant Anglo-Saxon material is limited and varied in genre.

The movement to expand the idea of the formula is not actually new. Parry's systems of formulas, as he elaborated them for the Homeric poems in 1928, could be thought of as expansions of the formula. The "formulaic expressions" that I discussed in general and described in detail for both South Slavic and Old English in *The Singer of Tales*, being based on the idea of Parry's "systems" of formulas, could also be considered expansions of the concept of the formula.[24] It is true, however, that we distinguished the formula from both the system, a group of formulas sharing a syntactic pattern and at least one word, and also from the formulaic expression, which might be thought of as a member of a system, or a partial repetition, a phrase sharing at least one word with the other phrases. It is also true that we considered the formula itself to be a verbatim repetition. In a seminar on medieval epic and romance that I used to offer regularly in the Department of Comparative Literature at Harvard, we accepted as formulas repetitions in which two words were metathesized, and we also counted as formulas phrases in which the elements of formula were declined or conjugated, taking into account necessary adjustments in metrical conditions. Riedinger calls such cases, I think often correctly, the "same formula." For example, she considers *hwær ic under swegle* (Wids 101a), "where beneath the heavens I," and *nænigne ic under swegle* (Bwf 1197a), "Of none I beneath the heavens" to be the same formula, although I would prefer to think of them as *aspects* of the same formula.[25] The poet of *Andreas* uses *ofer cald wæter, ond on cald wæter*, and *on cald wæter*, and I find no difficulty in calling all three expressions the same formula, although when Riedinger adds *ofer cald cleofu*, "across the fateful cliffs" (And 310a), I prefer to note that the phrase is a member of a system with *ofer cald* as its stable core and *wæter* and *cleofu* as the variables, before agreeing to call them the same formula. I hesitate, because these distinctions in "fine-tuning" may turn out under certain circumstances to be useful, and one is running the danger of calling everything a formula indiscriminately or on purely subjective or intuitive grounds.

Riedinger does make an important distinction between an "incidental" and a "significant" repetition. The first is determined by prosody and syntax, the formula, in short, with which we are familiar; the second is "intentional—the deliberate repetition of a verse such as *ofer cald wæter* or *wan under wolcnum* in order to convey a specific meaning."[26] The significant formulas are thematic formulas. They imply, or signify, a theme; receive their signifi-

---

24. See A. Lord, 1960, e.g., 37, 47–48, 297–301. For the importance of "sound-patterning" in the concept of the formula, see Creed, 1981, 19–20.
25. Riedinger, 1985, 303.
26. Ibid., 304.

cance from their traditional contexts; and are used by the poet in order to evoke the essence of those contexts.

There are at least two other kinds of expansion—or directions in which expansion may go—that should be mentioned here. One is by making the formula longer, that is, by extending it beyond the half-line and the whole line to encompass two and more lines. Another is contained in what I have called the "weaving style" of oral traditional poetry. Tod Luethans has described the interlocking of formulas both in the Old French chanson de geste *Gormont et Isembart* and in the *Chanson de Guillaume*.[27] A noun-epithet formula can have systems involving the noun and other systems involving the epithet. Each noun listed in the system based on the epithet may have its own system of epithets; each epithet listed in the nominal system may in turn have a system of its own, and so forth. Formulas are thus interrelated through such overlapping, or interwoven, systems.

Those are but two ways, however, of "expanding" the formula, and scholars in Old English have been moving forward very provocatively in others as well. Similar expansions also have taken place in other language areas, particularly Homeric studies, beginning with the work of Notopoulos, Hainsworth, and Hoekstra, and continuing with that of Nagy and Janko.[28]

Benson did not try to redefine the formula but accepted Parry's definition for application in Old English. Before Riedinger, the greatest modification of the definition of the formula had come from Fry. It seems that all scholars who have concerned themselves with the subject have thought of Parry's definition as not applicable to Old English, although it was applicable to Ancient Greek and South Slavic. I believe that it is time to point out that Parry's definition is not specific to either Greek or South Slavic. Consider each phrase in the definition: "A group of words" is appropriate to any language that uses words, and certainly Old English does. "Regularly used" is certainly general enough—it implies that the group of words is generally used in the practice of the singers in any given tradition; it does not say it must be used such-and-such a number of times. "To express a given essential idea" is also not language specific—the essential idea does not have to be Greek, or Slavic; as long as the Anglo-Saxons expressed ideas they were not excluded.

It is "under given metrical conditions" that has caused the difficulty. For

---

27. Luethans, 1990.
28. Notopoulos, 1959; Hainsworth, 1968 and 1978; Hoekstra, 1964; Nagy, 1976 [and 1990a, 50–51]; Janko, 1982, 11, 19–24, [and 1992; see index s.v. *formulae*].

some unknown reason it has been assumed that the phrase meant either dactylic hexameter or South Slavic decasyllables. Inasmuch as Old English poetry is in meter, Old English scholars should be able to translate the phrase into the metrical system of Old English, even as Greek scholars translate that general, nonspecific metrical term into dactylic hexameters, or South Slavs into asymmetric decasyllables. Russian scholars have found no problem in accommodating it to the tonic verse of the *byliny*, and Old French scholars have not found the assonance of the laisse difficult to include in the umbrella term of "metrical conditions." In short, surely Old English poetry has "metrical conditions," or Eduard Sievers, M. W. M. Pope, Robert Creed, and John Foley have lived in vain. I see no reason to change Parry's definition for the formula. I have already treated Fry's valiant attempts to define the Old English formula as the product of a system while limiting the formula to a half-line. Saying that a formula is the product of a system is not to define it but merely to say whence it came; and to limit it to a half-line is simply to read into Parry's generic definition the specific "metrical conditions," or part of them, that Fry sees as appropriate for Old English. Parry's definition still stands for any poetry that uses words and has some form of "metrical conditions." Each language area will set forth its own particular "metrical conditions," but there is no need to change the definition.

With that much behind us, let us look at Riedinger's concept of formula and system, because, although we may have problems of terminology, I believe that her distinctions are worthy of consideration. She defines a formula thus: "The repetition of one general concept + one system + one function = one formula."[29] Parry's "essential idea" has been replaced by "general concept." Her example is *x under (heavens)*. "Under" is constant; "heavens" may be expressed by several words, such as *swegle*, *wolcnum*, *roderum*, and so forth; and *x* may be anything, noun, pronoun, adjective, or adverb. The system involved in the example is *x under x*. If I understand Riedinger correctly, there are two functions possible. One is as a "tag," a way of making a line; the other function is a thematic formula, as described above. *Rume under roderum*, "spacious beneath the heavens," is a tag; in *Phoenix* 14a "the verse describes the forests of paradise," and in *Genesis* 1243a it "describes how the descendants of Noah multiplied." "The two share no contextual meanings, and therefore do not function as thematic formulas," she points out. The repetition of *rume under roderum* is "incidental." It is a tag the function of which is "chiefly prosodic." But *wan under wolcnum*, as we have seen in detail above, functions as a thematic formula.

---

29. Riedinger, 1985, 305.

The Formula in Anglo-Saxon Poetry   131

Riedinger's definition of a system is admittedly derived from Fry's and runs as follows: "A system is a group of verses usually sharing the same meter and syntax in which one word, usually stressed, is constant and the other stressed word or words may be varied to suit the alliterative and/or narrative context" (305). In Anglo-Saxon terms, this definition of a system is not much different from Parry's, or from mine, for that matter, and it is close to Fry's. There is nothing remarkable in it. But from it she derives another grouping of formulas, which she calls a "set" and defines as follows:

> A "set" may be defined as a group of verses usually sharing the same function and system in which one word, usually stressed, is constant, and at least one stressed word may be varied, usually synonymously, to suit the alliterative and/or narrative context. A system may contain several different sets, each of which is a different formula, but all the verses in a set constitute the same formula—whether or not they repeat one another verbatim. By making a distinction between verses that are members of the same system, but of different sets, one can identify word groups that are the equivalent of the "same formula," even though they contain variables. (306)

This is all somewhat confusing and perhaps unduly complex, but it is to be noted that a formula and a set share the elements of function and system. A formula is a repeated general concept + system + function. In other words, both a formula and a set belong to a system; and both a formula and a set have a function. For a formula, we saw that Riedinger acknowledged two clear functions, one as a tag, the other as a thematic formula in context. But we learn later that other functions, of a less precise nature, are adduced. Function does not enter the definition of system, and it is in respect to function that set is of significance. It is the component of function of Riedinger's groupings that saves her work from being just another reshuffling of terms for already familiar phenomena. The system and the set according to Riedinger will be clearer if we look at some of her examples.

She illustrates both system and set with an analysis of the system *x hremig* 'exulting in x'.[30] She finds two of the sixteen members of this system not to be formulas: *wuldrum hremge* 'exulting in glories' (Chr 54a) and *feðerum hremige* 'exulting in their wings' (And 864b). Riedinger comments: "They share neither concept nor function with any other members of the system and are therefore not demonstrably formulas." I believe that Fry would call them formulas because they are members of a system, and I would call them

---

30. Ibid., 310.

"formulaic expressions," although I am ready to admit that most "formulaic expressions" are really formulas. (I like to keep some distinction between verbatim repetitions and those with at least one constant and one or more variables). Both Fry and I, it seems to me, would find her decisions against these two verses too harsh.

The remaining fourteen members of the *x hremig* system fall into three sets. The first has only one verse, but it is used six times:

Set 1. *blissum hremig* 'exulting in joys' (And 1699a; Ele 1137a; ECL 64a; Glc 1106b; Phx 126b, 592b).

This verse, Riedinger tells us, "recurs in varying contexts and functions as a traditional expression of Christian happiness. The frequency of this verbatim repetition makes it an easily recognizable formula" (310). It is the function, nonthematic in this case, that makes this formula into a set. It is not clear to me that anything of moment is gained thereby.

The second set is the opposite of the first in respect to meaning. Its three members may be translated "clamorous with grief."

Set 2. *geohðum hremig* (SB1 9b)
gehþum hremig (SB2 9b)
sorgum hremig (SFt 208b).

Riedinger comments that these formulas "function as a traditional expression of Christian lamentation for man's sins" (310). The first two would be formulas according to both Fry and myself, and the third also according to Fry. I am perfectly willing to go along with this judgment, because all three are synonyms. It is worth pointing out that in spite of their having the same meaning, they do not violate the principle of thrift, because they have different alliteration.

The third and last set has five members, and there is somewhat greater variety in meaning:

Set 3. *huðe hremig* 'exulting in his booty' (Bwf 124a; Ele 149a)
since hremig 'exulting in his treasure' (Bwf 1882a)
frætwum hremig 'exulting in his treasures' (Bwf 2054a)
wiges hremige 'exulting in battle' (Brb 59b).

According to Riedinger, "Set 3 is a thematic formula whose function it is to signify the theme 'the victor's reward.' It usually appears with formulas expressing the general concept 'to seek home,' so that the complete theme may be identified as 'the victor returns home with his reward' " (310). In the first case, Grendel returns to his lair with thirty men from Heorot; in the second, Constantine returns home from his victory over the Goths and Huns; and in the third, Beowulf returns home from Denmark with his rewards. Riedinger has to stretch a point for the inclusion of the last two examples, because their contexts, especially in the third *Beowulf* example, are not so clearly related to the first three as one might hope. I find no problem in considering the *Brunanburh* passage with its depiction of the English forces returning victorious, even though they are "exulting in battle" instead of "booty" or "treasure," as belonging to the same theme as the first three. The fourth instance above occurs in one of the digressions in *Beowulf* and concerns the descendant of the victor exulting in the sword that had been previously won as booty. There is no returning home, except perhaps by implication, but the context is not so far removed from the sense of the other passages to quibble about its traditionality.

Riedinger closes her article with the following comment:

> I believe that with further study my definition of a set, which is the same as my definition of a formula—the repetition of one general concept + one system + one function—can be further narrowed and refined; but the key to that greater precision lies in the study of traditional contexts, which allows us to discern what the Old English poets themselves seem to have regarded as formulas. (317)

The principle of contextual analysis is a very worthy one, it seems to me, and should be pursued, as Riedinger urges, with greater precision. There are, of course, pitfalls, of which she is thoroughly aware. We have a limited body of Anglo-Saxon poetry and it is varied in its genres. To jump to the conclusion that a formula used five times in four poems in a given context is used "invariably" in that type of context is assuming a great deal, even though the statement is literally true. Moreover, one has to strain unduly to interpret some contexts as being of the nature that one would like them to be for the theory to fit. Subjective judgment comes into play more than Riedinger admits, albeit she tries hard to be careful and honest. Nor is context the only element in her analyses and definitions which lies open to the charge of "subjective." Her terms *general concept* and *function* are not models of precision; yet they are the cornerstones of her definitions of formula and set.

To turn now to another aspect of the formula, we note that the oral formulaic style is characterized by a high degree of "thriftiness," that is to say, there is usually only one way of expressing an essential idea under any given metrical and—for Anglo-Saxon, or Germanic in general—alliterative conditions.

Thrift is a rich subject for Anglo-Saxon poetry with its requirements of alliteration and its propensity for apposition. Nevertheless, few scholars have investigated it. One of the exceptions is William Whallon, who began writing about *Beowulf* in 1961.[31] In his 1969 paper, Whallon suggests that there are some cases of lack of thrift in *Beowulf*. He cites two noun-epithet phrases for the hero which have the same alliterative value, *rof oretta* 'the brave warrior' in line 2538 and *rices hyrde* 'the guardian of the kingdom' in line 3080, and two similar phrases for Providence, *ece drihten* 'the everlasting Lord' in line 108 and *ylda waldend* 'the Ruler of men' in line 1661.

Superficially it is true that *rof oretta* and *rices hyrde* have alliteration in *r* and each contains four syllables. But the distribution of long and short vowels and of stresses is different. *Rof oretta* has two long *o*s, with stresses on both and a possible weaker stress on *ett*, whereas *rices hyrde* has a long *i*, which is stressed, and a short *y*, which is also stressed. Thus the two verses are not equivalent except in number of syllables and in alliteration. The differences in distribution of long vowels and of stresses is important and should not be ignored. Moreover, *rof oretta* is found in the b-verse, whereas *rices hyrde* is used twice in *Beowulf*, and only in the a-verse, and belongs in a larger system that includes *folces hyrde*—used four times in *Beowulf* in the a-verse (610, 1832, 1849, 2981), *hordes hyrde*—once in the a-verse (887), and others. Only once does the *Beowulf* poet use a member of this a-verse system in the b-verse; that is *folces hyrde* in line 2644. *Oretta* is used only twice in *Beowulf*, once in the a-verse (*yrre oretta*, line 1532) and *rof oretta* in line 2538, where it alliterates with *ronde* in the a-verse, *Aras ða bi ronde* 'arose then by his shield'. To follow that a-verse with *rices hyrde* would break the poet's usage of that essentially a-verse formula. One should also note that *ronde* and *rof* share more than an *r*; they also share the following *o*. The poet is thrifty here.

As for *ece drihten* in line 108, and *ylda waldend* in line 1661, the story is much the same, although it is true that the distribution of stresses as well as the alliteration (or assonance in this case) is the same in both phrases. All the vowels in the two formulas are short, however, except for the first *e* of *ece*, which is long. It would be well to see the context of the two lines in question before we move further.

Lines 106–8 and 1659–64

siþðan him scyppend   forscrifen hæfde
in Caines cynne.   þone cwealm gewræc
ece drihten,   þæs þe he Abel slog;
. . . .

---

31. Whallon, 1961 and 1969.

> Ne meahte ic æt hilde   mid Hruntinge
> wiht gewyrcan,   þeah þæt wæpen duge;
> ac me geuðe   <u>ylda waldend</u>
> þæt ic on wage geseah   wlitig hangian
> eald sweord eacen   (oftost wisode
> winigea leasum),   þæt ic ðy wæpne gebræd.

... after the Creator had condemned them. On Cain's kindred did <u>the everlasting Lord</u> avenge the murder, for that he had slain Abel.... I could do nothing in the fray with Hrunting, trusty though that weapon be. Howbeit <u>the Ruler of men</u> granted me that I might see hanging in beauty on the wall a huge old sword (often and often has He guided those who are deprived of friends), so that I drew that weapon.[32]

Once again the two phrases inhabit different verses, one the a, the other the b. *Ylda waldend* would have been impossible in the a-verse of line 108, and *ece drihten*, while just possible perhaps, would be really unhappy in the sea of *us*, which start at line 1660 and roll on through line 1664. Actually, the *Beowulf* poet uses *wuldres waldend* three times in the a-verse (lines 17 [*wealdend*], 183, and 1752). Whallon has chosen too hastily. If anything, he has strongly confirmed the thriftiness of the *Beowulf* poet.

Let us take another instance, namely, the line *Beowulf maþelode, / bearn Ecgþeowes*, 'Beowulf spoke, the son of Ecgtheow' with which we are already familiar, and examine it from the point of view of thrift.[33] Are there other ways in which the *Beowulf* poet says "Beowulf spoke" in one line with b-verse alliteration? *Beowulf maþelode   bearn Ecgþeowes* is found nine times in the poem. *Beowulf maþelode* with some other b-verse occurs three times, the first time in lines 405–6:

> Beowulf maðelode   (on him byrne scan,
> searonet seowed   smiþes orþancum):

Beowulf spoke, the corslet on him shone, the armour cunningly linked by the skill of the smith.

When Beowulf first appears before Hrothgar in Heorot, the poet presents him to Hrothgar, and to us, in his shining byrnie in line 405b, followed by a typical appositional line, which is also, by the way, a good example of the adding style of oral traditional verse making, of unperiodic enjambment, to

---

32. The translations from *Beowulf* in this section are from Clark Hall, 1950.
33. For more on "Beowulf spoke," see A. Lord, 1991, 147–69.

use Parry's terminology. In this case "Beowulf spoke" is limited to the a-verse, and a new idea begins in the second half of the line.

There are two instances, however, in which the poet uses an appositional clause in the b-verse referring to the verb rather than to Beowulf. The first is in the introduction to Beowulf's final boast before fighting with the dragon (lines 2510–12):

> Beowulf maðelode, beotwordum spræc
> niehstan siðe: "Ic geneðde fela
> guða on geogoðe; gyt ic wylle . . ."

Beowulf discoursed—spoke a last time with words of boasting:—"I ventured on many battles in my younger days; once more will I, . . ."

Here again is a classic example of unperiodic enjambment. Were we to stop at the end of line 2510, we might have thought that here was an instance in which the poet was not being thrifty. But in the b-verse he introduces an idea that continues into the a-verse of the following line. One simply cannot stop at the end of line 2510, because the significant and emotion-filled words, *niehstan siðe* 'for the last time' come in the following line. Besides, *beotwordum spræc* introduces a new idea, that of boasting, in the b-verse. The appositive is not a colorless repetition of the verb of speaking but a meaningful addition.

The second instance of an appositive to the verb *maþelode* in the a-verse is in lines 2724–25:

> Biowulf maþelode (he ofer benne spræc,
> wunde wælbleate; wisse he gearwe,

Beowulf discoursed: despite his hurt, his grievous deadly wound, he spoke,—he knew full well. . . .

The unperiodic enjambment after line 2724 is followed by an appositive to its b-verse in the a-verse of 2725, which emphasizes the tragic poignancy of the situation. It is noticeable that when the poet leaves the pattern of *Beowulf maþelode, / bearn Ecgþeowes*, it is for significant emphasis. It is also worth noting that this gesture does not mean that the poet is departing from the traditional, because the departing itself is traditional.

We can conclude, therefore, that the Beowulf poet shows evidence of thriftiness and, in so doing, indicates an affiliation with the oral traditional style of Homer.

CHAPTER 6

The Theme in Anglo-Saxon Poetry

From my point of view the work on the theme in Anglo-Saxon poetics got off on what I always thought was the wrong foot. What Francis Peabody Magoun, Jr., called a theme was not what either I or Parry meant by the term. His meaning, nevertheless, was to prevail and is found in Riedinger's *Speculum* article—not under that name, however, but as a "cluster" of motifs.[1] Yet could it be that that is as close to my theme as can be expected in Anglo-Saxon poetry? Let us examine the proposition, because those who have sought "theme" there seem to have been frustrated, as was, for example, Francelia Clark, who has investigated this subject thoroughly.[2]

I think of a theme as "a repeated passage with a fair amount of verbal repetition." The "cluster" of ideas in the theme of "the beasts of battle," for example, or that of "the hero on the beach," might correspond to "a repeated passage," especially so as one would expect that the cluster would tend naturally to contain verbal repetition. So far so good, it would seem, but the verbal repetition in these clusters, when it occurs, is of key words, rather than of full formulas or of lines. This may account for the feeling that there is a difference between my theme, as it is found in Slavic or in Homer, and elsewhere, and the clusters in Anglo-Saxon.[3] The best thing to do in such a case is to go directly to a text, to a specific theme, and see what we have from this point of view.

1. Riedinger, 1985; see Chapter 5, above, at n. 23.
2. F. Clark, 1981 and 1995.
3. In the context of Parry's investigations, the earliest discussion of theme, although not using that term, is to be found in his review of Walter Arend's *Die typischen Scenen bei Homer*, Parry, 1971, 404–7. The opening sentence of the review is useful: "There are certain actions which tend to recur in the *Iliad* and *Odyssey*, and which each time they do recur, are told again with many of the same details and many of the same words." That is actually an excellent definition of the theme.

138   The Singer Resumes the Tale

Magoun was the first to write in very specific terms of the theme in Anglo-Saxon. In his article "The Theme of the Beasts of Battle in Anglo-Saxon Poetry," he describes the theme of the title as "the mention of the wolf, eagle, and/or raven as beasts attendant on a scene of carnage. They seem to appear in nine poems on twelve occasions, where their presence serves to embellish a battle scene or a reference to warfare. It is an ornamental rather than an essential theme."[4] He noted the occurrence as once each in *Battle of Brunanburh*, *Beowulf*, *Exodus*, *Genesis A*, *Battle of Maldon*, and *The Wanderer* and twice each in *Elene*, *Finnsburh*, and *Judith*. Magoun quotes the relevant passages and then gives references to support the formular status of their components. His first three instances provide us with material for discussion, beginning with *Battle of Brunanburh* 60–65:

>   Letan him behindan   hræw bryttian
>   saluwigpadan,   þone sweartan hræfn,
>   hyrnednebban   and þane hasewanpadan,
>   earn æftan hwit,   æses brucan,
>   grædigne guðhafoc   and þæt græge deor,
>   wulf on wealde.   [Ne wearð wæl mare.][5]

Here is Magoun's translation:

> They left behind them the dark-coated one, black raven with horny bill, and the dark-coated eagle with white tail-feathers to share the carcasses, greedy war-hawk, and the gray beast, wolf of the forest to enjoy the carrion. [Never was there more slaughter.]

The second passage is from *Beowulf* (3024b–27):

>   ac se wonna hrefn
>   fus ofer fægum   fela reordian,
>   earne secgan   hu him æt æte speow
>   þenden he wið wulf   wæl reafode.[6]

Again, Magoun's translation:

> quite the contrary, the dark raven, poised over men fated to die [will] talk a lot,

---

4. Magoun, 1955b, 83; cf. Diamond, 1961.
5. For the sake of consistency Magoun's citations are replaced with those from the *ASPR*, a change that does not substantially affect his arguments. The lines from the *Battle of Brunanburh* are from Dobbie, 1942.
6. The text is from Dobbie, 1953.

tell the eagle how it did at its meal while it and the wolf face to face plundered the slain.

Sweartan hræfn 'black raven' and *wonna hrefn* 'dark raven' are varied for purposes of alliteration. The *earn* 'eagle' and the *wulf* 'wolf' are mentioned in both passages, as is *wæl* 'the slain', but there are no other verbal correspondences between the two quotations. The first passage from *Elene*, 27b–30a, adds further responses:

> Fyrdleoð agol
> wulf on wealde,   wælrune ne mað.
> Urigfeðera   earn sang ahof,
> laðum on laste,[7]

The wolf of the forest sang its war-song, made no secret of its hope for a corpse. The dewy-feathered eagle raised its song in pursuit of the foe.

The formula *wulf on wealde* 'wolf of the forest' was found in the *Brunanburh* passage as well. The *hrefn* is missing here, but *wæl* appears again.

The second instance of the theme in *Elene* (109b–13a) increases the elements repeated:

> Byman sungon
> hlude for hergum.   Hrefn weorces gefeah,
> urigfeðra,   earn sið beheold,
> wælhreowra wig.   Wulf sang ahof,
> holtes gehleða.

The trumpets sang out loudly in the presence of the troops; the raven rejoiced in the work; the dewy-feathered eagle watched the march; the warfare of men cruel in war; the wolf raised its song, co-spoiler of the grove.

The *hrefn* is there in this second example from *Elene*, and the *urigfeðra earn* 'dewy-feathered eagle' as well as *wæl*, but note that in this case we have *wulf sang ahof* 'the wolf raised its song' rather than *earn sang ahof* in the first quotation. These examples are, I believe, sufficient to bring to mind Magoun's material and to demonstrate that there are not only elements but also verbal correspondences among the several occurrences of the theme.

In the same year in which Magoun's article appeared, Stanley B. Green-

---

7. The text is from Krapp, 1932.

field's "The Formulaic Expression of the Theme of 'Exile' in Anglo-Saxon Poetry" carried further Magoun's idea, quoting thus from Magoun:

> "Certain verbal similarities among poems may in a sense represent borrowing from one poem to another, for traditional singers perforce learn from other singers. But one verbal similarity or even a number of verbal similarities in themselves prove nothing beyond suggesting that given singers have found the same formulas useful to express a certain idea in a similar measure of verse."[8]

Greenfield then distilled "four aspects or concomitants of the exile state": (1) status, (2) deprivation, (3) state of mind, and (4) movement in or into exile. He noted the characteristic verbal correspondences among nine examples of the theme from nine separate poems. These he divided into three groups that shared some key words. His first group, for example, included:

WLa 9–10a

Ða ic me feran gewat   folgað secan,
wineleas wræcca.[9]

Then it fell to me to go   to seek following,
a friendless outcast.

Gen 1049b–51a

     Him þa Cain gewat
gongan geomormod,   gode of gesyhðe,
wineleas wrecca.

     Then it fell to Cain
to go sorrowful,   from the sight of God,
a friendless outcast.

The correspondences are in kind, like those in Magoun's "beasts of battle" theme, namely, a formula consisting of *þa ic me* (*him Cain*) *gewat* plus a verb of going, *feran* or *gongan*, and the formula *wineleas wrecca*. The lines are then filled out in typical fashion with paratactic alliterative phrases *folgað secan* and *gode of gesyhðe*, and, in the case of *gongan*, with an epithet modifying *Cain* in the preceding hemistich. Brief as it may be, this, it seems to me, is either a viable theme in itself or part of a viable theme, that is, "a repeated

---

8. Magoun, 1953, 460–61; in Greenfield, 1955, 200.
9. Greenfield's citations are adjusted to correspond with *ASPR*.

passage with a certain degree of verbal correspondence." The passages are made up of two formulas, as I have indicated, adapted to the specific metrical and alliterative conditions by parataxis.

In terms of the "aspects or concomitants of the exile state" as set forth by Greenfield, "status" is represented in the two examples above by *wineleas wrecca*. "Deprivation" is well represented in the second group of examples in his article:

Edw 15–17
Wæs a bliðemod   bealuleas kyng,
þeah he lange ær,   lande bereafod,
wunode wræclastum   wide geond eorðan.

Was ever happy   the innocent king,
although long before,   bereft of land,
he lived as an outcast   widely over the earth.

XSt 119–21a
Forðon ic sceal hean and earm   hweorfan ðy widor,
wadan wræclastas,   wuldre benemed,
duguðum bedeled.

Forthwith despised and poor I shall   turn then more widely,
wander as an outcast,   bereft of glory,
separated from retainers.

Sea 14–16
hu ic earmcearig   iscealdne sæ
winter wunade   wræccan lastum,
winemægum bidroren.

how I full of sorrows   the ice-cold sea
in winter inhabited   as an outcast,
deprived of friends.

"Deprivation" is signaled by *lande bereafod, wuldre benemed, duguðum bedeled,* and *winemægum bidroren.* "State of mind" is indicated by *hean and earm,* and *earmcearig,* and "movement in or into exile" is expressed by *wunode wræclastum, wadan wræclastas,* and *winter wunade   wræccan lastum.* In all these cases in both Magoun and Greenfield we can note a more or less stable core of formulas adapted to context. I have found such clusters of formulas or lines in oral traditional lyric poetry as well as in oral traditional narrative poetry, as discussed in previous chapters. Perhaps these smaller groupings, or clusters, are the next highest structural unit above the formula. We must investigate further their relationship to the theme; for it may be, indeed, that these smaller units are themselves the themes we are seeking in Anglo-Saxon.

There is no need to follow in further detail Greenfield's excellent article. It is clear, I hope, from these examples that, in spite of such categories as "status" or "deprivation," one is dealing with obvious cases of verbal repetition. In short, in "the theme of the beasts of battle," and "the theme of exile" the repeated passages do exhibit a certain degree of verbal correspondence, be they from the same poem or not. These seem to be recognizable as themes of the oral traditional type, whether they are in an oral or a written text. Moreover, they are themes known to and used by several authors, a fact that strengthens their claim to be traditional.

In the next development in the study of the "theme" in Anglo-Saxon poetry, verbal correspondence practically disappears, and what remains is a cluster of repeated elements of a more general than specific sort. This phenomenon was present actually in Greenfield's theme of exile, inasmuch as such categories as "status," "deprivation," or "state of mind" are general rather than specific. Nevertheless, as we saw, he found groups of formulas used regularly to express the constituent items of the theme.

The first example of a theme in which verbal correspondence seems minimal is found in an article by David Crowne in which he introduced the theme of "the hero on the beach."[10] He isolated these items that constitute the theme: "(1) a hero on the beach, (2) with his retainers, (3) in the presence of a flashing light, (4) as a journey is completed or begun."

Crowne lists two passages in *Beowulf* as examples of the theme of "the hero on the beach" which seem to me to be only sections of a larger theme, namely, lines 1880b–99 and 1963–66. In reality, I believe, the full theme—or perhaps more properly, the full context of the theme of a journey that

---

10. Crowne, 1960, esp. 368. For additional articles on this theme in Old English, see G. Clark, 1965a and 1965b. Although Clark cites Crowne's article with others, I believe that his theme of "the traveler recognizes his goal" was developed independently. Its subthemes are (1) continuing or completed motion, (2) verb of seeing, (3) goal gleams (towering wall, cliff, etc.), and (4) sometimes an indication of time, frequently dawn. To these may be added such elements as "a reference to the path traversed" or even a description of the hero's setting out. It is the glistening or shining *goal* that differentiates this theme from the "hero on the beach," at the same time joining the two themes with its brightness. See the very useful review article Olsen, 1986, which contains a section (IV), "Themes and Type-Scenes," 577–88; sections I–III treat "oral and written," the "oral-formulaic theory," and the "formula." For a digest of Old English themes, together with full bibliography through 1987, see Foley, 1990, 331–33.

includes departure and arrival—is interrupted by a digression. The full theme began with departure at line 1888, which ended only at line 1904, to be followed by a description of the journey, lines 1905–13, and of the arrival (1914–31a), which is interrupted by a digression about a cruel queen which extends from line 1931b to line 1962, at which point the account of arrival is continued. It would be, therefore, a mistake to treat lines 1914–24 and lines 1963–66 as separate examples of the theme of "the hero on the beach"; together, actually, they form the arrival section of the theme of a journey.

This full theme in *Beowulf* 1888–1966, the theme of a journey, from departure to arrival, should be compared with the same theme in *Beowulf* 208–307a. This earlier example of the theme of a journey is also lengthened, not by a digression but by the inclusion in it of the scene of the encounter of Beowulf and his companions with the coast guard and their ritual exchange of words.

No two departures are likely to be exactly the same, nor any two arrivals. The departure of the Geats from southern Sweden is not like their departure, after their adventures, from Denmark. The circumstances are different; yet there are some common elements, even if they may not be in the same formulas, or even the same words, owing in part, at least, to the immediate demands of alliteration. Here is the departure from southern Sweden in lines 207b–16:[11]

```
                XVna sum
        sundwudu sohte;    secg wisade,
        lagucræftig mon,   landgemyrcu.
210     Fyrst forð gewat.  Flota wæs on yðum,
        bat under beorge.  Beornas gearwe
        on stefn stigon;   streamas wundon,
        sund wið sande;    secgas bæron
        on bearm nacan     beorhte frætwe,
215     guðsearo geatolic; guman ut scufon,
        weras on wilsið,   wudu bundenne.
```

With fourteen men he went to the ship; skilled in sea-craft, he himself led the way to the shore.

Time passed on; the bark was on the waves, the boat under the lee of the cliff. The warriors, well prepared, stepped on to the prow; streams of ocean made the sea eddy against the sand; men bore into the bosom of the ship bright armour, splendid

---

11. The text of *Beowulf* is from Dobbie, 1953. Here and henceforth, the modern English version is from Clark Hall, 1950, with some modifications.

war-gear; the heroes, the warriors on their eagerly-sought adventure, pushed off the vessel of braced timbers.

The departure of Beowulf and his companions from Denmark runs as follows in lines 1880b–1904:

```
1880        Him Beowulf þanan,
        guðrinc goldwlanc,      græsmoldan træd
        since hremig;       sægenga bad
        agendfrean,     se þe on ancre rad.
        Þa wæs on gange     gifu Hroðgares
1885    oft geæhtcd;        þæt wæs an cyning,
        æghwæs orleahtre,       oþþæt hine yldo benam
        mægenes wynnum,     se þe oft manegum scod.
            Cwom þa to flode    felamodigra,
        hægstealdra heap,       hringnet bæron,
1890    locene leoðosyrcan.     Landweard onfand
        eftsið eorla,       swa he ær dyde;
        no he mid hearme        of hliðes nosan
        gæs[tas] grette,        ac him togeanes rad,
        cwæð þæt wilcuman       Wedera leodum
1895    scaþan scirhame     to scipe foron.
        Þa wæs on sande     sægeap naca
        hladen herewædum,       hringedstefna,
        mearum ond maðmum;      mæst hlifade
        ofer Hroðgares      hordgestreonum.
1900    He þæm batwearde        bunden golde
        swurd gesealde,     þæt he syðþan wæs
        on meodubence       maþme þy weorþra,
        yrfelafe.   Gewat him on naca
        drefan deop wæter,      Dena land ofgeaf.
```

Then Beowulf, champion brave with gold, exulting in his treasure, trod the greensward; the ship, which rode at anchor, waiting its owning lord. Then, as they went, was Hrothgar's bountifulness often praised. That was an altogether blameless king, until old age deprived him of the joys of power,—old age which has oftentimes caused harm to many.

Thus to the water came the troop of most courageous liegemen:—ring-mail they wore, corslets interlocked. The land-guard perceived the nobles coming back, as he had done before; not with contumely did he hail the visitors from off the headland's brow, but rode up towards them and said that they, the bright-mailed warriors who went to their ships, would be welcomed on their return by the people of the Geats.

Then was the spacious sea-boat on the beach laden with battle-gear, the ship with curved prow was loaded with horses and valuables; the mast towered above Hrothgar's hoarded treasures.

To the boat-keeper Beowulf gave a sword bound round with gold, so that henceforth he was more honored on the mead-bench for that treasure,—that heirloom.

Then the ship went on, to ruffle the deep water; it left the Danish land.

This second passage is about three times the length of the first, and, though there are some elements in common, there are also some specific to each. For example, lines 1884–87, telling how Hrothgar's gifts were admired as the men marched, and commenting on him as a king, are applicable only to the circumstances at that particular moment in the poem. This is true also of the lines concerning the coast guard in this passage: in lines 1890b–95, the coast guard spots the returning Geats, rides to meet them, and, in indirect discourse, bids them welcome again for their continuing voyage back to Geatland; and in lines 1900–1903a, Beowulf presents the coast guard with a sword, and the poet comments on how proudly he boasted of it on the mead-benches. These three passages specific to the circumstances of this particular departure occupy twelve of the twenty-four and a half lines. There is no coast guard in the scene of departure of Beowulf and his companions from southern Sweden, although he does appear, of course, at the time of their arrival in Denmark. In the *Beowulf* context he seems to belong to arrivals—and to departures on the way back after an initial arrival.

One might add the first lines of the passage to those already labeled specific to the particular occurrence:

> Him Beowulf þanan
> guðrinc goldwlanc,   græsmoldan træd
> since hremig;

Then Beowulf, champion brave with gold, exulting in his treasure, trod the greensward;

These lines, however, serve the same purpose as the opening lines of the first departure, namely, to move the hero to the shore and ship:

> XVna sum
> sundwudu sohte;   secg wisade,
> lagucræftig mon,   landgemyrcu.

With fourteen men he went to the ship; skilled in sea-craft, he himself led the way to the shore.

One might consider, perhaps with greater reason, that lines 1898b–99 could also be specific to this occurrence:

>   mæst hlifade
>   ofer Hroðgares   hordgestreonum.
>
> . . . the mast towered above Hrothgar's hoarded treasures.

The opening lines of the first departure set in a distinctive way a pattern of key words and sounds which recurs in the passage. The line "sundwudu sohte;   secg wisade," with an alliteration perhaps suggested by the previous hemistich, "XVna sum," is picked up a little later in line 213, "sun wið sande;   secgas bæron," and the *b* of *bæron* seems to suggest the alliterative pattern for the following line, "on bearm nacan   beorhte frætwe."

One should add that the *wudu* of *sundwudu* at the beginning of the passage is also picked up at the end of the passage in lines 215b–16:

>   guman ut scufon,
>   weras on wilsið,   wudu bundenne.
>
> The heroes, the warriors on their eagerly-sought adventure, pushed off the vessel of braced timbers.

This is an excellent example of a kind of "responsion," noted earlier by Foley and others as typical of Anglo-Saxon, which is akin to the progression from line to line in South Slavic epic through the alliterative and assonantal patterns of key words.[12]

Something similar may be observed in the second departure, where, for example, the *sægenga* of *sægenga bad* of line 1882b is picked up by *sægeap naca* in line 1896b, which in turn leads to *gewat him on naca* in line 1903b. And the *hringedstefna* of line 1897b echoes *hringnet bæron* in line 1889b.

If lines 1880b–82a and 1884–87 are specific to Beowulf departing from Hrothgar, lines 1882b–83 belong to departure itself and are not specific:

>   sægenga bad
>   agendfrean,   se þe on ancre rad.
>
> The ship, which rode at anchor, waited its owning lord.

---

12. Foley, 1981b; A. Lord, 1960, 54–58.

We can find verbal correspondences between these lines and others, such as lines 301–3a in the first journey theme, in which the boat remains at anchor while Beowulf and his men go inland after their arrival. Note that these correspondences occur in the arrival section of the larger themes in this instance and not in the departure section.[13]

>   Gewiton him þa feran.   <u>Flota stille bad,</u>
>   seomode on sale   <u>sidfæþmed scip,</u>
>   <u>on ancre fæst.</u>

They set out then to journey on;—<u>the ship waited still, the spacious vessel</u> rode on the painter, <u>held by its anchor.</u>

The "subtheme," if I may use that term tentatively, of the boat at anchor is also found in the second journey passage, but in its arrival section, in lines 1917–19:

>   sælde to sande   <u>sidfæþme scip,</u>
>   <u>oncerbendum fæst,</u>   þy læs hym yþa ðrym
>   wudu wynsuman   forwrecan meahte.

He tethered to the beach <u>the roomy ship, held fast with anchor-ropes</u>, lest the waves' force should drive the joyous craft away from them.

Here, the ship is waiting for the return of the heroes from inland. It seems that this subtheme belongs most commonly—if the few instances we have can justify such a statement—to a ship being anchored to await the return of its owners or which, having been previously anchored, is waiting at anchor for them to come back. The "anchored ship" subtheme is found in *Elene* and *Christ*, in addition to the above instances in *Beowulf*, and we should see whether the context of those passages confirms the usage in *Beowulf*. The pertinent lines in *Elene* extend from line 225 to line 255 and cover a journey from departure to arrival. The departure reads as follows:

>   225 Ongan þa ofstlice   eorla mengu
>   to flote fysan.   Fearoðhengestas
>   ymb geofenes stæð   gearwe stodon,
>   sælde sæmearas,   sunde getenge.
>   Ða wæs orcnæwe   idese siðfæt,

---

13. See Foley, 1990, chap. 9, for a discussion of the sea journey.

```
230    siððan wæges helm       werode gesohte.
       Þær wlanc manig         æt Wendelsæ
       on stæðe stodon.        Stundum wræcon
       ofer mearcpaðu,         mægen æfter oðrum,
       ond þa gehlodon         hildesercum,
235    bordum ond ordum,       byrnwigendum,
       werum ond wifum,        wæghengestas.[14]
```

A throng of men, then, quickly began to hasten down to the sea. Ships, the horses of the ocean, lay ready along the seashore, sea-steeds moored afloat upon the sound. The woman's expedition had then become common knowledge, when she came with her company to the ocean: many a high-mettled man stood on the shore there by the Mediterranean Sea. At once along the coast-roads advanced one troop after another, and then loaded the ships, wavehorses, with battle-coats, with shields and with spears, with armoured soldiers, with men and with women.

One should observe in passing the abundance of responsions. Note, for example, *feorodhengestas* 'a throng of men' in line 226b and *wæghengestas* 'wavehorses, ships' in line 236; and *stæð* 'seashore' and *gearwe stodon* 'they stood ready' in line 227, which are picked up in line 232a in *on stæðe stodon* 'they stood on the shore.' Such responsions indicate that the poet thought of the passage as a unit bound by internal tensions.

It is fascinating to see that this departure section of the journey theme in *Elene* depicts the ships as moored to the shore and standing waiting in lines 226b–228, but they are not *on ancre fæst*. But when the journey, which covers lines 237–50a, is over, the arrival is described as follows:

```
250              Ceolas leton
       æt sæfearoðe,    sande bewrecene,
       ald yðhofu,      oncrum fæste
       on brime bidan   beorna geþinges,
       hwonne heo sio guðcwen    gumena þreate
255    ofer eastwegas   eft gesohte.
```

They left the ships at the sea-shore whipped with sand, the ancient vessels <u>secure at their anchors</u>, to wait <u>on the surf</u> the warrior's fate, until the warlike queen with her company of men returned to them along the roads from the east.

The anchors seem to belong to the arrival section of the journey theme in

---

14. The text of *Elene* is from Krapp, 1932; the translation is from Bradley, 1982.

Elene as well as in *Beowulf.* Let us look, then, at the passage in *Christ,* a really different kind of poem. Here is the pertinent passage in lines 858b–63:

> Þa us help bicwom,
> þæt us to hælo   hyþe gelædde,
> godes gæstsunu,   ond us giefe sealde
> þæt we oncnawan magun   ofer ceoles bord
> hwær we sælan sceolon   sundhengestas,
> ealde yðmearas,   <u>ancrum fæste</u>.[15]

Then help came to us, that piloted us to salvation in port, God's Spirit-Son, and granted us grace that we might know a place where we shall secure our steeds of the deeps, our old horses of the waves, <u>securely with anchors</u> over the ship's side.

This example too confirms the fact that our subtheme of the ship at anchor belongs in the arrival section of the journey theme. There is as well considerable verbal correspondence among the occurrences of the subtheme and its environment: *sundhengestas* 'ocean horses' and *yðmearas* 'horses of the waves' in *Christ* and *fearoðhengestas, sæmearas* 'sea horses', and *wæghengestas* in *Elene.* Surely we are dealing with themes and sections of themes and subthemes within the sections. Yes, there are oral traditional themes in Anglo-Saxon poetry. Moreover, they are very similar to oral traditional themes in other poetries, namely, repeated passages with a certain degree of verbal correspondence between occurrences.

It is worthwhile to continue further with the larger theme of the journey, with its sections on departure, travel, and arrival. We must return, therefore, to the departure section of the two journey themes in *Beowulf* with which we began. The departure from southern Sweden is the simpler of the two. We saw that it differed from the departure from Denmark in respect to the ship. In the latter, the ship was at anchor awaiting the return of the Geats from their adventures at Hrothgar's court. In the former, the ship was in the water under the cliff (lines 210b–11a):

> Flota wæs on yðum,
> bat under beorge.

The bark was on the waves, the boat under the lee of the cliff.

The next action is embarkation of men and equipment. In the first departure this is accomplished in lines 211b–15a:

---

15. The text of *Christ* is from Krapp and Dobbie, 1936; the translation is from Bradley, 1982.

> Beornas gearwe
> on stefn stigon;   streamas wundon,
> sund wið sande;   secgas bæron
> on bearm nacan   beorhte frætwe,
> guðsearo geatolic;

The warriors, well prepared, stepped on to the prow; streams of ocean made the sea eddy against the sand; men bore into the bosom of the ship bright armour, splendid war-gear;

This almost stark description, broken only by the paratactic *guðsearo geatolic*, which is needed to alliterate with and to introduce *guman ut scufon* 'the men shoved off', is truly ornamented by the realistic detail of the sea surging against the beach as the men entered the boat.

The departure from Denmark, leaving aside the specific elements I enumerated earlier, especially those dealing with the coast guard, tells, as we have seen, of Beowulf proceeding to the shore after leaving Hrothgar and mentions the boat waiting for its captain and riding at anchor (lines 1882b–83):

> sægenga bad
> agendfrean,   se þe on ancre rad.

The ship, which rode at anchor, waited its owning lord.

After commenting on Hrothgar's gifts and on the man himself, the poet continues (lines 1888–90a):

> Cwom þa to flode   felamodigra,
> hægstealdra heap; hringnet bæron,
> locene leoðosyrcan.

Thus to the water came the troop of most courageous liegemen:—ring-mail they wore, corslets interlocked.

After five and a half lines devoted to the coast guard, the action continues with the loading of the ship (lines 1896–999):

> Þa wæs on sande   sægeap naca
> hladen herewædum,   hringedstefna,
> mearum ond maðmum; mæst hlifade
> ofer Hroðgares   hordgestreonum.

Then was the spacious sea-boat on the beach laden with battle-gear, the ship with curved prow was loaded with horses and valuables; the mast towered above Hrothgar's hoarded treasures.

There is not much verbal correspondence between these parts of the departure section, nor indeed between the departure sections themselves of our two examples of the journey theme in *Beowulf*. This is not very surprising, of course, because no treasure was loaded on the ship in southern Sweden, only armor, which the men are wearing in the second departure; and there the emphasis, as was to be expected, is on the treasure given Beowulf by Hrothgar. Moreover, the coast guard plays a large role in the second departure but is not present in the first. We did discover that a subtheme of the second departure, that of the ship riding at anchor, was to be found in arrival scenes as well. Let us turn now, then, to the arrival sections of the journey theme. The arrival of Beowulf and his companions in Denmark is notable for their encounter with the coast guard, who appears as soon as they have secured their ship. Here is their landing (lines 224b–28):

        Þanon up hraðe
  Wedera leode on wang stigon,
  sæwudu sældon (syrcan hrysedon,
  guðgewædo), gode þancedon
  þæs þe him yþlade eaðe wurdon.

After that the people of the Geats went quickly up on to dry land; they made fast the ship; their coats of mail, their armour, rang; they thanked God that for them the sea-paths had been easy.

The coast guard is now introduced and the famous interchange between him and Beowulf, ending with the march to Heorot, ensues. This elaborate coast guard episode contrasts with the arrival home of Beowulf and his men. They too are met by a coast guard (lines 1912b–19):

      Ceol up geþrang
  lyftgeswenced, on lande stod.
  Hraþe wæs æt holme hyðweard geara,
  se þe ær lange tid leofra manna
  fus æt faroðe feor wlatode;
  sælde to sande sidfæþme scip,
  oncerbendum fæst, þy læs hym yþe ðrym
  wudu wynsuman forwrecan meahte.

The keel pressed forward, driven by the wind; it stood upon the land. The havenward was quickly ready at the water's edge, he who before had long time looked out eagerly far over the sea for the dear men. He tethered to the beach the roomy ship, held fast with anchor-ropes, lest the waves' force should drive the joyous craft away from them.

There is some verbal correspondence between the arrivals up to this point, in spite of the differences of the coast guards. The word *hraþe* 'quickly' appears in both passages, but applied to different persons. Most noticeable is the securing of the ship. It is done in one hemistich in the first paragraph—*sæwudu sældon*—and in a line and a half in the second: "sælde to sande sidfæþme scip / oncerbendum fæst." Only the verb (*sælde / sældon* 'fastened') is common to both passages. I have discussed the subtheme of the ship at anchor above; now the seafarers set out for inland.

It is on this point that Crowne's work focuses most intensely, eventually leading far away from beaches and even from human actors, as when he equates the sea beasts at banquet in the Breca episode with the hero's companions, who would otherwise be missing from the scene. But in the early part of his article he treats themes, or subthemes, in the sense in which I also understand them, namely, as repeated passages with some verbal correspondence.

For example, in some of the instances given by Crowne there is actually a fair degree of verbal correspondence. The simplest form of "the hero on the beach" is found when Beowulf and his men arrive in southern Sweden on their return from Denmark in lines 1963–66. This is the second part of the arrival section of the second journey theme, as discussed above.

> Gewat him ða se hearda   mid his hondscole
> sylf æfter sande   sæwong tredan,
> wide waroðas.   Woruldcandel scan,
> sigel suðan fus.   Hi sið drugon, . . .

Then the strong one went forth himself and his companions, by the sand, treading the sea-beaches, the broad foreshores. The world's lamp shone, the sun hastening from the south;—they passed along their way, . . .

A more elaborate form is found in *Andreas* 235–47, in which Andreas starts out his journey to Mermedonia. The account begins:

> 235 Gewat him þa on uhtan   mid ærdæge
> ofer sandhleoðu   to sæs faruðe,

The Theme in Anglo-Saxon Poetry 153

	þriste on geþance,	ond his þegnas mid,
	gangan on greote.	Garsecg hlynede,
	beoton brimstreamas.	Se beorn wæs on hyhte,
240	syðþan he on waruðe	widfæðme scip
	modig gemette.	Þa com morgentorht
	beacna beorhtost	ofer breomo sneowan,
	halig of heolstre.	Heofoncandel blac
	ofer lagoflodas.	He ðær lidweardas,
245	þrymlice þry	þegnas gemette,
	modiglice menn,	on merebate
	sittan siðfrome,	swylce hie ofer sæ comon.[16]

So in the dawning with the first light of day he went over the sand-dunes to the edge of the sea, bold in thought, and his thanes with him, marching on the shingle. The ocean was roaring, the waters of the deep were pounding. The intrepid man was delighted when he found on the shore a broad-beamed ship. Just then the sun, brightest of beacons, came in its morning radiance, a holy thing, hastening out of the darkness across the deep; heaven's candle shone over the waters of the ocean. There on the ship he found the crewmen, three splendid thanes, valiant men, sitting ready for a voyage, as though they had come across the sea.

Both passages begin with *gewat him þa*, a common opening gambit for saying "Then he began to...."; both indicate the beach, using the word *sand*: *sylf æfter sande* and *ofer sandhleoðu*; and both speak of his companions, *mid his hondscole* and *ond his þegnas mid*. The difference between *hondscole* 'companions' and *þegnas* 'thanes' is dictated by the alliteration established by the first half of each line. In the selection from *Andreas*, still another word for beach is used in *gangan on greote* 'advance on the sand', employing an alliteration that seems to be governed by the verb *gangan*. The word *sæ* also is used in both passages, as *sæwong tredan* in *Beowulf* 1964 and as *to sæs faruðe* in *Andreas* 236. *Waroðe* 'shore' too is found in the *Beowulf* passage in *wide waroðas* and in line 240 in the quotation from *Andreas* in *syðþan he on waruðe*. And finally, the *woroldcandel scan* 'world's lamp shone' of the *Beowulf* passage above has its counterpart in *heofoncandel blac* 'heaven's candle shone' in line 243 from *Andreas*. In short, there is considerable verbal correspondence between those two passages. It has been suggested that the *Andreas* poet modeled his story and hero after *Beowulf*.[17] If this is true, the verbal similarities noted here are

---

16. The text of *Andreas* is from Krapp, 1932; the translation is from Bradley, 1982.

17. [See, e.g., Brooks, 1961, xxii–xxvi. This reference is owed to the kindness of Daniel Donoghue. For a discussion of the arguments about source for *Andreas* and the conclusion that *Andreas* is a traditional poem, see Foley, 1995, forthcoming, chap. 6.]

not surprising. The words repeated in one form or another are *gewat him þa, sand, mid his, sæ, waroðe*, and *-candel*, representing six of the eight hemistichs of *Beowulf* 1963–66. Only line 1966 of the *Beowulf* quotation seems to have no verbal correspondence that I have noted in the passage from *Andreas*.

Moreover, *sand* and *sæ* alliterate in a single line in both passages: "sylf æfter sande   sæwong tredan" and "ofer sandhleoðu   to sæs faruðe." When the two concepts of sand and sea are repeated in *Andreas* 238, the alliteration, governed now by *gangan*, brings forth two other words for sand and sea: "gangan on greote.   Garsecg hlynede."

Strangely enough, there is less correspondence between *Beowulf* 301–7, the second part of the arrival section of the first journey theme, and *Beowulf* 1963–66, given above, the second part of the arrival section of the second journey theme; *Beowulf* 301 begins with *gewiton him þa feran*; the words *sand, sæ, waroðe*, and *woroldcandel*, or equivalents, do not appear. But this passage does have correspondences with *Andreas* 235–37, as cited above. Here are lines 301–7a of *Beowulf*:

>   Gewiton him þa feran.   Flota stille bad,
>   seomode on sale   sidfæþmed scip,
>   on ancre fæst.   Eoforlic scionon
>   ofer hleorberan   gehroden golde,
>   fah ond fyrheard;   ferhwearde heold
>   guþmod grimmon.   Guman onetton,
>   sigon ætsomne, . . .

They set out then to journey on;—the ship remained still, the spacious vessel rode on the painter, held by its anchor. Above the cheek-guards shone the boar-images, covered with gold, gleaming and tempered. The fierce-hearted boar held guard over the warlike men. The warriors hastened; they went together, . . .

Sidfæþmed scip 'spacious ship' corresponds to *widfæðme scip* 'wide ship' in *Andreas*. There are other correspondences, too. For example,

>   fah ond fyrheard   ferhwearde heold
>   guþmod grimmon.   Guman onetton,

The fierce-hearted boar held guard over the warlike men. The warriors hastened;

reminds one of the following from *Andreas*:

>   ofer lagoflodas.   He ðær lidweardas
>   þrymlice þry   þegnas gemette,

> ... over the waters of ocean. There on the ship he found the crewmen, three splendid thanes,

It would seem that the kenning [metaphorical compound word] *ferhwearde* 'life-protector' governs the alliteration of the first hemistich, "fah ond fyrheard." The same is probably true also in the case of *lidweardas* 'ship-protector', which would govern the alliteration of *ofer lagoflodas* in the first hemistich. The following lines in both passages are governed by alliteration around the word for man: in *Beowulf* the word is *guman*, and it calls forth "guþmod grimmon"; in *Andreas* it is *þegnas*, which calls forth "þrymlice þry"—although in this instance, it might well be that the specialized *þry* 'three' is the governing word, in which case it is *þry* that calls forth both *þrymlice* 'splendid' and *þegnas*.

These passages include the "flashing light" element of the theme, which is thought by many to be the most significant and typical item in it.[18]

One of the reasons there is little verbal correspondence in some of the examples given is that in a few cases the elements are more general, let us say, than the raven, the eagle, and the wolf in the theme of "the beasts of battle." Another reason comes from the fact that as Crowne became more engrossed in the theme of "the hero on the beach," he moved further and further away from its literal elements. Although he kept the place as a beach, eventually even it gave way to include a doorway, or any liminal situation. Sometimes the hero was mentioned, sometimes not, and the companions became ever more variable. Finally the two merged into "the comitatus relationship," which could be manifested in innumerable ways.

The element of "a flashing light" has also been extended from "the sun," indicating the time of day, which could be expressed as "woruldcandel scan" in *Beowulf* 1965b, or "Leoht eastan com / beorht beacen godes" in *Beowulf* 569b–70a, to include anything shining, such as armor or a battle standard. Gradually the theme has been almost destroyed by overextension. The possibility for verbal correspondence was eliminated. The last element, "as a journey is completed or begun," is more stable and even has some characteristic verbal expressions, such as *fus forðwegas* 'ready for the journey' in *Exodus* 248a[19] and *fuse to farenne* 'ready to depart' in *Beowulf* 1805a.

Crowne finally rephrased the theme as containing "(1) a beach, (2) the *comitatus* relationship, (3) a bright light, and (4) a voyage." He has eliminated the hero and his companions in favor of their relationship to one another. The place was somewhat more stable verbally for a while longer with

---

18. See Renoir, 1988, 97, 112–30.
19. Krapp, 1931.

Crowne, as was the voyage. It may be that such a pattern exists, but I wonder if we should call it a "theme," thus confusing it with passages that are held together as discernible verbal units having a cohesive sense of textuality. The latter is another way of saying repeated passages with a certain degree of verbal correspondence, which are what I call themes. In the foregoing I have demonstrated that such passages do occur, but they are not long.

No scholar seems to have challenged Crowne's extension of the idea of the hero's companions to include the sea beasts in the Breca episode in *Beowulf*, nor his substitution of shining armor for the sun as a flashing light, nor Renoir's allowing of a door in the *Nibelungenlied* as a replacement for the beach.[20] Fry supported Renoir by invoking a door in *Finnsburh Fragment* in order to reduce the gap in time between *Beowulf* and the *Nibelungenlied* during which the theme of "the hero on the beach" had to be maintained in Germanic tradition.[21]

Fry soon turned his attention to *Judith* and to the "heroine on the beach."[22] Besides adding an example from *Judith* to those already listed on page 178 of his article, Fry, who was always interested in the aesthetics of formulaic composition (he was soon to drop the term *oral*, partly on the argument that orality would not change aesthetics involved), wrote, "The uses and resultant effects of the theme in *Judith* are threefold, for association, structure, and unity."[23] He quoted Crowne: "The real mnemonic utility of the theme is in the learning of songs by singers in the later stages of their training and in the creation of new songs" and added that "themes prove to be a mnemonic device as much for the audience as for the poet; they provide the audience with a supply of associations, which are used by the poet to enrich the narrative" (181). The principle involved here is an important one, although I would prefer to consider the theme as a "compositional" rather than as a "mnemonic" device. Earlier in the same article Fry pointed out very correctly that the thirteen passages containing the theme of "the hero on the beach" should be considered "as a pool of variants, whose common denominator is their narrative content, none of which is a norm from which the others represent departures" (179).

Another of Fry's articles marks an important step in the study of themes because it presents his definitions of both *theme* and *type-scene*, definitions that have been followed by later scholars more or less exactly. The article

20. Renoir, 1964.
21. Fry, 1966.
22. Fry, 1967a.
23. Ibid., 181.

begins with a review of the various meanings given to "theme," "motif," and "type-scene" and ends with the definitions, which run as follows:

> A type-scene in Old English formulaic poetry may be defined . . . as *a recurring stereotyped presentation of conventional details used to describe a certain narrative event, requiring neither verbatim repetition nor a specific formula content*; and a theme may be defined as *a recurring concatenation of details and ideas, not restricted to a specific event, verbatim repetition, or certain formulas, which forms an underlying structure for an action or description.*[24]

I must confess that these definitions are not crystal clear in themselves, nor is it easy to differentiate between them. Nevertheless, one can see that according to Fry, neither verbatim repetition nor any given formula content is to be expected in either a theme or a type-scene.[25] It is to these arguments that I address myself, because it is in respect to them that these two definitions depart most markedly from my own concept of a "theme." I have thought that a certain degree of verbal correspondence was needed to differentiate between a repeated action or description in oral traditional and in written nontraditional literature. That is to say, in a written nontraditional literary work there may be repeated battles, or repeated councils, or assemblies, or repeated descriptions of the hero, but the writer makes a point of varying the actions or descriptions. This introduction of variety does not exist to the same degree in oral traditional literature. Put simply, the oral traditional poet has learned how to describe a hero or a horse or how to convene an assembly and report speeches. Although he does not always use the same words, or formulas, if you will, there is a tendency to a fair degree of verbal repetition because he does not strive for variety for its own sake. That he does not value variety in itself does not mean that he may not vary nor that his variations may not be meaningful. He may make meaningful differences between several renderings of the same oral traditional theme.

An illustration of variation within a cohesive structure is provided by two

---

24. Fry, 1968b, 53; see also Fry, 1969 and 1972.
25. See Foley, 1976, who argues that a theme in Old English poetry may be held together by the recurrence of "stave-roots," "the roots of alliterating words, although non-alliterating words may at times be included" (221). One occurs near the beginning ("initializing") and one near the end ("termination") of the theme, but there are also several between these boundaries. By this means, Foley provides the theme with a kind of verbal correspondence, although his statement that this phenomenon is close to the theme in Homer and in South Slavic epic may be questioned. [Note that both in his 1976 article (231) and in Foley, 1990, Foley points out that each poetry, Greek, Old English, and South Slavic has its own way of constituting verbal correspondence and that each was tradition-dependent; see chap. 1 and passim.]

versions of the theme of an overnight visit made by Meho and Osman in Avdo Međedović's epic "The Wedding of Smailagić Meho." For a discussion of the two versions of this theme, see Chapter 9. We have similar "themes" in Anglo-Saxon, although of a somewhat different nature, to be sure. We have seen examples in Magoun's theme of "the beasts of battle," and in "the boat at anchor," which I isolated earlier in this chapter, as well as the theme of "the world's candle," the last two from Crowne's "the hero on the beach." They have a degree of verbal correspondence and a sense of textuality and are not abstractions. They are larger than formulas, although made up of formulas. In the references to arms and armor—the most common "alternative" to "the world's candle" in the "flashing light" category—one must allow for the use of several words for the same object, as, for example, words for "sword," such as *sweord*, *secg*, *bill*, and *mece*. A sword is often found associated with other weapons or pieces of armor. Let us see whether we have any cohesive "more or less stable core" for the expression of this group of related ideas.

In my analysis of introductions to direct discourse in *Beowulf*, *Elene*, and *Andreas*,[26] I have found in those passages of two and a half or more lines something different from a cluster of formulas, something that I have by chance designated as a "cluster of lexical units," in short, words rather than groups of words. A repeated subject is bound to contain a number of the same words. It would be normal, for example, for a description of a sea voyage to contain words for ship, for sea, or water, and the like.

In Beowulf's fateful journey, weapons and armor are first mentioned when he and his men embark from southern Sweden (lines 213b–15a):

         secgas bæron
    on bearm nacan beorhte frætwe,
    guðsearo geatolic.

Men bore into the bosom of the ship bright treasures, splendid war-gear.

Here our key words are *frætwe* and *guðsearo*, both general terms, not referring to specific armor or weapons. *Beorhte frætwe* occurs once in *Daniel*, once in *Christ*, and once in *Beowulf*. The passage from *Daniel* (lines 707b–10a) reads:

         ða hie Iudea
    blæd forbræcon billa ecgum,

---

26. A. Lord, 1991, 147–69.

and þurh hleoðorcyme, herige genamon
beorhte frætwe.

. . . when they destroyed the glory of the Jews with their swords' edges and in the process of their clamorous invasion seized the gleaming treasure in battle.²⁷

Two words for specific weapons or specific pieces of armor are to be seen in this passage, *billa ecgum* 'with the edges of the sword'; *ecg* is also used for "weapon" or "sword." The passage in *Christ* (lines 1634–37a) reads:

Þonne þa gecorenan   fore Crist berað
beorhte frætwe.   Hyra blæd leofað
æt domdæge,   agan dream mid gode
liþes lifs,

Then the elect will bring their bright treasures before Christ. Their splendour will survive at the day of judgment; they will possess the joy of a gentle life with God,

A word to "carry" appears in all three passages, *bæron*, *genamon*, and *berað*; and *blæd* 'glory' is found in the last two. Two "sword" words occur in the *Daniel* passage, *bill* and *ecg*.

In *Beowulf* when the Geats land in Denmark, a few lines after our beginning passage wih *frætwe* and *guðsearo*, their armor is again referred to in two successive sections of text (lines 224b–28 and 229–32a):

           [Þanon up hraðe
225 Wedera leode   on wang stigon,
     sæwudu sældon]   (syrcan hrysedon,
     guðgewædo),   [gode þancedon
     þæs þe him yþlade eaðe wurdon].
         Þa of wealle geseah   weard Scildinga,
230 se þe holmclifu   healdan scolde,
     beran ofer bolcan beorhte randas,
     fyrdsearu fuslicu;

After that the people of the Geats went quickly up on to dry land; they made fast the ship; their coats of mail, their armour, rang; they thanked God that for them the sea-paths had been easy.

Then from the rampart the watchman of the Scyldings, who had to guard the sea-cliffs, saw them lift bright shields and trim war-harness over the gangway;

27. The text of *Daniel* is from Krapp, 1931; the translation is from Bradley, 1982.

160   The Singer Resumes the Tale

Here we have corslets (*syrcan*) and shields (*randas*), each with an appositive of general significance, *guðgewædo* 'war-dress' and *fyrdsearu* 'accoutrements', needed for making lines.

Syrcan occurs frequently in *Beowulf*.[28] In line 334 it follows almost immediately after a *guðsearo* passage (329). Here are lines 333–36a:

> "Hwanon ferigeað ge   fætte scyldas,
> græge syrcan,   ond grimhelmas,
> heresceafta heap?   Ic eom Hroðgares
> ar ond ombiht."

"Whence have ye brought these plated shields, these hauberks, grey and visored helmets, this pile of battle-shafts? I am Hrothgar's herald and officer."

A word for "bring," *ferigeað*, a word for "shields," *scyldas*, a word for "helmets," *grimhelmas*, and a word for "spears," *heresceafta*, make up this "armor and arsenal theme."

Syrcan also occurs in line 1111 in the Finn episode, lines 1108b–13a:

>   Herescyldinga
> betst beadorinca   wæs on bæl gearu.
> Æt þæm ade wæs   eþgesyne
> swatfah syrce,   swyn ealgylden,
> eofer irenheard,   æþeling manig
> wundum awyrded.

The best of the War-Scyldings, the battle-heroes, was ready on the funeral pyre. At the pyre the blood-stained corslet, the swine-image all-golden, the boar hard as iron, and many a noble killed by wounds, were visible to all.

"Shield," in *Herescyldingas* (note *Scildinga* in line 229b above); corslet, *syrce*; and "helmet," metaphorically in *swyn* correspond to part of the combination in lines 333–36a. Only the spears are missing; and there is no word for "bringing," inasmuch as the corpses are inert on the ground or pyre.

Guðgewædo in line 227a above, in apposition with *syrcan*, is also often found in *Beowulf*. It is used in five other lines, the first two of which (lines 2617 and 2623) lead us to a rich lode of weapons and armor beginning in line

---

28. [Daniel Donoghue has brought to my attention the fact that *syrcan* appears in other Old English works, and within *Beowulf* it appears on six occasions in compounds: *beadusercean* 2755, *heresyrcan* 1511, *hiorosercean* 2539, *leoðosyrcan* 1505 and 1890, and *licsyrce* 550. Interestingly, in three of these a form of the verb *beran* appears (2755, 2539, 1890).]

2609 and extending through line 2625a. In this passage, it will be noted, *fyrdsearo* also appears, the only other time it is found. These two passages, lines 224b–32a and 2609–25a, have many verbal correspondences. Here are lines 2609–25a, which cover part of the account of Wiglaf's background:

```
         Ne mihte ða forhabban;      hond rond gefeng,
2610     geolwe linde,      gomel swyrd geteah,
         þæt wæs mid eldum      Eanmundes laf,
         suna Ohteres.      Þam æt sæcce wearð,
         wrǣcca[n] wineleasum,      Weohstan bana
         meces ecgum,      ond his magum ætbær
2615     brunfagne helm,      hringde byrnan,
         eald sweord etonisc;      þæt him Onela forgeaf,
         his gædelinges      guðgewædu,
         fyrdsearo fuslic,      no ymbe ða fæhðe spræc,
         þeah ðe he his broðor bearn      abredwade.
2620     He frætwe geheold      fela missera,
         bill ond byrnan,      oððæt his byre mihte
         eorlscipe efnan      swa his ærfæder;
         geaf him ða mid Geatum      guðgewæda
         æghwæs unrim,      þa he of ealdre gewat,
2625     frod on forðweg.
```

And then he could not forbear; his hand seized the disc, the yellow linden-shield, and he drew his ancient sword. This last was known among men as the legacy of Eanmund, the son of Ohthere, of whom, when a friendless exile, Weohstan was slayer in fight by edge of sword, and bore off to his kinsmen the burnished helmet, the ring-mail corslet and the ancient giant-made sword which Onela had given him—his kinsman's war-harness, a battle-outfit ready to his hand. Onela did not speak about the feud, although Weohstan had laid low his brother's son. He kept these treasures—sword and corslet—many years, until his son could compass doughty deeds, as his old father had done. Then when he passed away from life, full of years, on his journey hence, he gave to him among the Geats a countless number of habiliments of war of every kind.

Here are two words for "shield," *rond* and *linde*; three words for "sword" (one in two spellings), *swyrd*, *mece*, *sweord*, and *bill*; one word for "helmet," *helm*; and one word for "corslet," *byrnan*, used twice.

We are clearly defining a "theme," with sufficient verbal and ideational correspondence to assure a sense of textuality. The verbal core, or cluster of lexical units, with such variations of alliteration and metrics as are needed to make lines, is adapted to the ideas and action of the narrative.

Up to the point in the poem where Beowulf and his men enter Heorot and Beowulf first addresses Hrothgar, the word *sword* has not yet appeared. *Sweord* is actually, however, a frequent word in *Beowulf*; it is used twenty-two times in that form alone. It is combined with "shield" in the first passage in the poem in which it occurs, namely, in Beowulf's first speech to Hrothgar, in which he says that he will scorn sword and shield and rely on his grip (lines 433–40a):

>   "Hæbbe ic eac geahsod   þæt se æglæca
>   for his wonhydum   wæpna ne recceð.
> 435   Ic þæt þonne forhicge   (swa me Higelac sie,
>   min mondrihten,   modes bliðe),
>   þæt ic sweord bere   oþðe sidne scyld,
>   geolorand to guþe,   ac ic mid grape sceal
>   fon wið feonde   ond ymb feorh sacan,
> 440   lað wið laþum."

"Moreover, I have learnt that in his rashness the monster recks not of weapons. Hence—so that Hygelac, my prince, may be glad at heart on my account, I renounce that I should bear a sword, or ample shield, yellow buckler to the battle; but with the fiend I will close with grip of hand, and contend for our lives, foe against foe."

The structure in this passage is worth remarking on, typical as it is of the appositive style. *Scyld* is repeated in the rare *geolorand*, which anticipates the alliteration with the key word *grape* 'grip' in the b-verse. *Grape* is in turn reiterated in *fon* 'grasp,' and it leads into the alliterating key word *feorh* 'life'. We might note the common, and quite natural, use of the verb *beran* with *sweord*.

There is a fine "morning light" passage (lines 569b–72a) that I am pleased to insert here in the midst of many swords:

>   Leoht eastan com,
>   beorht beacen godes;   brimu swaþredon,
>   þæt ic sænæssas   geseon mihte,
>   windige weallas.

The sun, bright beacon of God, came from the east; the waters grew calm, so that I could descry sea-headlands, wind-swept cliffs.

>   574–75a
>   Hwæþere me gesælde   þæt ic mid sweorde ofsloh
>   niceras nigene.

The Theme in Anglo-Saxon Poetry 163

Yet it was granted me to slay nine sea-monsters with my <u>sword</u>!

> 581b–86a
> No ic wiht fram þe
> swylcra searoniða   secgan hyrde,
> <u>billa</u> brogan.   Breca næfre git
> æt heaðolace,   ne gehwæþer incer,
> swa deorlice   dæd gefremede
> fagum <u>sweordum</u>.

I have never at all heard such contests, such peril of <u>swords</u> related about thee. Never yet did Breca at the battle-play nor either of you, perform so bold a deed with shining <u>swords</u>.

J. Bryan Hainsworth noted that there are clusters of formulas in the Homeric poems and surmised that, as in everyday speech, when a phrase "surfaced" once into the mind of the singer, he kept using it for a while but dropped it eventually.[29] I wonder if we have something similar here?

In the description of Beowulf's fight with Grendel, familiar words for weapons emerge again (lines 801–5a):

> sawle secan,   þone synscaðan
> ænig ofer eorþan   <u>irenna cyst</u>,
> <u>guðbilla</u> nan,   gretan nolde,
> ac he <u>sigewæpnum</u>   forsworen hæfde,
> <u>ecga</u> gehwylcre.

. . . and to hunt out his life, that no <u>war-bill</u> on earth, not the <u>best of iron swords</u>, could touch the cursed foe, for that he used enchantment against <u>conquering weapons</u>, every sort of <u>blade</u>.

When the poet used *irena cyst* before, in line 673 in the doffing scene, it was in apposition with *sweord* in the preceding line. Note that in this passage, *guðbilla* is in apposition with *irenna cyst* in the preceding line. Alliteration plays a role in the choice of *guðbilla*, to go with *gretan* 'touch, harm' in the second half of the line. In line 802, *ænig ofer eorþan* 'any over the earth' calls for assonance in the b-verse and hence *irenna cyst*. Within the limits of alliteration, assonance, and metrics this passage is "thrifty."

In line 1020 begins a long armor and weapon passage as the poet describes the giving of gifts to Beowulf:

29. Hainsworth, 1976.

1020	Forgeaf þa Beowulfe	bearn Healfdenes
	segen gyldenne	sigores to leane,
	hroden hildecumbor,	helm ond byrnan;
	mære maðþumsweord	manige gesawon
	beforan beorn beran.	Beowulf geþah
1025	ful on flette;	no he þære feohgyfte
	for sceotendum	scamigan ðorfte.
	Ne gefrægn ic freondlicor	feower madmas
	golde gegyrede	gummanna fela
	in ealobence	oðrum gesellan.
1030	Ymb þæs helmes hrof	heafodbeorge
	wirum bewunden	walu utan heold,
	þæt him fela laf	frecne ne meahton
	scurheard sceþðan,	þonne scyldfreca
	ongean gramum	gangan scolde.
1035	Heht ða eorla hleo	eahta mearas
	fætedhleore	on flet teon,
	in under eoderas.	Þara anum stod
	sadol searwum fah,	since gewurþad;
	þæt wæs hildesetl	heahcyninges,
1040	ðonne sweorda gelac	sunu Healfdenes
	efnan wolde.	Næfre on ore læg
	widcuþes wig,	ðonne walu feollon.
	Ond ða Beowulfe	bega gehwæþres
	eodor Ingwina	onweald geteah,
1045	wicga ond wæpna,	het hine wel brucan.

Then the son of Healfdene bestowed on Beowulf as the meed of victory a gilded ensign, a decorated battle-banner, a helmet and a corslet; many saw the jewelled sword of honour borne before the hero. Beowulf drank of the cup in the hall; no need had he to be ashamed of the costly gift before the warriors. Not many men have I known to give more heartily four such treasures, decked with gold, to others on the ale-bench. [A crest around the crown of the helmet, wound about with wires, afforded head-protection from outside], that the sword wrought by files, hard in the storm of battle, might not sorely injure it, when the shielded warrior must go forth against foes. Then the protector of nobles bade eight horses with gold-plated bridles, be brought into the hall, within the building. On one of them was placed a saddle cunningly inlaid, adorned with treasure,—that was the war-seat of the mighty king, when Healfdene's son wished to take part in the play of swords. Never did courage fail the far-famed chieftain at the front, when men were falling dead. And then the lord of Ing's descendants, the Danes, gave Beowulf ownership of both the two, of horses and of weapons, bade him enjoy them well.

The Theme in Anglo-Saxon Poetry 165

This mighty passage illustrates, I believe, how the basic "theme" of arms and armor can be elaborated for special purposes. In the opening lines, the familiar cluster at the beginning, of *helm*, *byrne*, and *sweord*, is introduced by a splendid newcomer, *segen gyldenne* 'a golden standard', with its own appositive, *hroden hildecumbor* 'an ornamented battle banner'. In what follows, the helmet, with its own alliterating appositive *heafodbeorge* 'a head-protector', is described in lines 1030–34; then eight horses are introduced and the saddle of one of them is given special attention. Like the battle-standard, these are not "arms and armor" but are ornaments added to the basic theme for special purposes. The *sweorda gelac* 'swordplay' in line 1040 does not refer to any particular sword and does not come into consideration for describing the theme. The *wicga ond wæpna* of line 1045 sum up the gifts of "horses and weapons." The weapons listed at the beginning covered the basic theme; the rest was elaboration.

Two instances of *sweord* in *Beowulf* lead us into a maze of arms and armor words in lines 1280b–91, when the retainers of Heorot take to arms at the arrival of Grendel's dam:

```
1280b                    Þa ðær sona wearð
        edhwyrft eorlum,    siþðan inne fealh
        Grendles modor.     Wæs se gryre læssa
        efne swa micle      swa bið mægþa cræft,
        wiggryre wifes,     be wæpnedmen,
1285    þonne heoru bunden, hamere geþuren,
        sweord swate fah    swin ofer helme
        ecgum dyhttig       andweard scireð.
        Þa wæs on healle    heardecg togen
        sweord ofer setlum, sidrand manig
1290    hafen handa fæst;   helm ne gemunde,
        byrnan side,        þa hine se broga angeat.
```

Then forthwith there came a reverse for the nobles, when Grendel's mother entered within. The fear was less by just so much as women's strength, a woman's war-terror, is, as compared with that caused by an armed man, when the ornamented, hammer-forged blade, the blood-stained sword, trusty of edges, cleaves through the boar-image on the helmet of the foe. Then in the hall, from above the benches, the hard-edged sword was taken down; many a broad shield was raised, firm in the hand. When the terror seized him, none thought of helm or great corslet.

Swords, helmets, shields, and corslets form this arsenal, with only the spear missing.

By now we have established the classic core of four or five items that make up the arsenal theme, namely, for armor, corslets, helmets, and shields, and for arms, swords, and spears. They do not always all appear together, as we have seen, but they are what the singer has in mind for arms and armor. As the style demands, and as the specific occasion in the narrative context requires or suggests, the words may vary for purposes of alliteration, and appositives may be employed for making lines and couplets; but these five basic objects constitute the foundation of the arsenal theme in *Beowulf*.

When Beowulf and his companions reach the mere on the morning after the death of Æschere, his men kill with bow and arrows some of the creatures that inhabit the mere. This passage brings us new arms for our repertory, namely, *flan* 'arrow', *flanbogan* 'bow', and *herestræl* 'arrow' (lines 1431b–36):

> > bearhtm ongeaton,
> guðhorn galan.   Sumne Geata leod
> of <u>flanbogan</u>   feores getwæfde,
> yðgewinnes,   þæt him on aldre stod
> <u>herestræl</u> hearda;   he on holme wæs
> sundes þe sænra,   ðe hyne swylt fornam.

They had heard the noise, the war-horn sound. One the chief of the Geats severed from life, from his battling with the waters, by his <u>shafted bow</u>, so that the hard <u>war-arrow</u> stuck in his vitals:—he was the slower at swimming in the mere, for that death had carried him off.

From the examples given above, selected from many possible passages in *Beowulf*, one can justifiably refer to an "arsenal theme" in Anglo-Saxon poetry. Its elements are regularly not so much formulaic but, rather, single words or lexical units, used in recognizable groups of three, four, or five members. This concept of the theme in Anglo-Saxon poetry has much to offer the reader who heretofore has had problems in identifying in *Beowulf* a feature that is characteristic of other traditional poems believed to be oral in their origin.

CHAPTER 7

The Ballad: Textual Stability, Variation, and Memorization

It has become apparent that, because the study of oral traditional literature has so concentrated on epic, the application of the oral theory to other kinds of oral poetry may lead to difficulty. The ballad has presented one thorny problem, and short forms in general another, the one because of its stanzaic form, the other because of its comparative brevity. I have treated short lyric poems in Chapter 2. In the case of the ballad, it seems possible, as Bertrand Bronson once suggested, that some ballads were more fluid than others in their texts up to the time when they were written down and published, thus establishing a text such as one had for other literary poems.[1]

A glance at some of the texts of the 198 variants of "Barbara Allen" (Child No. 84) in Bronson's *The Traditional Tunes of the Child Ballads* makes one pause.[2] Bronson vividly summarizes "Bonny Barbara Allen" as follows: "This little song of a spineless lover who gives up the ghost without a struggle, and of his spirited beloved who repents too late, has paradoxically shown a stronger will-to-live than perhaps any other ballad in the canon."[3] The texts of this ballad are not as close to one another as one might have expected them to be from what is often assumed to be a tradition of memorization.[4] There are some close texts, but others are quite different. The idea that a memorized text is behind all of these variants would not be easy to defend.

1. Bronson, 1945.
2. Bronson, 1962, 321–91.
3. Ibid., 321. Note that Child No. 84 is accepted into Toelken's oral canon for the Child Ballads, qualifying by all three suggested criteria, Toelken, 1967, 89.
4. See Jabbour, 1969, 177; for more on Jabbour, see below, at n. 13.

An investigation of the textuality of this ballad is in order. I have chosen to examine the opening stanzas of eight variants from the group beginning with a form of "In Scotland I was born and bred." This group, a relatively small number of Bronson's 198 variants, provides a convenient unit for study.[5] The eight versions embrace three of the four classes of tunes described by Bronson for "Barbara Allen."[6] These variants begin:

1

In Scotland I was born and bred,
In Scotland is my dwelling;
A young man on his death-bed lay
For the love of Barb'ra Ellen.

She went to his bedside and said,
"Young man, I think you're dying;"
"A dying man! pray don't say so,
One kiss of yours will cure me."

9

In Scotland I was born and bred
And England is my nation
For a young man on his death-bed lay
For the love of Bar'ra Ellen.

[no second stanza]

12

In Scotland I was born and bred,
In Scotland I was dwelling,
When a young man on his death-bed lay
For the sake of barb'rous Allen.

He sent his servant to her house,
To the place where she was dwelling,
Saying: You must come to my master's house
If your name is barbarous Allen.

27

In Scotland I was bred aden born,
In Scotland was ė my dwellin';
And there I cörted a prutty mad;
And her name was Bäbrė (H)Ellen.

I courted her for a month or two,
Thinkin' I should gain her favor,
Then I went a servant to her house,
The house that she did dwell in,
Sähin', "My master wants to speak to you,
If your name be Bäbrė (H)Ellen."

51

In Scotland I was bred and born,
In Scotland was my dwelling,
And there I loved a pretty maid,
Her name was Barbary Allen.

94

In Scotland I was born and bred
O, there it was my dwelling;
I courted there a pretty maid,
O, her name was Barbara Allen,

---

5. Many more variants of "Barbara Allen" begin with " 'Twas in the merry month of May" or a similar line; still others, for example, begin "In Scarlet Town where I was born."

6. Bronson, 1962, 321. Nos. 1, 9, 12, and 27 belong to Group A; Nos. 51, 94, and 127 to Group C; and No. 156 to Group D.

[no second stanza]	I courted her in summer time, I courted her in winter; For six long years I courted her, A-thinking I should win her.

127	156
In Scotland I was born and bred, In London I was dwelling; I fell in love wi' a nice young girl And her name was Barbara Allan, Allan, And her name was Barbara Allan.	(In) London I was bred and born, (In) Scotland was my dwellin', O I fell in love with a nice young girl And her name was Barbru Allan, O And her name was Barbru Allan, O.
I courted her for seven long years, Till I could court no longer; I grew sick and very very ill I sent for my own true lover, lover, I sent for my own true lover.	I courted her for seven long years; I could nae court her langer, O, But I fell sick and very ill And I sent for Barbru Allan, O, And I sent for Barbra Allan, O.

From a study of these first stanzas it is clear that the unit of composition is mainly the couplet. One cannot predict with certainty from the first couplet in the stanza what the second couplet will be. Five of these eight variants begin with the line "In Scotland I was born and bred"; one reads "In Scotland I was bred and born," and another begins similarly, "In Scotland I was bred aden born." The eighth begins "(In) London I was bred and born." The second line is somewhat less predictable than the first. No. 1 has "In Scotland is my dwelling"; No. 9, "And England is my nation"; No. 12, "In Scotland I was dwelling"; No. 27, "In Scotland was è my dwelling'"; No. 51, "In Scotland was my dwelling"; No. 94, "O, there it was my dwelling"; No. 127, "In London I was dwelling"; and No. 156, "(In) Scotland was my dwelling', O." In spite of this lack of complete fixity, the couplet holds together pretty well as being something that is varied, usually beginning with "In Scotland" and ending with "dwelling."

The "In Scotland I was born and bred" couplet is usually followed by either "I courted there a pretty maid," which rhymes roughly with "bred," or its variant "And there I loved a pretty maid" or with "A young man on his death-bed lay," which, of course, rhymes with another opening couplet, "'Twas in the merry month of May." The opening couplets "In Scotland I was born and bred" and "(In) London I was bred and born" are also followed by a couplet beginning with "I fell in love with a nice young girl," a variant of "I courted there a pretty maid."

Although a singer may have arrived at a version that became habitual with him or her, probably by some form of "remembering" or memorization— but not memorization of a single already fixed text—somewhere along the line, couplets have moved from association with one other couplet to still another. The couplets, moreover, themselves are not stable. Of the eight "In Scotland" couplets, as we have seen, no two are exactly alike, although several are close.

When one proceeds to the second stanza, it becomes apparent that the eight versions differ in the pace of the narrative. Four of the second stanzas begin with some mention of courting. No. 27 has "I courted her for a month or two"; No. 94 has "I courted her in summer time"; Nos. 127 and 156 have "I courted her for seven long years." It is noticeable that in No. 27 and No. 94, the courting has begun already in the third line of the first stanza. The second stanza of No. 12 commences at a different moment in the story: "He sent his servant to her house," whereas in No. 1, Barbara already goes to the young man's bedside. In No. 27 a striking deviation is that the narrator is the servant not the young man himself.

We have thus seen something of the variations in text in the first two stanzas of six of the eight variants of "Barbara Allen"; (two of the eight lack a second stanza). We have observed the relative instability of the text in the traditional ballad and its propensity toward variation. An examination of these eight variants bears out Bronson's remarks on variability in the tunes and texts of the Child Ballads:

> There is no fixed original, like an author's signed autograph, to be memorized note for note, and word for word. Just as in the telling of a prose yarn by a practised raconteur, the true folk-singer carries in his or her memory the mental image of a song, malleable in verbal and melodic detail, to be given new realization in every fresh rendition. (This is not to deny the continual reappearance of what Samuel Bayard has called 'melodic formulae' or 'congenial idiomatic expressions' [see Bronson's footnote 8]). The differences may be almost unnoticeable, but it is next to impossible for a singer to give an identical repetition of the same song. The notes of the successive stanzas will be affected by the words; the unmemorized word will not be repeated verbatim. . . . Tradition is a fluid medium, never quite the same, ever renewed. That is what keeps it inexhaustibly interesting and alive.[7]

---

7. Bronson, 1976, xliii. [For a summary of David Buchan's 1972 presentation of three stages in the composition and transmission of ballads in the northeast of Scotland, see the Editor's Addendum at the end of this chapter. His first stage, the period of oral composition, corresponds closely to Bronson's statement just cited.]

Let me now turn to the variants of one of the shorter songs, a ballad, in Serbo-Croatian from the Milman Parry Collection.[8] What can we find out about its textuality? I have taken the beginning of five versions of *San usnila Hasanaginica*, "Hasanaga's wife dreamed a dream" (Bartók No. 12a, Parry No. 6391a) and compared them for their sense of textuality, or rather for stability of text in a song sung or dictated by women in a very closed group in Gacko, Herzegovina, in 1935.[9] I have numbered them 12a, A, B, C, and D for convenience of reference. Bartók 12a is sung in couplets, as is shown below. The dictated texts have some differences from the sung text purely because they are dictated and not necessarily written down well by the scribes, who were sometimes school children.

12a

1 San usnila Hasanaginica,
  San usnila, u snu se prenula.

  Hasanaga's wife dreamt a dream.
  She dreamt a dream, and from her dream awoke.

2 Ona budi šćerku Melećhanu:
  "Ustaj, sine, šćeri Melećhana!

  She awakened her daughter Melećhana:
  "Arise, daughter Melećhana,

3 Evo ti se razboljela majka,
  I Bog znade da preboljet neću,

  Your mother has fallen ill,
  And God knows that I shall not recover,

4 I Bog znade da preboljet neću,
  Jerbo sam ti ružan san usnila,

  God knows that I shall not recover,
  For I have had a bad dream.

5 Jerbo sam ti ružan san usnila,
  Da s' na meni zapalila diba,

  I have had a bad dream,
  That my brocade caught fire.

6 Da s' na meni zapalila diba.
  Svi mi desni izgorjeli skuti.

  That my brocade caught fire,
  And my skirts on the right-hand side were all burned away.

7 Što s' na meni zapalila diba,
  To će tvoja umrijeti majka.

  That my brocade caught fire
  Means that your mother will die.

8 Što su desni izgorjeli skuti,
  To će ti se babo oženiti."

  That the skirts on my right side were burned
  Means that your father will marry again."

---

8. For a treatment of the circumstances of singing South Slavic heroic or epic songs and of "women's songs," some of which are lyric songs and some of which are ballads, see Chapter 2, at n. 17.

9. For Bartók No. 12a, see Bartók and Lord, 1951, 290–97. Versions A–D are unpublished. There are thirty other texts besides 12a listed under the first line, "San usnila Hasanaginica," in the Parry collection, all from Gacko and all dictated.

A

San usnila Hasanaginica,	Hasanaga's wife dreamt a dream,
Đe se na njoj zapalila diba,	Wherein her brocade caught fire,
Svi joj desni izgorjeli skuti.	Her skirts on the right side all burned up.
San usnila, u snu se prepala,	She dreamt a dream, in her dreaming she took fright,
Pa doziva kćercu Melećhanu:	So she called her daughter Melećhana:
"Ustaj bolje, kćeri Melećhana!	"Arise quickly, daughter Melećhana!
Evo ti se razboljela majka,	Your mother has fallen ill,
I Bog znade, preboljeti neće,	And God knows she won't recover,
I tvoj će oženiti babo."	And your father will marry again."

B

San usnila Hasanaginica,	Hasanaga's wife dreamt a dream,
U snu se prenula,	While dreaming she started up,
Pa doziva šćerku Melećhanu:	Then she called her daughter Melećhana:
"Ustaj, šćeri Melećhana!	"Arise, daughter Melećhana!
Ružan (n)ti je sanak usnila,	I have had a bad dream,
Đe se na meni diba zapalila,	Wherein my brocade caught fire,
Desni mi se skuti zapalili.	My skirts on the right side caught fire.
Šćeri moja Melećhanu,	My daughter, Melećhana,
Što mi se je diba zapalila,	That my brocade caught fire
To će ti se majka umrijeti.	Means that your mother will die.
Što mi se skuti desni zapalili,	That my skirts on the right side caught fire
To će ti se babo oženiti."	Means that your father will marry again."

C

San usnila Alibegovica,	Alibeg's wife dreamt a dream,
San usnila, pa se probudila,	She dreamt a dream, then awoke,
Pa doziva Akjunu đevojku:	Then she called the maiden Ajkuna:
"Čudan sam ti noćas san usnila.	"I had a strange dream last night.
Brže će ti majka umrijeti.	Your mother will die soon.
Tvoj će se oženiti babo."	Your father will marry again."

D

San usnila Alibegovica,	Alibeg's wife dreamt a dream,
San usnila, u snu se prenula,	She dreamt a dream, while dreaming she started up
Pa dozivlja ćerku Melećanu:	Then she called her daughter Melećana:
"Ćeri moja, mila Melećana,	"My daughter, dear Melećana,
Majka ti se noćas razboljela,	Your mother fell ill last night,

I Bog znade i ljudi znaju,	And God knows, and mortals know,
Da ti preboljet' neću,	That I shall not recover.
Jerbo sam ti ružan san usnila.	For I have had a bad dream.
Još se na meni zapalila (diba)	My (brocade) caught fire,
Desni su mi skuti izgorjeli.	My skirts on the right side burned up.
Što se na meni zapalila diba,	That my brocade caught fire
To će mi se babo oženiti."	Means that your father will marry again."

Here is a summary of the 130 lines of Bartók-Lord No. 12a:

Hasanaga's wife has a dream which she interprets as portending her death and the remarriage of her husband to her neighbor, Kasum pasha's wife. (The latter is evidently a widow, although the song does not specify this.) Hasanaga's wife warns her daughter, Melećhana, to guard her possessions, which are locked behind ten locks in the attic, from Kasum pasha's wife and her pregnant daughter, Ajka.

After the death of Hasanaga's wife and Hasanaga's remarriage to Kasum pasha's wife, Melećhana asks her aunt to arrange her marriage with Mehmedbeg, a cousin. But when the wedding party comes to take Melećhana to Mehmed's house, Kasum pasha's wife locks Melećhana in the attic, and substitutes her daughter Ajka for her. After the wedding party departs, Mehmedbeg returns one last time to the house, to bestow presents on Kasum pasha's wife and female relatives. It is then that Melećhana breaks the window of the attic and calls to a street singer:

> "Sing, oh singer, my brother-in-God
> Perhaps Mehmedbeg will hear you.
> Woe to you, Mehmedbeg!
> You are not carrying away lovely Melećhana,
> You are not carrying away lovely Melećhana,
> But Kasum pasha's daughter Ajka."

Mehmedbeg hears the singer, rushes upstairs to free Melećhana, removes Ajka from the wedding party, and takes Melećhana "to his own white house."[10]

The first line is common to all the texts, except that the lady is Hasanaginica in some (12a, A, and B) and Alibegovica in others (C and D). The second line, sung together with the first in a couplet, *San usnila, u snu se prenula*, "She dreamed a dream and while dreaming she started up," repeats

---

10. [I am grateful to Thomas J. Butler for translating versions A–D and for preparing the summary of Bartók-Lord No. 12a.]

the first half of the first line and adds a new idea in the second half. This is a common method of line, or couplet, structure, which I have sometimes described as fitting three ideas into four metrical slots by repeating in the second line an idea introduced in the first. Text D has the same second line as 12a, although the lady is Alibegovica, not Hasanaginica. The second line in C, *San usnila, pa se probudila,* "She dreamed a dream, then awoke," uses a different verb in the second half of the line, with essentially the same meaning, "she woke up." Text B is defective in this line, *U snu se prenula,* "while dreaming she started up," the scribe not bothering to repeat the first half of the line and writing down only the second half, which is the same as in 12a and D.

In Text A, lines two and three:

> Đe se na njoj zapalila diba,
> Svi joj desni izgorjeli skuti.
>
> Wherein her brocade burst into flame
> Her skirts on the right side burned up.

"intervene" between what are lines one and two in the other texts, with the result that line two of the other texts is line four of Text A, and it (*San usnila, u snu se prepala,* "She dreamed a dream, in her dreaming she took fright") repeats the first half of line one but has still another verb in the second half. Lines two and three of Text A will be found in another position in the other texts. They are descriptive of the dream, and there are several places in which they might logically occur and, as a matter of fact, do occur.

In 12a, lines three and four go together in a couplet just as one and two did.

> Ona budi šćerku Melećhanu,
> "Ustaj, sine, šćeri Melećhana!"
>
> She awakened her daughter Melećhana
> "Arise, daughter Melećhana."

Bartók No. 12a is the only one of the five texts to use the verb (*pro*)*budi* 'awoke' (line three); the others use *doziva* 'called to'. The person called in 12a, A (line five), B, and D is "daughter Melećhana"; in C it is *Ajkunu devojku* 'the maiden Ajkuna'.

The second line of this couplet begins with *Ustaj* 'arise', in 12a, A, and B, followed by a vocative for the daughter. In D, the vocative is repeated in both halves of the line, *Ćeri moja, mila Melećana,* "My daughter, dear Melećana."

Once again, Text C is different (as in *Ajkuna djevojku*). The text has no vocative but begins immediately with *Čudan sam ti noćas san usnila*, "Last night I dreamed a strange dream."

The next couplet in 12a is:

> Evo ti se razboljela majka,
> I Bog znade da preboljet' neću,
>
> Your mother has fallen ill,
> And God knows I shall not recover.

This couplet is more or less the same in A, but it is amplified to three lines in D:

Majka ti se noćas razboljela,	Your mother fell ill last night,
I Bog znade i ljudi znaju,	And God knows and mortals know,
Da ti preboljet' neću,	That I shall not recover.

There is a balance in some lines of the poetry between *Bog* 'God', and *ljudi* 'people', in the traditional poetry, and that has lengthened the second line of the couplet, thus requiring a third line for its completion. Texts B and C omit the idea that the mother has fallen ill and take up, rather, the idea of her dying only in connection with the interpretation of the dream, which appears later in the other texts.

The next three new lines in 12a should be taken together because they introduce the lady's dream:

Jerbo sam ti ružan san usnila,	For I have had a bad dream,
Da s' na meni zapalila diba,	That my brocade caught fire,
Svi mi desni izgorjeli skuti.	And my skirts on the right-hand side were burned.

Text D gives a three-line equivalent to the three lines above, and they are in the same sequence:

Jerbo sam ti ružan san usnila.	For I have had a bad dream.
Još se na meni zapalila (diba)	My (brocade) caught fire,
Desni su mi skuti izgorjeli.	My skirts on the right side burned up.

Text B has also a three-line equivalent to the 12a lines in question, also with slight variations:

Ružan (n)ti[11] je sanak usnila,	I have had a bad dream,
Đe se na meni diba zapalila,	Wherein my brocade caught fire,
Desni mi se skuti zapalili.	My skirts on the right side caught fire.

These lines, however, follow immediately on the *Ustaj* 'arise', line because the mother's illness has been omitted; or rather, there is no mention of it. Text A has the *two* lines describing the dream but not the line introducing them, but they are placed immediately after the first line of the song, as we saw before, "interrupting" the first and second lines.

Text C does not give a description of the dream and keeps only the line *Čudan sam ti noćas san usnila*, "I had a strange dream last night," adding *Brže će ti majka umrijeti*, "Your mother will soon die." Text C telescopes the song, shortening it considerably.

Bartók No. 12a then gives the interpretation of the dream in four lines:

Što s' na meni zapalila diba,	That my brocade caught fire
To će tvoja umrijeti majka.	Means that your mother will die.
Što su desni izgorjeli skuti,	That my skirts on my right side were burned
To će ti se babo oženiti.	Means that your father will marry again.

Text B has approximately these same lines of interpretation but introduces them with a vocative line: *Šćeri moja, Melećhanu*, "My daughter, Melećhana." Text D gives only two lines of interpretation, corresponding to the first and the last lines of 12a:

> Što se na meni zapalila diba,
> To će mi se babo oženiti.
>
> That my brocade caught fire
> Means that your father will marry again.

Text C has only two of the four lines of interpretation found in 12a, namely:

> Brže će ti majka umrijeti.
> Tvoj će se oženiti babo
>
> Your mother will soon die.
> Your father will marry again.

Finally, Text A has only one line of interpretation, and it falls hard on the

---

11. The nasalization at the end of *ružan* is carried over to the beginning of the next word.

heel of the mother's illness: *I tvoj će se oženiti babo,* "And your father will marry again."

These sample versions present fewer variations than we saw in the "In Scotland I was born and bred" versions of "Barbara Allen." The South Slavic examples, as noted, are all from the same small district and represent a song that was well known. Even so, they reveal many differences in text. The analysis is sufficient, I believe, to illustrate what I mean by a sense of textuality, that is, a sense that a song has a recognizable text and that the singers recognize that fact. But the existence of such textuality does not by any means imply a fixed text or an attempt at rote memorization. The ballad of "Hasanaga's wife" is "remembered" rather than memorized.[12]

Questions concerning the nature of the transmission of some Anglo-Saxon poems and of Anglo-Scottish ballads arise in connection with the thesis proposed by Alan Jabbour in his article "Memorial Transmission in Old English Poetry."[13] His research has been thorough so far as the Anglo-Saxon texts are concerned, but there is room to reconsider his interpretation of the cause, or causes, of the variations that he has so skillfully and clearly set down. His evidence—other than the Old English texts themselves—for memorial transmission is founded in English and Scottish ballad tradition. There are clearly parts of traditional ballads that are comparatively stable, but also clearly, there are variations, as we have seen in the case of "Barbara Allen." In using the evidence of ballad transmission in attempting an interpretation of Old English poems, parts of which are stable and parts variable, one must remember that the ballads are traditional in subject and style, with a history of transmission over a fair, if varying, number of generations and singers. In contrast, *Soul and Body, Daniel,* and *Azarias* are scarcely traditional subjects and, so far as I know, were never sung by many of the populace over generations. To use ballad variation as an analogue to explain variation in some Old English poems seems to me to be methodologically unsound.

We are left, then, with two problems instead of one, neither of which is adequately explained: first, the variations in some Old English poems that cannot be accounted for by scribal error, and second, the processes of transmission or even of composition, or both, of traditional ballads. These are separate problems. I find it easier to approach that of traditional ballads, where material for analysis is abundant and more varied than that of the comparatively small group of Old English poems involved, which would have been known to a restricted number of persons. I might add that one

---

12. For the distinction between "remembering" and memorizing, see Chapter 1, after n. 26.
13. Jabbour, 1969.

need not confine one's observations to British, Scottish, or American ballads but should include Danish, Swedish, German, or any other ballads of similar form and tradition, whatever the language or culture may be.

Jabbour rejects comparative studies based on "modern foreign tradition." He says, "The aim of the foregoing discussion has been to disengage the speculations about Old English oral tradition from a point of view shaped by the study of a quite different tradition, and to suggest that, in the absence of first-hand evidence about Anglo-Saxon oral practices, the analogy of later British oral tradition should carry greater weight than the analogy of modern foreign traditions."[14] Yet, while having objected to a comparison between *Beowulf* and South Slavic epic tradition, he accepts for analogy with certain Old English religious poems the study of the far different tradition of ballad, albeit in the same geographic frame. Jabbour's, and others', primary difficulty is in not understanding the difference between a fixed and a fluid text, and in the case of ballad and epic, between stanzaic and stichic form.

In speaking of the English ballad, one must be careful. What ballads is Jabbour talking about? They are not all alike in fixity of text. If Jabbour wishes for a "memorial tradition" in English with which to compare *Soul and Body* or *Daniel* or *Azarias*, he might look to the fixed text of the nontraditional broadsides. The broadside sometimes starts with a fixed text composed by someone, whose name is known.[15] We know its first form, and knowing that, we can note divergences from it. That is memorial transmission of a fixed text, which is *not* an oral traditional process.

The solid "core" of traditional English ballad, the ballad tradition itself, is a different matter entirely. Here the case for memorial transmission is not open and shut; for the text of a ballad is not fixed, not even after it has been published, less so, of course, before. One is dealing with lines or couplets that may be used in more than one stanza and in more than one ballad, provided the meter and tune allow. The *exact* wording of such lines and couplets is not predictable, but they maintain a high degree of stability. The topoi of the ballads are too well known to need extended comment. Such lines as "She mounted her milk-white steed," "he on his dapple gray," and the like are useful with little change in a number of songs. These lines and couplets are like the lines and couplets of the formulaic style. On this level, the process of formation of stanza lines and probably their later re-creation seem at some

---

14. Ibid., 180.
15. Speaking of English balladry in the sixteenth century, Entwistle (1939) remarks, "The invention and application of printing was causing ballad-mongers to print their wares on broadsides; the censorship forced them to register their pieces and names at Stationers' Hall" (228).

time to have been much like formulaic composition. Here we have, or have had, not memorial but "improvisational" transmission, that is, composition in performance.

It is paradoxical that, on the one hand, in the ballads we find oral traditional texts displaying a kind of textual stability sometimes characteristic of nontraditional "written" processes; on the other hand, in the nontraditional written texts of Old English *Soul and Body* and parts of *Daniel* and in *Azarias*, we find textual variation characteristic of oral traditional texts. If we remember that Old English written Christian poetry, even that translated from Latin, uses a formulaic technique of composition derived from oral traditional poetry, then we can conclude that Old English written Christian poetry derived its technique of variation in reproduction of text as well as its composition from oral traditional poetry. On reflection, it is not surprising, because reproduction of text is a kind of recomposition.

It is not my purpose here to analyze fully balladic formation and structure. Suffice it to say that to call it as a whole "memorial" is simplistic, because that implies fixed texts, and such are not to be found, except possibly at this latest hour when all singings stem from the written, fixed texts of the collections. What is more for our present purposes, to use balladic formation and structure as an analogue to explain the variations in Old English *Soul and Body*, *Daniel*, and *Azarias* is misguided. The two groups of poems are quite different in all ways, even, I admit, *pace* Jabbour, in the reasons for variations of text.

Jabbour has done a real service, however, in calling attention to the multiple manuscripts of Old English poetry; for they are often ignored and his isolating of those poems in which variation is clearly not fully accounted for by scribal error is very useful. Still, I am not at all sure of the reason for the variations.

At the time when Jabbour was working on this subject for his dissertation at Duke University, Alison Jones at Canberra was also investigating the variations that occur between the "Prayer of Azariah" as given in the Old English *Azarias* and another version of it in the Old English *Daniel*.[16] This research was published and Jabbour referred to it in his own article. Jabbour and Jones, stressing the importance of memory, can account for variation only by *lapsus memoriae*, which does not by any means explain all the variants. Jabbour did not refer to a later article by the same scholar on the variations in *Soul and Body*, I and II.[17]

16. A. Jones, 1966.
17. Gyger (née Jones), 1969.

In her 1966 article on *Daniel* and *Azarias*, Jones examined in detail the variations in the corresponding passages of those two poems:

> The two poems show differences which are more attributable to the lapses of memory of an "oral singer" than to anything else, yet they are so similar that they must at the same time stem from the same "original" poem. It is not possible to decide which, if either, was the primary version. In view of gaps in both texts, it would seem that both were derived from some common original rather than that either was in a direct line of descent from the other.[18]

As Jones says, "The relevant sections of the poems are *Azarias* 1–75 and *Daniel* 279–364, where the two texts are roughly parallel, and *Azarias* 76–175 and *Daniel* 365–415, where some similarities of phrasing occur, but where the two poems go more their own way, which can be seen even from a comparison of the number of lines which the two poems take to deal with the same material."[19] In 1969 she said of *Soul and Body*:

> In I, 33b ... and II, 30b ... the difference is not simply the chopping off of a word at the end of a line (something that could be attributed to scribal carelessness), but the whole line has been re-shaped, so that a verb is left in the position of prominence at the end of the line. This ... shows that the transmission of the poem was not just a question of mechanical memorizing, but that a constructive and even creative attitude was felt by the transmitter, so that he tried to make sense of what he was remembering by adjusting his text if it departed slightly from the original. This, however, did not always work out, as can be seen from some of the confusions of transposed and omitted lines.[20]

She concludes:

> An examination of these two versions of the same poem, and a comparison of this with the *Daniel-Azarias* problem reveal two different patterns. Here there are very few alterations by the method of formula substitution, and in proportion a higher number of lines added or omitted, but although different kinds of lapses are involved in these processes, the relevant fact is that both are lapses of memory. It seems likely, too, that both *Daniel* and *Azarias* are further from their source than either of the *Soul and Body* poems is from the original, and it

---

18. A. Jones, 1966, 95.
19. Ibid., 96.
20. Gyger, 1969, 240.

is possible that the "singers" of *Daniel* and *Azarias* (or one of them) had a more creative attitude towards their material, remembering the general outline and improvising the details, where the two "singers" responsible for the two versions of *Soul and Body* were more conservative and relied more on straight memorizing. But while much of this can only be in the field of speculation, it can at least be said in both cases that the differences between the two versions are more understandable when attributed to oral transmission than anything else.[21]

Earlier Jones spoke of oral transmission as "a means of transmission which previous critics have noted to be facilitated by the formulaic nature of the verse, a characteristic revealed in the study of both of these poems."[22] Thus she notes the formulaic character of both *Daniel* and *Azarias*, and at the same time, she repeats the fallacy that formulaic verse is easier "to transmit" than nonformulaic. Later she reiterates, "Since it is the formulaic nature of Old English poetry that makes it so suitable for oral recitation, let us look first at some of the variations in formulaic phrases between the two poems."[23]

Formulas and the formulaic style are aids in *composition*, or were so in their inception, and not "intended to facilitate recitation or memorization," nor do they. If formulas made memorization easier, why are there so many formula substitutions among the variants? Indeed, they make word-for-word memorization more difficult because it is not easy to remember which of two or more similar formulas is used at any given place in a *fixed* original. The formulas are, I hazard to say, unnecessary and awkward in a purely "memorial" tradition.

In this regard, I was interested to read of a computer experiment attempting to determine the usefulness of rhyming words as a mnemonic device in poetry. Suzanne Petersen wrote:

> In order to ascertain whether or not rhyme has by its mere presence a mnemonic function in the oral Hispanic ballad ... the computer was asked to derive three *indexes of stability*: one for the total vocabulary of the ballad, one for the words in last position of "A" (non-rhyming) hemistichs and one for the words in last position of "B" hemistichs (rhyme-slot).... Contrary to our expectations, these three indexes revealed that in the 612 versions of "La condesita" the words in rhyme-slot were *less*—not more—stable than the

---

21. Ibid., 244.
22. A. Jones, 1966, 95.
23. Ibid., 96.

overall vocabulary of the ballad. The statistics seemed to indicate that, far from being a mnemonic device, rhyme was actually conducive to innovation.[24]

And finally, after other tests, which indicated that only the infinitive showed stability in rhyming position, Petersen concludes:

> The statistical analysis of rhyme function in this ballad clearly suggests that in the model of oral poetic discourse constituted by the Hispanic *romancero*, rhyme in and of itself does not operate as a mnemonic device—quite the contrary. Even for the one isolated case in which rhyme proved to exert a stabilizing effect on the vocabulary of "La condesita," that stability was achieved only indirectly.[25]

Petersen's evidence is corroborated by an incident recorded by Milman Parry in his unpublished journal "Ćor Huso" under the date of December 2, 1934. Parry tells of a poem dealing with the assassination of Archduke Franz Ferdinand, which he was reading into the dictaphone. He says, "The poem is written as most of the new poems are, in rhyme, and while the themes and phrases of the poetry show on the one hand a habitude of the old poetry, other verses clearly indicate the influence of the newspapers." Parry describes how, as he was reading the verses of Gavrilo Princip's speech before he fires the fatal shot, his assistant and scribe, Nikola Vujnović, himself a singer, recited the line that follows them. Parry says, "When I asked him to recite the poem from the beginning he was able to do so only for twelve verses, and then lost himself in making the rhymes. . . . His explanation which, in its way, is doubtless true, was that it is very easy to forget poems that are rhymed." This incident as well as the data from the computer studies cast doubt on theories urging the "memorial transmission" of some traditional ballads.

To return to Old English, it is to be noted, although Jones does not actually say so, that *Azarias* 76–175 and *Daniel* 365–415 are so far apart, in spite of occasional similar phrases such as *sunne ond mona* (*Azarias* 77) and *sunna and mona* (*Daniel* 369) that there can be no real question of "memorial transmission."[26]

---

24. Petersen, 1978, 92–93.
25. Ibid., 95; see also Beatie, 1964–65.
26. [Moffat, 1992, also comments on differences between the texts of *Daniel* and *Azarias*: "While in some passages they move in parallel, word for word, in others they are quite different" (814).]

Editor's Addendum

Lord's text of his chapter ends here. One is left, therefore, with serious doubts, *pace* Jabbour, of the "memorial transmission" both of the Anglo-Scottish traditional ballads and of the Old English *Soul and Body*, *Daniel*, and *Azarias*. With regard to the Anglo-Scottish ballads, the word *memorization* is deceptively enticing in a truly traditional setting. Lord liked to maintain a distinction between what the singer "remembers" by a natural and informal mental process and what he or she is alleged to have reproduced by memorization. The very process of oral composition makes an attempt at close or exact memorization unnecessary. First and foremost, in traditional poetry there is no fixed text to memorize. An "original" or archetypal text is the chimerical goal of literary critics. Behind Jabbour's memorial transmission there lies the assumption of an "original" text. He says, "If we discover . . . that in a certain tradition the variants of a song show a history of word-for-word or phrase-by-phrase oral transmission from a known or presumed archetype, we may describe the tradition as memorial."[27] For the Child Ballads accepted into Toelken's "oral canon,"[28] such a fixed text was nonexistent, as is the case with all truly traditional lore, with the exception of very short forms.

As for the religious Old English poems discussed by Jabbour (but not for all Old English poetry, notably *Beowulf*), Lord used the words *transitional or perhaps mixed* to describe them.[29] He modified his views on the "transitional text" as expressed in *The Singer of Tales* in later articles, especially in "The Merging of Two Worlds: Oral and Written Poetry as Carriers of Ancient Values" and in "The Nature of Oral Poetry."[30] The introduction of writing (and a new literary style) did not come, as Jabbour maintains, "at a stroke." For a considerable time, established formulaic habits continued into a period of style known to have been influenced by written literature.

Jabbour has a different view of the transitional text. Influenced by Lord's 1960 position that there is no transitional stage between oral and written style, Jabbour says:

> Those scholars who regard extant Old English poetry as transitional are, I believe, trapped in the same foreign perspective of the oral advocates. . . .

27. Jabbour, 1969, 178.
28. Toelken, 1967.
29. A. Lord, 1975, 23.
30. A. Lord, 1986 and 1987b.

There can be no transitional stage moving from oral to written tradition. . . . There can, however, be a transitional stage moving in the other direction. In the strictest sense, the cleavage between written and memorial tradition is simple and complete: a given work is passed along either memorially or scribally. . . . In this context one may speak of "transitional text" as a text which, though appropriated from written into memorial tradition, has not yet been subjected to the full gamut of traditional modification and remains close to its written exemplar.[31]

Katherine O'Brien O'Keeffe takes issue with Jabbour's advocacy of the memorial transmission of Old English poetry.[32] As I explained in the Addendum to Chapter 4, O'Keeffe by using very refined paleographic methods, plots for Anglo-Saxon manuscripts and their scribes the stages on the continuum from orality to literacy. Her voice adds support to Lord's position in regard to the transitional milieu of Old English religious poetry, even though she concentrates not on the poet but on his reader or scribe.

In regard to both the ballad and Old English poetry, we must return to the search for what is traditional and to methods of measuring the degree and the kind of traditional devices that the poetry shares. We need an understanding of a style that has remained fluid, subject to variation by a compositional process rather than by *lapsus memoriae* or by mere scribal error or incompetence.

In connection with Jabbour's thesis of memorization, the more recent work of Murray McGillivray comes to mind.[33] His carefully measured attempt to demonstrate the transmission by memorization of four Middle English romances is not entirely convincing. The parallel passages he cites for comparison among different versions of the same romance are anything but fixed in their text. The manuscripts of the romances, by McGillivray's admission, show "massive variation from text to text." Groups of two or three lines, moreover, which are found to be transposed and to be inserted at different points in the narrative, rather than proving faulty memorization of set passages, could possibly illustrate blocks of lines or formula clusters that are useful in composing a text that is essentially fluid in nature. The author's inability to define an archetypal text for a group of manuscripts of the same romance is ominous for a theory of memorization. An "original" version that was available for the minstrel to memorize, well or badly, fades into the

---

31. Jabbour, 1969, 180–82.
32. O'Keeffe, 1990, 41 n. 61.
33. McGillivray, 1990.

The Ballad   185

distance to the vanishing point. One is faced with a group of texts the variations in which are not fully explained.

Relevant to the problems treated by Lord in the present chapter on the ballad is Buchan's discussion of three stages in the composition and transmission of ballads in the northeast of Scotland. He defines the first stage as a period of oral composition, the second a transitional period, and the third and final stage as one of memorization when habits of literacy have taken complete hold. The oral period he describes as a time when "the Northeast was still largely nonliterate." The concept of a fixed text was not yet established, but ballad singers were creative, or at least "re-creative." They were not bound by the words of a ballad as they had heard it but maintained something closer to stability of narrative rather than to stability of text, freely making changes at will.[34] Buchan's choice of Mrs. Brown of Falkland, who learned her ballads mostly before 1789, as the exemplar of the oral period of northeast balladry has not met with the approval of several scholars; for she was an educated person even though she learned her songs in her youth from persons of the old oral tradition and herself carried on that tradition.[35]

The example of transitional texts provided by Buchan are the ballads of James Nichol of Strichen, who died in 1840. Buchan traces the tendencies that emerge in the ballads of the transitional period, many of them traits that stem from changing social conditions. He finds the transitional method of singing "re-creative but rather haphazardly so." In Nichol's ballads, "sometimes a sequence of balances is merely a string of paired stanzas rather than an organic scene whose units are intricately related."[36] What Buchan calls "the annular device," that is, ring composition, an artistic mark of nonliterate style, is found rather infrequently in Nichol's texts.

Buchan notes that "English, the language of literacy for Scots, made ever-increasing inroads into the old formulaic style. Everywhere in the texts we can see the results of the new education: in words like 'espied' . . . and in lines such as 'Lay gasping on the ground' " (231). The influence of the broadside is

---

34. Buchan, 1972, esp. 62–65.
35. Buchan, ibid., 64, believes the paradox of an educated singer of oral traditional ballads to be apparent rather than real. For opinions questioning Mrs. Brown as a conveyor of pure oral tradition and discerning possible signs that she "doctored" her texts, see Henderson, 1973, a largely favorable review of Buchan's book; Nygard, 1978; and Andersen and Pettitt, 1979. The fundamental description of Mrs. Brown's balladry was made by Bronson, 1945. For further controversy over the application of oral formulaic methods of analysis to English and Scottish ballads, see J. Jones, 1961; Friedman, 1961a, and Thigpen, 1973.
36. Buchan, 1972, 227.

evident in beginning lines with such detail as "Upon the eighteenth day of June." Especially telling in the ballads that Buchan calls transitional is the "religiosity that now incongruously appears in the ballad texts [which] may be traced to the spread of devotional literature. Evangelical terminology accords ill with the ballad context" (241).

The modern period of northeast ballad tradition, according to Buchan, began about 1830. With the introduction of the printed ballad texts into the tradition comes the memorization of the ballads, the third stage of transmission. For his exemplar of this phase Buchan chose the ballads of Bell Robertson, who was also a writer of pious and spiritual poems. Among the several signs of the memorization of Robertson's ballads is their incompleteness. He reports that only one-third of the eighty-four ballad pieces in her repertory could be called complete. Because she recited rather than sang her ballads, the lack of music to aid her memory may have helped to explain the fragmentary nature of her pieces. She often did not understand particular words in her text or believed that they could have been corrupt, but she insisted on giving what she had heard. "Not only was it a case of her memorizing texts sung by other singers but also of her learning by rote off the printed page" (251).

As we approach the end of the twentieth century, when ballad singing remains a continuing aspect of popular culture, whether performed before live audiences or brought to our ears by record albums or compact discs, it is helpful to look back to the tradition of the Scottish northeast. Of special importance for this volume is the information that the Anglo-Scottish tradition teaches us about comparative stability of text and matters of transmission and memorization, and it helps, moreover, to define when the term *memorization* is appropriate for the ballad.

CHAPTER 8

Rebuttal

Oralitas, sicut Gallia, est omnis divisa in partes tres, quarum unam incolunt philosophi, aliam qui recitatores spectant, sicut scripsit Juvenalis in satira prima, tertiam philologi, qui textūs spectant et explicant.

In the years since *The Singer of Tales* there have been some criticisms of the "oral theory" to which I have not responded. I have come to feel that I would be shirking my responsibilities in not commenting as fully as I ought on such criticisms. I want here to respond in particular to a *Speculum* article by D. H. Green, Fellow of Trinity College, Cambridge.[1] Green's article, which was originally a plenary lecture delivered at the Medieval Academy meetings in Madison, Wisconsin, in April 1989, is a significant contribution to the study of reading in the Middle Ages. He has also read widely on orality in general and on the "oral theory," and I appreciate his assembling in a few pages the most common reservations scholars have had on this discipline, some of which have arisen from misunderstandings.[2]

I am reminded of the three divisions mentioned in the epigraph (with apologies to Julius Caesar); for Green's first three paragraphs on the "oral theory" correspond roughly to the three schools of which I speak. One group of these critics, the "Belgians," the dwellers in the first of the three

---

This chapter, with certain alterations, was originally presented as a lecture before the Medieval Seminar at Harvard's Humanities Center in the fall of 1990.
 1. Green, 1990.
 2. After introducing the subject of "orality," Green made some very generous remarks on my contribution to the field: "If we now talk of the interplay between oral and written at all this is only because Lord first systematically drew our attention to an oral dimension which a discipline based on written texts was prone to forget. The debt must be borne in mind if I now mention some reservations about the theory and its applicability and question whether its concentration on orality alone does justice to the symbiosis of oral and written in medieval society" (ibid., 270). I am truly grateful for his courtesy.

parts of the epigraph, constitutes what I have termed the "philosophical" school. I recall that, fittingly enough, the Belgians were the most remote from the Province. The members of this school write about orality and literacy from a philosophical, psychological, or sociologic point of view. Their primary concerns are the illiterate and the preliterate, or nonliterate, and literate societies, and the "oral mind." Although they often give some attention to "literature," they are not primarily concerned with the more limited problems of composition and transmission—or, as I think I prefer, learning and performing—which are the focus of what I think of as the first stage, as it were, of the "oral theory." Inasmuch as some of them are interested in the "oral mind" and the social status of the poet, they do involve themselves with the quality and aesthetics of the poetries with which they deal. The best-known scholars in this group are Marshall McLuhan, Eric A. Havelock, Franz Bäuml, Walter J. Ong, Jack Goody, and Brian Stock.[3]

In the second part dwell the "Aquitanians," those who use the adjective "oral" in its literal sense of nonwritten. Oral poetry is any poetry that is heard, that is spoken or sung, no matter how it was composed.[4] The reciter of any poetry is an oral poet. To the dwellers in Aquitaine, oral composition and oral performance are two separate entities. If, as sometimes happens in some traditions in Africa, one composes a poem in one's head and teaches it to someone else, who memorizes it and recites, or "performs" it, both the composer and the reciter are oral poets and the poem is literally an oral poem. A person reciting Virgil's *Aeneid*, or even reading it aloud, is an oral poet. This view can lead to absurdities. I am reminded of Martial's thirty-eighth epigram:

> Quem recitas meus est, o Fidentine, libellus:
> sed male cum recitas, incipit esse tuus.[5]

3. McLuhan, 1962; Havelock, 1963, 1978, and 1986; Bäuml and Spielmann, 1975; Ong, 1982; Goody and Watt, 1963; Goody, 1977; Stock, 1983 and 1989.

4. The passage from Juvenal's first *Satire* referred to in the epigraph is *Satire* 1.1–14:

> Semper ego auditor tantum? numquamne reponam
> vexatus totiens rauci Theseide Cordi? . . .
> Frontonis platani conuolsaque marmora clamant
> semper et adsiduo ruptae lectore columnae
> expectes eadem a summo minimoque poeta.

"What? Am I to be a listener only all my days? Am I never to get my word in—I that have been so often bored by the Theseid of the ranting Cordus? . . . these are the themes with which Fronto's plane trees and marble halls are forever ringing until the pillars quiver and quake under the continual recitations; such is the kind of stuff you may look for from every poet, greatest or least." (Text from Clausen, 1959; translation by Ramsay, 1924.)

5. For Latin text, see Lindsay, 1929, 1.38.

> The little book that you are reciting, o Fidentinus, is mine,
> but when you recite it badly, it begins to be yours.

Any poetry with which writing is not involved at the time of its performance is literally oral poetry to the Aquitanians. In this school I believe that Ruth Finnegan is the most serious critic because she does treat matters of oral poetry extensively. In spite of some excesses, this school has legitimately pointed out that all oral poetic traditions are not the same in their methods of composition and transmission. I see that Finnegan is not offended by the term *oral literature*. She grants, if I read her correctly, that unlettered people can have a literature.[6]

Caesar's third region was inhabited by a people who call themselves Celts in their own language but whom the Romans called Gauls. In our domain the dwellers in this region are those who concentrate on the texts of the poetry or, more properly, on words and groups of words and on the many ways, often very subtle, in which they are put together to express the thoughts and feelings of the oral traditional poets and of their traditional societies. These scholars constitute, I suggest, the "philologists," who belong perhaps to a separate branch of philology concerned with a kind of oral poetry characterized by a special technique of *composition*, a technique peculiar to a significant group of traditional oral poetries. It is with that kind of oral traditional poetry that Milman Parry, as a classical philologist, was engaged. The members of this third school give a specialized meaning to the adjective "oral," indicating a specific technique of composing, performing, and transmitting a traditional literary composition. Although these scholars are all intent on the text, most of them are also, however, deeply concerned with poetics and poetic structure—in short, with "quality"—as well as with understanding the traditional meaning conveyed by that particular kind of text.

In the medieval field, I find that the kind of criticism of Parry's work that looks to the Anglo-Saxon text, to speak only of Old English, can in some ways be quite productive because it is backed up by the texts themselves. These "Gauls" or philologists include, for example, Robert Creed, Donald K. Fry, and John M. Foley and such works as Daniel Donoghue's *Style in Old English Poetry*, an admirable study of the auxiliary in Old English, and Alain Renoir's book *A Key to Old Poems*, Fred Robinson's *Beowulf and the Appositive Style*, and Geoffrey Russom's *Old English Meter and Linguistic Theory*, to

---

6. Finnegan, 1970, 1976, 1977, and 1988.

name only a few.⁷ In the Germanic field, Stephen A. Mitchell's *Heroic Sagas and Ballads* should be mentioned.⁸

Green initiates discussion of the "oral theory" with arguments drawn directly from Havelock's *Preface to Plato*:

> In the first place, in applying their findings in Yugoslavia to the Homeric epic Parry and Lord were basing their argument, not on proof, but on an analogy whose validity has been called into question, since it lumps together two different poetic situations, one where the oral technique of a Balkan peasantry was no longer central to the culture in which they lived and one where the poetry of a Homeric governing class represented the main vehicle of significant communication in its society.⁹

I am not sure I follow Havelock's and Green's logic here. Surely it is perfectly legitimate to compare the compositional technique of one poetry with that of another. One should note first of all Havelock's and Green's unconscious (I assume) class consciousness in contrasting the "oral technique of a Balkan peasantry" and "the poetry of a Homeric governing class." I trust that Havelock in referring to "a Homeric governing class" was speaking of the audience, not the poet, because there is little, if any, evidence that Homer belonged to the "governing class," although he may have sung for them.

In his research Parry was not comparing a "peasantry" with a "governing class" but the techniques of oral narrative verse making of two separate language cultures, one ancient and the other modern. He had reason to believe that the techniques were the same, or similar, and the comparison demonstrated by means of textual experiments that both cultures exhibited the same stylistic traits that Parry believed arose from the necessity of composition in performance.

I do not know what kind of "proof" Havelock and Green were looking for. That they were really concerned with the sociologic differences of classes in the English sense is clear when later both scholars seem perfectly willing to accept the same sort of analogy from some other cultures, such as some from Africa or the Pacific Islands, where there are chieftains and kings and no mention is made of "peasants."¹⁰

---

7. E.g., Creed, 1959 and 1962; Fry, 1967a, 1967b, 1968a, 1968b, and 1975; Foley, 1976, 1985, and 1990; Donoghue, 1987; Renoir, 1988; Robinson, 1985; and Russom 1978 and 1987a.
8. Mitchell, 1991.
9. Green, 1990, 270 = Havelock, 1963, 93–94.
10. See Havelock, 1978: "The analogues [to Homer] would lie if anywhere in the epics recoverable from African or Polynesian societies if uncontaminated by documentation. Yet the analogues are necessarily imperfect; the societies which have yielded such pure specimens of orality

They forgot that the ruling class in what was Yugoslavia consisted for some five hundred years of viziers and pashas, whose courts inherited the brilliance of Byzantium. These rulers had been preceded by Serbian kings and emperors and were eventually followed by more Slavic kings and princes. The Moslem epic in South Serbia, Bosnia, and Herzegovina was, up until the end of World War I, the poetry of the governing class. The Serbian Christian poetry also was that of the governing class, first in the Middle Ages—for example, in the time of Emperor Dušan in the fourteenth century, although we have no texts from that period—and again from the nineteenth century to 1945, and perhaps to the present day, as parts of Serbia began to be liberated from the Ottomans; the Christian poetry was that of the emerging or reemerging kings and princes, who were not ousted until World War II. Both the Moslem and the Christian poetry expressed the ideals of the governing class even when out of power. Havelock and Green have been too cavalier with the facts of Balkan history and social structure.

I choose not to use the word *peasant* pejoratively. Avdo Međedović, an outstanding case in point, although living in humble circumstances, was a tradesman and had been a sergeant in the Turkish army, seeing service in many parts of the Balkans. He was a man of great dignity and integrity and was highly gifted with poetic sensitivity.[11]

Perhaps most important to realize is that the phrase "oral theory" with regard to the investigations into South Slavic oral epic by Parry and me is a misnomer. These findings do not constitute a "theory"; rather, they provide demonstrated facts concerning oral traditional poetry. The particular singers whom Parry described as unlettered were designated as such after careful inquiry and not by guess or hearsay. Southern Serbia, Bosnia and Herzegovina, and Montenegro were chosen as places for conducting Parry's experiments because a living tradition of epic singing was still practiced there, and these regions were accessible, albeit with special effort. Where else but to a tradition continuing into modern times could a scholar go to look for clues to the nature of epics such as the Homeric poems and *Beowulf*, the method of whose composition is not documented and is subject to controversy?

Parry went into the field to study epics with a clear plan of operation in mind. His recording equipment was the best available and specially made for him. With two turntables, it could record the singers without losing a word

---

appear to be relatively simple in structure compared with the Greek" (10). See also Green, 1990, 271.

11. See "Avdo Međedović, *Guslar*," in A. Lord, 1991, 57–71.

from one record to another. Besides the songs themselves, invaluable conversations with the singers were recorded, revealing the singers' own thoughts about their poems, from whom they had learned, and explanations of difficult words that appeared in their songs. Epics from the same singer were taken down first in close proximity of time and then, in my later visits, after many years had elapsed. Such experiments were important in determining the role of memory and answering questions concerning composition in performance. Sometimes it was possible to record a song as it was sung by the singer and also by the one from whom he had learned it.[12]

Substantial portions of the epics recorded by Parry have been transcribed, with meticulous attention to every syllable. Many of the epics have been published, with every possible attempt to achieve accuracy and fidelity of transmission, and they have been made available also through English translation. For scholars who are debating whether a poem from antiquity or from the Middle Ages is "oral" or "written" to disdain Parry's investigations into South Slavic epic is to reflect a narrow elitism and is nothing short of perversity. Information about the poetics of unlettered singers, the range of their ability, the structure of their lines, the themes of their songs, and the cadences of their expression, all this is surely useful and valid for comparative study.

Green continues with two questions: "Is it, with Curschmann, 'legitimate at all to apply a theory developed pragmatically in the field of a living tradition to a medieval literary production';[13] is it justified to base a general definition of oral poetry on one tradition alone and then to force this definition on all oral poetry, no matter of what tradition?"[14] In regard to Curschman's question, I fail to see anything methodologically unsound in the proposition that the compositional style of one poetry may be compared with that of another. Is it proper to dismiss out of hand the possibility that any medieval literary work might contain traits of a style that is known to be that of an oral poetry? The answer to the second question is, of course, in the negative, but I might point out that the definition was developed in a different climate at a different time and that at that time, Parry was thinking primarily of Homer and South Slavic, although his horizons had been widening for some years before 1935. As his assistant, I used to reserve books for him in Widener, and they included W. Radloff and his central Asiatic

---

12. For my account of the Parry collection and Parry's methods of field collecting, see Parry, 1954, "General Introduction," 3–20.
13. Curschmann, 1977, esp. 64.
14. Green, 1990, 270.

scholarship insofar as it was known in those days and the Finnish *Kalevala*, with especially the important work of Domenico Comparetti.[15]

For his second question, Green refers in his note 24 to the following passage from Jeff Opland:

> One of the criticisms levelled at the comparative work of Parry and Lord, especially as applied to Anglo-Saxon studies was that . . . a study of contemporary Southslavic oral poetry could be of but little relevance to the study of Anglo-Saxon poetry. This attitude is partly unjustified and partly justified. It is correct that Lord erred in seeking a general definition of oral poetry based on the Yugoslavian experience. Magoun and his followers claimed to adopt from Parry a definition of an oral poet which apparently held good for all oral poets and hence for Anglo-Saxon poets, and forced this definition onto the facts of Anglo-Saxon tradition. (See, for example, Creed: 1958 and 1959; Magoun: 1955[b]; cf. Watts [1969], 195.)[16]

Thus Opland explained why he thought that the criticism was justified. Green should have included in his reference, however, the next page of Opland's book, on which Opland goes on to say:

> These objections are valid up to a point, but the guslar can serve as a model for useful comparison with the Anglo-Saxon poet if the proper methodology is observed. If we are aware that what we are studying in the two cultures is an *analogous* phenomenon, then it is not necessary that the cultures be either similar or contemporaneous. . . . A study of the craft of the guslar . . . , of his method of poetic composition and other elements of significance in his tradition, should produce a set of observations that might or might not be helpful in understanding other oral poets. The student of any one living tradition ought to find relevance in the study of any other living tradition; he will probably find some points of agreement and other points on which the two traditions differ; the earlier definition might well help him to arrive at a coherent definition of the phenomena he is observing. The student of a dead oral tradition can similarly find relevance in the study of living oral traditions. Some observations on the contemporary traditions will fit the extant facts of his dead tradition, others will not; he must pick and choose what seem to him to be illuminating points of comparison. He must never assume a one-to-one correspondence between any two traditions, an assumption that would lead him to force the facts of a living tradition onto those of a dead one. (7)

15. Radloff, 1885; Comparetti, 1898.
16. Opland, 1980, 6.

I apologize for the long excerpts, but Opland's words here make sense, it seems to me, and I want to place his criticisms in proper perspective.[17]

Let me return to Green's article and to the second point in his reservations about the "oral theory." He wrote, "Secondly, one may question whether the oral-formulaic practice described by Parry and Lord (the poet composes his work orally, by means of formulas, in the act of performing) may be equated with oral practice at large."[18] Green then turns to "Ruth Finnegan's critique":

> She reminds us that composition-in-performance is not the only kind of oral composition, that there are recorded cases where the process of composition, while still oral, can precede and be separate from the act of performance. (Finnegan, *Oral Poetry*, page 18) On the other hand, there is the situation, common in the Middle Ages, where a work may be composed in writing but delivered orally, so that by the criterion of performance such an example must be termed oral.[19]

The first quotation from Green found us in *oralitate prima* with Havelock, the second quotation brings us to *oralitatem secundam*, that of "literal orality," with Finnegan. Oral composition before performance is common, it would seem, in Somaliland and on some of the islands in the Pacific.[20] One should note that the examples from Somali poetry which Finnegan adduces in *Oral Poetry* are not epic but short occasional songs, which one could easily "make up in the head and memorize." They are not narrative and infrequently go beyond fifty lines. When speaking of memory, one should not lump together epics of thousands of lines and short songs of less than a hundred.

In her book *Literacy and Orality*, Finnegan cites the examples of some of the Pacific oral poetries in which composition takes place before perfor-

---

17. The reference to the opinion of Opland on the subject of the definition of oral poetry, while quite correct, is not without a touch of irony. At one time, Opland was worried because he thought that Parry's definition of oral poetry did not fit the praise songs in South Africa, and he was afraid that they might be excluded. He did not then believe that they were "improvised." Later he discovered that some of them were "improvised," rather than memorized, and that he did not have to worry on that score.

18. I have omitted the following sentence: "I leave on one side the logical error, sufficiently stressed by others, of suggesting that because all oral poetry is formulaic, therefore all formulaic poetry is oral (Claes Schaar, "On a New Theory of Old English Poetic Diction," *Neuphilologus* 40, 1956, 301–5) and turn instead to Ruth Finnegan's critique."

19. Green, 1990, 270–71.

20. Beyond the remarks of Finnegan one can learn much about the Somali songs from Andrzejewski and Lewis, 1964. One should also see the volumes by Enrico Cerulli, 1957–64, devoted to the Somalis.

mance and there are fixed texts that are memorized.[21] I have looked into some of Finnegan's sources on Pacific poetry, and the adventure has been very rewarding. I have learned of some fine peoples, of talented poets, and of dedicated, courageous, and amazing collectors. There was Sir Arthur Francis Grimble, for example, who spent years in the Gilbert Islands, learned the languages needed, and collected traditions and poetry.[22] And there was also Buell Quain from Bismarck, North Dakota, who collected epic songs ("true stories") on the Fiji Islands and who learned Fiji and at the ages of twenty-three and twenty-four, wrote down and published songs and tales,[23] then died at the age of twenty-seven. He reminded me of Parry, who was killed at the age of thirty-two. And then there was Richard C. Thurnwald, who made a large collection in the Solomon Islands, which was published in Berlin in 1912.[24]

It seemed to me at first that these poems differed from written literature only in their *literal* orality. Thus they would fall into the second category, that of *oralitatis recitatorum*. I should like, however, to know much more of the details of composition, whether, for example, the phrases used are traditional. One can learn this only from a study of the texts themselves. Let me turn, for example, to Grimble, speaking of the islander's ritual preparatory to composition of a poem:

> He removes himself to some lonely spot, there to avoid all contact with man or woman. He eats nothing but the flesh of coconuts, and drinks nothing but water.
>
> For three days he thus purges his body of its vicious humours. On the fourth morning he marks out a twelve-foot square on the ground, in some place where he can get a good view of the rising sun. This is his "house of song," wherein he will sit in travail with the poem that is as yet unborn. All the next night he squats there, bolt upright, facing east, while the song quickens within him.
>
> Dawn breaks. As the edge of the sun's disc appears over the eastern sea, the poet lifts his hands at arm's-length before him, with palms turned outwards to the rising flame:
>
> He intones an incantation to the sun.
>
> This incantation (age-old inheritance from his magic-loving ancestors) he repeats three times, then rinses his mouth with salt water, thereby making his

---

21. Finnegan, 1988.
22. Grimble, 1957.
23. Quain, 1942.
24. Thurnwald, 1912; see also 1936.

tongue "pure for song." Immediately after this ritual, he goes to his village to seek five friends. When he has found them he brings them back to his "house of song." . . . They make a small, acridly smoking fire in the middle of the "house." The poet sits, in such a position that the smoke may be blown upon him by the breeze, and his five friends face him in a semicircle on the other side of the fire.

Without further preamble, he begins to recite the "rough draft" of his poem, which he has ruminated over night. It is the business of his friends to interrupt, criticise, interject suggestions, applaud, or howl down, according to their taste. Very often they do howl him down, too, for they are themselves poets. . . . They will remain without food or drink under the pitiless sun until night falls, searching for the right word, the balance, the music that will convert it into a finished work of art.

When all their wit and wisdom has been poured out upon him, they depart. He remains alone again—probably for several days—to reflect upon their advice, accept, reject, accommodate, improve, as his genius dictates. The responsibility for the completed song will be entirely his.[25]

Two comments come immediately to mind. First, although I have no quarrel with Grimble's veracity, I note a certain romantic concept of the poet and some probable exaggeration. Second, as was the case in the Somali tradition, the songs created by the poet are short. We are not speaking of models for the creating of epic songs. Third, and most important, I long to know the details of composition, the relationship of one song to another of the same genre, how much the diction is used in more than one song, and whether the style is traditional or individual.[26]

In the foregoing discussions the word *tradition* has occurred very seldom, except in my replies to criticism, when I have adduced occasionally the compound term *oral traditional*. It is at this juncture, as we consider the Pacific traditions, especially the Gilbertese songs, that the element of the "tradition" begins to loom as significant. It is important to understand that Parry's studies of Homer when he was at Berkeley and in Paris were on the traditional character of the *Iliad* and the *Odyssey*. Years ago Nagy reminded me of the significance of the diachronic element in archaic Greek poetry; he

---

25. Grimble, 1957, 204–5.
26. [Stephen A. Mitchell has observed that Grimble's description of poetic composition in the Gilberts is remarkably similar to the Germanic situation, especially to the detailed description we have of a poet at work, namely, of Egill Skallagrímsson visiting the court of Eiríkr Blood-Axe in York in the tenth century. The similarity is in respect to the notion of composition and apparent memorization before the declamation and to the fact that, in both cases, relatively short, nonnarrative genres are involved. For a discussion of Cædmon's *Hymn* in this context, see below, after n. 35.]

was speaking of Hesiod particularly.[27] In some ways, the traditionality of the poetry is more pertinent than its orality, but both aspects must be understood. The point is to emphasize the diachronic character of the oral poetries concerned.

Parry's first tenet in regard to the traditionality of Homeric style was, I believe, that such a complex style could not have been invented by a single person but must have been created by a number of poets over several generations. I think this is true, for the epic at least, about the medieval vernacular poetries. It is also true, I suggest, that the poetics of that style antedated writing. Finally—and this seems to me to be the most important— the values inherent in oral traditional narratives, their "mythic" patterns, are very old, although they may have undergone changes and reinterpretations as there were changes in religion or social structure. Here I find myself in agreement with Havelocks' concept of the function, or functions, of oral traditional literature when he wrote, "Literate societies [conserve their mores] by documentation; pre-literate ones achieve the same result by the composition of poetic narratives which serve also as encyclopedias of conduct . . . and as continually recited constitute a report—a reaffirmation—of the communal ethos and also a recommendation to abide by it."[28]

Finally, Green continues to his third and last point:[29]

> This brings me, thirdly, to the theory's rejection of memorizing as the basis of performance (as opposed to extemporizing composition-in-performance). This is at variance with isolated references to a memorial tradition in Germanic sources[30] and Alan Jabbour's suggestion that ballad tradition in northern Europe might be more relevant than Yugoslav practice,[31] but more particularly with evidence from further afield, showing poetry composed before performance in a fixed, memorized form.[32] Confronted by this evidence, Lord said that such examples "may not be oral composition, but rather written composition without writing"—in this phrasing we may detect, I think, a desperate attempt to save the appearances of the theory by dismissing what does not conform to it. That the awkward evidence, coming from the Pacific islands, is not so remote as to be irrelevant is suggested by a case from medieval Europe, for whereas Caedmon constituted Magoun's case for oral-formulaic composi-

27. Nagy, 1982.
28. Havelock, 1978, 4.
29. Green, 1990, 271.
30. Lönnroth, 1971; Harris, 1983.
31. Jabbour, 1969.
32. Finnegan, 1988, 86–109.

tion, Donald K. Fry has used the same example to suggest prior composition and memorization as an alternative to improvisation.[33]

Perhaps this was intended to be the coup de grace, but I am sorry to disappoint D. H. Green. I do not feel at all desperate about the "oral theory" *and never have*. Occasionally I have felt a bit exasperated that my attempts to elucidate it have not been understood.

With regard to Finnegan's statements, supported as we have seen by Grimble,[34] concerning prior composition and memorized performance of poetry in the Pacific Islands, I do not deny the evidence. In my paradoxical description of such poetry as "written composition without writing," I was attempting to emphasize that the prolonged and to a very high degree premeditated nature of such composition and the strenuous efforts to transmit it to others by rote memorization resemble more closely a written than an oral mentality. To my mind, such poetry would appear to be "oral" mainly in its performance.

The "isolated references to memorial tradition in Germanic sources," namely, papers by Lars Lönnroth and by Joseph Harris on Eddic poetry and Alan Jabbour's 1969 article on memorial transmission in Old English poetry are to be reckoned with. Jabbour begins with a useful summary of the "oral theory" and the attitudes toward composition engendered by it. He focuses on the distinction between "primarily improvisational" and "primarily memorial" transmission, concluding that the South Slavic belongs in the first category and Old English, together with the English ballads, in the second. I have responded at some length to Jabbour's arguments in the previous chapter.[35]

33. Fry, 1975.
34. To the passage from Grimble, 1957, quoted by Finnegan, 1988, 96–97, I add the following: "The islander is a consummate poet. His songs . . . are clear-cut gems of diction, polished and repolished with loving care, according to the canons of a technique as exacting as it is beautiful. . . . This island poet thrilled as subtly as our own to the exquisite value of words, labouring as patiently after the perfect epithet. As a result his songs are literature, though they remained from the beginning unwritten" (Grimble, 1957, 200).
35. For my discussion of Jabbour, see Chap. 7, at n. 13. [In his lecture on which the present chapter is based, Lord did not respond to Green's reference to Lönnroth and Harris. Concerning Lönnroth, Stephen A. Mitchell kindly informs me that it should be noted that his early views, as expressed in his 1971 article—in which, incidentally, he already acknowledged the importance of "the oral-formulaic theory" for explaining "certain features of Eddic composition" (3)—seasoned considerably as he came increasingly to appreciate the theoretical ramifications of Parry's and Lord's findings for the Old Norse situation. In particular, his publications of 1976, 1979, and 1981 make clear that whatever his early reservations, Lönnroth found that a full understanding of the Icelandic materials without reference to their oral nature was an impossibility. See also Mitchell, 1987. With regard to Harris's work on Eddic literature, it is helpful to consider the survey in Mitchell, 1991, 92–103, of the Old Norse prosimetrical *fornaldarsogur* in particular, and other sagas in general. He

Let me turn finally to Green's last instance. Cædmon's *Hymn* is demonstrably formulaic. He was inspired to compose it after he excused himself from the postprandial group entertainment. He had his vision after he went out to the barn and fell asleep. That he kept it in memory is clear from Bede's account, because the next day the steward brought him to Abbess Hild, to whom he recited the nine verses.[36] It is credible that short songs can be composed in the formulaic style and memorized. After all, even I can remember nine lines.

It was not the formulaic style, however, that was noteworthy in Cædmon's *Hymn* but the new subject matter.[37] The legend about his inspiration is a version of the same kind of legend found in the Near East—in Turkey, for instance—and on the Pacific Islands, as we have just seen. The legends in those cases also had to do with the contents of poems.

A similar phenomenon occurs in the case of several of the songs composed in the traditional formulaic style by two of Karadžić's singers, Tešan Podrugović and Filip Višnjić. Under the influence of the monastery at Šišatovac they were told about some of the church legends and made songs of them, songs that were a new kind of creation: the formulaic style was the same, but the subjects were not the traditional ones. Thus, alongside Podrugović's traditional songs such as "Marko Kraljević and Musa Arbanasa" and "Marko Kraljević and Đemo Brđanin," we find a religious legend, *Nahod Simeun*, "The Foundling Simeun." Filip Višnjić gave Karadžić two religious songs, such as *Sveti Sava*, "Saint Sava," and a version of *Smrt Marka Kraljevića*, "The Death of Marko Kraljević," which contained clear reference to church legend. In the last, for instance, the dead Marko is found by Vaso, a monk from the Serbian monastery of Hilandar on Mount Athos, which was given by the Byzantine emperor in 1189 to Simeon and Sava Nemanja, the founders of the illustrious Nemanjić dynasty. Vaso and his deacon take Marko's body to Hilandar, where it is entombed. This element is found only in the version by Višnjić and those texts derived from it. Interestingly enough, other versions, including one in the Parry collection, tell of a monk discovering the body of Marko; the monk is not from Mount Athos, however, but from the church at Samodreže, an establishment found only in the traditional poetry, which scholars have not been able to locate either historically or geographically.

The parallel between the phenomenon of these two singers, Tešan Podru-

---

discusses what is, for Norse culture, the transitional thirteenth century, when a true court culture and attendant written literature develop. But, he states, they do so in addition to, rather than as a replacement for, traditional oral narration.

36. [The mention of these last details is owed to the kindness of Daniel Donoghue.]
37. [A. Lord, 1993. For a well-rounded article on Cædmon's *Hymn*, see Morland, 1992.]

gović and especially Filip Višnjić, and that of Cædmon is striking. The Serbian Orthodox Church was having a revival in the late eighteenth century and during the nineteenth. A significant sociologic change was taking place in the nineteenth century, and the old traditional Serbian epic was being adapted to the new circumstances. In Cædmon's time, a great religious change was taking place and the traditional songs were being adapted to the new religion. In both cases, traditional poets were using the oral traditional formulaic style in which they were already expert.

Presumably both Podrugović and Višnjić were dictating line by line to Karadžić, or possibly to the archimandrite Mušicki. Their performances were those of dictating—a kind of performance, by the way, of which not nearly enough has been written in detail. They may have, and probably did, think about the songs beforehand, just as extempore speakers usually think of what they are going to say before they rise to their feet, although they may not have put it into fixed words until the moment of performance, as it were. I suspect that we shall never know whether Cædmon fixed his nine lines in his mind—in other words, memorized them—before he performed them for his fellows, or expressed his well-thought-out ideas in the traditional style when at last his turn came to sing. In the first case, he was a memorizer of nine lines of oral traditional formulaic poetry; in the second, he was composing in performance.

Clearly the question of memorizing belongs as much in the land of the Aquitanians, because it is part and parcel of the separation of composition and performance, as in that of the philologists.

Let me begin a kind of summation with some considerations not raised by Green but often brought up. Early on, the tests for orality—(1) by formula density, (2) by thematic composition, and (3) by the presence of unperiodic enjambment—caused difficulty and misunderstanding. A fourth idea that belongs perhaps in the same category is that of thrift. This concept stems from Parry's Homeric studies and has been recently questioned by David Shive.[38]

The definitions of *formula* and *theme* have been much debated, and still are. Parry's definition of the formula was general enough that it could be easily adapted to the metrical requirements of any given cultural tradition. Fry's adaptations of the definitions of both it and the theme furnish a fine, if somewhat cumbersome, example. It is necessary to differentiate between a repetition and the formula: all formulas are repetitions by definition, that is, they are "regularly used"; but not all repetitions are formulas. This differen-

---

38. Shive, 1987. [See, however, Martin, 1989, 2, and n. 3; also Riggsby, 1992.]

tiation is often neglected. Larry Benson questioned the test of formula density in respect to *Beowulf* and other Anglo-Saxon poetry. I have only recently come to realize, after comparing the style of the Russian *byliny* with that of *Beowulf*—they both use tonic rather than syllabic metrics—that, because of the alliterative technique, we cannot expect an accurate assessment of formulas without a larger body of poetry available than there is in Anglo-Saxon.[39]

I consider the *theme* as a repeated *passage*—not a repeated *subject*—within the songs or poetry of a given individual, thus constraining it not only to a single poet but also to a more or less stable set of words. It is demonstrable that it exists as an entity that can be employed in the poetry whenever its subject is pertinent to the song at hand.

Something more has been made of unperiodic *enjambment* than it really deserves, I fear, but it is true that there is a decided tendency in the oral traditional poetic narratives with which I am acquainted to enclose an idea of sentence length—if that is the way to put it—within a line and not to run it over to the next. It is a tendency more noticeable in some traditions than in others. The Homeric poems contain run-on lines, but the unperiodic relationship between the first and the second lines of the *Iliad* is what Parry had in mind. The South Slavic poetry follows this concept fairly well, but Anglo-Saxon poetry, with its frequent cases of a sentence beginning in the b-verse, does not. The presence or absence of unperiodic enjambment is more a rule of thumb than a conclusive test.

A word on *thrift*: It is certainly a Homeric phenomenon but I am not sure that it has been properly investigated in medieval epic. One has to confine the test to songs or poems by a single person in order to arrive at reliable results, and such material is not readily available in medieval literature.

It seems to me that those difficulties came to be ignored by scholars, either because they were understood and taken for granted or, more likely, because they were not considered significant. In their place, as it were, the concept of composition in performance became most troublesome to both classicists and medievalists, because it was equated with extempore improvisation, which I have discussed above.

My insistence in *The Singer of Tales* that there is no such thing as a transitional text presented a difficulty for the medievalist. Associated with the idea of the transitional text is the dictum that a singer who learns to read or write loses the ability to compose orally. In Chapter 4,[40] I have addressed this matter, and to it I return again in Chapter 10.

---

39. [Lord, 1992.]
40. See Chapter 4 after n. 19.

Let me end this chapter not with criticism but with a positive statement, a creed, as it were. Literature, in the sense of the artistic use of words, began without writing and was already highly developed when writing was invented or introduced into a given society. The style created by many practitioners over several generations persisted long after writing came in. Only gradually, and under influences outside the traditional milieu and people, was the oral traditional style modified by conscious breaking with tradition and movement in the direction of conscious originality and nontraditional choice of words and constructions. It was easier to change subject matter than to change style, to adapt old words to new contexts, as did Cædmon in Old English, moving from pagan to Christian themes but preserving the old style.

The subject matter of the narrative poetry, its stories, originated, in the case of the epic, in myth, whence came its aura of the numinous, its atmosphere of the sacred in the broadest sense of the term. It is the nature of traditional literature to conserve old meanings even under heavy disguise placed on them through intermittent reinterpretation. It is, in my view, essential to know the relationship of any given text to the tradition so that one may be justified in discovering in it the latent traditional meanings, their vestiges or echoes, and thus rightly to read it with full understanding. Moreover, on the level of aesthetics, one needs to know whether a text is oral traditional or not in order correctly to apply the criteria of referentiality.[41] There *is* a difference between oral traditional poetics and written poetics, and one must know with what kind of poetry one is dealing in order correctly to appreciate its aesthetics and to describe and edit its texts.

41. For an example of unwarranted and excessive editing of oral texts according to "literary" standards, see the discussion in Chapter 1, after n. 21, of the changes made by Marjanović in texts that he had collected.

CHAPTER 9

*Two Versions of the Theme
of the Overnight Visit in*
The Wedding of Smailagić Meho

I have attempted throughout to define and illustrate the role of the theme, and I wish to pursue this subject further by calling attention to a fully developed theme as seen in two versions in Avdo Međedović's epic song *The Wedding of Smailagić Meho*.[1] In discussing the theme in Old English in Chapter 6, I remarked that this narrative device in oral traditional poetry should contain a certain degree of verbal correspondence if a theme in oral traditional literature is to be differentiated from one in written nontraditional literature. The oral poet tends to repeat some words or formulas in different singings of the same theme, although he is free to vary his lines as he wishes, and this variation may be significant. To what extent the singer may vary repeated versions of the same theme depends, of course, on the skill of each singer and on how often he uses a particular theme. Short themes frequently employed are likely to exhibit considerable verbal stability.

A means of gauging the amounts of repetition and variation which a highly talented oral poet can display in singing two versions of a theme can be found by comparing two episodes in which Avdo Međedović describes the journey of the Bosnian hero Meho and his companion, Osman, to Buda. They make two overnight stops en route.[2] At the first stop, their host and his wife see the approaching men and in conversation establish their identity. In the first episode the host Vukašin tells his wife that he will go to the

---

1. For an account of the life and the songs of Avdo Međedović, see my introduction to Parry, 1974a, 3–34; also A. Lord, 1991, 57–71. For previous discussions of the theme of the overnight visit in *Smailagić Meho*, see A. Lord, 1951 and 1971. See also A. Lord, 1986, 57–59, with a list of the narrative elements in this theme.

2. For the Serbo-Croatian text and my English translation, see Parry, 1974a, 108–18; and 1974b, 115–36.

courtyard to greet their guests and that she should take their rifles. This they do and servants take their horses. In the second episode the host—in this instance, Vujadin—instructs his sons to go down to the courtyard to welcome the young men. They do this, and then Vujadin comes to the courtyard and welcomes Meho and Osman, while the sons walk the visitors' horses and Vujadin's wife takes their rifles.

In the conversation before dinner in the first episode, after Vukašin has inquired after Meho's father and has received news of the Border, Meho tells of the purpose of their journey to Buda and remarks that the vizier in Buda is a good friend. The host, however, warns Meho and Osman that the vizier in Buda is a traitor. Avdo is preparing for the events to come the following day when the young men reach Buda; he is introducing in this casual, realistic way the complications that will shape the action of the rest of the song.

In the second overnight episode the preprandial conversation does not touch on these matters at all, but Vujadin asks after Meho's father and the Border, ending with: "How does it seem to you, Mehmed? Are the old men better, or would you say the young are?" Mehmed replies: "Opinions are divided, but mine shall ever be that the old men are better than the young." This is a favorite subject of Avdo's, because he had one dutiful and one rebellious son, and he sometimes brings this question into his songs. Vujadin replies to Meho: "Bravo! my dear son. If God grants you will be an honor to us." This is a fathers-and-sons conversation in a fathers-and-sons scene.

After dinner in the first episode, the young men's beds are prepared for them by two beautiful girls, after which the maidens leave and Vuk and his wife stand watch all night long as their guests sleep. At dinner in the second episode Vujadin's sons stand ready to serve while host and guests eat, served by the daughters-in-law, and during the night the sons stand watch over Meho and Osman as they sleep.

It is clear that Avdo has varied the contents of the theme and hence reduced the degree of verbal correspondence. Yet the theme is recognizable as a theme, with the main elements of (1) viewing the approaching heroes, 2) conversation determining their identity, (3) the welcoming of the guests, (4) preprandial conversation, (5) tending the horses, (6) dinner, (7) sleeping, and (8) awakening and departure. But verbal correspondence there is. Let us look briefly at the beginning of the texts to verify this point:

First Episode	Second Episode
	Koliko su zemlje Bosne prešli,
Đe li *h*i je akšam zateknuo,[3]	Do akšama došli đe su rekli,

3. The italicizing of single letters here and throughout indicates abnormal pronunciation.

Theme in *The Wedding of Smailagić Meho* 205

U nekako selo Vukašiće,	Do dvorova kneza Vujadina.
Pred dvorove kneza Vukašina,	Knez se beše pridesijo tuna,
Najboljega njihnog domaćina.	I kod njega Vujadinovica,
Vukašin se na dvor pridesijo,	I dva sina kneza Vujadina.
I gospoja Vukašinovica.	

At nightfall they found themselves in the village of Vukašići before the dwelling of Vukašin, the village elder and their family's best householder. Vukašin and his spouse were both at home.	They had covered as much of Bosnia as they said they would before nightfall, for they had come to the house of Vujadin. Vujadin happened to be at home, and with him his wife and their two sons.

The verbal correspondence is clear so far. The heroes reached their destination at evening, at the house of a named elder, and he and his wife, and in the second case also his two sons, are at home. The verbal similarity now disappears, to reappear later, as, for example, in the section describing the tending of the horses.[4] In the first episode the couple sees Meho on his horse, and both horse and rider are described; then Osman on his horse, with accompanying description also. Vukašin and his wife converse about the two newcomers at some length, finally recognizing them and expressing their joy that they are coming to their house. Vukašin then gives instructions as to how they should be received. In the second episode the couple looks from the window and sees the two "imperial dragons." They are described, and then the host's two sons go to the window and are amazed at what they see. They express their amazement to their father, who looks again and recognizes Meho and Osman. He then gives instructions as to how their guests are to be received. This part of the first episode is more than twice the length of the corresponding section of the second episode.[5]

There is, of course, some verbal correspondence between the two episodes, but it is not very extensive because of the difference in content between the two instances of the theme. Yet one notices considerable repetition, for example, in Avdo's treatment of the subtheme describing the

---

4. See the next excerpt.
5. [Shannon, 1975, 21, calling attention to Parry's distinction between "good" and "bad" oral poets according to their ability to expand and elaborate on any given theme, is mistaken in arguing: "Were that the case, every typical scene should be fully elaborated in the work of a 'good' oral poet." For the singer 'to ornament' (*kititi*) a theme did not mean to string out extraneous detail but rather to know how effectively to develop a theme—to caparison a horse, to arm a hero, to gather an assembly. Shannon admires the fact that, in Homer, elaboration and variation are used "with scrupulous selectivity." We should add that the differing length of Avdo's two versions of the theme of the overnight visit shows that he, like Homer, knew when to elaborate and when not to.]

tending of Meho's and Osman's horses. The following comparison, with similarities in wording underlined, shows how the singer had a fairly stable way of expressing this segment of his story. It is clear, however, that he had not memorized the passages but was composing as he sang.

First Episode	Second Episode
Mlađi <u>momci konje provedoše,</u>	Dokle <u>momci konje provedoše,</u>
Dok <u>h</u>im <u>vodu</u> konji <u>pokupiše.</u>	S ćelehana umor povrnuše,
Pa sa konja <u>sedla oboriše,</u>	Pa im zlatna <u>sedla oboriše,</u>
Svitu cjelu i njihno oružje;	Zlatna <u>sedla</u> i zlatne rahtove,
Pa na konje <u>čule navališe,</u>	I kalkane sa četiri strane.
Da umorni konji ne ozebu.	Na sunđer <u>h</u>im <u>vodu pokupiše,</u>
Pa <u>h</u>im sitnu <u>arpu</u> natakoše.	A na čaršaf dlaku namestiše.
U <u>podrum</u> hi za jasli svežaše,	Na pleći <u>h</u>im <u>čule navališe,</u>
Kod putalja kneza Vukašina	<u>Arpu</u> daše, pa <u>h</u>i pričekaše,
Dok atovi zobcu izedoše,	Dok hajvani <u>arpu</u> pozobaše.
Na atove timar navališe,	U jaslima seno utakoše,
Te <u>h</u>im kao i znoj otrljaše.	Pa na <u>podrum</u> vrata zatvoriše.
Na čaršafe dlake namestiše,	
Pa <u>h</u>im opet <u>čule navališe.</u>	

Then stewards walked their horses, and as they led them, the horses regained their spirits.[6] They stripped them of their saddles, their trappings, and armor. They flung blankets over the horses that the tired steeds should not become chilled, measured out barley for them, and tied them in their stalls beside Vukašin's stallion. When the horses had eaten their barley, the youths groomed them and rubbed the mud and sweat from them, drying their manes with cloth. Finally they replaced the blankets on the horses.

In the meantime the young men were walking the heroes' steeds, driving fatigue from them. They took off the golden saddles and trappings and all the girths. Then they sponged the horses and dried their manes with a towel. They covered them with blankets, gave them barley, and waited for the beasts to eat it. Then they put hay into the mangers [and] closed the door of the stable.

These descriptions, if different to some extent, are close to descriptions elsewhere in this song and in others by Avdo. He was trying to vary the

---

6. The translation of this line, 2382, is an attempt to render a misformed line. The dative *him* should be accusative. A word such as *silu*, acc. of *sila* 'strength' is to be supplied as object of the verb *pokupiše* 'gather', 'regain'.

Theme in *The Wedding of Smailagić Meho* 207

scene, and his repertory of descriptive formulas was so great that he did not have to repeat himself, if he did not choose to do so.[7]

We can take the individual items in the descriptions and find their counterparts in other poems of Avdo's to note that the sense of textuality belongs to a comparatively small group of lines. For example, in the early description of Meho in episode one above we find the lines (2162–64):

Oko konja njegova dorata	His forged saber glided over his horse's side
Plaza mu se sablja okovata,	like a serpent around a dry thistle.
Ka' i guja oko suhog trna.	

This theme, or "subtheme," is found at least twice in Avdo's other long song, *Osmanbeg Delibegović i Pavičević Luka*, in lines 664–69 and 4897–99:

A alatu čatal podigao.	He had drawn the bay's bridle up tight.
Kolik alat beše u visinu,	The bay carried itself so tall
Mača kleta od tri rastegljaja,	that the damned sword, a full three ells long,
Kaako (*sic*) se plaza oko konja,	which slithered about the horse
Baš k'o ono guja oko trna,	like a viper 'round a thorn bush,
Sve alata po čavlama tuče.	kept knocking against the well-shod hooves.
A zlatna se alamanka valja	His gilded German sabre fell
Oko tanke njihne bedevije,	about his finely-featured bedouin mare,
Bi rekao da je plaza guja.	one might say, like a viper slithering.[8]

Two of the key words are *plaza* 'glide' and *guja* 'snake'.

The next lines in *Smailagić Meho* present another subtheme, lines 2165–67:

Dorat dvije žvale razvalijo.	The chestnut steed spread his two jaws.
Da mu bugar-kabanicu baci,	Were you to cast a Bulgarian cloak into
Ne bi konju žvale zatisnula.	them, it would not fill his gaping jaws.

There are several related passages in *Osmanbeg Delibegović i Pavičević Luka*, but they do not express exactly the same idea. Here are two of them (lines 638–43 and 6781–83):

---

7. See Parry, 1974a, 256, n. 60, for a brief account of differences between the versions of the theme under discussion.
8. For the Serbo-Croatian text, see Parry, 1980. [David E. Bynum has kindly supplied translations of the passages cited from *Osmanbeg Delibegović i Pavičević Luka*.]

Pa je dvije žvale ražvalijo,	He was gaping
Pa iz žvala pene prebacuje	and blowing out great gobs of foam
Preko sebe i pr'o gazde svoga,	onto himself and his master
Na olukli sapi dočekuje.	so plentifully that it was accumulating along his flanks.
Ko nije vešt pa nije vidijo,	Someone unaccustomed to such a spectacle
Bi rekao, rađaju se ovce.	might have said that ewes were lambing there.
Alat skoči nekud na oblake,	His bay seemed to gambol somewhere aloft amidst the very clouds,
Pa razvali žvale obadvije.	and when it parted its jaws
Iz noždre mu maven plamen linu.	blue flame shot forth from its muzzle.

Another cluster in the description in the first episode with corresponding clusters in *Osmanbeg Delibegović i Pavičević Luka* is in lines 2168–70 of *Smailagić Meho*:

Bi rekao i bi se zakleo,	One would say and swear that it was an
Da je mušir carev na dorata.	imperial field marshal upon the horse; his
Saltanet mu bolji no muširov.	trappings were better than a field marshal's.

Compare the following clusters from *Osmanbeg Delibegović i Pavičević Luka*, lines 4683–85 and 4624–26:

E, kakav je Ljevak na alata!	Oh, how splendid Ljevak was as he sat his bay!
Bi rekao da je vezir čarski.	One might have said he was an Imperial Vizier.
Saltanet mu bolji od vezira.	But he cut a more majestic figure than any vizier would.
Taj je dečak baš k'o vezir carski,	That young fellow was like some Imperial Vizier,
Nekud bolji mlogo od vezira.	though in some respects he was far better than a vizier.
Saltanet mu viši od vezira.	He cut a more majestic figure than any vizier would.

A larger descriptive theme consists of a collection of such clusters of several lines which I think are the basic "compositional themes" of the oral traditional songs. Of course they correspond to the units we found in oral

Theme in *The Wedding of Smailagić Meho* 209

traditional lyric songs, namely, units consisting of a more or less stable core of lines with additions adapted to context.

The two versions of the theme of the overnight visit in *The Wedding of Smailagić Meho* can be divided into several segments, for each of which the line numbers in the first and second episodes are given in parentheses so that the relative length of the two episodes can readily be determined and the passages located.[9] The theme begins with the viewing of the approaching heroes (1:2152–76 and 2:2677–2700). This is followed by the determining of their identity (1:2177–2254 and 2:2701–29). Avdo takes the opportunity to emphasize the striking appearance of the heroes and the splendid caparisoning of their horses. The guests are then formally welcomed (1:2255–84 and 2:2730–43). They enter the house and refreshment is served (1:2285–2310 and 2:2744–2783). After conversation (1:2311–57 and 2:2784–2824), the first episode launches upon a description of preparation for dinner (2358–80), which is matched slightly later in the theme in the second episode (2837–56), with the account of tending the heroes' horses intervening (1:2381–94 and 2:2825–36).

At line 2395 and continuing through 2467, Avdo in the first episode presents the important conversation in which Vukašin warns Meho and Osman of the treachery of the vizier in Buda. Then follows, still in the first episode (2468–72) a brief treatment of the bounteous feast served in Vukašin's house. As the theme progresses to the sleep of the heroes, the segments of the second episode are greatly curtailed. In the first episode Avdo gives an elaborate account of the beds laid for the heroes (2473–2509), whereas the second episode in its turn devotes only two lines (2857–58) to this segment. The sleeping Meho and Osman are guarded in the first episode by Vukašin and his wife (2510–16), and in the second episode the two sons of Vujadin watch over them (2859–62).

When the young heroes awake, there is a long discussion in the first episode with their host, Vukašin, who is greatly disturbed that the guests cannot be persuaded to lengthen their stay (2517–87), whereas in the second episode Avdo is content merely to state that Vujadin and his two sons tried as best they could to make their guests stay, but to no avail (2863–68). There follows the preparation of the heroes and horses for departure (1:2588–2618 and 2:2869–80). Before leaving, there is a giving of gifts to Vukašin's daughters and to Vujadin's daughters-in-law, and farewells are said to the household (1:2619–65 and 2:2881–92).[10]

9. The passages are in Parry, 1974a and 1974b.
10. [In a letter dated November 30, 1992, David Bynum pointed out the thematically prescribed gift giving to the women of the family: "A guest may not 'tip' a patriarchal host, but anything presented to the host's subordinate householders will be gratefully received."]

In both versions Avdo gracefully describes the heroes' departure:

First Episode (2666–74)	Second Episode (2893–95)
Then [Meho] applied the spurs and slackened the reins. The chestnut understood, took to his hoofs, and tossed the bit. He would not go through the iron gateway, but cleared the wall and was off over the heath. He cantered playfully across the green plain, behind him Osman on his spotted gray. He flew over the verdant plain even as a star across the sky.	Then he rode his chestnut steed to the courtyard gate, Osman behind him on his gray stallion, like a star across a clear sky.

Even this brief account reveals unmistakably how the narrative structure of the theme remains essentially intact from one version to another. The second episode is much briefer than the first, but with the exception of minor shifts in the order of some subthemes, the narrative follows step by step from the first approach of the heroes to their departure.[11] The variations in the scenes of hospitality and the shortened pace of the second episode ensure against tedium in the audience. In only one section ("entering the house, refreshment") is the second episode longer than the matching first episode. In this particular instance, as in others during the course of the two visits, the scene comes alive because it was Avdo's manner to form a mental image of what he was describing. He saw in his mind's eye the master's room in Vujadin's house, with all its furnishings. As Avdo explained to me in talking about his singing, he visualized, for example, each piece of the trappings on a horse. From this mental image there flowed the words to describe the scene or the action, so that it became a reflection of what he envisaged in his mind in all its vivid detail.

The two versions of the overnight visit in Avdo's song show nice contrasts and balances. Vukašin had long lived among the Turks and "in their fashion." His relations with his overlord, Smail, in Kanidža were especially warm, but he still kept his Christian faith, as did Vujadin. At one point, Vukašin crossed himself, and once Lady Vukašin prayed in the name of God and all his saints. Lady Vukašin had an important part in the hospitality to the guests. She helped welcome them and later she "pushed back her sleeves and made pies and prepared wheat cakes." She also with her husband watched over the heroes at night. Vujadin's wife had a less prominent role, partly taken over by

---

11. The first episode of the theme extends for 523 lines of verse; the second episode fills 219 lines.

her daughters-in-law. Vukašin had two marriageable daughters, while Vujadin had two sons who were already wed. Vukašin and his household provided lavish hospitality for their guests, but Vujadin's welcome and his concern for the heroes were also unstinting. Although the description of the second visit is greatly shortened, especially in the closing segments of the theme, no step in the episode is omitted.

I have earlier compared the two versions of the theme of the overnight visit in Avdo's song with two visits of Telemachus in the *Odyssey*.[12] On his journey to consult Menelaus about Odysseus's fate, Telemachus made two overnight stops in Book 3. The first one, in the company of Athena in the guise of Mentor, was at the home of Nestor at Pylos, a visit that the poet elaborated at full length, constituting Book 3. On the second stop, Telemachus, accompanied by Peisistratus, the son of Nestor, stayed at the house of Diocles in Pherae. This second stay is sketched only briefly, *Odyssey* 3.487–94. The second visit in Avdo's song, in contrast, although much briefer than the first, receives the singer's considerable attention.

By studying Avdo's two versions, the reader is able to judge the possible range of stability and variation within a well-established theme in the repertoire of an accomplished oral traditional singer. The poet is able to expand a part of his theme by effective ornamentation or in another version to curtail the corresponding segment for the sake of narrative economy, or to suit the particular situation. The seasoned oral singer can produce at will a long or short version of a theme according to his assessment of the demands of his narrative.

Even above and beyond the critical interest this theme arouses in its structure, however, is its value in illustrating Avdo's depiction of the ideals of courtesy and hospitality sensitively shared between the young Moslem heroes and their hosts, the Christian *kmet*s 'village head's. In this theme are mirrored the artistry and the humanity of the whole poem.

12. A. Lord, 1951.

CHAPTER 10

The Transitional Text

One of the important differences between an oral traditional singer and a nontraditional one is the fact that the traditional singer does not think in terms of a fixed textuality, whereas the nontraditional singer does. If a traditional singer in the course of a lifetime becomes a nontraditional poet—as, I believe, one could argue in the case of Petar Petrović Njegoš II—at what point does this singer's sense of fixed textuality develop?[1] Can we pinpoint the moment when he becomes a nontraditional poet? In *The Singer of Tales*, I phrased the problem somewhat differently by saying that I could not conceive of a singer thinking at one and the same time in terms of both fluidity and fixity. He might go from one mode to the other but could not be in both at the same time.[2]

I have now come to realize, as I have analyzed themes in terms of textuality, that the traditional epic singer, composing characteristically in comparatively short passages—that is, themes—actually does work with a mixture of more or less stable core and optional lines. By "more or less stable lines" I mean that they are not fixed in wording—not irrevocably fixed, that is, although they do tend to stability. Stability does not necessarily mean fixity. This is true, of course, of most of the lines of a traditional song; core lines and optional ones are alike in their lack of fixity. After all, fluidity of wording is the true mark of this style. The core lines are those found in all (or nearly all) the occurrences of a theme; the optional lines may or may not be used in any single instance of it. The latter are of at least two kinds. One

---

1. For previous discussions of the transitional text, see A. Lord, 1986; also 1987b, 337–45. For a treatment of the developing poetic style of Njegoš, see A. Lord, 1986, 30–34.
2. See A. Lord, 1960, chap. 6, "Writing and Oral Tradition," 124–38.

functions as expansion or ornamentation, the other in adapting a theme to the specific context of a given song.

Singers vary greatly in the comparative stability of the core lines and in the number and character of the optional lines. It would not be accurate, therefore, to say that in composing any instance of a theme a singer is thinking in terms of both fixity and fluidity; for a more or less constant core of lines is ornamented or expanded according to the wishes of the singer at the moment or adapted to fit a particular situation in a particular song. All I am doing is describing in greater detail the fluidity of the traditional style. None of the lines is really fixed and predictable; the number and content of even the core lines is to a degree variable. In short, we can predict, let us say, that two out of a given three core lines may be found in any given instance of a theme, but we cannot predict with certainty which two nor exactly what form they will have. This is not fixity of text, nor does it require a sense of fixed textuality on the part of the singer.

It is common in the Homeric poems to find passages that recur nearly verbatim. George Goold drew our attention to such passages, arguing that they were fixed and memorized.[3] First, the passages are not quite as unchangeable as Goold implies, and second, with George Bolling, I believe that their exactness, when it occurs, is the result of editing.[4]

All this may suggest a possible answer to the question posed earlier, namely, at what point does a singer pass from being traditional to being nontraditional? Could it be that point when he does begin to think of really fixed lines, when he actually memorizes them? If so, then we might be able to observe and even measure that "moment" in the texts of a singer, that is, when we find that a singer has memorized passages verbatim. This line of investigation needs to be followed both rigorously and extensively.[5]

Two other aspects of the question What is a transitional text? have been brought to my attention and deserve further discussion. One is suggested by the work of such a selector, editor, and "reteller" of folktales as Italo Calvino, the reference by some of my friends to whose work on folktales as possible transitional texts brought this question to mind. The second aspect concerns the *writing* rather than the singing or dictating of formulaic verse texts, for example, Andrija Kačić-Miošić's *Razgovor ugodni naroda slovinskoga*, "A Pleasant Discourse of the Slavic People."[6]

3. Goold, 1977.
4. See Bolling, 1925. [For the editing of repeated passages in the *Iliad*, see Janko, 1990, esp. 332–34.]
5. For an earlier discussion of this question, see A. Lord, 1987b, under the heading "The Memorizing Oral Poet," 313–24. See also A. Lord, 1991, "The Influence of a Fixed Text," 170–85.
6. Discussed below.

In connection with Calvino's work, a question arises how one could tell his version of a folktale, his retelling of it, from the "naïve" version of the traditional teller. This is a question that could be applicable to other retellers who are themselves men of letters. Calvino's work, it must be remembered, is prose tale, but some of the principles involved may be applicable to verse narrative as well. His situation brings to mind that of the Montenegrin poet Petar Petrović Njegoš II, and we shall look too at three stages of Njegoš's poetic output to see if the middle one may be thought of as transitional.

Calvino came into this discussion first by way of the question whether his retellings of Italian folktales could be considered as transitional texts. Now, Calvino's retellings are primarily translations of dialect texts into standard Italian. So to the second question, How can you tell Calvino's retelling from the "naïve" original? the ready answer is that one is in dialect, the other in standard Italian. In one way, then, and very superficially, it is easy to distinguish Calvino from his original. But Calvino did something more than just translate; he also made changes. He himself stated his method in his introduction to *Italian Folktales* in the section entitled "Criteria for My Work":

> The method of transcribing folktales "from the mouths of the people" was started by the Brothers Grimm and was gradually developed during the second half of the century into "scientific" canons scrupulously faithful to the dialect of the narrator. The Grimms' approach was not "scientific" in the modern sense of the word, or only halfway so. A study of their manuscripts confirms what is abundantly plain to an experienced eye perusing *Kinder- und Hausmärchen*, namely that the Grimms (Wilhelm in particular) had added their own personal touch to the tales told by little old women, not only translating a major part from German dialects, but integrating the variants, recasting the story whenever the original was too crude, touching up expressions and images, giving stylistic unity to the discordant voices.
>
> The foregoing serves as an introduction and justification (if I may take refuge behind names so famous and remote) for the hybrid nature of my work, which likewise is only halfway "scientific," or three-quarters so; as for the final quarter, it is the product of my own judgment. The scientific portion is actually the work of others, of those folklorists who, in the span of one century, patiently set down the texts that served as my raw material. What I did with it is comparable to the second part of the Grimms' project: I selected from mountains of narratives (always basically the same ones and amounting altogether to some fifty types) the most unusual, beautiful, and original texts. I translated them from the dialects in which they were recorded or when, unfortunately, the only version extant was an Italian translation lacking the

freshness of authenticity, I assumed the thorny task of recasting it and restoring its lost originality. I enriched the text selected from other versions and whenever possible did so without altering its character or unity, and at the same time filled it out and made it more plastic. I touched up as delicately as possible those portions that were either missing or too sketchy. I preserved, linguistically, a language never too colloquial, yet colorful and as derivative as possible of a dialect, without having recourse to "cultivated" expressions—an Italian sufficiently elastic to incorporate from the dialect images and turns of speech that were the most expressive and unusual. . . .

In all this I was guided by the Tuscan proverb dear to Nerucci: "The tale is not beautiful if nothing is added to it"—in other words, its value consists of what is woven and rewoven into it. I too have thought of myself as a link in the anonymous chain without end by which folktales are handed down, links that are never merely instruments or passive transmitters, but—and here the proverb meets Benedetto Croce's theory about popular poetry—its real "authors."[7]

The term *transitional text* is a grab bag often used to avoid the stigma of an oral text. We should once and for all eliminate the connotations as well as the tendentious prejudices from both "transitional" and "oral" and establish the facts. Calvino's example leads us into the "spider's nest" and is a good one with which to begin, even if, or perhaps precisely because, it is not verse epic but folktale. We are thereby not encumbered with problems of verse, or of formulas.

The first fact that strikes one is that there are comparatively few purely transcribed folktale texts published. We are much of the time proceeding on the basis of modified texts. One comes to realize that many generalities about oral traditional literature stem from doctored texts, from texts that have been "edited," changed, or "improved," most commonly by a nontraditional person or, at best, by nontraditional persons who have steeped themselves as well as they can in the traditional material but who often have other axes to grind. They too want to use tradition for their own purposes, which are not necessarily those of tradition. This can be seen in such statements as "I have chosen what is beautiful or what is striking" or "I have tried to eliminate the rough spots." Yet the tradition includes much that is not so beautiful, much that may be mediocre, many rough spots. It is true that it would be an injustice to the tradition to stress those elements, but in some way we should be made aware of what the *whole* tradition is like. This is particularly true if we want to talk about "transitional texts."

7. Calvino, 1980, xix–xxi.

How can one recognize a text that is in a transitional position between an oral traditional text and a literary text, if one never has an opportunity to see a real oral traditional text? Myles Dillon in the introduction to his translations of several Irish folktales indicated his awareness of this problem. He said that he had translated everything including the repetitions, which are usually omitted![8] There certainly is a way of distinguishing the "naïve" version from the edited or retold version, unless some of the most characteristic elements have been omitted, as is frequently done. I repeat, how can we proceed unless we have some actual knowledge of the oral traditional text?

There is no doubt that Calvino steeped himself in the traditions of the Italian folktale. Although he says that he "plunged into that submarine world totally unequipped, without even a tankful of intellectual enthusiasm for anything spontaneous and primitive," he soon became completely immersed. His characterization of the "innermost particularities" of that world, "infinite variety and infinite repetition," captures the essence not only of the folktale but of all oral "literature." He describes his journey through folklore thus:

> For two years I have lived in woodlands and enchanted castles, torn between contemplation and action: on the one hand hoping to catch a glimpse of the face of the beautiful creature of mystery who, each night, lies down beside her knight; on the other having to choose between the cloak of invisibility or the magical foot, feather, or claw that could metamorphose me into an animal. And during these two years the world about me gradually took on the attributes of fairyland, where everything that happened was a spell or a metamorphosis, where individuals, plucked from the chiaroscuro of a state of mind, were carried away by predestined loves, or were bewitched; where sudden disappearances, monstrous transformations occurred, where right had to be discerned from wrong, where paths bristling with obstacles led to a happiness held captive by dragons. Also in the lives of peoples and nations which until now had seemed to be at a standstill, anything seemed possible.[9]

How could such a sensitive and impressionable apprentice to the folktale fail to put his own stamp on the stories he retold? In his collection, Calvino has edited, making changes in style and content, oral traditional stories

---

8. Dillon, 1971: "The book therefore gives a true account of oral tradition, such as not to be found in Curtin or Larminie, or indeed, for that matter, in Grimm. The repeated formulae and the runs, which are essential features of the folktale and correspond to the formulae in Homer, are the very flavor of the story and are lost in any summary or 'literary' retelling by an editor" (7).

9. Calvino, 1980, xviii.

written down from traditional storytellers and then retold in nineteenth-century Italian, which Calvino has himself retranslated into twentieth-century Italian. The collectors from whose texts Calvino worked, for example, Antonio De Nino and Domenico Comparetti,[10] were cognizant of variants, as was also Calvino. Let us look at De Nino's comments:

> The folktales of the Abruzzi like all traditional tales vary—if not substantially, at least in modalities and in circumstances of time and place—from village to village and even, within the same village, from quarter to quarter. Even stranger, it sometimes happens that the very same narrator will vary the tale when he or she is made to repeat it at infrequent intervals. These are no slight difficulties for a collector. Nor could I have overcome them, in the present collection, without a good dose of patience, listening to the same tale being told by several persons. Thus only, I believed, could I grasp the tale in its fullness and in its most appropriate aesthetic form; thus only, also, could I overcome another difficulty no less grave: the bizarre interweaving of several fables into one—fables that, in retrospect, could and indeed must be independent. I leave it to others to judge whether I have extricated myself well or ill from the midst of this thicket.[11]

We have seen what Calvino has said in his introduction about his criteria. We can observe him at work as well through his notes, where, indeed, he tells us what he has done.

In the case of "The Florentine" (*Il fiorentino*), No. 76 (from Comparetti, 44) and "One-Eye" (*Occhio-in-fronte*), No. 115 (from De Nino, 61), both versions of the story of Odysseus and Polyphemus, Calvino has felt free to place his imprint on the tale. His inventiveness is particularly striking in "The Florentine." He says in his notes to this story: "I have accentuated the character satire (of the misery of the Florentine who has nothing to boast of) in the way the story seems to demand." This characterization includes the addition of the Florentine's false explanation of how he lost his finger, which he had himself cut off when the giant's ring stuck fast to him and threatened his life: "As for the finger, he said he had cut it off mowing the grass."[12] By a flash of Calvino's wit, the reader is suddenly transferred from a realm inhabited by giants to the very contemporary and mundane world of mowing the lawn.

See what he says about No. 164, "The Dove Girl":

10. De Nino, 1883; Comparetti, 1875.
11. De Nino, 1883, vii–viii. [I owe this translation from De Nino to the kindness of James Hankins.]
12. Calvino, 1980, 280.

164. "The Dove Girl" (*La ragazza colomba*) from Pitrè, 50 (*Dammi lu velu!*), Palermo, told by a woman.[13]

The swan girl or dove girl, whose bird costume the hero takes away, thereby compelling her to remain a woman, is a universally known motif and often combines with the motif of the sorcerer's servant who must climb a mountain of precious stones. I began with the Palermo version, showing the "lad who led a dog's life" in search of work, and the Greek from the Levant. I departed from the text by having the boy go up the mountain, not on a winged horse, but in a horse's hide carried upward by an eagle, as in other Southern versions (taking into special account one from Lucania—La Rocca, 9). I also borrowed the final episode of the invisible cloak, a very widespread motif, to make the plot complete.[14]

Calvino began with one version, then departed from the text, yet still following "other Southern versions," and ended by borrowing an episode from elsewhere. He did not make up anything new (except for the final outcome) but consciously used and manipulated traditional material.

Or take No. 161, "Rosemary" (*Rosmarina*), where Calvino says, "The girl's dancing to the flute music is the only thing I added, but a dance rhythm is already in the Palermo original." Calvino's notes are invaluable for assessing his relationship to the "original." Calvino also appears as himself in them, as in No. 180, "The Peacock Feather" (*La penna di hu*), when he says, after a very moving comment on the theme of the sacrifice of the youngest and on the ugly cry of the peacock, "I followed this Sicilian version with an unhappy ending (no resurrection of the boy), which seems in keeping with the spirit of the tale. But I replaced the pipe made from a bone of the dead boy with a reed sprung from the grave, as in many other versions.[15]

Finally, it is necessary ourselves to compare some of his "originals" with his own Italian. Because both De Nino and Comparetti translated their texts collected from the Abruzzi and Pisa, respectively, from dialect to Italian, I have chosen a text from Giuseppe Pitrè's extraordinary collection from Sicily. This text, a variant of the Cinderella story, is *Gràttula-beddàttula*, No. 42 from Pitrè's collection, No. 148 in Calvino's Italian edition.[16] I have analyzed only the first page or so of the Sicilian and the Italian simply as an example of what Calvino did with a dialect "original."

The first short paragraph of No. 148 is a translation, but where the Sicilian

---

13. See Pitrè, 1875, 410–15.
14. Calvino, 1980, 749.
15. Ibid., 753.
16. Pitrè, 1875, 368–80; Calvino, 1956, 719–25.

speaks of "the biggest," "the middle one," and "the littlest" (*la cchiù grànni, la mizzana,* and *la nica*), Calvino calls them "the first," "the second," and "the third" (*la prima, la seconda,* and *la terza*). It is not clear to me why he made the change.

In the next paragraph Calvino substitutes *ragazze* 'girls' once where Pitrè has *figghi* 'children', perhaps to avoid using *figlie* 'daughters' twice in succession—a stylistic change. The traditional text does not mind the repetition, but the nontraditional editor considers it stylistically unacceptable. Later in the paragraph Calvino adds to walling up the doors *con noi dentro* 'with us inside', which is not in the Pitrè text, but omits *cu saluti* from Pitrè's *e quannu piaci a Diu nni videmu cu saluti* 'when it please God that we see you in health'. These changes seem arbitrary.

In the third paragraph Pitrè uses *Lu patri* 'the father' and Calvino *il mercante* 'the merchant', perhaps trying (as with the "first," "second," and "third" above) to avoid "folktale-ish" diction. A little further along, Pitrè's *tutti li survizza di fora* 'all the services of the market' becomes in Calvino simply *le commissioni* 'the shopping' or, translated, 'the errands'. The most striking difference so far, however, occurs at the end of the paragraph (the other differences are minor stylistic ones in the translation from dialect to standard Italian), when the father asks each girl what she wants him to bring her. In Pitrè, Rosa replies, "*Tri bell' abbiti di culuri differenti,*" 'Three beautiful dresses of different colors,' and in Calvino the answer is "*Un vestito color del cielo,*" 'A dress the color of the sky.' Giovannina in Pitrè wants "*Zoccu voli vassia,*" which means, I believe, 'Whatever your lordship wants,' but in Calvino she wants "*Un vestito color dei diamanti,*" 'A dress the color of diamonds.' The significant answer, of course, comes from Ninetta, and Calvino's translation is exact, except for transferring *vossignoria* 'your lordship' (Pitrè *vassia*) from the second sentence to the first ('Please bring me, father, a beautiful date-palm branch. If you don't may your ship move neither forward nor backward').[17] The changes of colors are perhaps an attempt to heighten the tone of the story, but Calvino's omission of the obedient daughter's modest reply is a loss to the modern version of the tale. Whatever the reasons for the changes I have indicated, the purpose of pointing them out has been to illustrate something of the character of Calvino's editing of the original folktale's language and style.

Calvino had been asked by those who commissioned his work to do for Italian folktales what the Grimm brothers had done for the German. Com-

---

17. "Io voglio che vossignoria mi porti un bel ramo di datteri in un vaso d'argento. E se non me lo porta, che il bastimento non possa piú andare né avanti né indietro."

pared with the Grimms, especially Wilhelm, of course, Calvino was rather conservative. If we turn our attention then to the *Kinder- und Hausmärchen* and ask whether they are made up of a group of transitional texts, the answer might be in the affirmative, from a quite different point of view, using criteria different from fluidity and fixity of textual sense or even from that of manipulating of texts from a nontraditional set of standards. These texts of the Grimm brothers created a *Märchenstil*, which was based on oral traditional tale style. This style was itself, however, to be the foundation for several kinds of *literary* "folktale"; for example, on the one hand the unsophisticated style of the kind of tale told to children and, on the other, the highly developed and self-conscious literary *genre*, neither being genuine, traditional folktale. It can be argued, I believe, that the Grimms' texts were transitional in that sense between traditional folktale and purely literary "folktale." In this sense, Calvino's texts, made on the model of the German collector-editors, are transitional texts. The case would be better if it turned out that Calvino had created in Italian a literary folktale style. But that consideration leads to another: it is possible that Calvino's texts might be considered transitional in still another way, namely, within his own writing and in the passage of narrative in his experience from oral traditional (that is, the bona fide folktales from oral tradition which he read and heard) to his own fantasy novels, such as *The Baron in the Trees*. The chief problem in that approach is that an outsider's "experiencing" of a folktale by reading or even hearing it, and even when it included many variants, as Calvino's did, is not the same as the telling, or even writing, of tales in the tradition of an insider. In this case, the base from which Calvino's transitional texts departed was not firsthand.

It might well be that Old English poems, such as *The Phoenix*, which were amplified translations or adaptations of Latin originals, for example, *De ave phoenice* attributed to Lactantius, can be thought of as transitional texts, using the formulaic style and traditional poetic devices of the oral traditional poetry but leading through the Latin influence to a fully developed Old English nontraditional poetry and poetics. Latin originals were translated into Anglo-Saxon poetry, but the Anglo-Saxon poets continued to compose in their traditional style and poetics for a very long period, in spite of their Latin sources. If anything, their style became more markedly and more mechanically formulaic as they lost the art of free oral formulaic composition in performance.

Robert E. Diamond and Geoffrey Russom have found indications of specific elements differentiating between oral and written style.[18] They have

---

18. Diamond, 1963; Russom, 1978 and 1987b.

shown that the translators, unlike the poet of *Beowulf*, have not been skilled in making Anglo-Saxon verses but have employed "fillers," for example, using the traditional style but without complete command of it. Their verses are mechanical, almost regressive in the sense that they resemble those of traditional singers not fully practiced in their art.[19] As I have observed earlier, "it may be that the transition at one end of the scale, that of learning, is paralleled by the transition at the other end, when the style is no longer dynamic, the tradition being no longer in its prime. On the other hand the new style has not yet perhaps asserted itself."[20]

But before we can go much further in trying to define and describe transitional texts, we must be clear about where they are moving from. There is one firm base, I believe, from which we may depart: oral traditional narrative and its style. I may be overestimating the firmness of the base, but I think I can defend the emphasis and describe the style and the process of composition and transmission of oral traditional narrative, be it prose or verse. After all, whichever the form, we are dealing with storytelling, and, except for the use of prose rather than verse, some of the principles of composition and transmission of stories are the same in both forms.

One should bear in mind from the outset that within the tradition the processes of both composition and transmission are by no means static; they are as dynamic as living organisms. De Nino's description, given above, stressed in its own way how difficult it was to make for an anthology a version of a tale that exists in so many variants even in the mouth of the same teller and when tales are constantly being interwoven in tradition. The problem was to harness untamed horses, to make the dynamic static. It is the dynamic process that we must first understand, a process that the traditional teller and the traditional audience comprehend instinctively.

But if there is movement, it is neither frenetic nor chaotic. There are varying tempos involved, and the mixtures are explicable through association of ideas and, we might add, also of sounds. And directing the flow and the tempo, as it were, are the tellers of tales themselves, men and women of varying talent and from various walks of life. Sometimes this variety of ability is forgotten and the teller is thought of as a passive hander-on of

---

19. A partly comparable situation is noted by Cantilena, 1990, who contrasts the rigidity of written Greek hexameter with the flexibility of oral hexameter: ["The literary hexameter is more rigid than the oral on several grounds: in arrangement of words, in placing of caesuras, in rhythmic variety (the 32 types of hexameter in Homer are reduced to 21 in Callimachus and to nine in Nonnus)" (79).] This is not to suggest that the style of Callimachus is mechanical but that his hexameter versification is under more constraints than that of Homer. Cf. Haymes, 1987, for Middle High German heroic epic.

20. A. Lord, 1987b, 338–39.

tradition. If this *creative* role is properly understood as the reason why there are so many "variants," then the inevitability of many different levels of quality of creation and of performance becomes quite clear. Variation and interweaving are creative processes not due to lapses of memory or to confusion or mindless mixing. Such do occur, of course, at times, as does corruption, but less frequently than is imagined. Lapse of memory, after all, implies a fixed something to remember and also a mental attitude that allows of only one way of telling the "same story."

We have, then, in tradition (1) a dynamic process of composition and transmission of narrative, which produces variants and interweavings; (2) traditional tellers of varying talent who use the process subconsciously and thus create those variants and interweavings that exist only at and during performance and are, between tellings, merely latent potentials; and (3) an aesthetic peculiar to that process and its results, namely, the variants and interweavings. Just as the process is dynamic and creative, so too the aesthetics are caused not by restraints but rather by the possibilities inherent in traditional associations of idea and sound and their overtones established by past usages and shared by all the members of that tradition, both tellers and listeners.

With those elements—a process, tellers, and an aesthetic—in mind, let us look at what "transitional" might mean. One might expect, first, that there would be some kind of change in process; second, that there would be some kind of change in personnel; and third, that there would be a change in aesthetics resulting from the first two changes. As the tellers are, I believe, the key to the process, because they probably originated and surely operate it, and they and the process they operate are the keys to the aesthetics, let us look at the tellers of tales, or other figures who produce texts, who may not be tellers themselves, but mediators.

I have divided those who deal with texts into insiders (that is, members of the traditional group, including singers) and outsiders (that is, those who are not members of the traditional group, who, therefore, approach the text without the assumptions and sense of values that members of the group share with one another). I have further divided all these people into (1) collectors, collector-editors, and editors, (2) retellers, and (3) imitators.

The outsiders, who come to the tradition and have an effect on some texts, are probably the first to try to harness the wild horses. Collectors, collector-editors, and editors deal directly with oral traditional texts, working with someone else's creations, which they record or modify in some way. Calvino as an editor is in this group. They do not themselves create the primary texts, except insofar as they may put into writing, through dictation, what the creator tells them. There are many kinds of collectors and collector-editors. What determines their species is that they write down a text and for the first time bring the idea of the static into the tradition. But most of the time, text in hand, they have left their informant and the tradition behind, in reality practically untouched. Collectors in such cases have frozen an infinitesimal part of tradition and carried it away to study, to enjoy, to show to others. Ideally they have written down their texts exactly as the story tellers have told them. If they have done so, then those texts are oral traditional, dictated texts. These people have, then, some respect for the primary text and either maintain it scrupulously or change it in varying degrees and for a variety of reasons. Their texts constitute the first move in the direction of a written literary text, because they manipulate an oral traditional text with other than traditional criteria and for nontraditional purposes: the text thus produced is intended for a nontraditional audience. It is not a transitional text, but it has moved away from the purely oral traditional one.

Milman Parry is a prime example of an outsider who respected the exact text of the epic singer. He collected some lyric songs and some tales as well and was as scrupulous in regard to their texts as he was with the epic songs. I believe that I myself and David Bynum qualify also as collector-editors. Like Parry's, our goal in collecting and editing has been to record texts as accurately as possible and to present them in print as exactly as possible.

In the nineteenth century in Sarajevo the Austrian Kosta Hörmann, a collector-editor, to judge from his texts and from his commentary and the later work on his manuscripts by Đenana Buturović, seems also to have been a respecter of texts.[21] In the last quarter of that same century, Luka Marjanović was a careful field collector among the Moslems in northern Bosnia in the Bihačka Krajina, but his editing left something to be desired. I have given in Chapter 1 an account of the practices of Marjanović as an editor and have noted examples of the changes he made in the published texts from the poems as they were written down in manuscript by dictation. The style of the poets has been changed according to an outsider's judgment of what is proper. Marjanović's texts, therefore, cannot be used with full confidence to study traditional style because they have in part been detraditionalized.

Another significant group consists of people who retell stories. They may be collectors also. They create their own text, without using any of the "original." When we are talking about folktale we say that the retellers are telling the story in their own words: that means that they ignore even more

---

21. Buturović, 1976. [For another assessment of Hörmann's texts, see Bynum, 1993, chap. 4, esp. 587–88 and 600.]

than some types of editors (and even collectors) the characteristic traits (such as repetition) of the oral traditional text. It is impossible to check the retellers' text against the "original" because the original, that is, the one or ones they heard, were not set down at the time. The retellers do not produce an oral traditional text, essentially because their style is not the traditional style of the traditional group—to which they do not belong. Are their texts transitional? I honestly do not see how they could be, because they have already made the leap by choosing as their creators nontraditional persons, who bring their own styles to the texts. The tales went into another world to be born again in these new forms. Their creators, being outsiders, had different criteria from those of the tradition. The retellers, as a matter of fact, belong only in the world of the folktale, because retelling in one's own traditional diction is what we mean by oral traditional composition and transmission.

At this point the question arises—and this might have a bearing on Calvino's case—Are there not outsiders who have made themselves as familiar with a given tradition as an insider? I am not sure that is entirely possible, but I expect that the answer should be a somewhat, even slightly, qualified, affirmative. Obviously the degree of familiarity would depend on length of stay in the tradition, sensitivity to it, and other personal characteristics. What we are talking about in essence is an outsider becoming an insider.

In addition to the collectors and editors and retellers, there are those who imitate the oral traditional style more or less effectively. If the content of their poems is pseudotraditional, they might be classified as transitional. Their texts may look as if they were oral traditional, but their subjects and stories are not genuine traditional subjects or narratives. If, however, the content of their poems is nontraditional, I would classify them as written literary texts.

Let us now consider the insiders. By insiders I mean members of the traditional community, those who listen to and know the traditional songs and stories. They are the singer's audience. This group includes, of course, the singer or storyteller. The traditional singer may himself create a new song, a "transitional" text. I am thinking here of such a singer as Filip Višnjić, who made up songs about the Serbian uprising at the request of Karadžić. These were new songs, that is, they were about events that had actually happened. When songs consist of traditional themes, they are traditional even if new and even if never sung by anyone else again. But when Višnjić tried to recount history, departing from the traditional themes (although his style was certainly authentic), he created a nontraditional song. No other singer could learn it and sing it without memorizing it. Was it "transitional"?

Whereas singers like Višnjić never learn to write and never produce new songs beyond an occasional tour de force at someone's request, the traditional singer who becomes a written poet goes all the way. The prime example is Njegoš, to whom I return later.

There is a transitional period in the life of epic in Serbo-Croatian beginning with Andrija Kačić-Miošić's *Razgovor ugodni naroda slovinskoga*, "A Pleasant Discourse of the Slavic People," in 1756 and including Vuk Stefanović Karadžić (1787–1864), Vuk Vrčević (1811–82), Sima Milutinović-Sarajlija (1791–1847), and Luka Marjanović in the later nineteenth century. Songs were collected, edited, and *created*. Collecting and editing were done to some extent by all of these figures, even Kačić (1704–60). Karadžić, Vrčević, and Marjanović were primarily collector-editors, not themselves singers or creators, although I am not sure but that Karadžić may have made up some songs, and perhaps Vrčević did also. Milutinović and Njegoš wrote epics of their own, that is, written literary epics, and they also collected traditional songs and created new ones.

After Kačić in particular, although beginning even earlier, it seems that everyone began to make up epic songs. It was a period of great creativity of sorts. From Kačić's time, the line between oral traditional epic and the new songs in its style became very blurred. The forces behind this thrust were didacticism and nationalism. These two forces met in an interest in history or expressed themselves in a preoccupation with history. Kačić wrote a history of the South Slavs in a medium all could understand, the traditional epic decasyllables. Milutinović and Njegoš, to say nothing of Karadžić, were also interested in the history of their own people, the Serbs and Montenegrins. The cults of the gusle and of the hero were under way. A tradition of local songs of stealing sheep or wives was rapidly becoming a history of Montenegro. The Serbian uprising was being documented in epic song at the request of Karadžić. The Orthodox South Slavs were rising against the Turks. New things were happening in history and in the culture as well. Modern Serbian and Montenegrin literature was being born. The Middle Ages in Serbia and Montenegro—in fact, in most of the Balkans—had lasted into the *eighteenth* century. Toward its end, a new cultural spirit was beginning, which was to grow and reach full strength very quickly in the nineteenth. And history meant epic song to these men. They sought to sing and write history as it was known to them and to fill in the gaps with their own creations. The old style was being recreated or remade, sometimes gradually, to suit the new requirements.

The transitional period, then, in the general culture of the area formed the natural background for the creation of several kinds of transitional songs together with the collection of hundreds of authentic oral traditional epics from the tellings and singings of traditional singers and poets. As transitional figures, Andrija Kačić-Miošić, the Franciscan monk in the Catholic regions of Dalmatia, Croatia, and among the Catholics of Bosnia and Herzegovina, and the Montenegrin prince-bishop Peter II Petrović Njegoš among the Orthodox Serbs and Montenegrins stand out, although they were not alone.

Although Kačić was a collector-editor by reason of two oral traditional songs he included in the *Razgovor* (which he himself identified as such), it is primarily as an outsider writing pseudotraditional songs and nontraditional poems in the oral traditional style, or an imitation thereof, that we are interested in him. As I have described in *The Singer of Tales*,

> Kačić's *Razgovor* is a chronicle of the South Slavs from the beginning to his own day, partly in prose and partly in verse. The verse part consists of epic songs almost entirely in the ten-syllable line of oral tradition. Kačić knew the oral epic very well and he wrote his songs in its style. His sources were in part oral epics that he had heard, but even more the available chronicles and histories, documents, accounts of eye witnesses. He aimed at historical truth as he saw it. He has set out to praise the heroes who have not been praised in the tradition, or not sufficiently.[22]

There are two questions about Kačić that one must keep separate. The first concerns formula density. Rudy S. Spraycar has demonstrated by means of computer analysis a high degree of formulicity in the poetry of Kačić, a literate monk, as high as the formula count in a sample of the poetry of the oral singer Salih Ugljanin.[23] That there are many formulas in Kačić's *Razgovor* is not surprising, as its poems were deliberately written in the oral style, based on the epics that he had often heard. To differentiate between the songs of a Salih Ugljanin and the poetry of Kačić, other aspects of style must be considered. The second question is whether Kačić's poems, or some of those in epic decasyllables at least, are transitional texts. The two questions are related, but it is only the second that concerns me here.

There are 157 poems in the *Razgovor*, a few of which are written in symmetrical (4 + 4) octosyllables, but most in asymmetric (4 + 6) epic decasyllables. I have investigated only the decasyllabic poems for this chapter, but I have observed the octosyllabic ones also. Moreover, among the decasyllabic poems I have been particularly interested in those that are like the oral traditional epic songs in content as well as in meter.

Of the first fifteen poems, two (Nos. 2 and 3) are octosyllabic and thirteen

---

22. A. Lord, 1960, 136; see also 132–33.
23. Spraycar and Dunlap, 1982.

are decasyllabic. The openings of Nos. 1, 5–15, and possibly 4 are like the openings of oral traditional epics. No. 1 begins:

Knjigu piše od Kotara kneže,	The knez of Kotar wrote a letter,
Po imenu starac Radovane,	namely the Old Man Radovan,
Ter je šalje pobratimu svomu,	and sent it to his blood-brother,
Mjelovanu od gorice crne.[24]	Mjelovan of the Black Mountain.

These lines certainly not only look like familiar openings of oral traditional epics but actually are such. We need to follow the song further, of course, and shall. But it would be interesting to look for their parallels in early pre-Kačić seventeenth- and eighteenth-century texts. Kačić had a great influence on the oral traditional epic in the nineteenth and even the twentieth centuries, as we shall see. To be on the safe side, let us look for earlier examples. Compare the opening of No. 1 with that of Valtazar Bogišić's No. 117, *Kako Ivan Krušić senjski kapetan hitro ugrabi Jelicu svoju sestru zarobljenu iz rukih Muje Jeleškovića Turčina*, "How Ivan Krušić, Captain of Senj, Cleverly Rescued Jelica, His Sister, Captured by Muja Jelešković, a Turk":

Knjigu piše turski šužanj Mujo,
ter je šalje Jelešković Muji:[25]

The Turkish prisoner Mujo wrote a letter,
and sent it to Jelešković Mujo.

Though the openings of Kačić's songs may be oral traditional beyond any doubt, as we proceed we see new nontraditional elements appearing. The second stanza of Kačić No. 1, which has the title *Pisma Radovana i Mjelovana*, "A Song of Radovan and Mjelovan," betrays an element foreign to the oral traditional epic, namely, consistent end rhyme:

U knjizi ga lipo pozdravlja<u>še</u>,	In the letter he greeted him well,
ter ovako starac besidi<u>aše</u>:	and thus the old man said:
"Mjelovane, sva je vjeka <u>na te</u>!	"Mjelovan, long life to you!
probudi se, biće bolje <u>za te</u>!"	Wake up, it will be better for you!"

The frame of the song is an exchange of letters. Radovan's letter to Mjelovan goes from line 7 to line 28; line 29 introduces Mjelovan's reply in

---

24. Citations from Kačić in this chapter are from Kačić-Miošić, 1942.
25. The text is from Bogišić, 1878, 326.

the traditional fashion—*odpisuje starac Mjelovane*: "Old Mjelovan wrote in reply:"—a regular and very familiar formula. Mjelovan's answer goes from line 30 to line 72, the end of the poem. An exchange of letters is a common theme in traditional epic, but it is generally part of a larger action, not a song in itself.

Moreover, the content of the letters is nontraditional; as a matter of fact, it is a contrived literary conceit. Radovan writes:

> "Wake up, Mjelovan! Last year when you travelled in Kotari with your gusle and sang a song of heroes, you glorified some and others you did not mention. Lika, Krbava, Slavonia, Bosnia, all Dalmatia, Romania, and Bulgaria are angry at you, because you left out many knights, specialists in single combat, bans and princes. Watch out or they'll pull out your beard, because heroes have no sense of humor. Either sing of all the heroes, so that there will be no complaint against you, or give up the gusle and singing and travelling in Kotari!"

Mjelovan answers:

> "Don't be crazy, Radovan! Who can gather the clouds in the sky? Who can sing of all the heroes in the world? If you couldn't, how can I? It's not easy to shout to the gusle and to call all the heroes by name! . . ."

This is not heroic epic. The line is the traditional epic decasyllable with an attempt at consistent rhyming couplets, as illustrated above, or an *abab* rhyme scheme, as in:

Ali ćeš se prija prestavi<u>ti</u>,	You will die sooner,
kano čvrčak pjevajuć do mra<u>ka</u>,	like a cricket singing until dusk,
nego li ćeš, pobre, izbroji<u>ti</u>	my blood-brother, than count out
koliko je na svijetu juna<u>ka</u>.	how many heroes there are in the world.

There are, of course, a number of traditional formulas or formulaic lines, such as the first seven lines of the poem and line 29, the formulaic introduction to a reply in writing, which constitute the frame of the exchange of letters. All these familiar marks of the traditional style and even theme are there to be sure. But to return to the content of the letters themselves, it is not traditional epic story. Whence does it come?

A literary epistolary genre was well developed in Dubrovnik and on the Dalmatian islands already in the sixteenth century. One thinks immediately of Hektorović's *Ribanje i ribarsko prigovaranje*, "A Fishing Excursion and Fishermen's Incidental Conversation," of 1556, which is in the form of a letter from Hektorović to an aristocratic friend of his in Dubrovnik.[26] The letters in Kačić No. 1 stem from that literary genre, not from the traditional epic, although the formulas of the frame are traditional. Hektorović and other epistolary writers wrote in literary dodecasyllables, not decasyllables. And the dodecasyllable, like rhyme, was an Italian import, with a long history through the Middle Ages in Italy and the Renaissance.

Kačić's poem is an imitation of the traditional style, a conscious writing in it, to make the content available, as Kačić himself said, to the larger public, the traditional audience whose style he is imitating. The use of that style was not because there was no other vernacular literary style he could use, as was the case in Anglo-Saxon. The content of the letters themselves actually reminds us that there *was* another vernacular literary style with a long literary tradition behind it. There was, indeed, known to Kačić a highly developed literature in a richly ornamented style, one that he used in his octosyllabic poems, one in which he had been brought up and which was several centuries old by his time. It had been formed under influences from Italian literature in the aristocratic milieu of the coastal cities. Kačić's use of the epic decasyllable is really a conscious imitation, not a natural and necessary development from traditional oral usage.

Traditional singers did not take up the singing in rhymed couplets, although there were eventually some poets who *wrote* and adapted traditional formulaic decasyllable to a consistent rhyme scheme, as did Kačić. In time also some singers occasionally memorized written poems in rhymed couplets, such as some of Kačić's poems themselves and a later Kosovo song in rhymed couplets which became very popular in Montenegro and Serbia. I last recorded it in the district west of Niš in 1967. The introduction of pervasive rhyme is not a change that would have come from within in the South Slavic tradition. It was brought in from outside; or perhaps it would be more correct to say that the traditional stylistic elements were brought into the literary tradition. Such a poem as Kačić No. 1 in *Razgovor* seems to me for these very reasons to be literary rather than transitional.

I do not know whether consistent rhyming is characteristic of written literature in all cultures; each case should be studied in its own context and history. I am thinking especially, of course, of the *Nibelungenlied*. Anglo-Saxon verse and the Old Norse Eddic poetry, the oldest Germanic poetries we have, do not have rhyme.[27] If the Middle High German *Nibelungenlied*'s

26. Hektorović, 1951.
27. [Stephen A. Mitchell comments that in Old Norse, although the introduction of the ballad into the region is not usually dated much earlier than the thirteenth century, Egill Skallagrímsson produced an end-rhymed scaldic verse, the Hǫfuðlausn', "Head-Ransom," composed at York in the tenth century.]

rhyming comes from literary influence, where does that influence come from? As I have said, the South Slavic case is clear. Italian influence in the early sixteenth century, if not earlier, in the Petrarchan sonnets of "The Collection of Vinko Ranjina,"[28] with twelve-syllable lines rhyming both in the middle and the end of a couplet, developed also in the octosyllables of Gundulić's *Osman* in the seventeenth century,[29] and was applied to the epic decasyllable both by Filip Grabovac and by Kačić in the eighteenth. Each culture has its own history.

Grabovac preceded Kačić in the literary use of decasyllables in writing history in the early part of the eighteenth century. Grabovac used them in his *Cvit razgovora naroda i jezika iliričkoga aliti rvackoga*, "An Anthology of the Entertaining Discourse of the Illyrian or Croatian People and Language." Of his three poems in decasyllables, two are developed-narrative, heroic epics, *but* he composed them throughout in rhymed couplets. The content in this case is traditional; the meter of the line is traditional; but the rhymed couplets are not. Although rhymed couplets occur occasionally in oral traditional epic, the songs do not consist solely of them. Their use makes a difference in the formulaic diction. Though the first line of the couplets is usually formulaic, the order of the words in the second line is sometimes changed to accommodate the rhyme, or the wording is forced and nonformulaic. A single example suffices for the moment. The lines

> Ne piše je, čim se knjiga piše,
> već njeg krvca iz obraza biše.[30]

> He did not write it with what a letter is written with,
> but it was his blood from his cheek.

are an accommodation of a very traditional pair of formulaic lines to the nontraditional written literary rhyme. These are traditional lines:

> Ne piše je, čim se knjiga piše,
> već od krvi iz svoga obraza.

> He did not write it with what a letter is written with,
> but with blood from his own cheek.

Biše 'it was' is awkward and distorts the natural flow of the traditional formulas. One can see in such examples the traditional style changing to a

28. *Ranjin zbornik*, 1937.
29. Gundulić, 1938.
30. Grabovac, 1951, 207.

literary style before one's very eyes. Because of the traditional type of content and the many traditional formulaic lines on the one hand and the nontraditional rhymed couplets on the other, one might call these poems by Grabovac transitional. For me, however, I must confess that the rhymed couplets in themselves place the poems in the literary rather than transitional category.

Kačić's poems were composed in quatrains. This is itself a nontraditional element, but it does not of necessity distort the formulas in the way in which rhyme does. Some quatrains consist of rhymed couplets; in some the rhyming follows an *abab* pattern, some have only a few rhymed couplets, and some are unrhymed. The quatrains themselves and the rhyming schemes were drawn by Grabovac and Kačić from the literary tradition in which both were brought up. They were, after all, in our terms, outsiders, with a written literary training and style of their own. They chose to use the traditional decasyllabic line and the formulaic style of the oral traditional epic so that what they wrote would be accessible to those for whom those stylistic elements were natural.

Both Grabovac and Kačić were clearly well versed in the oral traditional style. This is so true of Kačić that many of his poems are indistinguishable from pure oral traditional songs. In those, he shows himself as an outsider who has become an insider, or who can compose as one. He has *written* traditional songs. In the poems in which he uses rhyme in any consistent way, however, we may have imitation and transitional texts. One should be aware of the fact that not all of Kačić's poems are alike. Poem No. 4 on the four holy namesakes, four Saints Sava, is strongly medieval. The content is not characteristic of oral traditional style; the quatrains contain two rhymed couplets. Kačić praises a hermit Sava in Palestine; then he describes the martyrdom of two other Savas, one a monk martyred by King Atanarik, the other a captain in Rome, whose sufferings are set forth in detail. Kačić finally comes to the Serbian Saint Sava, founder of Hilandar monastery on Mount Athos. Some of the familiar formulas appear, such as in the enumeration of the four saints:

>   9–10   Jedan biše cvitak kalopere,
>   po imenu Savo kaluđere.
>
>   One was a carnation flower
>   by name Sava the monk.

(But *cvitak kalopere* belongs in lyric, not epic.)

21–22 Drugi biše Savo kaluđere
       koji suzam svoje lišće pere.

       The second was Sava the monk,
       who washed his face with tears.

(The second line is not traditional epic.)

33–34 Treći biše Sava kapetane
       od vojnika đenerale bane

       The third was Captain Sava
       General commander of the army

61–62 Četvrti je ruža izabrana
       od kolina Nemanić Stipana

       The fourth is a choice rose
       of the family of Stipan Nemanić

(But with *ruža izabrana* we are again with flowers and lyrics.)

And other formulaic lines such as the familiar *Malo vrime postojalo biše,* "A little time had passed" (97), followed in rhyme by the unfamiliar *za biskupa Sava učiniše,* "[when] they made Sava bishop," make us realize that the formulaic style is there in the background. To me, this poem is more "written literary" than transitional, although I can understand why some critics might disagree.

There are instances of familiar motifs, or short themes. For example, changing clothes happens from time to time in traditional epic, when the hero prepares himself for departure or battle. Sava in this poem changes in lines 73–74:

Svlači Savo sa zlatom aljine,
Kaluđere oblači mantije.

Sava doffed his golden clothes,
he donned his monk's cassock.

Or there is a theme associated more with hajduks than with saints:

81–82 zemlja Savi prostirač bijaše,
       a vedrim se nebom pokrivaše

the earth was Sava's blanket beneath him,
and he covered himself with the clear sky.

In No. 5, "The Song of Radoslav," a subject we know from the "Chronicle of the Priest of Duklja" in particular,[31] rhyming is only sporadic. The subject, namely, the ousting of Radoslav by his son, involves the gathering and moving of armies and is more heroic than the song previously considered. As a result the formulaic language is more familiar than in No. 4. Yet we are aware that it is not as purely traditional as, let us say, No. 42, although the latter has a few moments that are not traditional. Song No. 42 is about Janko Sibinjanin's defense of Belgrade from the Turks in 1456. It seems to me that Kačić's poems like Nos. 5 and 42 are excellent candidates for the transitional text.

I turn finally to Petar Petrović Njegoš II (1813–51). Unlike either Kačić or Calvino, who, although they were deeply immersed in oral traditional art, were not themselves actual practitioners of it, Njegoš began in his early youth as an oral traditional poet. He had learned to sing epic songs to the gusle, as had his father also.

It is not necessary here to treat Njegoš's career as a poet in full; for I have already given an account of it elsewhere.[32] For our present purposes it is important to note that Njegoš learned to read and write in the monastery at Cetinje in 1825. He studied under tutors, one of whom was Sima Milutinović-Sarajlija, to whom his development as a poet can be attributed. In general, Njegoš was, however, largely self-taught. Part of his library and correspondence has been destroyed and dispersed, but what remains helps to provide a knowledge of his wide reading, which included, for example, Homer, Pindar, and the ancient Greek tragedians.[33] He traveled, moreover, to Russia, Austria, and Italy. When he returned from Russia in 1834, he founded the first school in Montenegro and brought in the first printing press in 1835. Education was under way.

When Njegoš was still very young, before he was twenty, he began to make up songs himself. Milutinović published five of them in the second edition (1837) of his *Pjevanija crnogorska i hercegovačka*, "A Montenegrin and Herzegovinian Songbook," and noted that the first of these songs was written before Njegoš became prince-bishop (*vladika*) of Montenegro in 1833, succeeding his uncle, Bishop Petar I Petrović. It is in these new songs,

31. See *Letopis popa Dukljanina*, 1950.
32. A. Lord, 1986, 30–34.
33. Savić-Rebac, 1957, 114.

five of which are characterized by Vido Latković as folk epics,[34] that we trace the beginnings of written or literary influence on Njegoš's purely traditional style. One of the songs, No. 25, *Crmničani*, "The Crmničani," opens in a traditional way:

Četu kupi Lekić Hasan-bego	Hasan beg Lekič gathered a band
od krvave šeher-Podgorice,	from the bloody city Podgorica,
malu četu četrdeset drugah.[35]	a small band, forty comrades.

Another, No. 56, *Mali Radojica*, "Little Radojica," begins:

Muški plaču trideset hajdukah	Manfully thirty hajduks wept
u tavnici paše od Travnika;	in the prison of the pasha of Travnik;
cmile jako tri nedelje danah,	they screamed loudly for three weeks,
doklena se paši dojadilo,	until it annoyed the pasha,
te tavnici na kapiju pode,	and he went to the door of the prison,
upituje trideset hajdukah:[36]	and asked the thirty hajduks:

Except for *muški plaču* 'manfully wept', this is all traditional epic wording; it would be familiar to anyone knowing the traditional songs.

In still another song, however, *Nova pjesna crnogorska*, "A New Montenegrin Song," there are elements not belonging to traditional style which reflect the cult of the gusle and the influence of Serbian nationalism. After a contrived invocation to the vila asking that she "bring together all voices into the gusle," the song itself opens with a statement of the date, "In one thousand eight hundred / and half of the twenty-seventh year," an element not found in truly traditional epic.[37] Because of these nontraditional features we are justified in considering the period of Njegoš's output of "new songs" written by himself and not learned from singers, as transitional between the oral style and the written.

Later in life, Njegoš became a fully literary poet and used the ten-syllable line for his great poems, *Luča mikrokozma*, "The Ray of the Microcosm," and *Gorski vijenac*, "The Mountain Wreath." The philosophical and mystical poem *The Ray of the Microcosm* is described by William Jovanovich in his

---

34. Latković, 1963, 32–38.
35. Njegoš, 1953, 9.
36. Ibid., 38.
37. For the intrusion of nontraditional dating into epic songs, see A. Lord, 1960, 132–33. [See also Buchan's comments on the use of dating in certain Scottish ballads, cited in the Editor's Addendum to Chapter 7.]

preface to Milovan Djilas's book *Njegoš* thus: "Like *Paradise Lost* it attempts to comprehend the unresolved struggle between good and evil that is told in the myth of Satan's rebellion against Heaven. This is the conflict within each man that by extension delineates the affairs of all men."[38] This poem reverberates with echoes of Plato; the church fathers, especially Origen; Philo; Dante; Neomanichaeism; and Milton, as well as with native Montenegrin influences.[39]

The Mountain Wreath is about the massacre of Slavic converts to Islam in Montenegro at the end of the eighteenth century, an episode that is not authenticated by historical record. The work is replete with descriptions of the local life, beliefs, struggles, and aspirations of the Montenegrin people. A third work, *Šćepan mali* "Stephen the Small," is a historical drama recounting the rule in Montenegro in the late eighteenth century of a charlatan who posed as the legitimate czar of Russia.

Thus the remarkable life and literary career of Njegoš embraced all three stages, the oral traditional, the transitional, and the fully literate styles.

We have now considered various kinds of evidence for the existence of transitional texts. Calvino set out to translate, into modern Italian, folktales that had been collected in dialect from the lips of oral storytellers. His style reflects the directness and vividness of the original tales. Because he scrupulously recorded the collected source for each tale, one is able to compare the "original" with Calvino's version. It is apparent that he injected his own sense of style into his translation. We have seen, for example, that he elevated the "three beautiful dresses of different colors" to the more highly charged "a dress the color of the sky" and that he changed the modest request of "whatever your lordship wants" to "a dress the color of diamonds." In his helpful notes he states when he combines in one tale its different variants or when he adds whimsically satiric touches of character, as in the ending of "The Florentine." He was, therefore, not a mere conveyor of the tales he translated but a writer of texts that are reasonably to be regarded as transitional between their oral originals and a written literary version.

Kačić-Miošić in his *Razgovor ugodni narodna slovinskoga* not only introduced two songs taken from oral singers, identified as such, but also added many songs of his own, which are highly formulaic in style. Kačić was not himself a singer, but a literate Franciscan monk. It is difficult to distinguish some of Kačić's songs from oral poems, and some of these may be regarded as transitional in style. Many of his poems, however, reveal signs of the pen,

---

38. Djilas, 1966, x.
39. Savić-Rebac, 1957, 124–49.

namely, the use of rhymed couplets and quatrains. As this usage can be traced to previous learned tradition, it has seemed best to consider such poems as examples of a style that has already passed into the literary and learned, rather than the intermediate, transitional stage, of writing.

In the literary production of Njegoš it has been possible to identify all three stages of composition, the truly oral epics of his earliest youth, the transitional style of some of his "new songs," and the fully literate style of his masterpieces, *The Ray of the Microcosm* and *The Mountain Wreath*.

Our forays into the works of these three writers have shown that there is such an entity as the transitional text. The proof of its existence, however, has depended on an intimate acquaintance with the underlying oral tradition and likewise upon familiarity with the possible learned influences at play in each instance. To judge the bounds of the transitional stage one must have a firm foothold in both the oral and the learned literary traditions.

There is one field, I think, to which the foregoing remarks about transitional texts have less relevance than to others. That is the Homeric poems; for it is clear, I believe, that they are not transitional texts but the work of an oral traditional singer. The world of Homer was a far cry from the world of the Latin-surrounded medieval vernacular poetry or from that of Kačić or Njegoš with their learned traditions. On another level, the Slavic oral traditional literatures, including the Russian *byliny*, the Ukrainian *dumy*, as well as the South Slavic, both Serbo-Croatian and Bulgarian heroic songs, as noted down in the past two centuries, have served as a primary source for our knowledge of the way in which still-living traditions function in their societies.

One of the most striking things to note and to emphasize in this connection before I conclude is that the great poets in any of the oral traditional literatures with which I am acquainted—Homer, Avdo Međedović, the *Beowulf* poet, the poet of the Oxford *Roland* (and, I should like very much to add, of the *Nibelungenlied*)—stand out in their traditions because they go beyond such strictures as a rigidly formulaic style. One feels this in Homer, of course; one feels it as one listens to Avdo singing his tremendous songs, the lines of description and narrative pouring forth with an impatient intensity that at times reminds one of Homer; I have felt it, as have others also, in the way in which the *Beowulf* poet tells his story. These poets were not *thinking* of style; they were creating it. They were full of their story and completely engaged in the all-consuming task of telling it grandly.

In conclusion, the prospect of further elucidating the processes of the development of vernacular oral traditional literature is exciting as new insights are brought to bear on the poetry and prose of the Middle Ages and later times. In spite of the great progress already made, we have still far to go. But the rewards are great; in my mind, perhaps the greatest is simply to become more intimately acquainted with the extraordinarily intricate and variegated literatures themselves.

Bibliography

Alexander, Ronelle. 1995. "The Tension of Essences in South Slavic Epic." In *O Rus! Studia Litteraria Slavica in Honorem Hugh McLean*, ed. Simon Karlinsky et al. Berkeley: Berkeley Slavic Specialities.
——. Forthcoming. "The Tension of Essences: The Thematic Structure of Banović Strahinja." In *The Proceedings of the Second International Albert Bates Lord Memorial Symposium*, St. Petersburg, November 1993, ed. John M. Foley, Columbia, Mo.: Center for the Study of Oral Tradition. To be published simultaneously in Russian in St. Petersburg.
Alexiou, Margaret. 1974. *The Ritual Lament in Greek Tradition*. Cambridge: Cambridge University Press.
Andersen, Flemming G., and Thomas Pettitt. 1979. "Mrs. Brown of Falkland: A Singer of Tales?" *Journal of American Folklore* 92:1–24.
Andersson, Theodore M. 1976. *Early Epic Scenery: Homer, Virgil, and the Medieval Legacy*. Ithaca: Cornell University Press.
Andrić, Nikola, ed. 1909–42. *Ženske pjesme*. Vol. 5, 1909; vol. 6, 1914; vol. 7, 1929; vol. 10, 1942. Zagreb: Izdanje Matice Hrvatske.
Andrzejewski, B. W., and I. M. Lewis. 1964. *Somali Poetry: An Introduction*. Oxford: Clarendon.
Armstrong, James I. 1958. "The Arming Motif in the *Iliad*." *American Journal of Philology* 79:337–54.
ASPR. See Dobbie, 1942, 1953; Krapp, 1931, 1932; and Krapp and Dobbie, 1936.
Bannert, Herbert. 1984. "Die Lanze des Patroklos." *Wiener Studien* 18:27–35.
——. 1988. "Ein Formelproblem: Die Lanze des Patroklos." In *Formen des Wiederholens bei Homer: Beispiele für eine Poetik des Epos*. Vienna: Österreichische Akademie der Wissenschaften.
Barons, Krišjānis, and H. Visendorfs, eds. 1894–1915. *Latvju dainas*. 6 vols. Vol. 1, Booklets 1–4, Mitau (Jelgava): Dravin-Dravnieks, 1894–95; vol. 1, Booklets 5–10, Riga: Kalniņš & Deutschmans, 1895–98; vols. 2–6, St. Petersburg: Imperial Academy of Sciences, 1903–15.
Bartók, Béla, and Albert B. Lord. 1951. *Serbo-Croatian Folk Songs: Texts and Transcriptions*

of *Seventy-Five Folk Songs from the Milman Parry Collection and a Morphology of Serbo-Croatian Folk Melodies*. Foreword by George Herzog. New York: Columbia University Press.

Bartsch, Karl, ed. 1886. *Das Nibelungenlied*. Leipzig: F. A. Brockhaus.

Bäuml, Franz H., and Edda Speilmann. 1975. "From Illiteracy to Literacy: Prolegomena to a Study of the *Nibelungenlied*." In Duggan, 1975, 62–73.

Beatie, Bruce A. 1964–65. "Oral-Traditional Composition in the Spanish *Romancero* of the Sixteenth Century." *Journal of the Folklore Institute* 1:92–113.

Bellows, Henry Adams. 1969. *The Poetic Edda, Translated from the Icelandic with an Introduction and Notes*. 2 vols. in 1. New York: Biblo & Tannen.

Benson, Larry D. 1966. "The Literary Character of Anglo-Saxon Formulaic Poetry." *PMLA* 81:334–41.

Benson, Morton, with Biljana Šljivić-Šimšić. 1971. *Serbocroatian-English Dictionary*. Belgrade: Prosveta; Philadelphia: University of Pennsylvania Press.

Bessinger, Jess B., with Philip H. Smith, Jr. 1978. *A Concordance to the Anglo-Saxon Poetic Records*. Ithaca: Cornell University Press.

Bogišić, Valtazar. 1878. *Narodne pjesme iz starijih najviše primorskih zapisa*. Vol. 1. Glasnik srpskog učenog društva, Sec. 2 [Humanities], vol. 10. Belgrade: Državna Štamparija.

Bolling, George M. 1925. *The External Evidence for Interpolation in Homer*. Oxford: Clarendon.

Bowra, Cecil M. 1930. *Tradition and Design in the Iliad*. Oxford: Clarendon.

Bradley, S. A. J., trans. 1982. *Anglo-Saxon Poetry: An Anthology of Old English Poems in Prose Translation with Introduction and Headnotes*. London: Dent, Everyman's Library.

Brillante. Carlo, Mario Cantilena, and Carlo O. Pavese, eds. 1981. *I poemi epici rapsodici non omerici e la tradizione orale*. Proceedings of the Venezia Meeting, September 28–30, 1977. Padua: Editrice Antenore.

Bronson, Bertrand Harris. 1945. "Mrs. Brown and the Ballad." *California Folklore Quarterly* 4:129–40.

———. 1962. *The Traditional Tunes of the Child Ballads with Their Texts, According to the Extant Records of Great Britain and America*. Vol. 2. Princeton: Princeton University Press.

———. ed. 1976. *The Singing Tradition of Child's Popular Ballads*. Princeton: Princeton University Press.

Brooks, Kenneth R., ed. 1961. *Andreas and the Fates of the Apostles*. Oxford: Clarendon.

Buchan, David. 1972. *The Ballad and the Folk*. London: Routledge & Kegan Paul.

Budmani, Petar, and Tomislav Maretić, eds. 1904–10. *Rječnik hrvatskoga ili srpskoga jezika*. Vol. 6. Zagreb: Jugoslavenska Akademija Znanosti i Umjetnosti.

Buslaev, Fedor I. 1861. *Istoricheskie ocherki russkoj narodnoj slovesnosti i iskusstva*. Vol. 1, *Russkaja narodnaja poezija*. St. Petersburg.

Buturović, Đenana. 1976. *Studija o Hörmannovoj Zbirci Muslimanskih narodnih pjesama*. Sarajevo: Svjetlost.

Bynum, David E. 1964. "A Taxonomy of Oral Narrative Song: The Isolation and Description of Invariables in Serbo-Croatian Tradition." Ph.D. diss., Harvard University.

———. 1987. "Of Sticks and Stones and Hapax Legomena Rhemata." In Foley, 1987, 93–119.

———, trans. and comm. 1993. *Serbo-Croatian Heroic Poems: Epics from Bihać, Cazin, and Kulen Vakuf*. Additional translations by Mary P. Coote and John F. Loud. New York: Garland.

Byock, Jesse L. 1982. *Feud in the Icelandic Saga*. Berkeley and Los Angeles: University of California Press.
Calvino, Italo. 1956. *Fiabe italiane*. Turin: Einaudi.
———. 1980. *Italian Folktales, Selected and Retold by Italo Calvino*. Trans. George Martin. New York: Harcourt Brace Jovanovich.
Cantilena, Mario. 1990. "Approccio metrico alle teorie della composizione orale." In *Metrica classica e linguistica*. Proceedings of the Urbino Conference, October 3–6, 1988. Urbino: QuattroVenti.
Cerulli, Enrico. 1957–64. *Somalia: Scritti vari editi ed inediti*. 3 vols. Rome: A Cura dell' Amministrazione Fiduciaria Italiana della Somalia.
Child, Francis James, ed. 1882–94. *The English and Scottish Popular Ballads*. 5 vols. Boston: Houghton, Mifflin. Rpt. New York: Dover, 1965.
Clark, Francelia. 1981. "Flyting in *Beowulf* and Rebuke in *The Song of Bagdad*: The Question of Theme." In Foley, 1981, 164–69.
———. 1995. *Theme in Oral Epic and in Beowulf*. Milman Parry Studies in Oral Tradition, ed. Stephen A. Mitchell and Gregory Nagy. New York: Garland. Forthcoming.
Clark, George. 1965a. "Beowulf's Armor." *English Literary History* 32:409–41.
———. 1965b. "The Traveler Recognizes His Goal: A Theme in Anglo-Saxon Poetry." *Journal of English and Germanic Philology* 64:645–59.
Clark Hall, John R., trans. 1950. *Beowulf and the Finnesburg Fragment: A Translation into Modern English Prose*. Rev. ed. with notes and introduction by C. L. Wrenn, prefatory remarks by J. R. R. Tolkien. London: Allen & Unwin.
Clausen, Wendell V., ed. 1959. *A. Persi Flacci et D. Iuni Iuvenalis Saturae*. Oxford: Clarendon.
Comparetti, Domenico. 1875. *Novelline populari italiane*. Turin: Ermanno Loescher.
———. 1898. *The Traditional Poetry of the Finns*. Trans. Isabella M. Anderton, with introduction by Andrew Lang. New York: Longmans, Green. Originally published as *Il Kalevala; o, la poesia tradizionale dei Finni; Studio storico-critico sulle origini delle grandi epopee nazional*. Rome: Reale Accademia dei Lincei, 1891.
Conroy, Patricia, ed. 1978. *Ballads and Ballad Research*. Selected Papers of the International Conference on Nordic and Anglo-American Ballad Research, 1977. Seattle: University of Washington.
Creed, Robert Payson. 1958. "*Genesis* 1316." *Modern Language Notes* 73:321–25.
———. 1959. "The Making of an Anglo-Saxon Poem." *English Literary History* 26:445–54. Rpt. with "Additional Remarks" in *The Beowulf Poet: A Collection of Critical Essays*, ed. Donald K. Fry, Jr. 141–53. Englewood Cliffs, N.J.: Prentice-Hall, 1968.
———. 1962. "The Singer Looks at His Sources." *Comparative Literature* 14:44–52. Rpt. in *Studies in Old English Literature in Honor of Arthur G. Brodeur*, ed. Stanley B. Greenfield, 44–52. Eugene: University of Oregon Press, 1963.
———. 1981. Preface to Foley, 1981, 19–20.
Cross, Frank M. 1977. *Canaanite Myth and Hebrew Epic*. Cambridge, Mass.: Harvard University Press.
Crowne, David K. 1960. "The Hero on the Beach: An Example of Composition by Theme in Anglo-Saxon Poetry." *Neuphilologische Mitteilungen* 61:362–72.
Curschmann, Michael. 1977. "The Concept of the Oral Formula as an Impediment to Our Understanding of Medieval Oral Poetry." *Medievalia et Humanistica*, n.s. 8:63–76.
De Nino, Antonio. 1883. *Fiabe*. Vol. 3 of *Usi e costumi abruzzesi*. Florence: Leo S. Olschki.

Diamond, Robert E. 1961. "Theme as Ornament in Anglo-Saxon Poetry." *PMLA* 76:461–68.
———. 1963. *The Diction of the Anglo-Saxon Metrical Psalms.* Janua Linguarum, Series Practica 10. The Hague: Mouton.
Dillon, Myles, trans. 1971. *There Was a King in Ireland: Five Tales from Oral Tradition.* Austin: University of Texas Press.
Djilas, Milovan. 1966. *Njegoš: Poet, Prince, Bishop.* trans. with introduction by Michael B. Petrovich. New York: Harcourt, Brace and World.
Doane, A. Nicholas. 1991. "Oral Texts, Intertexts, and Intratexts: Editing Old English." In *Influence and Intertextuality in Literary History*, ed. Jay Clayton and Eric Rothstein, 75–113. Madison: University of Wisconsin Press.
Dobbie, Elliott Van Kirk, ed. 1942. *The Anglo-Saxon Minor Poems.* Vol. 6 of *The Anglo-Saxon Poetic Records.* New York: Columbia University Press.
———, ed. 1953. *Beowulf and Judith.* Vol. 4 of *The Anglo-Saxon Poetic Records.* New York: Columbia University Press.
Donoghue, Daniel. 1987. *Style in Old English Poetry: The Test of the Auxiliary.* New Haven: Yale University Press.
Ducrot, Oswald and Tzvetan Todorov. 1979. *Encyclopedic Dictionary of the Sciences of Language.* Trans. Catherine Porter. Baltimore: Johns Hopkins University Press.
Duggan, Joseph J., ed. 1975. *Oral Literature: Seven Essays.* New York: Barnes and Noble.
Edwards, G. P. 1971. *The Language of Hesiod in Its Traditional Context.* Oxford: Blackwell & Mott.
Edwards, Mark W. 1987. *Homer: Poet of the Iliad.* Baltimore: Johns Hopkins University Press.
Eliade, Mircea. 1961. *The Sacred and the Profane: The Nature of Religion.* Trans. Willard Trask. New York: Harper & Row.
Entwistle, William J. 1939. *European Balladry.* Oxford: Clarendon.
Evelyn-White, Hugh G., trans. 1943. *Hesiod, The Homeric Hymns, and Homerica.* Loeb Classical Library. Cambridge, Mass.: Harvard University Press.
Fennell, C. A. M. 1893. *Pindar: The Olympian and Pythian Odes.* Cambridge: Cambridge University Press.
Figueira, Thomas J., and Gregory Nagy, 1985. *Theognis of Megara: Poetry and the Polis.* Baltimore: Johns Hopkins University Press.
Finnegan, Ruth H. 1970. *Oral Literature in Africa.* Oxford: Clarendon.
———. 1976. "What Is Oral Literature Anyway? Comments in the Light of Some African and Other Comparative Material." In Stolz and Shannon, 1976, 127–66.
———. 1977. *Oral Poetry: Its Nature, Significance, and Social Context.* Cambridge: Cambridge University Press.
———. 1988. *Literacy and Orality: Studies in the Technology of Communication.* Oxford: Blackwell.
Foley, John Miles. 1976. "Formula and Theme in Old English Poetry." In Stolz and Shannon, 1976, 207–32.
———. 1980. "Hybrid Prosody: Single Half-Lines in Old English and Serbo-Croatian Poetry." *Neophilologus* 64:284–89.
———. ed. 1981. *Oral Traditional Literature: A Festschrift for Albert Bates Lord.* Columbus: Slavica.
———. 1985. *Oral-Formulaic Theory and Research: An Introduction and Annotated Bibliography.* New York: Garland.

———, ed. 1987. *Comparative Research on Oral Traditions: A Memorial for Milman Parry.* Columbus: Slavica.
———. 1990. *Traditional Oral Epic: The Odyssey, Beowulf, and the Serbo-Croatian Return Song.* Berkeley and Los Angeles: University of California Press.
———. 1991. *Immanent Art: From Structure to Meaning in Traditional Oral Epic.* Bloomington: Indiana University Press.
———, ed. 1992. *De Gustibus: Essays for Alain Renoir.* New York: Garland.
———. 1995. *The Singer of Tales in Performance.* Bloomington: Indiana University Press.
Ford, Andrew L. 1985. "The Seal of Theognis: The Politics of Authorship in Archaic Greece." In Figueira and Nagy, 1985, 82–95.
Friedman, Albert B. 1961a. "The Formulaic Improvisation Theory of Ballad Tradition: A Counterstatement." *Journal of American Folklore* 74:113–15.
———. 1961b. *The Ballad Revival: Studies in the Influence of Popular on Sophisticated Poetry.* Chicago: University of Chicago Press.
Fry, Donald K., Jr. 1966. "The Hero on the Beach in Finnsburh." *Neuphilologische Mitteilungen* 67:27–31.
———. 1967a. "The Heroine on the Beach in *Judith*." *Neuphilologische Mitteilungen* 68:168–84.
———. 1967b. "Old English Formulas and Systems." *English Studies* 48:193–204.
———. 1968a. "Variation and Economy in *Beowulf*." *Modern Philology* 65:353–56.
———. 1968b. "Old English Formulaic Themes and Type Scenes." *Neophilologus* 52:48–54.
———. 1968c. "Some Aesthetic Implications of a New Definition of the Formula." *Neuphilologische Mitteilungen* 69:516–22.
———. 1969. "Themes and Type-Scenes in *Elene* 1–113." *Speculum* 44:35–45.
———. 1972. "Type-Scene Composition in *Judith*." *Annuale Mediaevale* 12:100–119.
———. 1975. "Cædmon as a Formulaic Poet." In Duggan, 1975, 41–61.
———. 1981. "Formulaic Theory and Old English Poetry." In *Report of the Twelfth Congress, Berkeley 1977*, ed. Daniel Heartz and Bonnie Wade, 169–73. International Musicological Society. Kassel, Germany: Bärenreiter.
Giannini, Pietro. 1973. "Espressioni formulari nell' elegia greca arcaica." *Quaderni Urbinati di Cultura Classica* 16:7–78.
Göller, Karl Heinz, ed. 1981. *The Alliterative Morte Arthure: A Reassessment of the Poem.* Arthurian Studies 3. Totowa, N.J.: Rowan & Littlefield.
Goody, John R. 1977. *The Domestication of the Savage Mind.* Cambridge: Cambridge University Press.
Goody, John R., and Ian Watt. 1963. "The Consequences of Literacy." *Comparative Studies in Society and History* 5:304–45.
Goold, George P. 1977. "The Nature of Homeric Composition." *Illinois Classical Studies* 2:1–34.
Grabovac, Filip. 1951. *Cvit razgovora naroda i jezika Iliričkoga aliti rvackoga.* Ed. Tomo Matić. Vol. 30 of *Stari pisci hrvatski.* Zagreb: Jugoslavenska Akademija Znanosti i Umjetnosti.
Green, D. H. 1990. "Orality and Reading: The State of Research in Medieval Studies." *Speculum* 65:267–80.
Greenfield, Stanley B. 1955. "The Formulaic Expression of the Theme of 'Exile' in Anglo-Saxon Poetry." *Speculum* 30:200–206.
Grimble, Arthur Francis. 1957. *Return to the Islands.* London: Murray.

Gundulić, Ivan. 1938. *Osman*. Ed. Đuro Körbler and Milan Rešetar. Vol. 9 of *Stari pisci hrvatski*. Zagreb: Jugoslavenska Akademija Znanosti i Umjetnosti.
Gyger (née Jones), Alison. 1969. "The Old English *Soul and Body* as an Example of Oral Transmission." *Medium Aevum* 38:239–44.
Hainsworth, J. Bryan. 1968. *The Flexibility of the Homeric Formula*. Oxford: Clarendon.
———. 1976. "Phrase-Clusters in Homer." In *Studies in Greek, Italic, and Indo-European Linguistics*, ed. Anna Morpurgo Davies and Wolfgang Meid, 83–86. Innsbrucker Beiträge zur Sprachwissenschaft, vol. 16. Vienna: Becvar.
———. 1978. "Good and Bad Formulae." In *Homer: Tradition and Invention*, ed. Bernard C. Fenik, 41–50. University of Cincinnati Classical Studies, n.s. 2. Leiden: Brill.
———. 1981. "Criteri di oralità nella poesia arcaica non omerica." In Brillante, Cantilena, and Pavese, 1981, 3–27.
Hamel, Mary, ed. 1984. *Morte Arthure: A Critical Edition*. New York: Garland.
Harris, Joseph. 1979. "The *Senna*: From Description to Literary Theory." *Michigan Germanic Studies* 5:64–74.
———. 1981a. "Satire and the Heroic Life: Two Studies." (*Helgakviða Hundingsbana* I.18 and Bjorn Hítdoelakappi's *Grámagaflím*). In Foley, 1981, 322–40.
———. 1981b. "*Beowulf* in Literary History." *Pacific Coast Philology* 16, no. 2:16–23.
———. 1983. "Eddic Poetry as Oral Poetry: The Evidence of Parallel Passages in the Helgi Poems for Questions of Composition and Performance." In *Edda: A Collection of Essays*, ed. Robert J. Glendinning and Haraldur Bessason, 210–42. Manitoba Icelandic Series. Manitoba: University of Manitoba Press.
Harrison, Ernest H. 1902. *Studies in Theognis*. Cambridge: Cambridge University Press.
Hatto, Arthur T., ed. 1965. *Eos: An Enquiry into the Theme of Lovers' Meetings and Partings at Dawn in Poetry*. The Hague: Mouton.
———, trans. 1969. *The Nibelungenlied: A New Translation*. Harmondsworth: Penguin.
Havelock, Eric A. 1963. *Preface to Plato*. Cambridge, Mass.: Harvard University Press, Belknap.
———. 1978. "The Alphabetization of Homer." In *Communication Arts in the Ancient World*, ed. Eric A. Havelock and Jackson P. Hershbell, 3–21. Humanistic Studies in the Communication Arts. New York: Hastings House.
———. 1982. *The Literate Revolution in Greece and Its Cultural Consequences*. Princeton: Princeton University Press.
———. 1986. *The Muse Learns to Write: Reflections on Orality and Literacy from Antiquity to the Present*. New Haven: Yale University Press.
Haymes, Edward R. 1987. "Ez Wart ein Buoch Funden: Oral and Written in Middle High German Heroic Epic." In Foley, 1987, 235–43.
Heidel, Alexander. 1951. *The Babylonian Genesis*. 2d ed. Chicago: University of Chicago Press.
Hektorović, Petar. 1951. *Ribanje i ribarsko Prigovaranje*. Ed. Ramiro Bujas. Zagreb: Jadranski Institut Jugoslavenske Akademije Znanosti i Umjetnosti.
Henderson, Hamish. 1973. "The Oral Tradition." Review of *The Ballad and the Folk*, by David Buchan. *Scottish International Review* 6, no. 1:27–32.
Herter, Hans. 1981. "L'inno omerico a Hermes alla luce della problematica della poesia orale." In Brillante, Cantilena, and Pavese, 1981, 183–201.
Hesiod, 1966. *Hesiod: Theogony*. Ed. with prolegomena and commentary by Martin L. West. Oxford: Clarendon.

———. 1970. *Hesiodi Theogonia Opera et Dies Scutum*. Ed. Friedrich Solmsen, with *Fragmenta Selecta*, ed. Reinhold Merkelbach and Martin L. West. Oxford: Clarendon.
Hilferding, A. F. 1938. *Onezheskie byliny*. Collected, summer of 1871 by A. F. Hilferding. 3d ed. Vol. 2. Moscow/Leningrad: Academy of Sciences of the Union of Soviet Socialist Republics (ANSSSR), 1938.
Hirtz, Miroslav, ed. 1941. *Rječnik narodnih zoologičkih naziva*. 2 vols. Zagreb: Hrvatska Akademija Znanosti i Umjetnosti.
Hoekstra. Arie. 1957. "Hésiode et la tradition orale: Contribution à l'étude du style formulaire." *Mnemosyne* 10:193–225.
———. 1965. *Homeric Modifications of Formulaic Prototypes: Studies in the Development of Greek Epic Diction*. Verhandelingen der Koninklijke Nederlandse Akademie van Wetenschappen, afd. letterkunde, n.s., vol. 71, no. 1. Amsterdam: Noord-Hollandsche Uitgevers Maatschappij.
The Holy Bible: Revised Standard Version. 1952. Containing the Old and New Testaments. New York: Thomas Nelson.
Homer. 1965. *Homeri opera*. Vol. 5, *Hymnos Cyclum Fragmenta Margiten Batrachomyomachiam Vitas Continens*. Ed. Thomas W. Allen. Oxford: Clarendon.
———. 1976. *Homeri opera*. Vols. 1–2, *Iliad*. 3d ed. Ed. David B. Munro and Thomas W. Allen. Vols. 3–4, *Odyssea*. 2d ed. Ed. Thomas W. Allen. Oxford: Clarendon.
Hony, H. C., ed. 1947. *A Turkish-English Dictionary*. Oxford: Clarendon.
Hrvatske narodne pjesme. 1896–1942. 10 vols. Zagreb: Matica Hrvatska.
Jabbour, Alan A. 1969. "Memorial Transmission in Old English Poetry." *Chaucer Review* 3:174–90.
Janko, Richard. 1982. *Homer, Hesiod, and the Hymns: Diachronic Development in Epic Diction*. Cambridge: Cambridge University Press.
———. 1990. "The *Iliad* and Its Editors: Dictation and Redaction." *Classical Antiquity* 9:326–34.
———. 1992. *The Iliad: A Commentary, Volume IV: Books 13–16*. Gen. ed. G. S. Kirk. Cambridge: Cambridge University Press.
Jones, Alison. 1966. "*Daniel* and *Azarias* as Evidence for the Oral-Formulaic Character of Old English Poetry." *Medium Aevum* 35:95–102.
———. See also Gyger, 1969.
Jones, James H. 1961. "Commonplace and Memorization in the Oral Tradition of the English and Scottish Popular Ballads." *Journal of American Folklore* 74:97–112.
Kačić-Miošić, Andrija. 1942. *Djela Andrije Kačića Miošića*. Ed. T. Matić. Vol. 1, *Razgovor Ugodni*. Vol. 27 of *Stari pisci hrvatski*. Zagreb: Hrvatska Akademija Znanosti i Umjetnosti.
Karadžić, Vuk Stefanović, 1824. *Narodne srpske pjesme*. Vol. 1. Leipzig: Breitkopf & Härtel.
———. 1932–36. *Srpske narodne pjesme*. 9 vols. Belgrade: Državna štamparija.
———. 1958. *Srpske narodne pjesme*. 4 vols. Belgrade: Prosveta.
Katzenelbogen, Uriah. 1935. *The Daina: An Anthology of Lithuanian and Latvian Folk-Songs*. Chicago: Lithuanian News Publishing.
Kinsley, James, ed. 1969. *The Oxford Book of Ballads*. Oxford: Clarendon.
Kirk, Geoffrey S. 1981. "Orality and Structure in the Homeric 'Hymn to Apollo.'" In Brillante, Cantilena, and Pavese, 1981, 163–82.

———. 1985. *The Iliad: A Commentary, Volume I: Books 1–4*. Cambridge: Cambridge University Press.
Klaeber, Frederick, ed. 1950. *Beowulf and the Fight at Finnsburg*. 3d ed. with 1st and 2d supplements. Boston: Heath.
Krapp, George Philip, ed. 1931. *The Junius Manuscript*. Vol. 1 of *The Anglo-Saxon Poetic Records*. New York: Columbia University Press.
———, ed. 1932. *The Vercelli Book*. Vol. 2 of *The Anglo-Saxon Poetic Records*. New York: Columbia University Press.
Krapp, George Philip, and Elliott Van Kirk Dobbie, eds. 1936. *The Exeter Book*. Vol. 3 of *The Anglo-Saxon Poetic Records*. New York: Columbia University Press.
Krishna, Valerie, ed. 1976. *The Alliterative Morte Arthure*. Critical ed. with introduction, notes, and glossary. Preface by Russell Hope Robbins. New York: Burt Franklin.
———. 1982. "Parataxis, Formulaic Density, and Thrift in the *Alliterative Morte Arthure*." *Speculum* 57:63–83.
———, trans. 1983. *The Alliterative Morte Arthure: A New Verse Translation*. Lanham, Md.: University Press of America.
Küllenberg, Richard K. 1877. *De imitatione Theognidea*. Strasbourg: K. J. Truebner.
Latković, Vido. 1963. *Petar Petrović Njegoš*. Belgrade: Nolit.
Lattimore, Richmond, trans. 1951. *The Iliad of Homer*. Chicago: University of Chicago Press.
———, trans. 1967. *The Odyssey of Homer*. New York: Harper and Row.
Letopis popa Dukljanina. 1950. Ed. Vladimir Mošin. Zagreb: Matica Hrvatska.
Lindsay, W. M., ed. 1929. *M. Val. Martialis Epigrammata*. 2d ed. Oxford: Clarendon.
Lobel, Edgar, and Denys Page, eds. 1955. *Poetarum Lesbiorum Fragmenta*. Oxford: Clarendon.
Lönnroth, Lars. 1971. "Hjálmar's Death-Song and the Delivery of Eddic Poetry." *Speculum* 46:1–20.
———. 1976. *Njáls Saga: A Critical Introduction*. Berkeley and Los Angeles: University of California Press.
———. 1979. "The Double Scene of Arrow-Odd's Drinking Contest." In *Medieval Narrative: A Symposium*, ed. Hans Bekker-Nielsen et al., 94–119. Odense: Odense University Press.
———. 1981. "Iorð fahnz æva né upphiminn: A Formula Analysis." In *Speculum Norroenum: Norse Studies in Memory of Gabriel Turville-Petre*, ed. Ursula Dronke et al., 310–27. Odense: Odense University Press.
Lord, Albert B. 1951. "Composition by Theme in Homer and Southslavic Epos." *Transactions of the American Philological Association* 82:71–80.
———. 1960. *The Singer of Tales*. Harvard Studies in Comparative Literature, 24. Cambridge, Mass.: Harvard University Press.
———. 1962. "Homer and Other Epic Poetry." In *A Companion to Homer*, ed. Alan J. B. Wace and Frank H. Stubbings, 179–214. London: Macmillan.
———. 1971. "An Example of Homeric Qualities of Repetition in Medjedović's 'Smailagić Meho.'" In *Serta Slavica Aloisii Schmaus: Gedenkschrift für Alois Schmaus*, ed. Wolfgang Gesemann. 458–64. Munich: Rudolf Trofenik.
———. 1975. "Perspectives on Recent Work on Oral Literature." In Duggan, 1975, 1–24.
———. 1980. "Interlocking Mythic Patterns in *Beowulf*." In *Old English Literature in Context: Ten Essays*, ed. John D. Niles, 137–42. Tototwa, N.J.: Rowan and Littlefield. Rpt. in A. Lord, 1991, 140–46.

———. 1981. "Memory, Fixity, and Genre in Oral Traditional Poetries." In Foley, 1981, 451–61.
———. 1986. "The Merging of Two Worlds: Oral and Written Poetry as Carriers of Ancient Values." In *Oral Tradition in Literature: Interpretation in Context*, ed. John Miles Foley, 19–64. Columbia: University of Missouri Press.
———. 1987a. "Characteristics of Orality." In *Festschrift for Walter J. Ong. Oral Tradition* 2, no. 1:54–72.
———. 1987b. "The Nature of Oral Poetry." In Foley, 1987, 313–49.
———. 1989. "Theories of Oral Literature and the Latvian Dainas." In *Linguistics and Poetics of Latvian Folk Songs: Essays in Honour of the Sesquicentennial of the Birth of Kr. Barons*, ed. Vaira Vīķis-Freibergs, 35–48. Montreal: McGill-Queen's University Press.
———. 1991. *Epic Singers and Oral Tradition*. Myth and Poetics, ed. Gregory Nagy. Ithaca: Cornell University Press.
———. 1992. "Beowulf and the Russian Byliny." In Foley, 1992, 304–23. Published posthumously.
———. 1993. "Cædmon Revisited." In *Heroic Poetry in the Anglo-Saxon Period: Studies in Honor of Jess B. Bessinger, Jr.*, ed. Helen Damico and John Leyerle, 121–37. Studies in Medieval Culture 32. Kalamazoo: Western Michigan University, Medieval Institute Publications. Published posthumously.
Lord, Mary Louise. 1967. "Withdrawal and Return: An Epic Story Pattern in the Homeric Hymn to Demeter and in the Homeric Poems." *Classical Journal* 62:241–48. Rpt. in *The Homeric Hymn to Demeter: Translation, Commentary, and Interpretive Essays*, ed. Helene P. Foley, 181–89. Princeton: Princeton University Press, 1994.
Lorimer, H. L. 1950. *Homer and the Monuments*. London: Macmillan.
Luce, T. James, ed. 1982. *Ancient Writers: Greece and Rome*. New York: Scribner's.
Luethans, Tod N. 1990. *"Gormont et Isembart": The Epic as Seen in the Light of the Oral Theory*. New York: Garland.
McGillivray, Murray. 1990. *Memorization in the Transmission of the Middle English Romances*. The Albert Bates Lord Studies in Oral Tradition, vol. 5, ed. John Miles Foley. New York: Garland.
McLuhan, Herbert Marshall. 1962. *The Gutenberg Galaxy: The Making of Typographic Man*. Toronto: University of Toronto Press.
Magoun, Francis P., Jr. 1953. "The Oral-Formulaic Character of Anglo-Saxon Narrative Poetry." *Speculum* 28:446–67. Rpt. in *An Anthology of Beowulf Criticism*, ed. Lewis E. Nicholson, 189–221. Notre Dame: University of Notre Dame Press, 1963; and in *The Beowulf Poet: A Collection of Critical Essays*, ed. Donald K. Fry, Jr., 83–113. Twentieth Century Views. Englewood Cliffs, N.J.: Prentice-Hall, 1968.
———. 1955a. "Bede's Story of Cædmon: The Case History of an Anglo-Saxon Oral Singer." *Speculum* 30:49–63.
———. 1955b. "The Theme of the Beasts of Battle in Anglo-Saxon Poetry." *Neuphilologische Mitteilungen* 56:81–90.
Martin, Richard P. 1989. *The Language of Heroes: Speech and Performance in the Iliad*. Myth and Poetics, ed. Gregory Nagy. Ithaca: Cornell University Press.
Mitchell, Stephen A. 1987. "The Sagaman and Oral Literature: The Icelandic Traditions of Hjörleifr Inn Kvensami and Geirmundr heljarskinn." In Foley, 1987, 395–423.
———. 1991. *Heroic Sagas and Ballads*. Myth and Poetics, ed. Gregory Nagy. Ithaca: Cornell University Press.

Mladenović, Živomir, and Vladan Nedić, eds. 1973. *Srpske narodne pjesme iz neobljavljenih rukopisa Vuka Stef. Karadžica.* Vol. 1, *Različne ženske pjesme.* Belgrade: Srpska Akademija Nauka i Umetnosti.

Moffat, Douglas. 1992. "Anglo-Saxon Scribes and Old English Verse." *Speculum* 67:805–27.

Morland, Laura. 1992. "Cæmon and the Germanic Tradition." In Foley, 1992, 324–58.

Muižniece, Lalita Lace. 1981. *Linguistic Analysis of Latvian Death and Burial Folk Songs.* Ann Arbor: University Microfilms International.

Nagy, Gregory. 1974. *Comparative Studies in Greek and Indic Meter.* Cambridge, Mass.: Harvard University Press.

———. 1976. "Formula and Meter." In Stolz and Shannon, 1976, 239–60. Rewritten as chap. 2 in Nagy, 1990a.

———. 1979a. *The Best of the Achaeans: Concepts of the Hero in Archaic Greek Poetry.* Baltimore: Johns Hopkins University Press.

———. 1979b. "On the Origins of the Greek Hexameter." In *Festschrift for Oswald Szemerényi*, ed. B. Brogyanyi, Amsterdam Studies in the Theory and History of Linguistic Science 4, Current Issues in Linguistic Theory, vol. 11, 611–31. Rewritten as part of app. in Nagy, 1990b.

———. 1982. "Hesiod." In Luce, 1982, 43–73. Rewritten as part of chap. 3 in Nagy, 1990a.

———. 1985. "Theognis and Megara: A Poet's Vision of His City." In Figueira and Nagy, 1985, 22–81.

———. 1990a. *Greek Mythology and Poetics.* Myth and Poetics, ed. Gregory Nagy. Ithaca: Cornell University Press.

———. 1990b. *Pindar's Homer: The Lyric Possession of an Epic Poet.* Baltimore: Johns Hopkins University Press.

———. 1992a. "Homeric Questions." *Transactions of the American Philological Association* 122:17–60.

———. 1992b. "Mythological Exemplum in Homer." In *Innovations of Antiquity*, eds. Ralph Hexter and Daniel Selden, 311–31. London: Routledge.

Neckel, Gustave, ed. 1983. *Edda: Die Lieder des Codex Regius nebst verwandten Denkmälern I. Text.* 5th rev. ed. Hans Kuhn. Heidelberg: Carl Winter Universitätsverlag.

The New Jerome Biblical Commentary. 1990. Ed. Raymond E. Brown, Joseph A. Fitzmayer, and Roland E. Murphy. Englewood Cliffs, N.J.: Prentice-Hall.

Niles, John D. 1981. "Formula and Formulaic System in *Beowulf.*" In Foley, 1981, 394–415.

———. 1983. *Beowulf: The Poem and Its Tradition.* Cambridge, Mass.: Harvard University Press.

Njegoš, Petar Petrović. 1953. *Pjesme.* Vol. 2. Ed. Radovan Lalić and Mihailo Stevanović. Belgrade: Prosveta.

Notopoulos, James A. 1959. "Originality in Homeric and Akritan Formulas." *Laographia* 18:423–31.

———. 1966. "Archilochus, the Aoidos." *Transactions of the American Philological Association* 97:311–15.

Nygard, Holger Olof. 1978. "Mrs. Brown's Recollected Ballads." In Conroy, 1978, 68–87.

O'Keeffe, Katherine O'Brien. 1990. *Visible Song: Transitional Literacy in Old English Verse.* Cambridge: Cambridge University Press.

Olsen, Alexandra Hennessey. 1986. "Oral-Formulaic Research in Old English Studies: I." *Oral Tradition* 1, no. 3:548–606.
Ong, Walter J. 1982. *Orality and Literacy: The Technologizing of the Word*. New Accents Series. New York: Methuen.
Opland, Jeff. 1980. *Anglo-Saxon Oral Poetry: A Study of the Traditions*. New Haven: Yale University Press.
Page, Denys L. 1963. "Archilochus and the Oral Tradition." In *Archiloque*, Entretiens sur l'Antiquité Classique Fondation Hardt, vol. 10, 117–63. Geneva: Vandoeuvres.
Parks, Ward. 1986. "The Oral-Formulaic Theory in Middle English Studies." *Oral Tradition* 1, no. 3:636–94.
Parry, Milman, col. 1953. *Serbocroatian Heroic Songs: Collected by Milman Parry*. ed. Albert Bates Lord, Vol. 2, *Novi Pazar: Serbocroatian Texts*, introduction and notes by A. B. Lord, preface by A. Belić. Belgrade: Serbian Academy of Sciences; Cambridge, Mass.: Harvard University Press.
———, col. 1954. *Serbocroatian Heroic Songs: Collected by Milman Parry*. Ed. and trans. Albert Bates Lord. Vol. 1, *Novi Pazar: English Translations*, musical transcriptions by Béla Bartók, prefaces by John H. Finley, Jr., and Roman Jakobson. Cambridge, Mass.: Harvard University Press; Belgrade: Serbian Academy of Sciences.
———. 1971. *The Making of Homeric Verse: The Collected Papers of Milman Parry*. Ed. Adam Parry. Oxford: Clarendon.
———, col. 1974a. *Serbo-Croatian Heroic Songs: Collected by Milman Parry*. Vol. 3, *The Wedding of Smailagić Meho, Avdo Međedović*, trans. Albert B. Lord, with introduction, notes, and commentary, with a translation of conversations concerning the Singer's life and times by David E. Bynum. Cambridge, Mass.: Harvard University Press.
———, col. 1974b. *Serbo-Croatian Heroic Songs: Collected by Milman Parry*. Vol. 4, *Ženidba Smailagina Sina, Kazivao je Avdo Međedović, s popratnim Razgovorima s Međedovićem i drugim*, ed. David E. Bynum with Albert B. Lord. Cambridge, Mass.: Center for the Study of Oral Literature.
———, col. 1979. *Serbo-Croatian Heroic Songs*. Vol. 14, *Bihaćka Krajina: Epics from Bihać, Cazin, and Kulen Vakuf*, col. Milman Parry, Albert B. Lord, and David E. Bynum; ed. David E. Bynum with prolegomena and notes. Cambridge, Mass.: Publications of the Milman Parry Collection; distributed by Harvard University Press.
———, col. 1980. *Serbo-Croatian Heroic Songs: Collected by Milman Parry*. Vol. 6, *Ženidba Vlahinjić Alije, Osmanbeg Delibegović i Pavičević Luka, Kazivao I Pjevao Avdo Međedović*, ed. David E. Bynum wih prolegomena and notes. Cambridge, Mass.: Distributed by Harvard University Press.
Pavese, Carlo O. 1972. *Tradizioni e generi poetici della Grecia arcaica*. Istituto di Filologia Classica, Filologia e Critica, 12. Rome: Ateneo.
Peabody, Berkley. 1975. *The Winged Word: A Study in the Technique of Ancient Greek Oral Composition as Seen Principally through Hesiod's Works and Days*. Albany: State University of New York Press.
Pearsall, Derek. 1977. *Old English and Middle English Poetry*. London: Routledge & Kegan Paul.
Petersen, Suzanne. 1978. "A Computer-Aided Analysis of the Mechanism of Variation in Orally Transmitted Parts." In Conroy, 1978, 88–100.
Pitrè, Giuseppe. 1875. *Fiabe novelle e racconti popolari siciliani*. Vol. 1. Biblioteca delle

Tradizioni Populari Siciliani, vol. 4. Palermo: Luigi Pedone Lauriel. Rpt. Bologna: Forni, n.d.
Preziosi, Patricia G. 1966. "The *Homeric Hymn to Aphrodite*: An Oral Analysis." *Harvard Studies in Classical Philology* 71: 171–204.
Pritchard, James B., ed. 1950. *Ancient Near Eastern Texts relating to the Old Testament.* Princeton: Princeton University Press.
Quain, Buell H. 1942. *The Flight of the Chiefs: Epic Poetry of Fiji.* New York: Augustin.
Radloff, Wilhelm von, col. and trans. 1885. *Proben der Volksliteratur der nördlichen türkischen Stämme.* Part 5. St. Petersburg: Kaiserliche Akademie der Wissenschaften.
Ralston, William Sheddin. 1872. *The Songs of the Russian People Illustrative of Slavonic Mythology and Russian Social Life.* 2d ed. London: Ellis & Green. Rpt. New York: Haskell House, 1970.
Ramsay, G. G., trans. 1924. *Juvenal and Persius.* New York: Putnam's.
Ranjin zbornik: Pjesme ranínina zbornika. 1937. Ed. Milan Rešetar. Vol. 2 of *Stari pisci hrvatski.* Zagreb: Jugoslavenska Akademija Znanosti i Umjetnosti.
Rečnik srpskohrvatskoga književnog jezika. 1967–76. 6 vols. Novi Sad: Matica Srpska, Matica Hrvatska.
Renoir, Alain. 1964. "Oral-Formulaic Theme Survival: A Possible Instance in the *Nibelungenlied.*" *Neuphilologische Mitteilungen* 65:70–75.
———. 1988. *A Key to Old Poems: The Oral-Formulaic Approach to the Interpretation of West-Germanic Verse.* University Park: Pennsylvania State University Press.
Reynolds, Dwight. 1990. "The Poet and the Poem in Egyptian Oral Epic Performance" (lecture) presented at the Center for Middle East Studies, Harvard University, February 15, 1990.
———. 1995. *Heroic Poets, Poetic Heroes: The Ethnography of Performance in an Egyptian Oral Epic Tradition.* Myth and Poetics, ed. Gregory Nagy. Ithaca: Cornell University Press, forthcoming.
Riedinger, Anita. 1985. "The Old English Formula in Context." *Speculum* 60:294–317.
Riedy, Nicolaus. 1903. *Solonis elocutio quatenus pendeat ab exemplo Homeri.* Munich: Kutzner.
Riggsby, Andrew M. 1992. "'Becoming Homer': An Exchange." Letter to the editor. *New York Review of Books* May 14, 51.
Ritzke-Rutherford, Jean. 1981. "Formulaic Microstructure: The Cluster." In Göller, 1981, 70–82, 167–69.
Robinson, Fred C. 1985. *Beowulf and the Appositive Style.* Knoxville: University of Tennessee Press.
Russom, Geoffrey R. 1978. "Artful Avoidance of the Useful Phrase in *Beowulf, The Battle of Maldon,* and *Fates of the Apostles.*" *Studies in Philology* 75:371–90.
———. 1987a. *Old English Meter and Linguistic Theory.* Cambridge: Cambridge University Press.
———. 1987b. "Verse Translations and the Question of Literacy in *Beowulf.*" In Foley, 1987, 567–80.
Savić-Rebac, Anica. 1957. "'The Ray of the Microcosm,' by Petar Petrović Njegoš: Translation and Introduction." *Harvard Slavic Studies* 3:105–200.
Schaar, Claes. 1956. "On a New Theory of Old English Poetic Diction." *Neophilologus* 40:301–5.
Segal, Charles. 1981. "Orality, Repetition, and Formulaic Artistry in the Homeric 'Hymn to Demeter.'" In Brillante, Cantilena, and Pavese, 1981, 107–62.

Shannon, Richard S., III. 1975. *The Arms of Achilles and Homeric Compositional Technique*. Mnemosyne, supple. 36. Leiden: Brill.
Shive, David. 1987. *Naming Achilles*. Oxford: Oxford University Press.
Škaljić, Abdulah. 1966. *Turcizmi u srpskohrvatskom jeziku*. Sarajevo: Svjetlost.
Šmits, Pēteris, ed. 1936–39. *Tautas dziesmas*. Supplement to Krišjānis Barons, *Latvju dainas*. 4 vols. Riga: Latviešu Folkloras Krātuves Materiāli.
Spraycar, Rudy S., and Lee F. Dunlap. 1982. "Formulaic Style in Oral and Literate Epic Poetry." *Perspectives in Computing* 2, no. 4:24–33.
Stender, Gotthard Friedrich. 1783. *Lettische Grammatik*. Mitau: J. F. Steffenhagen.
Stock, Brian. 1983. *The Implications of Literacy: Written Language and Models of Interpretation in the Eleventh and Twelfth Centuries*. Princeton: Princeton University Press.
———. 1989. *Listening for the Text*. Baltimore: Johns Hopkins University Press.
Stolz, Benjamin A., and Richard S. Shannon III, eds. 1976. *Oral Literature and the Formula*. Ann Arbor: Center for the Coordination of Ancient and Modern Studies.
Švabe, Arveds, Kārlis Straubergs, and Edīte Hauzenberga-Šturma, eds. 1952–56. *Latviešu tautas dziesmas*. 12 vols. Copenhagen: Imanta.
Svenbro, Jesper. 1984. "La stratégie de l'amour: Modèle de la guerre et théorie de l'amour dans la poésie de Sappho." *Quaderni di Storia* 10, no. 19:57–59.
———. 1988. *Phrasikleia: Anthropologie de la lecture en Grèce ancienne*. Paris: Découverte.
———. 1993. *Phrasikleia: An Anthropology of Reading in Ancient Greece*. Trans. Janet Lloyd. Myth and Poetics, ed. Gregory Nagy. Ithaca: Cornell University Press.
Thigpen, Kenneth A., Jr. 1973. "A Reconsideration of the Commonplace Phrase and Commonplace Theme in the Child Ballads." *Southern Folklore Quarterly* 37:385–408.
Thomas, Rosalind. 1992. *Literacy and Orality in Ancient Greece*. Cambridge: Cambridge University Press.
Thurnwald, Richard C. 1912. *Forschungen auf den Salamo-Inseln und dem Bismarck-Archipel*. Vol. 1, *Lieder und Sagen aus Buin*, with appendix: *Die Musik auf den Salamo-Inseln*, by E. M. V. Hornbostel. Berlin: Dietrich Reimer (Ernst Vohsen).
———. 1936. *Profane Literature in Buin, Solomon Islands*. Yale University Publications in Anthropology 8. New Haven: Yale University Press.
Toelken, J. Barre. 1967. "An Oral Canon for the Child Ballads: Construction and Application." *Journal of the Folklore Institute* 5:75–101.
Vīķis-Freibergs, Vaira. 1981. "Daina, Latvian." In *The Modern Encyclopedia of Russian and Soviet Literatures, Including Non-Russian and Emigré Literatures*, ed. Harry B. Weber, 5:41–49. Gulf Breeze, Fla.: Academic International Press.
———. 1984. "Creativity and Tradition in Oral Folklore, or the Balance of Innovation and Repetition in the Oral Poet's Art." In *Cognitive Processes in the Perception of Art*, ed. W. R. Crozier and A. J. Chapman, 325–43. Amsterdam: North Holland.
Vīķis-Freibergs, Vaira, and Imants F. Freibergs. 1978. "Formulaic Analysis of the Computer-Accessible Corpus of Latvian Sun-songs." *Computers and the Humanities* 12:329–39.
Vivante, Paolo. 1982. *The Epithets in Homer: A Study in Poetic Values*. New Haven: Yale University Press.
Wadstein, Elis. 1903. *Beiträge zur Erklärung des Hildebrandsliedes*. Göteborg: Wald, Zachrissons Boktryckeri.
Waldron, Ronald A. 1957. "Oral-Formulaic Technique and Middle English Alliterative Poetry." *Speculum* 32:792–804.

Watkins, Calvert. 1987. "How to Kill a Dragon in Indo-European." In *Studies in Memory of Warren Cowgill, 1929–1985*, ed. Calvert Watkins, 270–99. Berlin: Gruyter.
——. 1992. "The Comparison of Formulaic Sequences." In *Reconstructing Languages and Cultures*, ed. Edgar C. Polomé and Werner Winter, 391–418. Hawthorne, N.Y.: Mouton de Gruyter.
——. Forthcoming. *How to Kill a Dragon: Aspects of Indo-European Poetics.* Oxford: Oxford University Press.
Watts, Ann Chalmers, 1969. *The Lyre and the Harp: A Comparative Reconsideration of Oral Tradition in Homer and Old English Epic Poetry.* New Haven: Yale University Press. Rpt., Ann Arbor: University Microfilms, 1980.
Whallon, William. 1961. "The Diction of *Beowulf*." *PMLA* 76:309–19.
——. 1965a. "Formulas for Heroes in the *Iliad* and in *Beowulf*." *Modern Philology* 63:95–104.
——. 1965b. "The Idea of God in *Beowulf*." *PMLA* 80:19–23.
——. 1969. "Who Wrote Down the Formulaic Poem?" In *Actes du Ve Congrès de l'Association Internationale de Littérature Comparée*, Belgrade, 1967, ed. Nikola Banašević, 469–72. Amsterdam: Swets.
Whitman, Cedric H. 1958. *Homer and the Heroic Tradition.* Cambridge, Mass.: Harvard University Press.

Index

Achilles, 2, 12, 90–91, 93, 107, 110
    arming of, 76, 81–83, 95
    fight with river, 71–73
    Pelian ash spear of, 79, 82–85, 94
Aeneas, 87, 93–94
Æschere, 109, 166
aesthetics:
    of Homer, 69
    oral, 123, 156, 202, 222
    See also poetics, oral traditional
Agamemnon, 90, 93, 110
    arming of, 76, 79–81, 87, 92
Ajax, 88–90
Alcaeus, 63–64
Alexander, Ronelle, 49n33. *See also* tension of essences
Alexandrov, Vladimir, 10n10
Alfred's *Pastoral Care,* 115
alliteration, 13, 58, 76–78, 83, 99, 134–35, 139, 153, 155, 161–63, 166
Alliterative Morte Arthure, 100
anaphora, 13, 19
Andersson, Theodore M., 103
Andreas, 124–25, 127–28, 152–55, 158
Andrić, Nikola, 22n3, 32–33
Anglo-Scottish ballads, 177–78, 183
Apollonius Rhodius, 104
appositive style, 98, 134–36, 162, 166
Archilochus, 65n44
Arend, Walter, 137n3
Ares, 86
Argonauts, 110
Armstrong, James I., 76n16
assonance, 13, 163

Athena, 12, 82–85, 89, 91, 94, 211
Athos, Mount, 199, 231
awaking songs, 51, 56
Azarias, 177–82

Baal, 71n5
Babylonian creation epic (*Enuma Elish*), 12, 72
Bacchylides, 67
Baligant, 73
Ballad, 20, 32–33, 45, 50, 167–86, 197
    Anglo-Scottish, 177–78, 183, 186
    Hispanic (*La condesita*), 181–82
    in northeast of Scotland, 185–86
    South Slavic (*Hasanaginica*), 171–77
Bannert, Herbert, 84n22
"Barbara Allen," 4, 167–70, 177
Barons, Krišjānis, 22, 30–31
Bartók, Béla, 22n1, 59–60, 62
    Bartók-Lord No. 12a, 171–76
Battle of Brunanburh, 133, 138–39
Battle of Maldon, 138
Bäuml, Franz H., 188
Bayard, Samuel, 170
Bede, 123, 199
    Historia ecclesiastica, 114
Benson, Larry, 101, 113, 115, 117–20, 124n19, 129, 201
Beowulf, 11, 73, 98n8, 183, 191, 201, 221, 236
    arsenal theme in, 158–66
    compound diction in, 120–21
    formula in, 117–36
    and oral epic, 96–116
    theme in, 137–66
blind singers, 3, 32

253

Index

blocks of lines, 62–63, 66–67, 98–99, 101, 184
boasting songs, 55, 111
Boethius, Anglo-Saxon translation of, 101
Bogišić, Valtazar, 227
Bolling, George M., 213
Bosnia, 14, 16, 32, 191, 203, 205, 223, 226
Bowra, Cecil M., 75
Breca episode, in *Beowulf*, 152, 156, 163
broadside, 178, 185
Bronson, Bertrand, 167–68, 170, 185n35
Brown, Mrs., of Falkland, 185
Buchan, David, 170n7, 185–86, 234n37
Bulgarian heroic songs, 236
Butler, Thomas J., 173n10
Buturović, Đenana, 223
byliny, 2n1, 5–10, 15–16, 201, 236
Bynum, David E., 10, 36n25, 52n37, 122n16, 207n8, 209n10, 223
Byock, Jesse, 13
Byzantium, 191

Cædmon, 112, 114–15, 123, 196n26, 197, 199–200, 202
Cain, 108–9, 111, 135, 140
Callimachus, 104, 221n19
Calvino, Italo, 213–20, 224, 233, 235
Cantilena, Mario, 221n19
"Captivity of Đulić Ibrahim," 11
"Capture of Temišvar," 14
Cerulli, Enrico, 194n20
Chanson de Guillaume, 129
Charlemagne, 73
chiasmus, 13–14
Child, Francis James, 50–51
  Child Ballads, 50–51, 167, 170, 183
Chomsky, Noam, 106
choral poetry, Greek, 67
Christ, 96, 147, 149, 158–59
Chronicle, Anglo-Saxon, 115
Circe, 110
Clark, Francelia, 137
Clark, George, 142n10
"clusters":
  of formulas, 5–7, 127, 141, 158, 184
  of lexical units, 158, 161, 166
  of lines, 208
  of recurrent motifs, 125, 137
collector-editor, 220, 222–23
Comparetti, Domenico, 193, 217, 218
composition in performance, 34, 58, 62, 67, 98, 101, 103, 179, 190, 192, 195, 197, 200, 206
"Ćor Huso," 182

"core of lines, more or less stable," 30–31, 47, 61–62, 209, 212
creation, biblical account of, 108
Creed, Robert P., 130, 189, 193
Croatia, 226
Crowne, David K., 142–56, 158
Curschmann, Michael, 192
Cynewulf, 119–20

dainas. *See* Latvian *dainas*
Dalmatia, 226, 228
Daniel, 158–59, 177–82
Dante, 235
dawn songs, 13
Demodocus, 2n1
De Nino, Antonio, 217–18, 221
Denmark, 143–45, 149–50, 152, 159, 164
diachronic, 74, 197
Diamond, Robert E., 138n4, 220–21
dictation of texts, 102, 112–13, 171, 200, 213, 223
Dillon, Myles, 216
Diomedes, 71, 90
Djilas, Milovan, 235
Donoghue, Daniel, 107n31, 153n17, 160n28, 189, 199n36
Dream of the Rood, 125
Dubrovnik, 228–29
dumy, Ukrainian, 236
duplication, 108–9
Dušan, Emperor, 191

Edda, Poetic, 96–97, 106, 198, 198n35, 229
Edwards, Mark W., 81n19
elegiac poetry, Greek, 63–66, 111
Elene, 96, 99, 119–20, 124, 138–39, 147–48, 158
Eliade, Mircea, 12, 106
enjambment, unperiodic, 135–36, 200–201
epic, oral traditional, 20, 74
  function of, 12, 102
  performance of, 1–3
epithet, 5, 15, 75–78, 83–95
Euripides, 67
Exodus, 124, 138, 155

Figueira, Thomas J., 65, 66n50
figures of speech, 13, 18–19
Finn, episode of, in *Beowulf*, 109, 111, 160
Finnegan, Ruth, 18n24, 67, 189, 194–95, 197n32, 198
Finnsburh fragment, 103, 138, 156

fixity of text, 20, 75, 102, 178–79, 181, 183, 185
  lack of, 66, 169, 177, 212–13
fluidity of text, 66, 170, 178, 184, 212–13
flyting, 24
Foley, John M., 98n8, 107n32, 130, 142n10, 146, 147n13, 153n17, 157n25, 189
folktale:
  Italian, 214–18
  literary, 220
  Sicilian, 218–19
  traditional, 220
Ford, Andrew L., 66
formula, 4, 5n6, 58, 63, 66–68, 75, 101, 179, 181, 194, 199
  in *Beowulf,* 7n9, 117–36, 158
  in *byliny,* 5–7
  cluster of, 5–7, 127, 141, 158, 184
  definition of, 4–5, 121–22, 124n20, 130, 200
  density, 200–201
  melodic, 170
  whole-line, 5
formulaic style, 98, 181, 200, 220, 226, 230–32, 235–36
Freibergs, Imants, 28–29
Friedman, Albert B., 185n35
Fry, Donald K., 120–24, 129–32, 156–57, 189, 198, 200
"function," definition of in Old English, 130–31, 133

Gacko, Herzegovina, 22n1, 44, 46, 48, 52, 55, 58–59, 171
Geats, 99, 143–45, 149, 151, 159
Genesis, 71n5, 111
Genesis (Anglo-Saxon), 119
  Genesis A, 138
genre, 1, 4, 20, 220
Giannini, Pietro, 65, 66n47, 66n50
Gilgamesh, 12, 104, 107
glof 'glove,' 112–13
Goody, John R., 188
Goold, George P., 213
Gormont et Isembart, 129
Grabovac, Filip, 230–31
Green, D. H., 187–200
Greenberg, Nathan A., 66–67
Greenfield, Stanley B., 139–42
Grendel, 73, 107, 112, 124, 126, 163
  mother of, 107–9, 165
Grimble, Arthur F., 195–96, 198
Grimm, Wilhelm, 214, 216n8, 220
  Brothers Grimm, 214, 219–20

Gudrun, 96, 98
Gundulić, Ivan, 230
gusle, 31–33, 225, 234
guslar, 193
Guthlac B, 125
Gyger (née Jones), Alison, 179n17

Hainsworth, J. Bryan, 65n46, 129, 163
Halle, Morris, 31n16
Hankins, James, 217n11
Harris, Joseph, 111, 197n30, 198
Hasanaginica, 171–77
Hatto, Arthur T., 13n18, 98n8
Havelock, Eric, 67, 188, 190–91, 194, 197
Haymes, Edward R., 98n8, 221n19
Hector, 73, 82n21, 91
Hektorović, Petar, 228–29
Heorot, 104, 106, 108–9, 111, 119, 126, 133, 151, 162, 165
Hephaestus, 72, 82n20
Hera, 72, 92, 110
Heracles, 12, 107, 110
"Hero on the Beach," 142, 152–56, 158
Herzegovina, 32, 191, 226
Hesiod, 65, 197
  Theogony, 72, 107
  Works and Days, 64
Hilandar, 199, 231
Hildebrandslied, 96, 98n8, 103
Hilferding, A. F., 5, 15
Hoekstra, Arie, 65n46, 129
Homer, 2–3, 63–65, 68–95, 98, 104–5, 110, 120–21, 136–37, 157n25, 190–92, 196–97, 201, 213, 216n8, 221n19, 233, 236
Homeric Hymn, 64
  to Aphrodite, 65n46
  to Apollo, 2–3, 65n46, 91–92
  to Demeter, 12n14, 65n46
  to Hermes, 65n46
Hondscio, 107, 112
Hörmann, Kosta, 223
Hrothgar, 109, 126, 146, 149–51, 162
Hygelac, 104, 112, 119, 162

Iliad, 11–13, 64, 71–73
  arming scenes in, 75–95
"Il'ja Muromec and Car' Kalin," 6–7, 15
improvisation, 11, 58, 101–3, 179, 181, 198
incantations, 13, 23
"insiders," 2, 220, 222, 224, 231

Jabbour, Alan A., 167n4, 177–79, 183–84, 197–98

Janko, Richard, 36n27, 65n46, 78n17, 129, 213n4
Jones, Alison, 179–82
Jovanovich, William, 234–35
Judith, 138, 156
Juvenal, 187, 188n4

Kačić-Miošić, Andrije, 213, 225–33, 235–36
  Razgovor ugodni naroda slovinskoga "A Pleasant Discourse of the Slavic People," 213, 225–29, 231–33, 235
Kalevala, 193
Karadžić, Vuk Stefanović, 22, 31–60, 199, 224–25
Katzenelenbogen, Uriah, 24–25
Kirk, Geoffrey S., 65n46, 76n16
kolo (ring dance), 32–33
Konrad, Kristine, 31n16
Kosovo, 229
Kraljević, Marko, 4, 199
Krishna, Valerie, 100, 124
Küllenberg, Richard K., 64, 65n44

Lactantius, 220
laments, 4, 13, 111
lapsus memoriae, 179–80, 184, 222
Latković, Vido, 234
Latvian *dainas*, 22–31, 33, 45, 62
  performance of, 24–26
  sound patterns in, 28
  variants in, 26–27
letter writing, 14, 228–29
literacy, 101–2, 113
literary style, 231–32, 234–36
Lönnroth, Lars, 197n30, 198
Lorimer, H. L., 76n16, 92n25
Luethans, Tod, 129
lyric songs, 13, 20, 33, 66
  Greek lyric poetry, 63–68
  See also women's songs, South Slavic

McGillivray, Murray, 184
McLuhan, Herbert Marshall, 188
Magoun, Francis Peabody, Jr., 101, 137–41, 158, 193, 197
Makić, Sulejman, 18–19
Marduk, 12, 72, 107
Marjanović, Luka, 16–18, 202n41, 223, 225
"Marko Kraljević and Musa the Highwayman," 73
Martial, 188
Martin, Richard P., 111n34, 200n38
Matica Hrvatska, 16, 22, 32

Međedović, Avdo, 74n11, 104, 158, 191, 203–11, 236
  Osmanbeg Delibegović and Pavičević Luka, 207–8
  Wedding of Smailagić Meho, 158, 203–11
  memorial transmission, 178–79, 181–84, 198. *See also* memorization
memorization, 11, 33, 62, 167, 170, 178, 181, 183–84, 186, 194, 197–99, 200, 213
Menelaus, 88–90, 211
Mermedonians, 124, 127, 152
meter, 66, 69, 74–75, 96, 98, 122, 130, 161, 163, 174, 221n19, 230
Middle English romances, 184
Milman Parry Collection, 16, 22n1, 31, 33, 44–45, 48, 58, 70, 171, 192n12, 199
Milton, John, 235
Milutinović-Sarajlija, Sima, 225, 233
Mimnermus, 65
Mitchell, Stephen A., 97n2, 190, 198n35, 229n27
mixing of songs, 35–36, 52, 104
Mladenović, Živomir, and Vladan Nedić, 33–58
Moffat, Douglas, 115n38, 182n26
monsters, 106
  "monster slayer," 106–7, 109
Montenegro, 32, 191, 214, 225–26, 229, 233, 235
Morland, Laura, 199n37
MS BL, Cotton Vitellius A. XV, 115
Muižniece, Lalita Lace, 25–26, 29–30
multiform, 23, 95, 108
Mušicki, Lukian, 200
myth, 11–13, 71–73, 197, 202
  in *Beowulf*, 106–8
  Canaanite, 71n5
mythic return pattern, 12n14, 106

Nagy, Gregory, 3n4, 12, 64–67, 73n10, 105n26, 129, 196–97
Nahod Simeun, 199
Nausikaa, 91
Nemanjić dynasty, 199
Neomanichaeism, 235
Nestor, 90, 211
Nibelungenlied, 96, 98, 156, 229–30, 236
Nichol, James, 185
Niles, John D., 117–18, 120, 124
Njegoš, Petar Petrović II, 212, 214, 225–26, 233–36
Notopoulos, James A., 65n44, 129

Odysseus, 12, 89–90, 92, 211, 217
Odyssey, 2n1, 2n2, 11–12, 64, 110, 211
O'Keeffe, Katherine O'Brien, 113, 184

Ong, Walter J., 100, 188
Opland, Jeff, 193–94
oral tradition, 196–97
    content of, 4, 11–12
    definition of, 1–3, 100
    five aspects of, 3–4
    poetics of, 4
    subject to social changes, 100
oral traditional literature, 98, 157, 179, 187, 189, 227, 235–37
    content of, 4
    definition of, 1
    function of, 197
    genres of, 1, 20
    transmission of, 181, 185
    See also poetics, oral traditional
orality, 113, 115, 187–88, 194–95. *See also* oral tradition; oral traditional literature
Origen, 235
"original" text, 183–84
ornamentation, 90, 95, 165, 205n5, 211, 213
"outsiders," 100, 220, 222–24, 231

Pacific Islands, 190, 194–99
Panathenaean festivals, 3n4
pan-Hellenism, 65
parataxis, 19, 99, 141
Paris, arming of, 76, 78, 95
Parry, Milman, 4, 5n6, 14, 63–65, 67–69, 75, 98, 101, 104, 117, 120–22, 128–30, 136–37, 182, 189, 190–97, 198n35, 200–201, 223. *See also* Milman Parry Collection
Patroclus, 90
    arming of, 76, 78–79, 84, 95
patterns:
    semantic, 99
    sound, 95
    story, 11–13
    syntactic, 99
Pavese, Carlo O., 65n46
Peabody, Berkley, 65n46
Pearsall, Derek, 102–5
Penelope, 91
performance, 188–89, 197
    of Greek epic, 2–3
    of Greek tragedy, 67
    of Latvian *dainas*, 24–26
    of South Slavic women's songs, 31–33
Petar I Petrović, Bishop, 233
Petersen, Suzanne, 181–82
Petrarchan sonnets, 230
Phemius, 2n1
Philo, 235
Pindar, 67, 233

Pitrè, Giuseppe, 218–19
Plato, 235
Podrugović, Tešan, 199–200
poetics, oral traditional, 4, 13, 15, 18–19, 105. *See also* aesthetics
Polyphemus, 217
Pope, M. W. M., 130
Poseidon, 94
praise poems, 20, 111, 194n17
Preziosi, Patricia G., 65n46
Priam, 91

Quain, Buell, 195

Radloff, Wilhelm von, 192
Ralston, William S., 50
Ramadan, 2
Ranjina, Vinko, 230
remembering, not memorization, 11, 20, 39, 41, 57, 99, 170, 177, 180–81, 183
Renoir, Alain, 100, 155n18, 156, 189
repetition, 16–17, 70, 95, 122–23, 128, 200, 203, 205, 216
    of epithets, 15
    not all repetitions formulas, 200
    of sound, 13
"responsion," 146, 148
retellers of tales, 222–24
Reynolds, Dwight, 11n13
rhapsodes, 3n4
rhyme, 13, 58, 169, 181–82, 227–33, 236
    internal, 13, 19, 58
riddling songs, 13, 20, 36–56
Riedinger, Anita, 124–33, 137
Riedy, Nicolaus, 64, 65n44
Riggsby, Andrew M., 200n38
ring composition, 13–14, 185
ritual origin, 106
ritual preparation, 195–96
ritual songs, 13, 20, 33
Ritzke-Rutherford, Jean, 100
Rjabinin, Trofim Grigor'evich, 5–10, 15–16
Robertson, Bell, 186
Robinson, Fred C., 98, 189
Rodić, Antun, 32
Roland, Song of, Oxford, 7, 236
Russom, Geoffrey R., 189, 220–21

Samodreže, 199
Sappho, 36n27, 63–64
Sarpedon, 93–94
satiric songs, 57
Savić-Rebac, Anica, 233n33, 235n39
scop, Anglo-Saxon, 2n1, 109, 111

Segal, Charles, 65n46
Serbia, 32, 191, 225, 229
Serbian Orthodox Church, 200
Serbian poetry, 65, 200
    Serbo-Croatian heroic songs, 236
    See also South Slavic epic
"set," definition of, 124, 131–33
Shannon, Richard S., 79n18, 205n5
Shield of Heracles, 87, 95
Shive, David, 200
Sievers, Eduard, 130
Sigmund, 111
Singer of Tales, The, 12n15, 34, 101, 105, 117, 128, 183, 187, 201, 212, 226
Šišatovac, 199
Slava, 2
Šmits, Pēteris, 23
Solomon and Saturn I, 114–15
Solon, 63–66
Somali poetry, 194
"Song of Bagdad," 18–19
Sophocles, 67
Soul and Body, 177–81
South Slavic epic, 45, 49, 104, 110, 146, 157n25, 171n8, 192, 201
Speiser, E. A., 72n8
Spraycar, Rudy S., 226
stability of lines, 212–13
Stender, Gotthard Friedrich, 24
Stock, Brian, 188
storytelling, 3–4
Svenbro, Jesper, 63–64
Sveti Sava, 199, 231–33
Sweden, 143, 145, 149, 151–52, 158
"system," definition of, 120, 122, 124, 128, 131, 133

Telemachus, 211
tension of essences, 49, 62
textuality, 21, 33, 35, 37–39, 41–43, 56–57, 156, 158, 161, 168, 171, 177, 207, 212–13
theme, 4, 5n7, 34, 58, 63, 81, 101, 128, 200–201, 212
    compositional, 208
    definition of, 5, 201
    in Anglo-Saxon poetry, 137–66
    in Avdo Međedović, 203–11
    in *byliny,* 7–10
    in South Slavic lyric songs, 34
    stability of, 211
Theognis, 64–66
    Theognidea, 65

Thomas, Rosalind, 65n46, 74n11
thrift, 133–36, 163, 200–201
Thurnwald, Richard C., 195
Tiamat, 12
Toelken, J. Barre, 167n3, 183
tragedy, Attic, 67–68, 233
transitional text, 105, 113, 183–86, 201, 212–36
Turkey, 199
    Turks, 210, 225, 233
"type-scene," 156–57
Typhoeus, 12
Tyrtaeus, 65

Ugljanin, Salih, 226
Unferth, 106, 124

variants, 23, 26–27, 29–31, 33–49, 53, 56–62, 156–57, 168–70, 183, 214, 221–22. *See also* variation
variation, 27, 29, 47, 55, 177, 179–81, 184–85, 203, 205, 211
Vīķis-Freibergs, Vaira, 28
vila, 49n32, 52, 234
Virgil, 103–5, 112, 188
Višnjić, Filip, 199–200, 224
Vivante, Paolo, 69–71, 76
Vǫluspá, 97, 98n8
Vrčević, Vuk, 36n25, 225
Vujnović, Nikola, 182

Waldere, 103
Waldron, Ronald A., 100
Wanderer, 138
Watkins, Calvert, 106n30
Watts, Ann Chalmers, 101, 117–18, 193
weapon, special, 82, 107
weaving style, 122, 129
wedding songs, 33
"Wedding of Dushan," 104
"Wedding of Maksim Crnojević," 104
Wedding of Smailagić Meho. See Međedović, Avdo
Whallon, William, 134–35
Whitman, Cedric H., 82n20
Wiglaf, 119, 161
women's songs, South Slavic, 2n1, 31–62, 171n8
writing, 105, 183, 197–98, 202, 212n2, 213, 231, 234–35
    absence of, 1, 15

Xanthus (Scamander), 71–73

Zeus, 12, 71, 73, 94, 107, 110
Žunić, Murat, 14

MYTH AND POETICS
A series edited by
GREGORY NAGY

Helen of Troy and Her Shameless Phantom
by Norman Austin
The Craft of Poetic Speech in Ancient Greece
by Claude Calame
translated by Janice Orion
Masks of Dionysus
edited by Thomas W. Carpenter and Christopher A. Faraone
The Poetics of Supplication: Homer's Iliad *and* Odyssey
by Kevin Crotty
Poet and Hero in the Persian Book of Kings
by Olga M. Davidson
The Ravenous Hyenas and the Wounded Sun: Myth and Ritual in Ancient India
by Stephanie W. Jamison
Poetry and Prophecy: The Beginnings of a Literary Tradition
edited by James Kugel
The Traffic in Praise: Pindar and the Poetics of Social Economy
by Leslie Kurke
Topographies of Hellenism: Mapping the Homeland
by Artemis Leontis
Epic Singers and Oral Tradition
by Albert Bates Lord
The Singer Resumes the Tale
by Albert Bates Lord, edited by Mary Louise Lord
The Language of Heroes: Speech and Performance in the Iliad
by Richard P. Martin
Heroic Sagas and Ballads
by Stephen A. Mitchell
Greek Mythology and Poetics
by Gregory Nagy
Myth and the Polis
edited by Dora C. Pozzi and John M. Wickersham

Knowing Words: Wisdom and Cunning in the Classical Traditions of China and Greece
by Lisa Raphals
Heroic Poets, Poetic Heroes: The Ethnography of Performance in an Arabic Oral Epic Tradition
by Dwight Fletcher Reynolds
Homer and the Sacred City
by Stephen Scully
Singers, Heroes, and Gods in the Odyssey
by Charles Segal
The Mute Immortals Speak: Pre-Islamic Poetry and the Poetics of Ritual
by Suzanne Pinckney Stetkevych
Phrasikleia: An Anthropology of Reading in Ancient Greece
by Jesper Svenbro
translated by Janet E. Lloyd
The Jewish Novel in the Ancient World
by Lawrence M. Wills